The Cambridge Companion to Berg

The Cambridge Companion to

BERG

Edited by Anthony Pople

CAMBRIDGE
UNIVERSITY PRESS

PUBLISHED BY THE PRESS SYNDICATE OF THE UNIVERSITY OF CAMBRIDGE
The Pitt Building, Trumpington Street, Cambridge CB2 1RP, United Kingdom

CAMBRIDGE UNIVERSITY PRESS
The Edinburgh Building, Cambridge CB2 2RU, United Kingdom
40 West 20th Street, New York, NY 10011–4211, USA
10 Stamford Road, Oakleigh, Melbourne 3166, Australia

First published 1997

Printed in the United Kingdom at the University Press, Cambridge

Typeset in Adobe Minion

A catalogue record for this book is available from the British Library

Library of Congress cataloguing in publication data

ISBN 0 521 56374 7 hardback
ISBN 0 521 56489 1 paperback

AP

in memory of Derrick Puffett

Contents

Acknowledgements

A book of this kind is made by many people. Above all my thanks go to the contributors, some of whom have shown inordinate patience in waiting for their work to appear in print and several of whom have given assistance that extended well beyond authorship of their chapters. I am especially grateful to Douglas Jarman for a series of encouraging conversations when the book was in the planning stage, and to my friend and colleague Neil Boynton for many stimulating conversations about Berg and his Viennese musical environment in the 1920s.

At the London office of Universal Edition, Berg's principal publisher, Eric Forder and Robert Hahn showed me great kindness. For Cambridge University Press, Emma Smith and Caroline Murray offered friendly help and advice, and Penny Souster's patience and encouragement did much to guide the book through its long gestation. I should also like to thank Craig Ayrey, Ian Darbyshire and Ronald Woodley for their assistance. The University of Lancaster gave me a period of study leave in 1996, some of which was devoted to work on this volume. Above all I must thank Angela, Lucy and Flora (who arrived in the midst of it all) for striving to maintain home conditions that were conducive to bringing the enterprise to fruition.

Copyright materials are reproduced as follows:

Alban Berg, op. 1 Sonata for piano
© 1926 by Robert Lienau Edition/Germany (formerly Schlesinger)
Copyright renewed. All rights reserved. Reprinted by permission.

Alban Berg, op. 2 Four Songs
© 1928 by Robert Lienau Edition/Germany (formerly Schlesinger)
Copyright renewed. All rights reserved. Reprinted by permission.

All other excerpts of works by Alban Berg, Josef M. Hauer, Arnold Schoenberg and Anton Webern, and a music example from *Alban Berg Studien*, 2, are reproduced by permission of Universal Edition (London) Ltd. Reproductions and transcriptions of Berg's sketches, and music examples from Berg's letter to Schoenberg of 13 July 1926, are by kind permission of the Österreichische Nationalbibliothek and the Alban Berg Stiftung, Vienna.

Chronology

year	Berg's life	musicians and others
1885	Albano Maria Joannes Berg born (9 February)	Helene Nahowski born; 'King' Oliver, Varèse and Kern born
1886		Liszt dies
1887		
1888		serial killer 'Jack the Ripper' active in London
1889		
1890		Franck dies
1891		Prokofiev born
1892		
1893		
1894		
1895		Hindemith born
1896		Bruckner dies
1897		Brahms dies
1898	begins friendship with architect Hermann Watznauer	Gershwin born
1899		'Duke' Ellington born; Johann Strauss II dies; Karl Kraus begins publication of *Die Fackel*
1900	father dies (30 March), receives *The Golden Book of Music* as a gift from Watznauer	Copland and Weill born
1901	composes first songs	Verdi dies
1902	friendship with Paul Hohenberg; acknowledges paternity of Albine Scheuchl (born 4 December to Marie Scheuchl, a member of the Berg family staff)	Schoenberg: *Verklärte Nacht* performed (composed 1899); Debussy: *Pelléas et Mélisande* completed (begun 1893)
1903	friendship with Frida Semler; attempts suicide (autumn)	Wolf dies
1904	begins studies with Schoenberg (October) while working as an unpaid civil servant	
1905	attends Kraus's private production of Wedekind's *Die Büchse der Pandora* (29 May); family moves into inherited accommodation	Strauss: *Salome*

1906	resigns from civil service post (October)	Shostakovich born; Mahler: Symphony No. 6; Schoenberg: Chamber Symphony No. 1; Hauptmann: *Und Pippa tanzt!*
1907	passionate friendship develops with Helene Nahowski by Easter; composes 'Die Nachtigall' (spring), Fugue for piano quintet (summer); these and two further songs performed (7 November)	Mahler resigns his post at the Vienna Hofoper and leaves for New York
1908	impressed by Dukas's *Ariane et Barbe-bleue* (2 April); composes Twelve Variations on an original theme (performed 8 November); begins work towards a piano sonata (autumn)	Messiaen and Carter born; Strauss: *Elektra*; Schoenberg: String Quartet No. 2; Mathilde Schoenberg's tragic affair with the painter Richard Gerstl
1909	completes Piano Sonata Op. 1 and composes some of Op. 2 songs	Schoenberg: *Erwartung*
1910	finishes Four Songs Op. 2; composes String Quartet Op. 3; engagement to Helene	Stravinsky: *The Firebird*
1911	Piano Sonata Op. 1 and String Quartet Op. 3 performed (24 April); marries Helene (3 May); finishes studies with Schoenberg	Mahler dies; Schoenberg's *Harmonielehre*; Schoenberg leaves Vienna to work in Berlin
1912	composes *Altenberg Lieder* Op. 4; sketches fragments of a symphonic movement on Balzac's *Seraphita*	Cage born; Strindberg dies; Schreker: *Der ferne Klang*; Schoenberg: *Pierrot lunaire*; Mahler's Symphony No. 9 performed (composed 1908–9)
1913	the *Skandalkonzert* (31 March): first performance of two of the *Altenberg Lieder* leads to uproar; composes Four Clarinet Pieces Op. 5; receives criticism from Schoenberg (June); begins work on Three Orchestral Pieces Op. 6	Britten and Lutoslawski born; first performance of Stravinsky's *The Rite of Spring* leads to uproar in Paris (29 May)
1914	rift with Schoenberg (March); sees production of Büchner's *Woyzeck* (14 May); sketches parts of *Wozzeck* while composing Op. 6	Austria declares war on Serbia (28 July) after assassination of Archduke Franz Ferdinand, leading to First World War
1915	finishes Three Orchestral Pieces Op. 6; trained for military service; physical breakdown	sinking of the *Lusitania*
1916	intensive work at War Ministry	Emperor Franz Josef dies
1917	resumes composition of *Wozzeck*	Bolshevik revolution in Russia

1918	working with Schoenberg again, in the Society for Private Musical Performances	Austria surrenders (2 November); Wedekind dies; Debussy dies; Bernstein born
1919	first performance of Four Clarinet Pieces Op. 5 (17 October)	Treaty of Versailles; Peter Altenberg dies
1920	assumes editorship of 'Anbruch'; later resigns through ill-health	Stravinsky: *Pulcinella*
1921	finishes composition of *Wozzeck* (October); begins orchestration	
1922	finishes score of *Wozzeck* (April)	
1923	performances of String Quartet Op. 3 (2 August) and Op. 6 Nos. 1–2 (5 June) bring Berg to public notice; begins to compose Chamber Concerto	Schoenberg makes known his ideas for a twelve-note technique; Mathilde Schoenberg dies
1924	*Three Fragments from 'Wozzeck'* premiered (15 June)	Puccini dies; Gershwin: *Rhapsody in Blue*
1925	finishes Chamber Concerto (9 February), amorous exchanges with Hanna Fuchs-Robettin (from 20 May); composes twelve-note setting of 'Schliesse mir die Augen beide'; begins *Lyric Suite*; first production of *Wozzeck* (Berlin, 14 December)	Boulez and Berio born
1926	finishes composition of *Lyric Suite* (September); Berg's mother dies (19 December)	Sibelius: *Tapiola*
1927	first performances of *Lyric Suite* (8 January) and Chamber Concerto (20 March); signs exclusive publication contract with Universal Edition; *Wozzeck* produced in Leningrad [St Petersburg]; begins work towards opera on Hauptmann's *Und Pippa tanzt!*	Bartók: String Quartet No. 3; Hindemith: *Hin und zurück*
1928	prepares *Seven Early Songs* in orch. version (performed 6 November) and with revised piano accompaniments; abandons *Pippa* over contractual difficulties and begins to compose *Lulu* (June)	Stockhausen born; Schoenberg: Variations for Orchestra, Weill: *Die Dreigroschenoper*
1929	interrupts work on *Lulu* to compose *Der Wein* (completed 23 August); string orchestra arrangement of *Three Movements from*	Wall Street crash; Schoenberg: *Von heute auf morgen*

	the *'Lyric Suite'* performed (31 January); gives lecture on *Wozzeck* in connection with successful production in Oldenburg	
1930	Three Orchestral Pieces Op. 6 performed complete for the first time (14 April); elected to membership of the Prussian Academy of Arts; buys Ford cabriolet	Stravinsky: *Symphony of Psalms*
1931	*Wozzeck* performed in Philadelphia under Stokowski	Bartók: Piano Concerto No. 2
1932	buys 'Waldhaus' to improve working conditions away from Vienna	Schoenberg: *Moses und Aron* (left unfinished in two acts)
1933	intensive work on *Lulu*	Hitler becomes Chancellor of Germany (30 January)
1934	finishes composition of *Lulu* (May); begins orchestration; *Lulu Suite* performed (30 November)	Birtwistle and Maxwell Davies born; Elgar dies
1935	composes Violin Concerto to commission from Louis Krasner (completed 12 August); health deteriorates rapidly after insect sting (mid-August); hears *Lulu Suite* in Vienna (11 December); dies of blood poisoning around midnight on 23/24 December	Gershwin: *Porgy and Bess*

Select list of works

This list is selective in that, of his earliest works (preceding Op. 1), it in
cludes only those either performed publicly at the time or later published
by Berg himself. Many of the other *Jugendlieder*, in particular, are of considerable musical interest. Forty-six of these have been published in two
volumes, ed. Christopher Hailey (Vienna: Universal Edition, 1985). The
chapter references are given for convenience but are not exhaustive.

title	date	chapter
c. 85 early songs (*Jugendlieder*), including	1901–8	4
'Im Zimmer' (*Seven Early Songs*, No. 5)	1905	
'Liebesode' (*Seven Early Songs*, No. 6)	1906	
'Die Nachtigall' (*Seven Early Songs*, No. 3)	1907	
'Traumgekrönt' (*Seven Early Songs*, No. 4)	1907	
'Schliesse mir die Augen beide' (first setting)	1907	
'Nacht' (*Seven Early Songs*, No. 1)	1908	
'Schilflied' (*Seven Early Songs*, No. 2)	1908	
'Sommertage' (*Seven Early Songs*, No. 7)	1908	
Fugue for piano quintet	1907	4
Twelve Variations on an original theme	1908	4
Piano Sonata Op. 1	1908–9	4
Four Songs Op. 2	1909–10	4
String Quartet Op. 3	1910	4
Altenberg Lieder Op. 4 [Five songs on picture- postcard texts by Peter Altenberg]	1912	5
Four Pieces for Clarinet and Piano Op. 5	1913	5
Three Orchestral Pieces Op. 6	1913–15	6
Wozzeck	1914–22	7, 8, 9
Three Fragments from 'Wozzeck'	1924	
Chamber Concerto	1923–5	8, 10, 11
'Schliesse mir die Augen beide' (second setting)	1925	9, 10, 11
Lyric Suite	1925–6	8, 10, 11
Seven Early Songs (see above)	1928	11
Three Movements from the 'Lyric Suite' (arr. string orch.)	1928	
Der Wein	1929	11
Canon [from Alban Berg to the Frankfurt opera house]	1930	
Lulu	1928–34*	9, 11, 12
Lulu Suite [Symphonic pieces from the opera *Lulu*]	1934	11
Violin Concerto	1935	8, 11

* *Particell* (short score) completed in 1934; orchestration incomplete at Berg's death

Contributors

KATHRYN BAILEY taught for many years at the Universities of British Columbia and Western Ontario before moving to Cambridge in 1989. Her publications, including *The Twelve-Note Music of Anton Webern* (CUP, 1991), have primarily been analyses of the works of Webern and studies of his sketches.

ANDREW BARKER is Head of the Department of German and Russian at the University of Edinburgh. Specialising in the literature and cultural history of Vienna from the late nineteenth to mid-twentieth centuries, he is author of *Telegrams from the Soul: Peter Altenberg and the Culture of fin-de-siècle Vienna* (1996) and has also published on such figures as Nestroy, Bahr, Hofmannsthal, Mahler, Wittgenstein, Doderer and Joseph Roth.

NEIL BOYNTON is Lecturer in Music at the University of Lancaster. His publications are principally concerned with the music of the Second Viennese School composers, and include a study of formal combination in Webern's Variations Op. 30 based on the composer's sketches for the work. He is currently preparing an edition of notes from Webern's 1934–8 lectures on musical form.

RAYMOND GEUSS taught Philosophy at Heidelberg, the University of Chicago, and Princeton, before moving to Cambridge in 1993. He is the author of *The Idea of a Critical Theory* (CUP, 1981) and has published various articles on topics in ethics and the philosophy of history.

CHRISTOPHER HAILEY is Director of the Franz Schreker Foundation, Inc., and is the author of a biography of Schreker (CUP, 1993) and editor of the correspondence between Schreker and the critic Paul Bekker (1994). He is a co-editor of *The Berg–Schoenberg Correspondence* (1987) and a co-translator of Theodor W. Adorno's monograph on Berg (CUP, 1991).

PATRICIA HALL is Associate Professor of Music Theory at the University of California, Santa Barbara. She has published widely on Berg's music and other topics, and is the author of *A View of Berg's Lulu Through the Autograph Sources* (1996). Among her current projects is a database with visual access to the sketches for *Wozzeck*.

DOUGLAS JARMAN is Principal Lecturer at the Royal Northern College of Music, Manchester. He has published widely on Berg, and his *The Music of*

Alban Berg (1979) is a landmark in modern Berg scholarship. He has edited the Cambridge Opera Handbooks to both *Wozzeck* and *Lulu*, and also *The Berg Companion* (Macmillan, 1991). His scholarly edition of the Violin Concerto was published in 1996.

JUDY LOCHHEAD is Associate Professor of Music at the State University of New York at Stony Brook, where she teaches the theory and history of music in the twentieth century. Her current research focuses on phenomenological approaches to the analysis of recent music, the idea of musical postmodernism, and graphic transcription of musical timbre for the purposes of analysis. She has a long-standing interest in Berg's *Lulu*.

DERRICK PUFFETT taught at the University of Cambridge until his retirement in 1994 and was Editor of *Music Analysis* for eight years. He edited the Cambridge Opera Handbooks to Strauss's *Salome* and *Elektra*, and published notable studies of Tippett, Berg, Schoenberg, Stravinsky and Debussy towards the end of his life. The present volume was in press when Derrick Puffett died in November 1996.

ANTHONY POPLE is Professor of Music Theory and Analysis at the University of Lancaster, and Editor of *Music Analysis*. He has published widely on theory, analysis and twentieth-century music and his books include the Cambridge Music Handbook to Berg's Violin Concerto (CUP, 1991).

ARNOLD WHITTALL was Professor of Musical Theory and Analysis at King's College, University of London until his retirement in 1996. His many publications on nineteenth- and twentieth-century music include influential studies of Schoenberg, Stravinsky, Webern, Birtwistle and others, together with *Music Since the First World War* (1977) and *The Music of Britten and Tippett: Studies in Themes and Techniques* (CUP, 1982).

Introduction

Anthony Pople
University of Lancaster

If the quantity of performances and recordings is anything to go by, and the warmth of their reception, Berg's music is reaching a wider audience as the twentieth century ends than it has at any previous time. Since the appearance in 1979 of Friedrich Cerha's edition at last allowed *Lulu* to be heard in its entirety, this opera has arguably overtaken *Wozzeck* in both popularity and critical esteem. Recordings of the *Lulu Suite* threaten to outnumber those of the ever-popular Violin Concerto in the catalogues.

It is no longer remotely fashionable to ask 'what if?' questions about composers who died prematurely, but the popular emphasis on Berg's final compositions makes my mind, at least, turn occasionally to such idle speculation. Berg's compositional technique in the final act of *Lulu* and in the Violin Concerto is remarkably focused and fluent, and belies the opera's long gestation. His willingness to consider a substantial list of future projects as he neared the end of his work on the opera – a third string quartet, a piece of chamber music with piano, a symphony, a piece for radio or film[1] – might be taken to suggest that he was ready to unleash an outpouring of creativity, following a long period of frustration whilst composing the first two acts. The Violin Concerto would have fitted into such a pattern, for though one can certainly see signs of the speed at which it was put together, it remains a work that almost unerringly forges what was for Berg a new balance between the intricate and the communicative. At 50, he knew himself and his ways as a composer well enough to organise his working methods so that the music would flow.

All this, of course, overlooks a number of crucial negative factors. The Nazis were in power in Germany and already had a strong influence on Austrian life. Berg's financial and domestic situation was precarious, yet so profound was his Viennese sensibility that he was not inclined to move abroad like so many others. Even biology was against him: his own father had died in his mid-50s, and poor health dogged Berg in his final years. Had he lived, his music would have been officially reviled in Austria at least until 1945, and in post-war Europe he might well have been regarded as a kind of musical dinosaur. It is factors such as these that render detailed speculation about an older Berg's achievements quite impossible.

So we are grateful, as Willi Reich wrote in an obituary, 'for every smile of his bright yet still so puzzling countenance, for every note of his inconceivably intense and inspired work!'[2] What is more, we may observe that Berg's present popularity represents something of a rediscovery, rather than a direct continuation of his contemporaries' appreciation of the living man.[3] Recognising both these things, the present volume seeks both to discuss every major work, and to contextualise Berg's cultural outlook and musical output against the background of his own time and in terms of its resonances within the musical culture of the twentieth century.

In the first part of the book, Christopher Hailey takes us inside Berg's home territory in the Vienna suburb of Hietzing, Andrew Barker provides a profile of the composer's formative connections with major figures in Viennese cultural life, and Raymond Geuss examines how his music was treated in (and itself informed) the writings of a man who was both a talented composition pupil of Berg and one of the twentieth century's greatest philosophers, Theodor W. Adorno. Subsequent chapters in Part II examine the music itself, beginning with Berg's earliest compositions and culminating with his greatest success during his lifetime, the opera *Wozzeck*. The pivotal nature of this masterpiece for Berg's development is pursued at the beginning of the third part of the book, in three chapters which examine how Berg expanded his musical horizons in the early 1920s. For perhaps his greatest gift of all was to build constantly on his experience, accumulating and re-synthesising, so that almost everything he did was turned to good use later on. From this remarkable human nature, rather than from any reluctance to accept the challenge of the new, came the tendency of so much of his work to find its roots either in the Vienna of the 1900s, or in his complex personal life and his world of friends and acquaintances. Part III also examines all the post-*Wozzeck* music, and features a consideration by Judy Lochhead of the Lulu character in the light of recent feminist theory.

This chapter reminds us that the subsequent impact of Berg's music, whilst latent in whatever we might consider to be the music's substance, is nonetheless developing and multi-faceted. The final part of the book is devoted to Arnold Whittall's masterly examination of this topic, which shows how aspects of a Bergian synthesis may be detected in music that is either more single-mindedly constructive or single-mindedly referential, or – perhaps most of all – both pluralistic and historically sensitive. That these latter characteristics are so often seen as definitive for a post-modern age, and also of Berg's own artistic temperament, suggests in part why he has now become, not the foreign minister of his own land of dreams, as Adorno suggested to his face,[4] but to later generations a posthumous and much-loved ambassador from the world of modernism to our own times.

PART I

Culture and environment

1 Defining home: Berg's life on the periphery

Christopher Hailey

Old Hietzing natives were never in a hurry and others, like myself, who moved there later in life were drawn there because in Old Hietzing one never had to hurry.   *Soma Morgenstern*[1]

The effervescence of Vienna's turn-of-the-century culture, its spontaneous combustion of ideas, was an explosion of pent-up energies, of unstable ingredients long compacted under the pressure of Vienna's remarkably dense social, cultural and physical geography. Vienna's central first district was a magnet of extraordinary power, the centre, as it were, of a solar system around which its outer districts spiralled in uneven orbit. The sources of that power – the Hofburg and its bureaucratic appendages, the parliament and city hall, the banks and stock exchange, the university and academies, the Court Opera, Burgtheater and Musikverein – produced enough noteworthy activity, intrigue and gossip to fill the columns of the city's more than two dozen newspapers and tabloids, and to fuel agitated coffee-house debates on art, politics, philosophy and sex. But if the first district was the place where everyone met, only a few chose to live there. Peter Altenberg, of course, occupied a small hotel room in the Dorotheagasse, and Karl Kraus slept by day at his apartment in the Dominikanerbastei, but such creatures of the first district were the exception. It was in the city's orbiting outer districts that the rumblings within Vienna's core found their resonating chamber.

The twenty-one administrative districts of early twentieth-century Vienna were established between 1850 and 1904 (see Map 1) and were part of a process, along with the removal of the inner-city fortifications, the construction of the Ringstraße and Gürtel, the canalisation of the Wien river and the construction of the Stadtbahn, that would forge the city's scattered communities into a single sprawling metropolis.[2] But differences remained. Geography, history and architecture, local industry and economy, and above all the income, class, occupation or ethnicity of its inhabitants gave each district a distinctive identity, its own perspective; and it was the concert of those perspectives that diffracted the impulses of the first district into the prismatic cultural and intellectual rainbow of *fin de siècle* Vienna.

Map 1 Present-day administrative districts of Vienna (during Berg's lifetime much of what is today the fourteenth district was part of Hietzing). The shaded area shows the location of Alt-Hietzing and the Schönbrunn grounds.

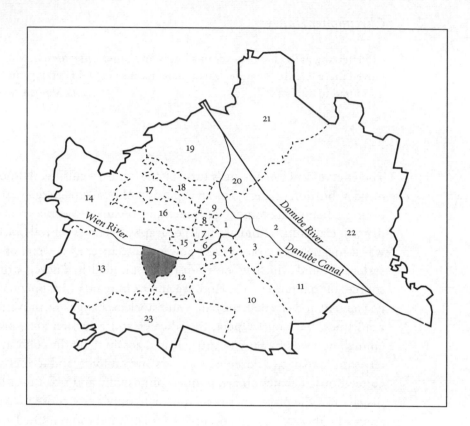

Key

1	Inner city	9	Alsergrund	16	Ottakring
2	Leopoldstadt	10	Favoriten	17	Hernals
3	Landstrasse	11	Simmering	18	Währing
4	Wieden	12	Meidling	19	Döbling
5	Margareten	13	Hietzing	20	Brigittenau
6	Mariahilf	14	Penzing	21	Floridsdorf
7	Neubau	15	Rudolfsheim-	22	Donaustadt
8	Josefstadt		Fünfhaus	23	Liesing

By their proximity to the centre the inner districts two to nine shared in the allures of the first district. Those who lived here often did so out of convenience. Mahler's apartment in the Landstraße district was within walking distance of the Opera, Franz Schreker and Josef Marx chose Margareten for its proximity to the Academy, and Sigmund Freud lived in Alsergrund near the University. But these third, fifth and ninth districts were also known as being home for diplomats, vendors and bureaucrats, just as the second district of Leopoldstadt was home for many of Vienna's working- and lower middle-class Jews, and the eighth district of Josefstadt a fashionable address for many of their upwardly mobile cousins. Beyond the Gürtel, the outer ring that had been completed in 1873, lay districts ten to twenty-one. These were the neighbourhoods that anchored Vienna in the surrounding countryside, from the Vienna woods to the Hungarian plain. Here the pace of life slowed. Carl Moll lived in the leafy olympia of the Hohe Warte near the vineyards of the nineteenth district, and Arthur Schnitzler had his villa in the more urban elegance of the eighteenth. For those yearning for the countryside itself, Vienna was ringed by quaint towns and villages such as Rodaun, where Hugo von Hofmannsthal lived and worked, or Mödling, where Anton Webern tended his modest alpine garden.

The inner city served up the world's imponderables; in the surrounding districts one could assert control over the more manageable dimensions of the *Alltag*, one's daily routine. Here, too, there were restaurants and cafés, but they were neighbourhood establishments with a local clientele. Here in the outer districts were the shopkeepers and tradesmen one knew by name and the neighbours with whom one could discuss such truly profound issues as the weather, the price of meat – and the other neighbours. Here were those first-hand encounters with the earthy wisdom of the *Ur*-Wiener, those interchanges and experiences of everyday life that nourish our deepest notions of calling a place home. These outer districts offered vantage points from which to triangulate the distance from Vienna's inner city to the world beyond.

The heart of Vienna's thirteenth district, Alt-Hietzing, or Old Hietzing, lies along the west wall of the Imperial summer palace of Schönbrunn, where a cluster of shops, bakeries, cafés and hotels gives the spot an air of tidy self-sufficiency.[3] At one end the parish church, dating from the early fifteenth century, and the post office, housed in the former summer palace of the emperor's foreign minister, are palpable reminders of the larger spheres of church and state; at the other end tram lines that converge at the beginning of Hietzinger Hauptstraße are the visible links to the metropolitan *Innenstadt* twenty minutes to the east.

Hietzing is a comfortable place. It is a district of Imperial yellow and varying hues of green, a district of elm, maple, chestnut, birch and plane trees, of squares and gardens, and of shady inner courtyards. In addition to the stately grounds of Schönbrunn, whose palace and gardens were laid out in the early eighteenth century, there are numerous parks, including Maxing Park and Hügel Park, several well-populated cemeteries and the expansive Lainzer Wildlife Preserve.[4] Despite the traffic that in recent decades has overtaken its principal arteries, the prevailing impression is one of settled quiet. Birds and the odd screech from the Schönbrunn zoological garden (founded in 1752, it is Europe's oldest) punctuate the stillness. There are villas here – it is what is called a Nobelbezirk, an elegant district – but little ostentation. Just as the Schönbrunn Palace and grounds manage to preserve a rural quality despite their formal splendour, Hietzing's estates and high-ceilinged apartment buildings integrate themselves among their less prepossessing neighbours in the shambling warren of its streets.

At the time of its incorporation in 1892, Alt-Hietzing and the surrounding communities of Ober St-Veit, Unter St-Veit, Speising and Lainz, were still predominantly agricultural, with nurseries, dairy farms, vineyards and pastures making up the bulk of commercial activity, as well as a few small industries such as meat processing, and textile and clothing manufacture. By the turn of the century Hietzing had established itself as a place where aristocrats, upper-level bureaucrats and professionals, and a sprinkling of artists, musicians, writers, actors, actresses and singers made their home. Gustav Klimt and Egon Schiele worked here, Johann Strauss, who had celebrated early successes at the Dommayer Casino on Hietzinger Platz, built his villa in the Maxingstraße opposite the Schönbrunn grounds; Emil von Sauer lived on the Hietzinger Hauptstraße, and the writers Berta von Suttner and Hermann Bahr were residents, as were the Court Opera soprano Marie Gutheil-Schoder, the actor Hans Moser and the Burgtheater star – and mistress to the Emperor – Katharina Schratt. And it was to Hietzing that Johanna Berg moved with her two youngest children, Alban, 20, and Smaragda, 19, in 1905. With the exception of three years, 1908 to 1911, it was in Hietzing that Alban Berg was to spend the rest of his life, and it was in Hietzing, rather than the inner city where he had grown to manhood, that he developed the strategies by which he transformed the impulses of his youth into the artworks of his maturity.

In the autumn of 1920, Soma Morgenstern – then a law student in his late twenties – moved from a modest furnished room near the University to the outlying thirteenth district, where he hoped to find the peace to study for his doctoral exams. It was to be a temporary dislocation, for after obtaining his law degree he fully intended to move back into the inner city and begin his career. Instead, he remained in Hietzing for the next twelve years.[5] One pleasant Friday afternoon in late September 1920 Morgenstern was on his way into the inner city to meet friends in a café before attending a concert. He boarded the 59 tram, which travelled from Hietzing to the inner city, and as he looked around among the handful of passengers his glance fell upon an attractive-looking couple studying a volume held between them. He was struck as much by the intensity of their study (the volume was a score of Mahler's Second Symphony, the work that he, too, was going to hear later that evening) as by their refined appearance. 'Das hohe Paar', he thought 'a lofty couple' – an impression, he admits, that was stimulated more by his fascination with the woman than by any interest in her companion.[6]

In the autumn of 1920 Helene and Alban Berg were in their mid-thirties and had been married for nearly ten years. Since May 1911 they had made their home in a ground-floor, three room apartment on Trauttmansdorffgasse, a quiet, tree-lined street of two- and three storey apartment houses that arcs in a bow from the Maxingstraße to the intersecting Gloriettegasse, creating a configuration of clean, angular lines that reminded Theodor W. Adorno quite plausibly, if incongruously, of Cezanne.[7] The Berg apartment, which fronts directly onto the corner of Trauttmansdorffgasse and Woltergasse, also looked out upon a large, unruly garden to the rear, a characteristic Hietzing combination of urban rectitude and sylvan lassitude. Hietzing's centre and the Schönbrunn grounds were just a few steps away, as was the villa in which Helene Berg had been born and where her parents still lived.

Helene Berg was the third of four children in the household of Franz (b. 1849) and Anna (b. 1859) Nahowski. The oldest, a daughter Carola (b. 1877), was the child of Anna's first marriage with Johann Heyduck, which had ended in divorce. Anna (b. 1882), Helene (b. 1885) and Franz Josef (b. 1889) were to all appearances the children of Franz Nahowski, although family legend has maintained that Helene and Franz were the illegitimate offspring of an eleven-year liaison that their mother had with the Emperor Franz Josef II between 1878 and 1889.[8] The Nahowski villa on Hetzendorferstraße (today Maxingstraße 46) is indeed located conveniently close to Schönbrunn. For his early morning trysts (usually a breakfast around 4am) the Emperor would leave the palace grounds by a small, inconspicuous garden door, cross the street, and, by a side entrance in the Weidlichgasse, let himself into the villa – he had his own key – and climb a winding staircase to Anna Nahowski's private salon.[9] With the end of the affair (after the Emperor began his liaison with Katharina Schratt, who lived in nearby Gloriettegasse), tensions in the Nahowski household sub-

sided and the children were raised in an atmosphere of bourgeois respectability and practised discretion.

It was during the 1906–7 season that Alban Berg had first noticed
Helene Nahowski at concerts and in the Opera. When he discovered she
was a neighbour who lived no more than five minutes' walk from his home
he began to haunt her street, dipping out of sight as soon as she appeared.
Tall, thin, and youthfully awkward, he was easily spotted by his quarry.
Finally, on Good Friday 1907, Helene's brother Franz, sympathetic to the
young man's predicament, engineered an encounter, lured Berg to the
family garden, and then ran to fetch his sister.[10] At a time when marriages
were not infrequently a race against the calendar the four-year courtship
that ensued is a testament to strictly observed proprieties. It is also testi-
mony to the strong misgivings that Franz Nahowski had about his daughter's spindly suitor.

There was nothing objectionable about Alban Berg's background.[11] His
family was very nearly the social equal of the Nahowskis. Indeed in 1905
Alban's sister Smaragda married the son of Alexander Freiherr von Eger,
President of the Imperial rail line (k.k. Privilegierte Südbahngesellschaft)
in which Franz Nahowski was an official.[12] Alban and Smaragda (b. 1886),
who had an extremely close relationship not unlike that of Helene and her
brother Franz, were the youngest of four children. Their father, Conrad (b.
1846), had run an import/export firm while their mother, Johanna Braun
(b. 1851), managed the family religious supplies shop. Their older broth-
ers Hermann (b. 1872), who lived in America, and Charly (b. 1881), who
remained in Vienna, both followed their father in the export business. It
was a comfortably prosperous first-district household with several serv-
ants, a governess, and a regulated schedule that included leisurely summers at the Berghof, the family's lakeside estate in Carinthia, no more than
a hundred miles from the Nahowski's country property in neighbouring
Styria.

Berg's parents encouraged cultural pursuits and enjoyed their contacts
with some of Vienna's musical celebrities, including the pianist Alfred
Grünfeld, a one-time summer neighbour, and Anton Bruckner, an occasional customer in the family shop and visitor in their home. The children
were bright, attractive, musical, and quick to take advantage of the cultural opportunities around them. Charly was an ardent Wagnerian, a
devout reader of *Die Fackel*, and an enthusiastic supporter of the controversial Court Opera director Gustav Mahler. Smaragda, a student of
Leschetizky, was an accomplished pianist who in later years would coach
leading singers, including Lula Mysz-Gmeiner, Anna Bahr-Mildenburg,
Marie Gutheil-Schoder and Frieda Leider. She was also an intimate in the
circles around Karl Kraus, Peter Altenberg, Gustav Klimt, Max Oppenheimer and Egon Friedell, and after her brief marriage she became an

outspoken lesbian. Alban, whose modest vocal and keyboard resources betrayed attentions divided between music, literature and art, was the coddled amateur composer whose Lieder were a centrepiece of family musical occasions.

Though Conrad Berg's untimely death in 1900 left the family in some financial uncertainty, the death in 1905 of Julie Weidmann, Johanna Berg's childless sister, brought the inheritance of a small fortune and extensive real-estate holdings, including the villa on Hietzinger Hauptstraße to which the family moved in October of that year. This sudden turn of fortune may well have provoked Berg to rethink his future. He had just begun his second year as an unpaid accounting apprentice in the Austrian civil service, a coveted opportunity for a secure position with generous pension benefits that had been obtained only through the influence of a highly placed family friend. A year later, however, having completed his apprenticeship and won his regular appointment, Berg abandoned this promising career in order to devote himself to music. His freedom had not come easily, but he assuaged his mother's misgivings by agreeing to administer the family's properties. As a marginally employed would-be artist Berg was thus a poor candidate for marriage, and around 1909 even a sympathetic Peter Altenberg gave the couple some half-serious advice. 'A young artist like yourself,' he told Alban, 'doesn't marry the daughter of a court official!'; 'Such a beautiful, genteel girl,' he told Helene, 'doesn't marry such a young Bohemian. He won't amount to anything.'[13]

It was not until June 1923 that Soma Morgenstern finally met the Bergs. By that time they had seen each other frequently and had realised that they had a number of mutual friends. One day as he entered the tram – again it was the 59, this time on its way out to Hietzing – Morgenstern was greeted by Alban Berg. The exchange was cordial but ended abruptly when Morgenstern, who was going to visit his mother in Mariahilferstraße, jumped out with a hasty farewell (having, out of politeness, already travelled well past his stop).

Some days later he met Helene Berg on the steps of the Hietzing post office. When he told her how pleased he had been to make her husband's acquaintance she looked surprised. Berg, it seems, had returned home that day out of sorts because Morgenstern's sudden departure – 'at a stop where no Hietzinger would ever have had any reason to go' – seemed like an excuse to end the conversation. When Morgenstern explained the circumstances Helene was visibly relieved and urged him to call on her husband: 'He seriously believed that he had annoyed you. That's the way Alban is. That's the way they all are, the Schönbergians, all of them [...] On the one hand very arrogant and then on the other full of feelings of inferiority. I don't understand how those two things go together. Perhaps you can explain it to me some time.'[14] That afternoon Morgenstern paid his first visit to Trauttmansdorffgasse 27.

To enter the Bergs' apartment was to enter a domain of well-ordered bourgeois comfort. The furniture was solid and tasteful, though of no prevailing style. The pictures and photographs that hung on the walls or cluttered the surfaces depicted admired personalities – mostly musicians and writers – or were reproductions of masterworks, interspersed with a few cherished originals. As one entered Berg's study, one of the two front rooms that faced Trauttmansdorffgasse, one found along the back and left walls the floor-to-ceiling bookshelves that housed his library. Berg's library was not particularly large, but it was well selected. The major classics of literature and music were there, as were numerous reference books. The heart of the collection was a body of works that belonged to the canon of *fin de siècle* Viennese predilections. The plays of Ibsen, the works of Strindberg, scattered volumes of Balzac and Maeterlinck, and above all works by Vienna's own: Kraus's *Die Fackel*, Peter Altenberg's slender volumes, writings by Bahr and Kokoschka, Hofmannsthal and Loos, among others.

Among those men Morgenstern identified a central pantheon of five *Hausgötter*, or household gods – Peter Altenberg, Karl Kraus, Gustav Mahler, Adolf Loos and Arnold Schoenberg – who were formative influences and continuing guides for Berg. They were the reflection of that fusion of acerbity and sentiment, fatalism and passion, so characteristic of his own psychic constitution. Mahler was, of course, a childhood idol, whose symphonies were redolent of the Austrian character and countryside. The admiration for Loos, Vienna's architect of austere villas and functional office buildings, came during the Schoenberg years, when the deaf architect was a vocal supporter of unpopular music he could not hear. Altenberg, the gentle apostle of fresh air, nature, a vegetarian diet and pre-pubescent girls, was for most Viennese a source of harmless bemusement, as if their good-natured toleration of his eccentricities were sufficient inoculation against the jaded callousness he exposed in their midst. For Berg he was a saint. Kraus, on the other hand, was opinionated, strident, mistrustful and litigious – an irate moral prophet whose tirades against the status quo aroused fierce passions. The flourishing readership for his journalistic alter-ego, *Die Fackel*, was likewise a tribute to Vienna's capacity for self-inoculation.[15]

Berg's association with Schoenberg went back nearly twenty years, to the time when the older man, in Vienna again after two-and-a-half years in Berlin had failed to make his career, began taking private students. Schoenberg was a self-taught outsider, a second-district Jew with no connections to the Academy or the University and few of the skills that might have distinguished him as a performer or conductor. His brash personality and evident genius had won him some prominent supporters, including Gustav Mahler, but that support had been of little use when in 1904, together with his brother-in-law, Alexander von Zemlinsky, he launched an ambitious concert organisation, the Vereinigung schaffender Tonkünstler (Association of Creative Musicians), for the propagation of new music. It folded after one season.[16] Of greater long-range significance were the energies Schoenberg devoted to teaching, for in Vienna an outsider could derive a significant measure of authority from his capacity to attract disciples. Karl Kraus had done as much for himself through the readership of *Die Fackel*.

Slowly Schoenberg had gathered his own circle – the first generation of what came to be called a 'school' and included Anton Webern, Heinrich Jalowetz, Erwin Stein, Josef Polnauer and Alban Berg – that would authenticate his presence in the Viennese cultural landscape.[17] Those early years, roughly 1904 to 1911, had been both exhilarating and harrowing for the teacher and his flock, and included in rapid succession artistic breakthroughs, premieres, openings, scandals and controversies, as well as personal and marital crises and a dramatic suicide.[18] The Chamber Symphony, Second String Quartet and George-Lieder established notoriety for Schoenberg the composer, his paintings thrust him into the vortex of the Austrian avant-garde, and performances of his students' compositions earned him esteem as a teacher. These were years during which lasting allegiances and alliances were formed. Mahler, Kraus, Loos, Altenberg, Klimt, Kokoschka, Wedekind, Strindberg, Balzac, Dehmel, George: for the Schoenberg circle these were more than the names of admired heroes, they were a call to arms. These were the years when this circle, drawn closer by conviction, made stronger by opposition, took on those brittle qualities of arrogance and inferiority that Helene Berg found so puzzling twenty years later. These were the years that transformed a clique of disciples into a phalanx of true believers.

At the time of Morgenstern's first acquaintance with Berg, Berg's association with Arnold Schoenberg was perhaps his chief claim to fame. Schoenberg was a frequent topic of their conversations, and Berg never failed to speak of his teacher with love and reverence, prompting Helene once to interject: 'You'd never believe how infatuated they all are with Schoenberg! Whenever they were discussing something and Schoenberg got up and wandered around the room, one of them always ran around after him with an ash tray.' – 'Even Alban?' I asked. – 'Him? He was the worst!'[19]

Such idolisation bespeaks an equal measure of awe and trepidation, and Berg was candid about his difficulties in freeing himself from the overbearing influence of his teacher. It was a dilemma that Berg once described as the central problem of his life, 'a problem I've carried around with me for decades without being able to solve it and which will be my downfall'.[20]

By 1911 most of Schoenberg's first-generation students were on their own. Webern, Jalowetz and Stein had embarked on their conducting careers, and in May of that year Berg had finally been allowed to marry Helene Nahowski.[21] Berg still derived his living from administering the family real-estate income, but proof-reading, preparing piano-vocal scores and teaching a few private students gave him at least the appearance of professional consequence, as did the couple's Hietzing address.[22]

Things were falling into place for Schoenberg as well. In 1909 he had signed a general contract with Universal Edition, Vienna's newest and most prestigious music publisher, and among the first works to appear was his widely heralded *Harmonielehre* of 1911. Schoenberg was at last being recognised as a teacher of consequence, and during the 1910–11 academic year he was granted permission to teach private courses in harmony and counterpoint at the Academy. The success of these courses gave him every expectation of an official appointment to the regular faculty – an offer that finally came in 1912.

Music history might have taken a different course had Schoenberg remained in Vienna, accepted the position at the Academy, and allowed himself to become a settled member of the city's establishment. But in the summer of 1911 he abruptly left Vienna and in the autumn moved again to Berlin.[23] It was an ill-considered decision that put Schoenberg's Viennese students and supporters in a state of disarray and over the next five years, from 1911 to 1915, consumed inordinate quantities of their time, energy and resources in supplying their master with his needs.[24] The concerts, lectures and publications they arranged during these years, which included the triumphant *Gurrelieder* premiere and the notorious *Skandalkonzert* of 1913, served to keep the absent Schoenberg a controversial presence in Vienna. But these years of proven devotion were also years of increasing tension, a tension that sprang from Schoenberg's artistic crises and self-doubts as well as from those of his students, who were attempting to establish their own artistic and professional identities.

Anton Webern may have suffered the most. He came to Schoenberg as a self-assured young man of considerable training and accomplishment. When he left Schoenberg he was a bundle of nerves and insecurities – as well as a composer of genius. His attempts at establishing a conducting career failed miserably, and he spent more than a decade hovering near the teacher who rewarded him with the intimacy of a friendship that left him scarred. Schoenberg's domination lay not just in his demands upon his students' time and loyalty; it was also the result of his capacity to get his students to suffer his agonies and to internalise the moral imperatives that drove him.

Unlike Webern, Berg did not initially come to Schoenberg with much more than his enthusiasms. Lacking Webern's skills and training he was more naturally diffident, and in consequence more unproblematically dependent. He had too much to learn to suffer profound doubts; those would come later. For fifteen years Berg was Schoenberg's most diligent student and chief fund-raiser; he wrote guides to his works, proof-read his scores, prepared the index to the *Harmonielehre*, and was throughout that time – and until the end of his life – a loyal correspondent.

Such loyalty was sorely tested, for Berg's psyche was the frequent object of blistering assault by a man who maintained the right to interfere with nearly every aspect of his life. In his letters and their intermittent personal encounters Schoenberg made it clear that he felt his student was by turns lazy, slovenly, passive, too slow a worker, a cloudy thinker, negligent of his health, preoccupied with his ills, too financially and emotionally dependent upon his mother and his wife's family, and too much caught up in their petty gossip and taken in by their social pretensions. 'You're angry that I accused you of dreaming!', Schoenberg wrote in May 1915, 'But I would like to make you still angrier. So angry that you jump up and bash me over the skull ... !'[25] Berg's many convoluted confessions, abject apologies and resolutions of reform did little to assuage his teacher, or indeed to alter his own patterns of behaviour, and by the end of 1915 there was a rupture between the two men that lasted more than a year.[26]

One evening in March 1925 Soma Morgenstern went to the Konzerthaus to purchase a ticket for a performance of Mahler's First Symphony. At the door he saw a very agitated Helene Berg, who implored him for help. Apparently a young man from Frankfurt who wanted to study with her husband had been invited over at three that afternoon and then had simply refused to leave:

He stayed for *Jause* and even after the *Jause* he didn't leave, and he talked away at Alban until Alban was quite pale from exhaustion. Alban had no idea what he was babbling on about. After the *Jause* we told him that we had arranged to go to the concert with Alma and had to leave early to go into the city. He said he'd come along. And he did not leave. He rode with us, bought himself a ticket, came straight to our box, and now is standing in front of Alban talking away at him. Alban sent me down here. After the concert we are invited to join Alma. He'll certainly want to go. You must rescue us![27]

Morgenstern entered the hall, and what he saw confirmed Helene's description. 'Standing in the box where Alma and her entourage sat, was Alban and in front of him a small and, compared to Alban, very short figure that was indeed talking away at him. When Alban saw me he raised both arms high above his head, but not in greeting but like a drowning man.'

No picture so tidily captures the difference between Alban Berg and Arnold Schoenberg as this image of Berg gasping for air under the importunate attentions of the young Theodor Wiesengrund Adorno.[28] Schoenberg would never have suffered such an assault without immediately asserting control and giving the puppy a few swipes for good measure. But the difference goes beyond Berg's lack of assertiveness or deficient authoritarian instincts. It was also a question of capacity. Berg simply could not process a barrage of new information and ideas quickly. Adorno implies that there was a certain coyness to Berg's claim that he was unable to grasp a Karl Kraus poem on first hearing,[29] but it was no pose. Hermann Watznauer, the fatherly mentor of Berg's youth, made these telling observations of his teenage friend:

His features and bearing often seemed tired and weary, and when in concert or in the opera he listened to a new piece of music he held his mouth a little open, which made an unfortunate impression. It was as if he were unable to grasp what he was hearing. He was different at times of relaxation and peace, of security, in the quiet circle of his friends. Then the compelling magic of his spiritualised youth glowed from his large clear eyes.[30]

In the security of his Trauttmansdorffgasse apartment Berg could take in the impulses from the outside world at his own pace and, with the help of liberal doses of his favourite cognac, even engage in heated debate, although Morgenstern tells us that his debating skills stood in an inverse ratio to his eagerness to wade in.[31] At home Berg could likewise give himself over to pleasures that in earlier times had earned him Schoenberg's haughty disdain.

One afternoon, Morgenstern, who was now himself living on Trauttmansdorffgasse, stopped by the Bergs' apartment to find them in the middle of a very lively *Jause*. Berg, surrounded by five women – Helene, Smaragda and three of her friends – was clearly having a grand time. Morgenstern stayed only a moment and as Berg accompanied him to the door he said with obvious glee, 'You have no idea how they gossip! It is intoxicating!'[32]

The truth is that Alban Berg liked gossip, he liked card games, and he enjoyed the little ceremonies of entertaining and socialising that were the rituals of his class. For the mildly bohemian Morgenstern, the Bergs, who lived in a world in which invitations to lunch, tea and dinner played a large role, were decidedly bourgeois. Even during the early 1920s, when inflation severely reduced their income, Helene's careful management of their resources made it possible for her to cater to her husband's sensuous appetites. Berg, Adorno noted, 'dignified everyday events relating to pleasure'. He recalled their home in these terms:

> The atmosphere always had something upper-class about it, to use the term in its proper sense. This was primarily because of the matter-of-fact attitude of those accustomed to a good life. [...] Nothing in their lifestyle was bohemian. Rarely have I seen a home in which I felt more comfortable; there was something spacious, large, corresponding precisely to Berg's ideal of the jovial.[33]

The comfort of routine fostered Berg's slow, methodical work habits and afforded him the means of partitioning his day to allow him his share of rewards and satisfactions. Such domesticity was seductive, and under its influence even Adorno learned the value of a little self-deprecation. 'I was deadly earnest in those days,' he later wrote, 'which could get on a mature artist's nerves. Out of pure veneration I tried never to say anything I did not consider particularly profound.' 'At times,' Adorno further noted, 'Berg no doubt relegated my own philosophical ballast to the category he termed tedious [*fad*]; I joked about it once and he did not seriously contradict me.'[34]

Tolerant and liberal are words that Adorno uses to describe Berg the teacher. Berg's teaching had none of the hectoring quality that kept Schoenberg's students on their toes. He was a patient and methodical guide through harmony and counterpoint, and taught composition by means of measured, carefully considered encouragement. Although Schoenberg's teaching lay at the core of his own, there was nothing doctrinaire about Berg's approach. His musical tastes were catholic and included a number of contemporary French, German, Italian and Eastern European composers who had little or no relationship to the atonal revolution. Berg's approach was never threatening, edgy or aggressive, and he was distinctly ill at ease with the presence of those qualities in his teacher's teaching and music. Lessons were usually given in his study and often concluded with four-handed music making at the piano, a visit to a café, or a lengthy stroll around the Schönbrunn palace grounds.

Berg's students were no circle of fawning disciples. They helped their teacher as Berg had helped Schoenberg – in preparing his scores, copying parts and correcting proofs – but they did not join him on his vacations and only rarely accompanied him on his travels, although they were generally welcome to participate in certain cherished routines of everyday life, including concerts, theatre, cinema and football matches.[35] Only a few of his students developed lasting personal ties with their teacher; most went their way after their studies. There was no doubt a good deal of friendly indoctrination into those topics dear to Berg – above all those Viennese *Hausgötter* Altenberg, Kraus, Loos and Mahler – and he certainly tried to instil an overriding sense of allegiance to the larger Schoenbergian cause. But Berg's students were not sent into the trenches of cultural warfare as Schoenberg's had been. Times had changed. More importantly, as Adorno observed, Berg's tolerance set him apart from other Schoenbergians, as did 'the need of this extremely sensitive and vulnerable man to avoid as far as possible the tyranny of the collective'.[36]

After their rupture in 1915 Berg's relationship with Schoenberg had slowly healed, and by 1918 Schoenberg had proffered his former student the familiar 'Du' form of address. During the early post-war years the Schoenberg circle cut a lower profile on Vienna's cultural horizon. The great pre-war scandals and controversies were a thing of the past, legends of another age. Now the sporadic public performances of their music were greeted with respect from a self-selected audience of new-music enthusiasts and with equanimity from the public at large. Their Verein für musikalische Privataufführungen (Society for Private Music Performances), founded in 1918, inherited the mantle of the Vereinigung schaffender Tonkünstler, although the modest scope of its performing forces, members-only audiences and ban on reviewers considerably reduced its public exposure.[37] The cessation of regular concerts in 1921 and the organisation's official demise in 1923 were scarcely noticed by Vienna's cultural community.

When Adorno arrived in Vienna two years later he was surprised to find the Schoenberg circle less tight-knit than he had supposed:

> Schoenberg, remarried, lived in Mödling; his elegant young wife, so it
> seemed to the old guard, kept him rather isolated from the friends of the
> old heroic days. Webern probably already lived out in Maria Enzersdorf.
> They did not see much of one another. Berg particularly lamented the
> fact that he so seldom saw Webern and Steuermann, of whom he was very
> fond, and blamed it on Vienna's size, which was hardly formidable.[38]

Post-war Vienna, reduced to little more than the provincial capital of a small alpine republic, was no longer the cultural powerhouse it had once been, and the honour of being one of her outsiders was losing its savour. Her creative artists began to look beyond the narrow confines of the Austrian hinterlands for cultural resonance. The Verein, for example, established links to new-music circles abroad and served as a model for the International Society for Contemporary Music, founded in 1923. Indeed the Vienna chapter of the ISCM, the Verein für neue Musik, essentially resurrected the Vienna chapter of the Verein für musikalische Privataufführungen, mixing familiar faces from the old guard with such younger members of the circle as Schoenberg's brother-in-law Rudolf Kolisch, whose quartet became an international champion for new music.

Schoenberg, too, sought teaching and conducting opportunities abroad, and at the beginning of 1926 he left Vienna to accept a master class at the Prussian Academy of the Arts in Berlin. It was his third sojourn in the German capital, and when he arrived an opera by Alban Berg was the talk of the town.

Recognition as a composer came late to Berg. His first wide exposure, the 1913 premiere of two of the *Altenberg Lieder* Op. 4, had ended in a scandal, after which the work disappeared without trace.[39] Other works, including his Piano Sonata Op. 1, Four Songs Op. 2, String Quartet Op. 3 and the clarinet pieces Op. 5, had appeared in student recitals or within the confines of the Verein concerts, but they had had little exposure outside Vienna. It was not until April 1923 that Berg signed a contract with Universal Edition, having by then already published his first three opus numbers and the *Wozzeck* piano-vocal score at his own expense. Later that year, performances of two of his Three Orchestral Pieces Op. 6 in Berlin and his String Quartet at the Salzburg Festival created a stir, but it was the performance of the *Wozzeck* excerpts at the International Music Festival in Frankfurt in the summer of 1924 that transformed Alban Berg into the celebrity whom Adorno was trying so hard to impress a few months later. It was also this performance that laid the groundwork for the stunning triumph of the Berlin *Wozzeck* premiere in December 1925. At the age of forty Berg was no longer just a member of the Schoenberg entourage but a personality in his own right. The *Wozzeck* premiere had made him famous and, for a time, financially prosperous.

During the last ten years of his life Berg assumed the public persona of a celebrated composer. Performances of his works took him to cities around

Germany, and to Prague, Brussels, Paris, Winterthur and Leningrad. Even
Vienna paid tribute to its native son with a brilliant production of *Wozzeck*
at the State Opera. He lectured on his music, received honours for his
achievements, and was quoted in newspapers and interviewed on the radio. He sat on juries and attended festivals in England, Switzerland, Germany and Italy, where he conferred with colleagues and numbered among
his professional acquaintances Béla Bartók, Edward J. Dent, Gregor Fitel-
berg, Zoltán Kodály, Charles Koechlin, Gian Francesco Malipiero, Albert
Roussel and Ernst Toch. He socialised with politicians, blue-blooded aristocrats and red-blooded financiers. Through his friendship with Alma
Mahler and Franz Werfel he was introduced to Gerhart Hauptmann and
Sinclair Lewis; Viennese literary figures such as Hermann Broch, Stefan
Zweig and Elias Canetti boasted his acquaintance; and admirers from
abroad, including George Gershwin, found their way to his Trauttmansdorffgasse door. Affluence enabled Berg to buy a car, a Ford cabriolet; he
now wrote his letters with a typewriter; and in 1932 he purchased a villa,
the Waldhaus, on the Wörthersee. Like Schoenberg, Berg was offered en-
ticements to leave Vienna. Positions in France, England or even America
would have been his for the asking, and at least twice, in 1925 and 1930,
Franz Schreker offered him a position at the Berlin Hochschule für Musik.
Despite strong encouragement from Schoenberg, Berg turned down both
offers.

It was not the flattery of official recognition that kept Berg in Vienna. In
1924 he graciously accepted the Kunstpreis der Stadt Wien, but when he
was offered the honorary title of professor he is said to have turned it
down with the laconic observation, 'too late – Alban Berg suffices!'[40] Perhaps he had spent too many years on the periphery to feel comfortable on
the inside, that milieu to which, unlike Schoenberg, he had been born and
bred. Even after the success of *Wozzeck* it is said that he occasionally returned to see an opera from the standing room. He continued to be an
avid reader of *Die Fackel* and in 1932 was a founder of the *Fackel*-inspired
cultural journal *23. Eine Wiener Musikzeitschrift*, edited by his student
Willi Reich.[41]

One reason for staying in Vienna was that family affairs and responsi-
bilities continued to play a large role in the Bergs' life, particularly as their
parents grew older.[42] Berg remained close to Smaragda and Charly (Hermann had died in America in 1920), and Helene's brother Franz, to whom
both she and Alban were bound by deep affection, was becoming increasingly incapacitated by severe and dangerous bouts of paranoia. Ties of
friendship were no less important reasons for remaining in Vienna, especially now that Berg's enhanced income enabled him to enjoy more fully
the sensuous comforts of his native city.

But the most important factors keeping Berg in Vienna were the requirements of his own creative persona. During the last decade of his life
Berg worked hard to overcome the predisposition toward indolence and
vacillation that had slowed his productivity in earlier years. As Soma Morgenstern observes, 'From the time of the sensational success of the *Wozzeck* Suite at the Music Festival in Frankfurt am Main, where he had, as it
were, tasted blood, he had become an extremely diligent worker.'[43] In this
he had the full support of his wife, who did everything she could to create
an environment conducive to his needs. Morgenstern reports that she
would even lock him into his study to force him to work, although Berg
claimed that on such occasions he consoled himself with the bottle of
cognac he kept hidden under the sofa.[44]

It is of little import whether Helene knew about the cognac or not. After
Berg's death she claimed that she did; Morgenstern is sure she did not.
What is important is that Berg thought he had a secret, one secret more he
could share with a friend. Berg's love of secrets and his compulsion to
gossip kept each other good company.[45] His marital infidelities – the relationship with Hanna Fuchs-Robettin was but one of several affairs and
sexual liaisons – were a favourite topic, and friends like Soma Morgenstern and Rudolf Kolisch, as well as the closest of his students, were frequently enlisted as confidants and go-betweens. Nor should one attribute
undue significance to the confessional contents of Berg's correspondence.
Letters were his preferred medium for cultivating friendships and chan-
nelling passions, but they were at bottom another strategy of reserve, a
method of using others to mask the location of a self that lay at some point
of infinite regress beyond. In any event Helene Berg probably knew about
or suspected most of these affairs and may well have had several of her
own, including a near-affair with Soma Morgenstern, who had Berg's permission and encouragement. Morgenstern changed his mind, not, as he
insists, out of bourgeois scruples, but because Helene's love for Berg and
his profound dependence upon her seemed more important.[46]

The sacrifices of those around Berg were inspired by his own detached
regard for his creative needs. Adorno once remarked that Berg

> treated his own person with both care and indifference, like the musical
> instrument he was to himself. He liked talking and writing about him-
> self, still more about his music. But there was no trace of vanity in this; it
> scarcely sounded as if he identified the two aspects of himself with one
> another, rather as if he were reporting about the composer Alban Berg
> whom he esteemed.[47]

'Berg's empirical existence,' Adorno writes elsewhere, 'was subordinate to
the primacy of creative work; he honed himself as its instrument, his store

of life experiences became solely a means of supplying conditions that would permit him to wrest his œuvre from his own physical weaknesses and psychological resistance.'[48] Food, drink, gossip and romantic entanglements were among the elements supplying the conditions of that creativity, and it was Berg's capacity for sharing his enjoyment that effaced any hint of egoism. But the physical precondition for Berg's creativity, the pendant of his own detachment from the creative self, was an environment that allowed him to participate in the world from a secure remove.

It is the irony of the last decade of Berg's life that the more fame drew him into the mainstream the greater his physical and psychological detachment became, and the more his comforts and passions created a wall around his works and were integrated into their texture. And the more the political horizon was darkened by events that doomed his cultural universe, the more he withdrew – to his life in Hietzing and to his rural retreat at the Wörthersee, a place he called his 'concentration camp' because it enabled him to shut out the distractions of the outside world. It was black humour tinged with the shame of a man who was incapable of overt resistance.[49] Adorno observed that in his last years Berg counteracted his growing isolation with a strategy of diplomatic dissimulation. 'I called him the foreign minister of the land of his dreams and he laughed.'[50]

Artistic choices are about perspectives and a point of view. Every artist must find a centre and Berg, a creature of habit, a product of place and environment, found his centre in a world he created in an outlying district of Vienna, a place he variously referred to as 'the back of beyond' and 'the end of the world'.[51] It was a place of bourgeois respectability and discreetly shared secrets, a place sheltered from confrontation, where he could absorb at his own pace the impulses from Vienna's inner district and assimilate the stimuli from the world beyond, a place where he could gently shoulder his way into the future while gazing back at the world of his parents. Its comforts were a precondition for his work and a context for his languorous, layered and secretive scores. Those comforts were also his buffer against challenges to his equilibrium, whether from the consequences of emotional entanglements, the moral compromises exacted from a world descending into madness, or the imperatives of the restless and driven man who was his teacher and master.

Of the household gods Morgenstern enumerates, Schoenberg stands apart. In Kraus, Loos, Altenberg and Mahler, Berg found reminders of his own identity and experiences – of the acerbity of the first-district coffee-house tirade, of the utopian vision for a regulated life in the districts beyond, of the fragile, tragic beauty of the human soul, or of the grand and melancholy solitude of his beloved Carinthian landscapes. Ultimately these lives and the works they produced reinforced Berg's own sense of place and belonging. Arnold Schoenberg, on the other hand, knew no home, was neither contained within space nor defined by place. His erratic moves, frequent travels, agitated summers and bewildering succession of apartments reinforced no pattern of belonging. They speak rather of a man who inhabited a sphere of ideas, of history and destiny; a man of ambition, of propulsive, protean energy, always in the process of transforming himself, always restless to conquer new terrain and move on. Berg's lifelong allegiance to Schoenberg was an exhilarating and terrifying orbit around a continually shifting axis. Schoenberg offered a traveller's compass to a man clinging to an anchor.

For all his loyalty to Schoenberg, Berg kept his distance. He resisted Schoenberg's urgings, both before and after the First World War, to join him in Berlin, and in later years he used evasion to avoid Schoenberg's repeated invitations that they vacation together. He may even have felt some relief when in 1933 Schoenberg left for America, a place where Berg knew he could not follow. Throughout his relationship with Schoenberg, Berg used his sedentary life, his family, his habits and environment as a bulwark behind which to construct his own very different identity and æsthetic persona, a persona forged from a synthesis of the dichotomous impulses of his native city, of sensual instinct with critical analysis, of timbral voluptuousness and emotive affect with painstaking design and structural intricacy.[52]

Berg constructed the land of his dreams on the outskirts of his youth. The models he followed, the texts he chose and the themes he pursued derive from that agitated and contradictory pre-war world of first-district passions. These impulses were filtered through a life on the periphery, through a world of unhurried comfort where within the sanctuary of settled propriety Alban Berg could indulge the sweet decay of his character and create a body of works that spring from the lingering embrace of two worlds.

2 Battles of the mind: Berg and the cultural politics of 'Vienna 1900'

Andrew Barker
University of Edinburgh

On the evening of 31 March 1913 the Great Hall of the Vienna Musik-verein erupted as Arnold Schoenberg conducted two of Berg's songs Op. 4, the *Fünf Orchesterlieder nach Ansichtskartentexten von Peter Altenberg*. The audience bawled for composer and poet to be sent to the madhouse, knowing full well that Altenberg was already a patient in the State Mental Institution at Steinhof on the outskirts of the city. Fights broke out, the police were called, and Erhard Buschbeck, a friend of Berg's and an organiser of the concert, was arrested after trading blows with the operetta composer Oscar Straus. At the trial Straus remarked that the thud of the punch had been the most harmonious thing in the whole concert.[1]

Although the *Skandalkonzert* has entered the folklore of modern musical history, it is perhaps not fully appreciated just how symbolic this event was, nor how indicative (albeit in a fairly extreme form) of cultural life in the city as a whole. For the glorious cultural florescence of 'Vienna 1900' – now almost as clichéd as is the other Vienna of Johann Strauss and Sacher-torte – was riven with factions, spite and, on occasions, violence. As often as not, the aggression focused on a man revered by Alban Berg: the satirist Karl Kraus (1874–1936), a close friend of Altenberg and no stranger to non-verbal altercation. As early as 1897 fists replaced brains when Felix Salten, author of *Bambi*, boxed the satirist's ears for suggesting that the Budapest-born Salten's command of German grammar was less than perfect.[2] In 1906 Kraus was knocked senseless by Marc Henry, *conférencier* of the 'Cabaret Nachtlicht' after Kraus had attacked him in his journal *Die Fackel* (*The Torch*).[3] Other feuds remained at the level of deep personal antipathy, sometimes even amongst artists moving within the same restricted circles and sharing a similar æsthetic. From 1910 onwards the painters Oskar Kokoschka and Max Oppenheimer, both close to the 'Superior Triple Alliance' of Kraus, Loos and Altenberg,[4] were at loggerheads after Kokoschka became convinced that 'Mopp', as he styled himself, was plagiarising his work. It is no coincidence that each artist produced distinguished portraits of Kraus, Loos and Altenberg as well as Schoenberg and Webern.[5]

The hostile, even violent reception of his *Altenberg Lieder* cannot have entirely surprised the languid, dreamy young composer, for Berg too was an enthusiastic partisan in the intellectual battlefield of late Imperial Vienna. Simply to have set the deranged poet was an act of solidarity almost calculated to inflame the bourgeois Viennese public. Nor would Berg have been shocked that his friend Altenberg, instrumental in bringing him and his future wife Helene Nahowski together in 1907, thought little of his songs.[6] After the concert Altenberg wrote to Franz Schreker, who had shortly before conducted the uniquely successful Viennese premiere of Schoenberg's *Gurrelieder*:

> I understand nothing of this latest 'modern music', my brain-soul still hears, feels, understands only Richard Wagner, Hugo Wolf, Brahms, Dvořák, Grieg, Puccini, Richard Strauss! But the countenance of the modern woman I understand like an alpine pasture and my beloved Semmering.[7]

In a letter to Adolf Loos (1870–1933), undated but probably from around 1910–11, Altenberg berated the architect for his excessive admiration for Schoenberg, Kokoschka and the avant-garde poet Else Lasker Schüler, who featured regularly in *Die Fackel*. The tone is typical of Altenberg when expressing a forceful opinion:

> Your preference for Oskar Kokoschka – Else Lasker-Schüler – Arnold Schoenberg demonstrates exactly the *nadir* of your *intellectual-spiritual machinery*.[8]

Yet when implored by Berg to support the public appeal in Autumn 1911 on behalf of the near destitute Arnold Schoenberg, Altenberg's answer was unequivocal: 'Naturally and with deep commitment'.[9]

Of the Kraus–Loos–Altenberg triumvirate, it was to Altenberg (né Richard Engländer, 1859–1919), the oldest of the group by some years, that Berg was personally closest. They first met in 1906, and in the following year his sister Smaragda introduced the composer to the Altenberg côterie which met in the Löwenbräu bar in the Teinfaltstraße. It is obvious that the older poet took a shine to him, for amongst his numerous letters to Smaragda are several references to Berg's nobility, a typical formulation being 'Alban, most noble of youths'.[10] Although fully aware of Smaragda's lesbianism, Altenberg was for a time extravagantly enamoured of her. The 'relationship' was especially intense between September 1909 and January 1910, and the fifty-year-old poet was not shy of soliciting Berg's direct intervention when things were going badly:

> I come as an artist to you as an artist —. *Help* me! I have offended and wounded your sister whom I worship —. Put in a good word for me with the dear lady, *I implore you*, so that I may *once again become capable of*

life, capable of suffering —. May God reward you. I implore your help in *relieving* my torments. Smaragda should forgive me *for your sake*.[11]

Altenberg's feelings for Helene Nahowski-Berg went equally deep, for with her willowy tallness and long blond hair she embodied his physical ideal. Knowing that the eccentric poet posed no real threat, for he famously loved the unobtainable, Berg seems to have harboured neither resentment nor jealousy. Instead, he knew that Altenberg had provided him with an entrée into an artistic circle which he admired with a fervour bordering on reverence. Frequently referring to Altenberg in his letters to Helene, Berg often points to shared features with the poet, not merely in terms of artistic outlook, but even of a personally trivial kind, such as a propensity for nailbiting.[12]

Altenberg was at the heart of a group to which both Kraus and Loos belonged, and which also included the polymath, actor and raconteur Egon Friedell (1878–1938) as well as Gustav Klimt (1862–1918), of whose paintings Kraus thought rather poorly. In June 1908 Berg accompanied Klimt and Altenberg to the great 'Kunstschau' exhibition dominated by Klimt's work,[13] and to which Altenberg dedicated a glowing sketch in which he talks of 'Room 22, Gustav Klimt-cathedral of modern art'.[14] A letter of 1 July 1908 to his future wife reveals just how well integrated Berg now felt in this seminal group of Viennese artists and intellectuals:

> In the afternoon I then went to the 'Kunstschau' … It was so quiet there to begin with … then I fled the café terrace, for the piano started tinkling and then they all came marching up: those from the Altenberg party – then the Klimt group – then Karl Kraus by himself – we joined each other, two lonely people. In the evening I then met up with Smaragda at the Altenberg table … at the Löwenbräu, and then Smaragda went off home with Ida!! I met up with Karl Kraus, Dr Fritz Wittels was there too, and that was really nice.[15]

Yet how typical of Berg's servility that as late as 1920 he could still write to Webern, in the course of a letter expressing his proximity to Zemlinsky:

> my ignorance in matters of painting and in particular Kraus's condemnation of Klimt [prevented] me from letting my enthusiasm for him be too widely known.[16]

Though absent from the *Skandalkonzert* itself, Altenberg had been granted leave from the asylum to attend the dress-rehearsal on the morning of 31 March. Despite hearing all about the uproar at the concert proper, he did not respond directly to the event. Instead, he sent Berg a copy of his latest book *Semmering 1912*, which Berg in fact already possessed.[17] Even inside Steinhof, however, the poet continued writing obsessively, reacting in inimitable fashion to 'what the day brings' (*Was der Tag mir zuträgt* is the title of the book from which Berg's earlier Altenberg songs of 1906 had been taken).[18] On 3 April, just three days after the *Skandalkonzert*, Altenberg composed a short prose sketch entitled 'Alma' which can only refer to events he had witnessed at the dress-rehearsal. This sketch avoids any reference to Berg's settings of his words, concentrating instead on the frivolous reactions of Alma Mahler, a close friend of the Bergs, during the rehearsal of the *Kindertotenlieder*. These songs were scheduled to conclude the public concert but in the event had to be abandoned because of the rumpus triggered off by the *Altenberg Lieder*. The sketch depicts Alma, decked out in widow's weeds, canoodling with a young man while 'the third *Kindertotenlied* wept' ('das dritte *Kindertotenlied* weinte').[19] In a few succinct lines Altenberg delivers a devastating cameo of Alma's facile reactions to the *Kindertotenlieder*, which had eerily pre-dated the death of her daughter Anna Maria in 1906 – an event which she apparently regarded as a punishment for their composition.[20] Although he is not named, the young man in the sketch can only be Oskar Kokoschka (1886–1980), and, as Altenberg knew, would be instantly recognised as such by a contemporary Viennese readership with a well-trained nose for scandal.[21] Their affair, which was the talk of the town, was commemorated in one of Kokoschka's greatest works, *Die Windsbraut* (1913), depicting the ecstatic union of the artist and his lover. Altenberg's garrulous miniature was not published until 1915, along with a dedication to Gustav Mahler conspicuously absent from the original manuscript. The entire sketch, but especially the dedication, must have been intentionally provocative, especially as Alma had by then finished with Kokoschka and taken up with the German architect Walter Gropius, a leading light in the 'Bauhaus' movement. She went to law, and the sketch disappeared from all further editions of the book *Fechsung*.[22] Soon afterwards, Alma gave birth to her daughter Manon Gropius, whose premature death inspired Berg to write what transpired to be his last work, the Violin Concerto.[23]

I open with this essentially anecdotal material because it demonstrates the extent to which the world which formed Alban Berg was an incestuous one where everyone not only knew everyone else, but also to a large degree knew everyone else's business. These lives have even been diagrammatically realised as the 'Vienna Circles', at the very centre of which intersect those of Kraus, Loos and Schoenberg, within whose common segments can be found the names of both Berg and Altenberg.[24] This was also the world which shaped Helene Nahowski (1885–1976), rumoured to be the illegitimate daughter of the aged Emperor Franz Josef (1830–1916).[25] Having spent her life in a world of at best partial privacy may well explain why in later years Frau Berg so fiercely resisted any public knowledge of her husband's passion for Hanna Fuchs-Robettin. Hanna, of course, was not only the sister of Franz Werfel (one of the most popular authors of the day, whom Kraus thoroughly despised) but also the sister-in-law of Alma Mahler-Werfel. True to his literary master, Berg also thought little of Werfel, but because of the close relationship between the Bergs and Alma Mahler he maintained what he described in a letter to Helene as a 'quasi-friendship' ('Quasi-Freundschaft') with him.[26] As if these relationships were not already intertwined enough, Anna Mahler, the surviving daughter of Gustav and Alma, was married for a time to the composer Ernst Krenek, who in turn was close to Alban Berg.

Although the Schoenberg–Kraus–Loos–Altenberg–Kokoschka axis by no means tells the whole story of the Vienna which dominated Berg's early artistic life, it is nevertheless the one with the most meaning for him. In a letter of June/July 1903 Berg wrote to his friend Paul Hohenberg: 'So we share the same tastes, which pleases me greatly, for in some things they diverge: Kraus, *Altenberg*!'[27] Moreover, this early enthusiasm never wavered, and more than thirty years later, in his oration at Berg's funeral, Soma Morgenstern remarked of the dead composer that he possessed 'the nobility of a new era, which Peter Altenberg, its greatest prophet, heralded: the nobility of naturalness'.[28] This naturalness, manifested in an æsthetic functionalism which reduced literature to its essence, was a feature of Altenberg's writing which appealed to a generation of Viennese intellectuals, foremost amongst them Karl Kraus. It formed a literary parallel to what Adolf Loos was trying to achieve in architecture, and for a brief while Altenberg and Loos even tried to co-operate in a joint publishing venture. The short-lived journal *Kunst* (1903–4) was edited by Altenberg, with a section edited by Loos entitled *Das Andere*, whose purpose was nothing less than the 'introduction of Western culture into Austria' ('Einführung Abendländischer Kultur in Österreich').

In matters literary, what went for Berg went also on the whole for his teacher Schoenberg and for his fellow-pupil Webern, and as the following quotations reveal, there was an almost uncanny consensus amongst them as to who was important. Thus Schoenberg, writing in memory of Webern in 1945, declared:

> [It] is clear that [Webern] never changed his opinion about Karl Kraus, Peter Altenberg, Peter Rosegger, Gustav Mahler and me. They were his 'fixed stars'.[29]

Reminiscing about his years in Vienna, the Paris-based Schoenberg pupil Max Deutsch (1892–1982) was quite specific in his recollections of who set the tone for Berg and his contemporaries:

> This special style, you had four people – Schoenberg the musician, Karl Kraus the writer, Adolf Loos the architect, and Peter Altenberg the poet – four people, this German writing.[30]

In a letter to Berg dated 13 December 1911, by which time Schoenberg had been forced from Vienna to try his luck in Berlin, Webern declared:

> It would be so nice if all the people who these days are something were together in one town, interacting vigorously: Schoenberg, Klimt, Altenberg, Loos, Kraus, us, Kokoschka and many others.[31]

Very noticeably, however, this list of great names does not include such eminent, quintessentially Viennese figures as Freud, Hofmannsthal and Schnitzler, and the reason is again best summarised in two words: Karl Kraus. As it happens, Kraus had a vacillating opinion of Mahler too, but in this respect at least Berg was able to maintain his independence. The extent of his intellectual reliance upon the satirist emerges, however, in a draft letter which Berg penned on the occasion of Kraus's fiftieth birthday on 28 April 1924. Addressed to the 'Venerated Master' ('Verehrter Meister'), and signed 'in eternal fealty' ('in ewiger Gefolgschaft'), Berg writes that because of his timidity he has spent twenty-five years suppressing the need to express his devotion. Now at last, in a tone of excessive deference reminiscent of his letters to Schoenberg, he expresses what he feels:

> My thanks to the lead which your exemplary figure has given me in all questions of art and life since the days of my youth, and which it still gives today as I approach forty. My thanks for the immeasurable bliss with which your written work provides me ... My thanks for the spiritual support which you have provided me with time and again in life's most unpleasant situations.[32]

Through the medium of *Die Fackel*, published between 1899 and 1936, as well as through direct personal contact, Kraus was indeed central to the development of Berg's overall perspective on life and art. He was equally important to Schoenberg, although in this instance the relationship was more obviously one between equals. Berg, however, found it difficult, if not impossible, to assert himself in a mature manner with those he stood in awe of. Perhaps most importantly for the future development of Berg's art, it was Kraus who introduced the banned German playwright Frank Wedekind (1864–1918) to a select Viennese audience. Because of censorship, *Die Büchse der Pandora* (*Pandora's Box*), the second of Wedekind's Lulu plays – the first was *Erdgeist* (*Earth Spirit*) – was to remain unperformed in public until after the dramatist's death, but on 29 May 1905 Kraus put on a private performance, even playing a small role himself, frustrated actor that he was. For both the dramatist and the composer it was an event with lasting consequences. Wedekind, who took the role of Jack the Ripper in the final scene, found his future wife Tilly in the young actress playing the victim, Lulu. She recalls the occasion:

> In the hall, filled to capacity, there sat, one among many, a young man of twenty who looked like an angel. Decades later the world became aware of the lasting impression that the play, the production, and the [intro-ductory] talk by Karl Kraus had made on him. His name was Alban Berg, and one day he was to compose the opera, *Lulu*.[33]

Writing to congratulate Kraus on his sixtieth birthday in 1934, Berg enclosed a six-bar excerpt from *Lulu* with Alwa's words to Lulu: 'Eine Seele, die sich im Jenseits den Schlaf aus den Augen reibt' ('A soul rubbing the sleep out of its eyes in the next world'), this being the very quotation with which Kraus had opened his introductory lecture to *Die Büchse der Pandora* nearly thirty years previously.[34]

Wedekind was also enthusiastic about the then virtually unknown Georg Büchner (1813–1837), who provided the dramatic source for Berg's *Wozzeck*. Büchner had essentially been discovered by the Galician/Jewish writer Karl Emil Franzos, who had first published the *Woyzeck* fragment in the Viennese *Neue Freie Presse* in 1875.[35] Thereafter, his cause was taken up with particular vigour by Hugo von Hofmannsthal, for whom Karl Kraus had little but contempt. While Kraus was busy trying to restore the reputation of the great Viennese farceur Johann Nestroy (1801–62), Hofmannsthal published Büchner's short story *Lenz* in his hugely influential anthology of German stories entitled *Deutsche Erzähler* (1912). Büchner's triumphal march through the dramaturgical history of our century can be dated back to the Viennese performance of his comedy *Leonce and Lena* in 1911, while Hofmannsthal went so far as to provide his own reworking of *Woyzeck*, including a new ending to the fragment. At his instigation, *Woyzeck* was brought to the stage for the first time, in Munich in November 1913, to mark the centenary of Büchner's birth, and one year later the Viennese premiere took place, an event which led to Berg's decision to compose his first great opera.

Kraus may have thought very highly of Frank Wedekind, but it is entirely typical of the diversity within unity that characterised the 'triple alliance' that Altenberg should have held Wedekind in particularly low esteem. Berg, who responded so sensitively to all three, might well have heard Egon Friedell (who had a role in the private performance of *Die Büchse der Pandora*) recite his 'Altenberg anecdotes' at the Cabaret Fledermaus, which was patronised by Vienna's intellectual élite from its inception in 1907 until its transformation into a strip-joint in 1913:

The Frank Wedekind Conversation

We were sitting one night in the café when Frank Wedekind came by.
Peter Altenberg said: 'Ha, here comes that pasty-faced wretch!'
   'Come on, Peter,' I said, 'make it up again with him.'
   'What!?!' said Peter Altenberg, '*me* make it up with him?? That's *quite out of the question*! I'd rather make it up with any *other* of my mortal enemies!! But not with him! And why not? With all the others it would be more or less private and personal, *subjective* animosity! But him I hate *objectively*! *Worlds* divide him and me! He is Satan, Beelzebub, the *Antichrist* here on earth!'
   'Fine,' I said, 'but supposing he lends you three hundred crowns?'
   'What do you mean!?! He's not going to lend me it anyway!!'[36]

Through *Die Fackel*, with its promotion of both Wedekind and Altenberg, a whole generation of young artists and intellectuals in Central Europe learnt to perceive the world in a very specific way. Ludwig Wittgenstein, for instance, even took copies of Kraus's journal with him to the fastness of his hideaway perched above a Norwegian fjord. By means of the most precise and targeted use of German, over which he had a supreme control – no language doubter he! – Kraus cast a critical and often hilarious eye upon the social, political and artistic foibles of the dying Habsburg Empire. It was a very partial view, its prejudices (against, for example, Klimt's paintings and Freud's psychology) as forcibly articulated as its enthusiasms. High among the latter was the miniaturist Altenberg, health fanatic, drug-addict, alcoholic, wooer of young girls, and for many quite simply the biggest fool in Vienna. For Kraus, however, he was the most important writer in a city full of literary talent, most of which he despised. Where others in Vienna were given over to artifice and superficial decoration, Kraus believed that Altenberg, with his love of children and nature, was genuine, and that a single word of his was worth more than an entire lending library.[37] Of especial importance was Altenberg's view, shared with the notoriously misogynistic philosopher Otto Weininger,[38] that women were essentially of æsthetic and/or sexual importance. In no way could they match the 'intellectual' genius of men, for woman's genius was an 'æsthetic' one. As has been pointed out, Weininger's notion of the 'otherness of women' ('Anderswertigkeit der Frau') soon became associated in Kraus's mind with the writings of Frank Wedekind.[39]

   Alongside Altenberg and Adolf Loos, whose pioneering new building on the Michaelerplatz (1910–11) caused at least as much offence as the *Altenberg Lieder* – 'a horror of a building' ('ein Scheusal von einem Haus') is how one contemporary critic described it[40] – Kraus often stood shoulder to shoulder. Perhaps especially significant in the shared perceptions of the triumvirate were their reactions in two important areas. First, their insistence on the centrality of female sexuality, and a woman's right to exercise control over her body in the way she thought fit. This included an unusual tolerance of prostitution which Berg seems to have shared not only artistically but in his everyday life too, for writing to Helene in 1910 he says 'a prostitute's position [is] no more or less offensive than associating with people whom you and many others consider quite unobjectionable'.[41] Smaragda Berg's girlfriend of the moment was a prostitute, and a general tolerance of homosexuality was a notable feature of the Kraus set. The second distinguishing feature of this 'triple alliance' was its disdain for excrescence, and a belief in the primacy of function over decoration: Kraus famously said that he and Loos between them had taught the world to recognise the difference between an urn and a chamber pot. Reading *Vita Ipsa* (1918), the last book Altenberg published in his lifetime, Berg noted in the margin those aspects of the book which instantly brought Loos to mind. Not surprisingly, he reacted positively to a text like 'Applied Art' ('Kunstgewerbliches') which confirms Altenberg's continuing adherence to the Loos–Kraus æsthetic:

> My little inkwell is made of brown glass, fabulously easy to clean, costs
> two Crowns, and moreover is called 'Bobby', well 'Robert' nowadays. It
> is thus a work of art, it fulfils its purpose, disturbs nobody and is a
> beautiful brown.[42]

In Berg's copy of *Vita Ipsa*, this not unironic passage is annotated with a single word: 'Loos'.

Central though they were for Berg, and indeed to Viennese culture as a whole, Kraus, Loos and Altenberg have nevertheless to be seen in the context of a larger and more heterogeneous Viennese picture. For the city in which Berg came to maturity was the centre of an artistic and intellectual renaissance probably unparalleled in modern times. Whereas Paris, with which Vienna might best be compared, had seldom stagnated, many felt that in the latter part of the nineteenth century Viennese artistic life had languished. Although this artistic decline has to be understood in relative terms – for the city was after all home to Brahms, Wolf and Bruckner – there is no doubt that in the course of the 1890s a new generation of artists and thinkers, many of them Jewish, had set the place alight. A major centre in this revitalisation was the Café Griensteidl, a venerable establishment opposite the rear entrance to the Hofburg, the Imperial Palace. Forming what one critic has described as a 'sub-society', the cream (as they saw themselves) of Viennese intellectual and artistic life would meet there to drink, read newspapers, debate, and to stay warm and dry in winter.[43] This was the place where Schoenberg (1874–1951) and his future brother-in-law Alexander von Zemlinsky (1872–1942) met for coffee and discussion, along with painters, writers and revolutionary politicians. Indeed, it should not be forgotten how important in world terms were these 'politics in a new key', as Carl Schorske has dubbed the activities of Griensteidl habitués like the Socialist leader Victor Adler, the radical pan-German extremist Georg von Schönerer who was so admired by Hitler, and Theodor Herzl, the founder of Zionism.[44] The Café Griensteidl was the chief meeting place for the writers and poets of 'Young Vienna' who had put the city back on the map of European literature. With the critic and essayist Hermann Bahr at its hub, 'Young Vienna' – whose members included Hofmannsthal, Schnitzler, Salten and Beer-Hofmann as well as, briefly, Altenberg – took it upon itself to rejuvenate Austrian letters from a consciously cosmopolitan perspective. Generally rejecting the Naturalist tendency newly popular in Germany, where Gerhart Hauptmann enjoyed considerable success with such socially-committed dramas as *Vor Sonnenaufgang* (*Before Sunrise*, 1889) and *Die Weber* (*The Weavers*, 1893), the 'Young Viennese' placed the accent firmly upon a poeticisation of reality and an acute examination of the individual, often pathological, psyche. The social and biological determinism of the Naturalists gave way to works dealing with dream-states and visions; depictions of physical distress yielded to portrayals of extreme psychological subtlety. The forms beloved of the 'Young Viennese' were the lyric, the fairy-tale, the short story and the dramatic sketch. Not Zola and Hauptmann but Maeterlinck, Baudelaire and Jens Peter Jacobsen were their models. A glance through the poets who inspired Berg's early songs will suffice to demonstrate the prevailing literary tastes of Vienna 1900. Alongside Goethe and Romantics like Heine, Mörike and Eichendorff, all of whom were perennial favourites with earlier generations of composers, are ranged such names as Mombert, Hofmannsthal, Dörmann, Rilke, Holz, Schlaf and Liliencron.

Along with 'Young Vienna's' fascination for morbid states went a notable tendency towards posing and self-stylisation, all of which proved too much for Kraus, who in 1896 took the impending demolition of the Café Griensteidl as the opportunity to launch his first great satire *Die demolirte Literatur* (*Literature Demolished*). Its opening sentence 'Vienna has been demolished into a metropolis' ('Wien ist zur Großstadt demolirt worden') was followed by a string of cruel but hilarious pen-portraits of the 'Young

Viennese' gathered round Hermann Bahr, the 'gentleman from Linz' who indicated his talent by letting a lock of hair fall over his brow. Schnitzler is dismissed as a cliché maker who cannot get beyond death-bed scenes and sweet young girls seduced by middle-class lechers. The precociously gifted Hugo von Hofmannsthal, later to become Richard Strauss's most treasured librettist, is written off as 'Goethe at his school-desk' ('Goethe auf der Schulbank'). With unerring aim, Kraus unmasked the pretensions of what he felt was a self-selecting literary élite blessed with no special talent. Significantly, the only writer spared the lash of the satirist's pen was Peter Altenberg.[45]

Parallel with the writings of 'Young Vienna', the artistic scene in Vienna entered the modern era with the painters of the Secession ranged around the dominant figure of Gustav Klimt. Kraus belittled the work of Klimt,[46] just as he despised 'Young Vienna'. Linking 'Young Vienna' and the artists of the Secession was both a love of allegory and a fascination with decoration. They also shared a strong awareness that however 'modern' they appeared, they also were rooted in the past, and it is this awareness of a common heritage in nineteenth-century art, and earlier, which provides an overarching link (a 'family resemblance' as Wittgenstein would have called it) not only with such an apparently revolutionary figure as Schoenberg, the creative reworker of Brahms and Johann Strauss, but also with Kraus and Loos.[47]

Indeed, a major factor in Loos's and Kraus's disapproval of Klimt, the Secession, and later the arts-and-crafts-oriented 'Wiener Werkstätte', lay in their self-confessed ethical rejection of ornamentation. One of Loos's most celebrated essays is tellingly called 'Ornament and Crime' ('Ornament und Verbrechen', 1908), and its message was one which appealed especially to Schoenberg as he moved towards a new musical language. Given originally as a lecture, it is very probable that Berg was present when Loos delivered it again at the Akademischer Verband für Literatur und Musik in 1910.[48] Intriguingly, although Loos and Altenberg rejected decoration on intellectual and ethical grounds, their strident æsthetic functionalism might also be linked to the nature of their sexuality. It has been convincingly suggested not only that Loos's loathing of ornamentation was linked at a deeper level to his fear of mature female sexuality (he was married three times, to progressively younger women),[49] but that 'Ornament und Verbrechen' can be interpreted as a document which 'amounts to the criminalization of women'.[50] Hence the 'Haus am Michaelerplatz' can conceivably be regarded both as a revolutionary step in the development of functional modern architecture and, in its denial of sensuality, as realising the 'utopia of the disavowal of mature female sexuality'.[51] Whether Berg understood it as such must remain a moot point, but the widespread fear of women at the turn of the century, recorded so starkly in Wedekind's Lulu tragedies, was something to which the composer could respond with searing intensity. He will have been equally alive to Altenberg's endless fascination with pre-sexual and pubescent girls, typical not only of the *fin de siècle* preoccupation with adolescence, but also of its dual perspective on women: the *femme fatale* on the one hand, the *femme fragile*, the apparently asexual 'child-woman', on the other.

The 'frozen music' of architecture is the art-form most immediately affecting everyday life, and in few other places had developments in architecture made more of an impact than in 'Vienna 1900'. From the 1850s onwards, central Vienna had been rebuilt on a scale at least as great as that of Haussmann's reworking of the Parisian cityscape. Monumental and historicist, also quintessentially style-less in the view of the novelist (and friend of Berg) Hermann Broch,[52] the new Vienna with its patchwork of mock-Gothic, Classical, Palladian and Renaissance buildings horrified Loos. In an essay of 1898 he compared the emptiness of these theatrical façades, which made them so appealing to at least one aspect of the Viennese temperament, with the paste villages which Potemkin had erected in an attempt to fool Catherine the Great that the endless steppes were being successfully populated and that out of emptiness was coming forth plenty.[53] It was, therefore, entirely consistent that Loos should in time have come to support the new music of Schoenberg and his followers with a financial generosity that often left the architect in dire straits. It says nothing for Schoenberg's better nature that he could (or would) never appreciate the sacrifices which Loos made on his behalf, and also for the art of other revolutionaries such as Kokoschka who offended against bourgeois Viennese taste. It is yet another of Vienna's ironies that Loos, celebrated for his iconoclastic views and an architectural spareness that shocked and offended in equal measure, was also profoundly hard of hearing. Altenberg, with his usual bluntness, described him in a uniquely Viennese phrase as 'der terische Adolf Loos' ('that Mutt'n Jeff Adolf Loos').[54] Understandably enough, Loos's deafness was meat and drink to a section of the Viennese press, as Berg reported in a letter to Schoenberg soon after the *Skandalkonzert*. The anonymous critic 'Veritas', who had described Altenberg's texts as 'anal poetry' and Berg's songs as a 'hoax', also took the opportunity to describe Loos, who had been present at the concert, merely as 'the well-known deaf architect', for whom such works probably represented the 'music of the spheres'.[55] Kraus himself, who had been absent from Vienna in late March, was unable to experience directly the poisonous atmosphere surrounding the concert, but in mid-April he gave a highly successful public reading from Altenberg's latest book, attended by Berg,[56] and in *Die Fackel* of 8 May 1913 he commented belatedly on the scandal. It was not, he contended, a response to the 'New Music' as such, but rather an example of a negative response in which the Viennese press had managed to stoop below even its own execrable standards.[57]

For their part, Berg and Schoenberg were supportive of Loos when obloquy was heaped upon him on account of what his critics saw as the alien functionalism of his building on the Michaelerplatz. In a letter to his teacher dated 6 December 1911, accompanied by a quite effective pencil sketch of the building which was causing so much offence (Schoenberg was now living in Berlin), Berg reports how Loos had given him some practical advice on how to further the public awareness of Schoenberg's music. He also tells Schoenberg how he naturally intends going to Loos's lecture on his Michaelerplatz building. He continues:

> By the way, one Viennese paper implied that Loos had gone mad as a
> result of the building and was seeking treatment in an institution. That's
> typically Viennese![58]

By this time, as both Berg and Schoenberg knew, Loos's friend Altenberg was already undergoing treatment in the Inzersdorf Sanatorium. Both had learned from Kraus, however, that the press in Vienna was as fickle as it was venal. Sympathy for Loos's functional æsthetic was central to all the composers of the 'New Music' in Vienna, but they also responded to the architect as a human being, expressing their support for him in 1928 when his alleged involvement in pædophile activities resulted in a suspended prison sentence of four months.[59] When a *Festschrift* came out to celebrate his sixtieth birthday, there were contributions from both Schoenberg and Webern as well as a nine-line double acrostic by Berg in which the initial letters spelled 'Adolf Loos' and the last letters 'Alban Berg'.[60]

Although the 'Haus am Michaelerplatz' had turned Loos into the most famous architect in Vienna, it remained (typically) the only large-scale design he was able to realise in the city. If searching today for other Viennese buildings which express something of the spirit of Loos, above all in their functionalism and movement away from decoration, then it is to the work of Otto Wagner (1841–1918) that one must look: buildings such as the pumping station at the Nussdorf dam on the Danube-cut, the Postsparkasse in the city centre and the block at No. 40 Neustiftgasse in the seventh district all indicate a new attitude towards function in architecture which parallels the new musical language being developed by Schoenberg and his pupils in the dying years of the Habsburg empire.

When late in 1911 Schoenberg published his *Harmonielehre*, which he dedicated to Mahler, he also paid fulsome tribute to the example which Karl Kraus had set him, even admitting that there was more of Kraus in the work than was perhaps proper. A year previously, in the 300th edition of

Die Fackel, Kraus, whose understanding of modern music was probably not great (his favourite composer remained Jacques Offenbach), had expressed his appreciation of the relationship between Schoenberg's innovations and the writings of Peter Altenberg by publishing on facing pages a facsimile of Schoenberg's setting of Stefan George's poem 'Sprich nicht immer vom Laube', from *Das Buch der hängenden Gärten*, and Altenberg's sketch 'Widmung [Sommerabend in Gmunden]', soon to be republished in *Neues Altes*, where of course Berg found his texts for the *Altenberg Lieder*.

Throughout their lives, the triumvirate of Berg, Webern and Schoenberg retained an allegiance to the 'triple alliance' of Kraus, Altenberg and Loos, whose desire for a new simplicity coupled with a frank assessment of the role of female sexuality proved to be of lasting importance. However, the world in which these ideas first came to fruition ended for ever with the outbreak of war in the summer of 1914. To begin with, Berg and Schoenberg, who both donned uniform, took a rather more patriotic and bellicose view of events than Kraus, whose linguistic clarity scythed unerringly through the popular jingoism of the day. Significantly, however, in his fiftieth-birthday letter to Kraus, Berg made a point of thanking him for the spiritual support he had given him during the war, 'in life's most unpleasant situations ... not to mention my military service of more than three years'.[61]

The spirit of Kraus, which meant so much to Berg, was nowhere better articulated in wartime than in the rhetorical masterpiece 'In dieser großen Zeit' ('In these great times'), first delivered as a lecture and finally published in *Die Fackel* in December 1914. Whereas the unpredictable Altenberg reacted in his usual instantaneous manner with an outspoken attack on France fairly typical of the response amongst intellectuals in Austria at the outbreak of war, Kraus had initially remained mute.[62] When eventually he broke his silence, Kraus examined the causes of war, providing an analysis of twentieth-century civilisation and its discontents which remains in crucial respects as valid today as when the lecture was first delivered. War is the outcome of a catastrophic failure of the imagination, Kraus argued, for if its consequences could be imagined, it would never happen. Once it has broken out, its iniquities are fuelled by a press whose ultimate function is not public illumination but the creation of wealth within the capitalist system. Horrified by the bombardment of Rheims Cathedral, Kraus recognised that 'culture' is an early victim of a world where people now count only as consumers: 'Menschheit ist Kundschaft' ('To be human is to be a customer'). When, he asks, with a demand still resonating, unanswered, at the end of the twentieth century, will the greater age break, when cathedrals make war against people?[63]

3 Berg and Adorno

Raymond Geuss
University of Cambridge

When Berg was in Frankfurt for the premiere of the *Three Fragments from 'Wozzeck'* in 1924 he was introduced to a twenty-one-year-old student named Theodor Wiesengrund. Wiesengrund was about to submit a doctoral dissertation in philosophy on the then fashionable topic of Husserlian phenomenology, but he also had some training as a musician and had published a number of journalistic pieces on contemporary music. Later, Wiesengrund would claim that at the time he saw in Berg a representative of the 'true new music' – 'at the same time Schoenberg and Mahler'.[1] He proposed to move to Vienna to study composition with Berg as soon as the formalities for the granting of his doctoral degree were completed. Berg agreed to take him as a student.

Wiesengrund was the only son of a wealthy Jewish wine merchant, Oskar Wiesengrund, and of Maria Calvelli-Adorno, a French singer. He was a highly intelligent, deeply cultured and æsthetically sensitive young man, but had in some ways a not very attractive character. Schoenberg found his oily, self-important manner, arrogance and beady-eyed stare repulsive,[2] and certainly Wiesengrund's writings give the impression of being the work of a more than usually self-absorbed person. Despite this, Berg seems to have had a genuine affection for him and a high opinion of his compositions, although no interest at all in his philosophical speculations.[3]

For a time Wiesengrund composed while also pursuing a university career in philosophy, but during the 1930s he gradually gave up composition altogether,[4] although he continued to write about music until his death in 1969. The Nazis deprived him of his university post in 1933, but he didn't believe Hitler would last long in power[5] and also, according to one of his friends, 'couldn't believe that anything could happen to *him*, the son of Oskar Wiesengrund',[6] so he temporised. In 1937, just after Berg's death, a number of analyses of Berg's work by Wiesengrund appeared in the volume edited by Willi Reich;[7] these had a certain influence on early interpretations of Berg. Finally in 1938 Wiesengrund emigrated to New York. At about the same time he began to use his mother's maiden name, Adorno, as his surname.[8]

In the early 1940s Adorno (as he now was) wrote the work that was to be his major contribution to thinking about music, *Philosophie der neuen Musik*.[9] He was working on the manuscript at just the time when his neighbour in the German exile community in California, Thomas Mann, was beginning to write his fictional life of the German composer 'Adrian Leverkühn' which eventually appeared as the novel *Doktor Faustus* (1947). Mann wanted to include some detailed descriptions of imaginary compositions by 'Leverkühn' in the novel and Adorno's presence was a godsend. In 1943 Adorno gave Mann a copy (in manuscript) of the theoretically most interesting part of *Philosophie der neuen Musik*, the chapter on Schoenberg, and he served in general as musical advisor to Mann.[10] Adorno was later to point to some similarities between Berg and Leverkühn, but these seem actually to be relatively superficial.[11] Thomas Mann himself always claimed that Leverkühn was a fictional creation with composite traits derived from a variety of sources. It is certainly hard to see much of the Austrian-Catholic Berg, who was so given to the enjoyment of good food and drink (and whose comment on German cuisine was: 'the Germans only ever eat muck')[12] in the cold ascetic German-Protestant Leverkühn.[13]

After the war Adorno returned to Frankfurt and was active in the reconstruction of musical life there. He tried to enlist Thomas Mann's help in preventing the reopening of Bayreuth[14] and was a regular feature of the Darmstadt scene. He continued to publish copiously on music – in 1968, the year before his death, he published a monograph on Berg which incorporated the material he had originally written for the 1937 Reich volume – but his work never again attained the energy, imaginativeness and acuity it had had in the 1940s.[15]

Art and affirmation

Adorno took a basically Hegelian approach to art characterised by three theses:[16]

- the central æsthetic category is not 'beauty' (for instance), but 'truth'

- (æsthetic) 'truth' stands in a close inherent relation to history

- the history of music should be understood as a dialectic between Subject (in this case the 'musical' or 'compositional' subject, a composer with characteristic powers and sensibilities) and Object (in this case what Adorno calls 'the musical material').

There is, Adorno assumes, a single unilinear historical path of development of music. At any point in time a composer confronts a pre-given musical language, and a set of musical forms and æsthetic demands – this is the 'material' – and tries to structure this 'material' into a coherent work of art, using existing compositional techniques, or more or less radical modifications of such techniques. It is essential to keep firmly in mind that what Adorno calls 'the material' is not the physical (e.g. the acoustic) basis of music, not notes considered as natural phenomena; rather 'the material', what the composer finds already there and must deal with in order to produce a work, is a historically and culturally formed body of expectations, demands, expressive features, etc. Such 'material' is itself at any given time the *result* of previous compositional activity, and highly innovative compositional activity *now* will, as it were, become absorbed in and thus change the 'material' the next generation of composers will confront.

A further feature of Adorno's account is his claim that up to now (or at any rate up to Adorno's death in 1969) no fully satisfactory, stable state of compositional practice has been attained. The demands and expectations embodied in the musical material are not at any time fully consistent, and attempts by the 'musical subject' to use existing (or newly invented) techniques to introduce coherence into works shaped from that material will never be fully successful. One can look at the same historical process in two complementary ways: depending on which perspective one adopts, that of the subject (the composer) or that of the object (the musical material), one can see the whole process as one in which active agents (composers) imaginatively invent new forms and techniques, thereby continually transforming the 'material' of music; or one can see the process as one in which the material is itself making demands, setting puzzles to which composers respond as best they can, finding more or less satisfactory solutions.

There is always a state-of-the-art of music, a set of techniques of composing, æsthetic canons of correctness and expressivity; there is also a set of demands the material (at that particular time) makes. Serious music is state-of-the-art music which addresses the demands of the musical material. Æsthetically successful music advances the state-of-the-art; it is innovative and progressive. This innovation or originality, however, is historically located in two ways. First, no matter how radically 'new' a given procedure or form is, it will always turn out to be a modification of existing techniques; second, for an innovation to be more than an idiosyncrasy or theoretical trifle, it must be used to deal with historically specific problems posed by the musical material. What is genuinely 'new' thus has high positive value, but it is this historical element in 'the new' that distinguishes Adorno's conception from an apparently very similar one found in French modernism. Baudelaire's *voyageurs* who sail under their captain

Death 'pour trouver du *nouveau*' are motivated by ennui, horror and perhaps disgust, or by the sheer desire for novelty for its own sake.[17] Ever since the Epicureans at least, it has been pointed out, however, that Death is the radical Other of life, not a modified form of living; thus whatever new thing might exist 'au fond du gouffre' it is not something the *voyageurs* intend to bring back to improve existing techniques either of living or of making music.[18] Ennui is not the most obvious motivation of a composer trying to respond to the demands of the musical material, and indeed it is hard to imagine any of Baudelaire's *voyageurs* exhibiting the loving, meticulous devotion to tradition required to write a book like Schoenberg's *Harmonielehre* – although writing such a book is a perfectly reasonable thing to do for a composer who is trying to learn how to respond to the historically given demands of the musical 'material'.

The idea that in successful æsthetic activity there is a kind of reconciliation of 'freedom' and 'necessity' – that the highest exercise of spontaneous freedom is precisely to find the 'necessary' solution to a problem – is one that goes back to the end of the eighteenth century and finds full and explicit expression in Schelling's *System des transzendentalen Idealismus* (1800). I merely note at this point that the notion of 'necessity' involved here is problematic and seems to presuppose some very strong claims about the 'demands' the 'material' makes. To speak of successful composition as reconciling freedom and necessity would seem to require that the 'demands' of the material have great specificity and that there is a unique 'correct', or at least uniquely 'best' way to satisfy them.[19]

Up to this point, Adorno's account in *Philosophie der neuen Musik* follows a generalised Hegelian position rather closely. Now he adds two novel twists. First of all he identifies 'progressive' music in the historical–æsthetic sense – music that embodies new techniques to solve the problems posed by the material – with music that is 'progressive' in a political sense. Correspondingly, music that does not advance the state-of-the-art along the uniquely determined path required by the demands of the material is not just æsthetically unsatisfactory, but also politically reactionary. In *Philosophie der neuen Musik* Schoenberg (and his school) function as the exemplary representatives of 'progressive', genuinely 'new' music and Stravinsky as the representative of reactionary 'neo-classicism'. No compromise between Schoenberg and Stravinsky is possible, no intermediary position can be found.[20] To try to support this view Adorno has to engage in quite a lot of not very convincing dialectical manœuvres. Thus the second half of *Philosophie der neuen Musik* tries to argue that Stravinsky's music is 'psychotic', 'infantile', 'hebephrenic', 'depersonalised', 'alienated' and politically reactionary, despite the lack of evidence that Stravinsky himself held right-wing political views or was in any way supported or even especially warmly received in right-wing circles.[21] A continuing theme of Adorno's discussion of Berg will be his attempt to 'defend' him against the view that he represents a 'moderate' form of modern music, that is, occupies a kind of intermediate position the viability of which Adorno is committed to denying.

The second deviation from Hegelianism is connected with Adorno's doctrine of the 'dialectic of enlightenment'.[22] At a first approximation, the distinction between the members of the Second Viennese School and representatives of 'neo-classicism' seemed to be a division between sheep and goats, between the saved and the children of perdition, but on closer inspection the 'progress' represented by Schoenberg and his students is not an unmixed blessing. The central tenet of the Enlightenment, according to Adorno, is that the human subject by gaining instrumental control over nature can escape from blind subjugation to 'fate' (and 'myth') and attain autonomy and happiness. For complex and not perhaps finally very clear philosophical reasons which Adorno expounds at great length in *Die Dialektik der Aufklärung*,[23] the process of enlightenment has an inherent tendency to turn against itself, so that the system of tools, social institutions, imperatives of rationality, etc., which was supposed to give us mastery of our fate, instead enslaves us. Effective long-term control of nature requires that we inhibit our spontaneous reactions to the world and adapt our mode of behaviour (and eventually even our mode of feeling) to the laws we discover in nature. In the long run such loss of spontaneity empties our subjectivity of content and can eventually deprive us of the very possibility of human happiness. Nature, mastered and objectified, has its revenge.

Adorno interprets Schoenberg's development through atonality to the method of composing 'with twelve notes related only to each other' as an instance of the dialectic of enlightenment. The musical material of tonality has become a kind of (second) nature by the end of the nineteenth century. The breakthrough to atonality is a process in which the musical subject frees itself from the constraints of the material and establishes a kind of rational mastery over it. However, the absolute freedom of atonality leads by a 'necessary' progression to the even more rationally effective twelve-note method. In twelve-note music the 'material' (i.e. second 'nature') seems once again to be dictating to the subject after the brief fling of free atonality.[24]

> The subject dominates music through the rationality of the system, only in order to succumb to the rational system itself. ... The new ordering of twelve-tone technique virtually extinguishes the subject.[25]

The 'musical subject' in Schoenberg can thus become as 'depersonalised' as that which one finds in Stravinsky. So the two antipodes, Schoenberg and Stravinsky, are not after all that far apart.[26] Rather, they are held together in a fellowship of necessary failure, because the unredeemed state of the world makes fully realised, adequate, satisfactory art impossible. The only form of even relative 'success' accessible to art is to indicate through its own very fragmentariness, inconsistency, its defects and sharp edges, the inherent inadequacy of the world we live in.[27] To do this would be for art to attain the truth to which it can aspire.

Adorno sometimes puts this point by saying that a traditional work of art is 'affirmative': it operates by means of a logic of tension/conflict and resolution and is successful when it observes the Leibnitzian principle of economy or parsimony[28] in developing and resolving the tension – making the greatest variety of forms out of the least material with the least 'effort' – and when in addition that *formal* resolution is also experienced as an affirmation of the fact that the world, despite appearances to the contrary, is basically in order, 'rational', and 'good'. 'Affirmative' art, Adorno claims, is now 'false' because our world is not fundamentally in order but radically evil. 'New' music must therefore satisfy the almost impossible demand of creating works of coherence which satisfy the highly developed æsthetic sensibilities of the best contemporary practitioners, while avoiding the use of any device or form that would allow one to experience or interpret the æsthetic properties of the work as an affirmation of the world as it is. Unfortunately art by its very nature is affirmative. The very fact that an internally coherent, æsthetically satisfying work has been produced tends to promote reconciliation with the world. If 'new' art *must* be non-affirmative, it must in some sense be trying not to be art at all, trying to undermine the very idea of the rounded, æsthetically satisfying art-work: 'Today the only works which really count are those which are no longer works at all.'[29] Thus art may now simply be impossible.

Berg and the avoidance of affirmation

This idea that genuinely 'new' (and thus 'true') art in the twentieth century must be non-affirmative is of great importance, so to get a clearer view of what is meant it might be useful to look at an example.

As is well known, after completing *Wozzeck*, Berg hesitated for a long time between two projects for a second opera. One was for an opera based on Hauptmann's *Und Pippa tanzt!*, the other for an opera to be based on two plays by Frank Wedekind about 'Lulu' (*Erdgeist* and *Die Büchse der Pandora*).[30] Some of Berg's friends thought *Und Pippa tanzt!* more promising,[31] and Adorno tried to take some credit for encouraging Berg to use the Lulu plays rather than Hauptmann's text.[32] Berg, however, initially ignored Adorno's advice and set to work on *Und Pippa tanzt!* Only when the financial negotiations for the rights to Hauptmann's play broke down did he turn instead to Wedekind.

Und Pippa tanzt! is a kind of *Zauberflöte* without the happy ending. The Tamino and Pamina figures (Michel and Pippa) fail their test. She dies; he is blinded and sent off to wander from Silesia to 'Venice' (i.e. through virtually the whole length of Habsburg Austria) to live by begging and playing his ocarina. The text presents a number of obvious opportunities for superficially striking musical effects. Apart from Michel's ocarina there is a scene in which Pippa runs her finger around the rim of a glass, the sound gradually getting louder and transforming itself into music.[33] Pippa and her father, Tagliazoni (who is lynched at the end of Act I for cheating at cards) speak in a mixture of German and Italian; the Monostatos figure ('Old Huhn') speaks in Silesian dialect and has a fine repertory of groans, shouts and other inarticulate noises; he kills Pippa by breaking a glass while she is dancing. It is true, as Adorno points out, that the play has some signal dramatic deficiencies: it is disjointed and uneven in tone and pace, and the plot rather loses momentum half way through. These need not, however, have been fatal to the work considered as a possible libretto. After all, a play could scarcely have *less* dramatic momentum than large parts of *Tristan* or a sillier and less integrated plot than *Zauberflöte*, and Berg would no doubt have introduced improvements when he produced the libretto. What would disqualify the play as 'new' art for Adorno lies deeper.

Und Pippa tanzt! begins in a world much like that of *Wozzeck*, a tavern in a small mountain village in which the only local industry, a glassworks, has closed. The tavern is full of unemployed and casual workers. Act I ends with a realistically presented disaster, the death of Tagliazoni and the abduction of Pippa by Old Huhn, but as the play progresses this real catastrophe is dissolved into a series of fairy-tale events culminating in a very traditional ending in which the blinded hero Michel, now off to a life of begging, is offered illusory consolation for his suffering: 'If people threaten to throw stones at you, tell them you are a prince ... tell them about your water-palace.' It is just this kind of 'transfiguration' of suffering, 'tragic reconciliation' with fate, which Adorno believes to be characteristic of traditional 'affirmative' art and which he thinks 'new' art must reject on both æsthetic and political grounds.[34]

The ending of *Wozzeck* is quite emphatically not 'affirmative' in this sense. Perhaps it might have been just barely possible to take it in that way if the opera had ended with the orchestral interlude after Wozzeck's death (Act III scene 4): the (tonal) interlude might have been thought to suggest that a certain pharisaical kind of moral order had been established ('Poor man murders faithless wife and then drowns himself'). This way of taking it won't work, though, because Act III scene 5 shows us Wozzeck and Marie's young son. *He* isn't mystified into thinking real suffering has some deeper meaning or significance. He simply doesn't even yet realise what has happened, but we can be reasonably sure he will soon enough. It is quite wrong to suggest, as Fritz Heinrich Klein did in his review in *Musik-blätter des Anbruch* in 1923, that 'the sight of the innocent orphaned child arouses a deep melancholy in the sympathetic soul and the hope that fate will be kinder to him than it has been to his parents'.[35] Berg points out in his lecture on *Wozzeck* that the opera ends with a '*perpetuum mobile* movement' and suggests that 'the opening bar of the opera could link up with [the] final bar and in so doing close the whole circle'.[36] The clear implication of this is that any hopes aroused in the 'sympathetic soul' are grossly illusory and that the child's future will be the same kind of cycle of confusion, pain, violence and despair we have just seen Wozzeck endure and exhibit.

There does seem to be a clear distinction between plays like *Und Pippa tanzt!* which are in some sense 'affirmative' and dramas like *Wozzeck* (or *Woyzeck* if we are speaking of the play)[37] which are not. Adorno, however, when he is at his most uncompromising, drawing out the implications of his own position with the greatest dialectical rigour, argues that even *Wozzeck* (the Berg opera) is in its own way 'affirmative'. It is, after all, still a coherent 'work' exhibiting æsthetic closure, and thus to that extent something that transfigures pain and leads to a resigned acceptance of it.[38] In the passage in which Adorno makes this argument (early in *Philosophie der neuen Musik*) he is contrasting *Wozzeck* (and *Lulu*), on the one hand, with Schoenberg's *Erwartung* and *Die glückliche Hand* on the other. The implication seems to be that the latter really *are* non-affirmative non-works of art.

One might think that Adorno is simply confused here. It seems very odd to argue that *Erwartung* is not as much a *work* as *Wozzeck*. In addition, it is perfectly reasonable to present arguments against art in general: art won't cure real pain; perhaps it does foster the wrong attitudes in people. It isn't obvious, though, that such general arguments against the very existence of art can easily be transformed into internal æsthetic standards, ways of telling better art from worse art. True, art doesn't abolish the pain of the world, but that won't tell us anything about the relative merits of Schoenberg and Stravinsky.

But to argue in this way against Adorno is to misunderstand his basic procedure (which is not, of course, to defend that basic procedure, but only to assert that criticism which wishes properly to engage Adorno would have to be differently couched). As Adorno repeatedly emphasises, he is engaged in 'dialectics' – in what he later came to call 'negative dialectics' – and such a dialectic is a corkscrew that is in principle *indefinitely* further extensible. What assertion one makes depends on where one is in the dialectical process. *Wozzeck* is non-affirmative (compared to *Und Pippa tanzt!*), but is still affirmative because still a work of art (relative to *Erwartung*), but *Erwartung* itself is still art and so committed to an affirmation which it itself tries to undermine. To adopt this position, however, would seem to mean accepting that art is impossible (because a work of art would have to be a work that is not a work), but great composers are precisely those who can make the impossible possible, who can square the circle: 'every piece of Berg's was extracted by subterfuge from its own impossibility'.[39] For Adorno, the dialectical process can have no natural stopping place. This is a good thing too, because such a dialectic is the expression of free human subjectivity. The end of the dialectic would be a kind of mental (and emotional) death.

As Adorno also points out,[40] Wedekind's second play about Lulu (*Die Büchse der Pandora*) does *not* end with the Countess Geschwitz's 'Liebestod' but rather with her calling out 'O, verflucht' ('Oh damn!'). Friedrich Cerha holds that it was Berg's final intention that Geschwitz *not* sing (or speak) the word 'verflucht', so his edition of the score very oddly gives her a final C♮ and B♮ after '… in Ewigkeit', but no text to sing to these two notes.[41] I must say that I agree with what I take to be the implications of Adorno's account in *Philosophie der neuen Musik*: to delete the final 'verflucht' spoils the whole ending, and if Berg did not intend to use this last bit of Wedekind's text he made a serious mistake. Geschwitz is *not* going to be joined with Lulu 'in Ewigkeit'; she is a frustrated woman whom we have seen to be capable of great and selfless love, but who is now dying miserably in a garret in London. Her final curse will tend to keep the audience's collective mind appropriately focused on that fact.

Of Berg's later works, the *Lyric Suite* is relatively easy to fit into this scheme of an essentially non-affirmative music: the Largo desolato which ends the piece is about as despairing and lacking in any form of transfiguration, metaphysical hope or consolation as one could imagine. The piece even has a structural feature which makes it less affirmative than *Wozzeck*, namely the ending in which the three other instruments successively drop away leaving only the viola, which is to repeat the same sequence of D♭–F, *diminuendo* and *morendo* 'until it is extinguished completely', but the point at which the violist is to stop is not unequivocally indicated. Berg's instructions are 'repeat the final third D♭–F *possibly* once or twice'. This 'open' ending can be seen as a way of dissolving the æsthetic closure characteristic of a 'work of art' from within.[42] This effect is perhaps even more striking on the page than it is when simply listening to the piece, because when the violinists and the cellist stop playing they are not given written-out rests in full score: instead, their very staves disappear.

Adorno connects this avoidance of metaphysical affirmation with a technical feature of Berg's music. In it, Adorno claims, one does not generally find fully-formed distinct themes, each with its own clear identity, which can be stated in full at the beginning, then developed and transformed and finally reinstated in triumph. Rather, each of Berg's works is like an infusorium in which tiny units of structure are constantly transforming themselves into other microscopic structures.[43] The units involved are so small and the process of transformation is so continuous that one never gets the sense of a determinate point at which one 'theme' begins and another ends, or of what is the 'original' form of a 'theme' and what a modification. To the extent to which there *are* any 'themes', Berg allows them to arise through a series of gradual, almost imperceptible transitions. The moment any 'theme' with a determinate structure *does* succeed in getting itself stated, Berg immediately begins gradually to decompose it back into the minimal elements from which it arose. So the basic structure of Berg's music is not 'tension/resolution' but 'construction/deconstruction' ('Aufbau/Abbau'), or one of asserting and taking back what was asserted. This 'taking back' is the opposite of traditional forms of musical affirmation.[44]

One might be tempted to see this Bergian gesture of 'taking back' as another point of similarity to Mann's 'Adrian Leverkühn', who at the end of the novel wants to write a work that 'takes back' the affirmation of life found at the end of the last movement of Beethoven's Ninth Symphony. Adorno himself might seem to foster this identification by referring at one point to Berg's 'dynamic nihilism'.[45] 'Dynamic nihilism' is perhaps an appropriate way to characterise the attitude of Leverkühn and of his political analogues, the Nazis, but, as Adorno writes in other places,[46] Berg's own attitude was not one of active, engaged nihilism, but of passive, melancholy resignation: sad contemplation of the transitoriness and frailty of a world in which all structures crumble under their own weight, rather than a desire to kick down what is already about to fall.[47]

If one asks, then, in what the 'truth' of Berg's music consists (according to Adorno), an important part of the answer is Berg's refusal of 'affirmation'. The basic sadness of his music shows that he is not 'reconciled'; his 'resignation' is that of a person who makes utopian demands on life and sees them eternally unsatisfied, but does not give them up.[48]

Historicity

The other component of Berg's 'truth' is his acceptance of historicity. Berg does *not* take the path down which later serialism would go in the direction of 'bad ahistoricity', but rather continues to attempt to combine in a coherent way 'the most advanced techniques of composition' with modified versions of historically received musical forms.[49] Since music is inherently historical, it is a mere illusion to pretend one could ignore the history of forms and start afresh. Applying this to Berg, Adorno writes: 'Allowing the ruptures between the modern and the late romantic to stand is more appropriate than trying to let music begin absolutely *ab ovo*; if music attempted this, it would fall prey to a past that was not understood and overcome.'[50]

Berg's Violin Concerto presented a particular problem for Adorno in this context.[51] He obviously found it deeply embarrassing and felt the need to explain it away by referring to the fact that Berg had had to compose it to commission with uncharacteristic haste; thus it didn't really represent his work at its best.[52] What really bothered Adorno was not the continued presence of some traditional elements (e.g. of tonal centres): this can be seen as a novel (i.e. 'new') appropriation of the tradition and hence an expression of the 'truth' that music is embedded in history. Nor even was it the 'ruptures of style' ('Stilbrüche') involved in the use of the Bach chorale; though Adorno writes that he doesn't want to 'defend' these, they too could in principle be dealt with as forms of honest recognition of historical discontinuity.[53] What Adorno couldn't tolerate was above all the easy comprehensibility of the work and its resulting popularity, for in a world as pervasively evil as Adorno thought ours was, the 'truth' would have to be highly esoteric.[54] Furthermore, the Violin Concerto seemed to be an 'affirmative' work in the traditional sense, one that cast an æsthetic glow of consolation over pain and fostered a metaphysical acceptance of death. It followed, he said with ironic reference to Richard Strauss, a scheme of 'Death and Transfiguration'.[55]

I do not find Adorno's treatment of Berg's relation to history and tradition very satisfactory, and the inadequacies of his account are, I think, deeply rooted in his general philosophical approach. Adorno does point out some of the retrograde forms that occur in Berg's music – he could hardly have failed to mention them, given that Berg himself explicitly draws attention to them[56] – but he fails to give these circular and retrograde forms the prominence in his analysis they deserve. One might even think that there could be a natural affinity between large-scale retrograde forms and the principle of 'construction/deconstruction' on which Berg's mature works, according to Adorno, are based.

As Robert Morgan points out, the prevalence of these retrograde and circular forms seems to be connected with a basically cyclical conception of time.[57] For Adorno, as for the Hegelian–Marxist tradition in æsthetics out of which his work arose, the threefold distinction between fundamentally ahistorical, fundamentally linear-progressive and fundamentally cyclical views of time and history is of central philosophical, æsthetic and political significance. The late nineteenth-century bourgeoisie which (correctly) feels itself threatened by the rising proletariat must give up its ideology of inevitable progress and retreat from history either into the timeless present of 'positivism' – this is, as it were, the 'soft' Western liberal option – or, when the going really gets tough, into cyclical or other mythic forms of historical thought – this is the proto-fascist option. To protect Berg's progressivist credentials, it was thus highly politic for Adorno to understate the importance of circular and cyclical forms. To be sure, Adorno rejects not just 'positivism' and 'mythic' thought, but also eighteenth- and nineteenth-century 'linear' conceptions in which an underlying 'logic of history' guarantees inevitable progress. There is, Adorno thinks, no guarantee of such 'progress' – at least if that means moral progress or progress in the quality of art. From the fact that the 'modern' artist confronts what are in some sense more stringent historical demands (made by the material) than previous artists did, it does not follow that 'new' art will necessarily be 'better' than older forms of art were. It is central to Adorno's project that this kind of *internal* criticism of Enlightenment views of historical progress should *not* be taken to imply a reversion to any of the archaic modes of thought which are the natural precursors (and concomitants) of fascism,[58] a metaphysical view of time as circular would be one such archaic conception.

In principle, Adorno could have tried to argue 'dialectically' that Berg was showing that in our world, as modern barbarism grew (in the 1930s), time was circular. In presenting our world in this way Berg would not be making a metaphysical claim, but a tacit (and correct) quasi-empirical criticism of our society (as it looks in the light of a redeemed messianic future), and in this sense his music could be called 'true'.[59] The Third Reich was in some sense the archaic past redivivus. Lacking, however, the fixed points which Hegel's dialectic still retains – a system of logical categories and an affirmative relation to at least some basic features of contemporary society – Adorno's 'negative dialectics' can easily come to seem not the expression of a free, sophisticated cognitive subjectivity, but a form of special pleading.

Adorno would have no truck with astrology, numerology, the occult, or any of the theories of a biologically based life-rhythm that were popular among the members of the Schoenberg circle.[60] He thought belief in such things a sign of rigidity, conformism, depersonalisation and a predisposition to proto-fascist attitudes.[61] What seems to have bothered him about numerology and astrology was their pretence to scientific standing, for Adorno himself had no objection in principle to trying to 'read' the meaning of things or people from their appearance. Onomastics and physiognomy, if carried out in conjunction with an informed experience of 'Geist'

(and if dispensing with any claim to objectivity), were perfectly accept-
able; so were psychoanalytic interpretations. Thus Adorno refers Wagner's
ungenerous characterisation of Mime in *Siegfried* to the composer's fear
at recognising part of himself in Mime: Wagner, too, had a large head, was
virtually a dwarf and talked too much.[62] Adorno also emphasises that Berg
was 'like' his name: he was tall and gaunt like an alpine landscape ('Berg')
and also elegantly old-fashioned and Catholic ('Alban');[63] remarkably, this
is a claim he made not just about Berg's person, but also about his music.[64]

Indeed, despite the great documentary value of Adorno's recollections
of Berg and the occasional brilliance of his analyses, the work on Berg is
not one of the stronger parts of Adorno's œuvre. The reason for this that
immediately suggests itself is that Adorno's negative dialectics work best
when pointing out why, for one reason or another, a certain kind of artistic
project is doomed to failure. As I have shown, at the deeper reaches of
Adorno's philosophising, Berg's work is obliterated altogether, along with
virtually all of twentieth-century music (except perhaps a handful of
pieces from Schoenberg's period of free atonality), but assuming one does
not follow the dialectic out that far, the project of analysing relative failure
and success remains. Occasionally Adorno's animosity is too overwhelming, as in the case of Wagner,[65] or his fear is too great – what if, after all,
Stravinsky and not Schoenberg was the representative of truly 'new' music? – and then the gears of the dialectical machinery can fail to engage, but
in the case of Berg it seems instead to be Adorno's genuine love of his
subject and his desire to present Berg's work as a great æsthetic success
that get the better of him.

PART II

From song to opera

4 Early works: tonality and beyond

Anthony Pople
University of Lancaster

First songs and instrumental music

Berg's dozen or so 'official' compositions, from the Piano Sonata Op. 1 through to the Violin Concerto he composed more than a quarter of a century later, are many times outnumbered by the songs he wrote between the ages of sixteen and twenty-three. Only eight of these were published during Berg's lifetime – the 1907 setting of Theodor Storm's 'Schliesse mir die Augen beide' and the selection of *Seven Early Songs* that Berg revised and orchestrated in 1928 – though one more was made available by Willi Reich shortly after the composer's death.[1] The publication of two volumes of *Jugendlieder* in 1985 changed the picture entirely: it meant that roughly two-thirds of the approximately eighty-five early songs were available in published form; within a short while the same could be said of a significant proportion of the piano music Berg wrote in his early twenties. Between them, and almost exclusively, these two genres – solo song and piano music – carried him from his first teenage efforts as a composer through to atonality in the manner of Schoenberg.

One of the most striking features of this development is the disparity of Berg's achievement in the two genres. In a famous and characteristic letter written in 1910, Schoenberg described the situation without mercy:

> Alban Berg ... is an extraordinarily gifted composer. But the state he was in when he came to me was such that his imagination apparently could not work on anything but *Lieder*. Even the piano accompaniments to them were song-like in style. He was absolutely incapable of writing an instrumental movement or inventing an instrumental theme. You can hardly imagine the lengths I went to in order to remove this defect in his talent.[2]

Schoenberg's criticisms were reasonable enough. There is no doubt that even among Berg's earliest songs there are several that possess great charm and show an apparently effortless facility for the synthesis of words and music that was one goal of the Romantic *Lied*. They also show an ability to pick up idioms we now associate with Schumann, Mahler and Wolf without resorting to slavish imitation. In contrast, the piano pieces he wrote a few years later as exercises for Schoenberg, culminating in the Twelve Variations on an original theme (1908), are accomplished rather than distinguished and would be of little artistic interest were they not by Alban Berg.

Berg's first songs date from 1901. Composing them seems to have been just one expression of a self-consciously artistic sensibility which developed rapidly under the perhaps unlikely mentorship of the architect Hermann Watznauer (1875–1939), a friend of the Berg family since 1898.[3] Through Watznauer's later biography of the composer, which was checked by Berg himself and seems generally reliable as far as c. 1907, we know much of the chronology of the early songs up to this time, and in particular we know which of them were shown to Arnold Schoenberg in October 1904 as examples of Berg's recent work.[4] These songs, which led Schoenberg to accept the nineteen-year-old Berg as a pupil without charge, were 'Liebe', 'Wandert, ihr Wolken', 'Im Morgengrauen', 'Grabschrift' and 'Traum', the last two being dated 16 August 1904.[5] The very opening of 'Liebe' is impressive in its handling of the complexities of post-Wagnerian tonal harmony on a small scale (Example 4.1). Most of the chords, considered as individual sonorities, have the quality of dominant or half-diminished sevenths: Berg is adept at linking these by chromatic voice-leading, and occasionally through root motion through a tritone (see bars 1–2, 4–5). Tonally functional progressions – marked with brackets below Example 4.1 – are not employed as a matter of routine but rather *de*ployed from time to time, their qualitative difference from the chromatic progressions being held in balance by the composer as one aspect of the musical expression. 'Grabschrift' is perhaps the most remarkable of these songs, not least in that the music achieves tonal focus only in its third bar. Berg's writing for both performers encompasses a broad range of figuration, the vocal line taking in both stark declamation and animated sequence, the piano writing moving from bare chromaticism in the manner of late Liszt, by way of routine chordal accompaniment, to the middle section's florid arpeggio writing. The overall sense of tonal direction is hair-raising rather than secure, however, and the fact that the song ends by recapitulating the music of the opening a semitone higher seems scarcely calculated.

Nonetheless, these songs represent a level of achievement that might make one question why Schoenberg did not at first regard Berg as a student of composition *per se*: instead, he was to take instruction in harmony and counterpoint for three years. If the reason for this was to do with the shortcomings Schoenberg later described, then it must be said that his claim that 'even [Berg's] piano accompaniments ... were song-like in style' is something of an exaggeration. Some of Berg's earliest piano writing is

Example 4.1   'Liebe' (1904, wds. Rainer Maria Rilke), bars 1–7

indeed awkward, but many of the textures he employs in the untutored songs are adapted from his likely models, and most – probably all – of his accompaniments were written for actual performance, frequently by the composer himself. But what is missing from these songs, at least by comparison with those that we must take to embody the fruits of Schoenberg's teaching, is an element of musical concentration and coherence which can be put down, in the broadest terms, to the constant re-use of musical material.

In the later works this shows itself variously. Firstly, in the use of motives: whether to generate the phrases of a melodic line, to link it with the music of the piano, or to bind together the texture of the piano writing itself through internal counterpoint. Secondly, in a heightened articulation of musical form, brought about during the course of a song both through carefully placed allusions to earlier moments and through the varied reprise of more extended passages. By mid-1908 these were aspects of compositional technique which Berg had mastered, at least in the field of song-writing. Even 'Die Nachtigall', written as early as the spring of

1907 and later chosen by the composer for publication as one of the *Seven Early Songs*,[6] demonstrates such skills in the flowing, motivically saturated piano writing of the outer sections and the manner in which its motive forms the basis of the ever more prominent anacruses in the vocal line. And all of this is done without a loss of immediacy or charm – qualities which the song possesses in abundance.

Yet, as he wrote this song, Berg was but a student of harmony and counterpoint. It is much to Schoenberg's credit that whilst taking Berg through the fundamentals of the composer's craft, he nonetheless allowed his student to continue writing songs for pleasure. Indeed, he must have taken a professional interest in them as well, since three songs, 'Die Nachtigall' among them, together with an evidently ambitious double fugue for string quintet with piano, comprised Berg's contribution to the concert of music by Schoenberg's pupils that took place in Vienna on 7 November 1907.[7] Schoenberg thought highly of the fugue, at least within its pedagogical context:

> I could do counterpoint with [Berg] in a manner rare amongst my pupils. [The] double fugue for string quintet ... was overflowing with ingeniosities. But I could see already to what lengths he could be pushed: when the fugue was ready I told him to add a piano accompaniment in the manner of a continuo. Not only did he execute this with all excellence, he found ways of adding a further host of minor devilries.[8]

This was the culmination of Berg's work as a counterpoint student. The academic session that began in the autumn of 1907 saw him transfer to 'free composition'.

To start with, Berg was engaged on various short pieces mainly for piano, and these in due course led to a piano variations project which came to fruition in the summer of 1908 with the Twelve Variations on an original theme. There is much to admire in this music, which specifically recalls the Beethoven of the Diabelli Variations but adds many Brahmsian turns of phrase; indeed the layout of Berg's theme, and its unassuming nature, seem to have been designed to offer opportunities similar to those Beethoven found in the musical substance he extracted from Diabelli's 'cobbler's patch'. Berg's work is not on the same scale, and it almost totally lacks the cumulative sense of form across the variations which is one of the seminal achievements of Beethoven's towering masterpiece; but at a bar-by-bar level his technical accomplishment in following an established path stands up to comparison with variation sets by Beethoven's nineteenth-century successors surprisingly well.

Simply on account of their lack of individuality, however, the Twelve

Variations are quite limited in conception compared with the songs that Berg was writing at this time: 'Nacht' and 'Schilflied' (*Seven Early Songs*, nos. 1 and 2), 'Das stille Königreich' and 'Leukon' (*Jugendlieder*, Vol. II nos. 22 and 23). At least the first two of these are fully worthy of their place in the concert repertoire alongside songs by Berg's older contemporaries, whereas for all their accomplishment the piano variations are, by the very highest standards, no more than a curiosity. 'Nacht' is notable for its extensive use of the whole-tone scale, with which Berg was familiar from Schoenberg's Chamber Symphony No. 1 (1906) and more recently from Paul Dukas's opera *Ariane et Barbe-bleue*, which had impressed him at the Vienna Volksoper on 2 April 1908. Although the pure whole-tone character of the song's opening material perhaps makes this aspect over-prominent, Berg demonstrates a remarkable ability to move convincingly between such whole-tone writing and the other elements of his harmonic repertoire. The song also shows the art-that-conceals-art in Berg's control over its tonal direction, the key signature of A major being justified by two well-prepared climactic moments clearly focused on that key (bars 9 and 16) despite both the music's perpetual tendency to move flatwards – chords rooted on F, Bb and Eb are numerous – and the key-evading whole-tone sonorities that saturate the opening, the principal reprise at bar 26, and the concluding bars.

But, even more so than in the case of 'Die Nachtigall', a large part of what makes 'Nacht' and 'Schilflied' so impressive as music is their constant recycling and recombination of material to create a fully woven musical texture rather than simply a string of ideas. This was undoubtedly something that had come from Schoenberg's tuition in instrumental genres. After all, the very *raison d'être* of fugue and variation movements is their re-use of material. Even the counterexample of 'Das stille Königreich', described with some justification by Nicholas Chadwick in his pioneering study as 'far and away the most interesting of all Berg's [then] unpublished songs', is instructive.[9] Whilst, on the page, the song's principal motive and its treatment bear a close resemblance to the corresponding features of the slightly later 'Sommertage' (*Seven Early Songs*, no. 7), the song never takes wing as 'Sommertage' does. 'Leukon' is also only partly successful – its motivic material too bland to make anything of Gleim's poem. But all of these songs, embodying the young composer's sophisticated and far from uncritical literary tastes, and responding in their momentary musical gestures to the inflections of the texts he chose, retain that innate strength of purpose that Schoenberg saw even in Berg's untutored work, and it is this which distinguishes even the less successful of them from the Twelve Variations.

Piano Sonata Op. 1

The Piano Sonata Op. 1 is the first of Berg's completed instrumental compositions in which the debt is reversed. For the Sonata undoubtedly builds on the musical achievement of the songs as well as on the technical benefits Berg had taken from Schoenberg in the instrumental sphere. In fact, there was more than one sonata: five numbered sonatas preceded Op. 1, all of them similarly in one movement, though none was completed. The piano sonata 'project', if we may characterise it so, seems to have occupied Berg under Schoenberg's tuition during the 1908–9 season,[10] and it is in this sense that the Op. 1 Sonata may be said to date from 1908, the date which Reich gives in his authorised biography.[11] Even the fifth of the preliminary sonatas would appear to have been composed rather later than this, however, since in Berg's working manuscript it is interrupted by a draft of the second song from his Op. 2.[12] Perhaps the strongest circumstantial evidence that Op. 1 itself was not composed until the latter part of the season is that the Twelve Variations were chosen for performance in another concert of music by Schoenberg's pupils which took place on 8 November 1908 – a choice which, as George Perle has noted, would have been musically inexplicable had the Piano Sonata already been available at that time.[13]

The preliminary sonatas may have been conceived as exercises in writing different sections of a sonata form, though each begins at the beginning of the movement.[14] Of these, Nos. 3, 4 and 5 are particularly noteworthy. The opening dotted rhythm of No. 3 and its application to a leaping motivic shape clearly prepare the ground for Op. 1, whilst both the rising figure that follows and the counterpoint that develops it anticipate the opening of the song 'Nun ich der Riesen stärksten überwand', Op. 2/iii. The first eight bars of No. 4 were to be famously re-used some years later by Berg in the D minor interlude from Act III of *Wozzeck*;[15] but of more immediate chronological relevance is that this sonata, too, anticipates the third song of Op. 2 – even if its relation to the song's middle section is less substantial than is the relation of the third sonata to the same song's outer sections. The fifth and last of the preliminary sonatas, which resembles Op. 1 closely in several of its turns of phrase, is by far the longest and could probably be 'completed' without too much difficulty, but the attractiveness of this prospect is reduced by the meandering way in which the material is developed, making even the unfinished work seem over-extended by comparison with the definitive Sonata that was to follow.

Indeed, one of the principal characteristics of the Op. 1 Sonata is its tautness. Its one-movement format does not seek ambitiously to incorporate aspects of scherzo, slow movement and finale genres – bundling the four movements of a sonata design into the span of a single sonata-form – as had been one aim of Schoenberg's String Quartet No. 1 (1905) and first Chamber Symphony. At the same time, Berg's (and his teacher's) decision to let the single sonata-form movement of Op. 1 stand alone as a complete work reflects the devaluation of the other movement-types that was implicit in Schoenberg's project. The mundane explanation for this, according to Josef Polnauer (1888–1969), who studied with Schoenberg from 1909 to 1911 and thereafter with Berg for two years, was that Berg had originally planned a slow movement and finale to follow the sonata-form movement, but nothing suitable for these movements came to him. Seeking Schoenberg's advice, Berg was told 'Well, then, you've simply said all you had to say', and so decided to let the single movement stand alone.[16]

The course of the Sonata is articulated through the interaction between, on the one hand, the ongoing development of its motivic material and, on the other hand, the basis of its Brahmsian sonata-design in stable, contrasting thematic areas. The technique that allowed Berg to square this circle was that of *developing variation*, a compositional principle which Schoenberg was not yet ready to elaborate formally in his writings but which he surely imparted verbally to his pupils. All the same, Berg's Sonata must be counted a more thoroughgoing instance of developing variation than, say, Schoenberg's first Chamber Symphony, which is frequently cited as a model for the Sonata in other respects.[17]

The music begins in mid-flow, harmonically speaking (Example 4.2a): its cadential trajectory to the tonic gives bars 1–4 clear identity as a musical phrase and emblematic status as a source of motivic material, which is immediately taken up in a counterpoint of fragments. Through this, the characteristic shapes and rhythms established at *a*, *b* and *c* in the opening phrase are combined and recombined, and in the process adapted almost imperceptibly, until they are realigned in a newly thematic presentation (bars 12–14, Example 4.2b). This in turn is taken up and varied, the metamorphosis of motivic shapes gliding neatly into a re-presentation of the opening theme (bars 17–19). Whether this theme is now heard as a repetition that begins a larger formal unit, or as a step in a journey of transformation which is free to turn back on itself and so traverse the same material in different ways, is one of the games which this work plays: it becomes an issue at precisely this juncture, as noted by Adorno in his richly argued analysis of the movement, in which he suggests that 'transition and principal theme are combined in such a way that in retrospect the theme assumes a tripartite form'.[18] Adorno argues, in other words, that the music of bars 12ff. seems at first to be transitional, and then not to be.

At the root of this is the perceptibility of a distinction – even as the combination and recombination of materials proceeds in all its fluidity –

Example 4.2   (a) Piano Sonata Op. 1, opening (*Mäßig bewegt*), showing motives *a*, *b* and *c*

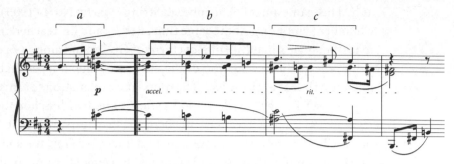

(b) bars 12–14 (*Rascher als Tempo I*)

between a sense at some moments of thematic delineation, and at other moments of transitional motivic working. In the hands of many performers this distinction will perhaps rightly remain a subtle one, though the establishment of a play of ideas at the broader formal level depends on it. Janet Schmalfeldt, in an analysis even more comprehensive than Adorno's, concurs with and clarifies his view, labelling bars 12ff. as a 'false transition' which 'becomes' the B-section of the main theme. Later in the movement, however, their analyses diverge: indeed a comparison among various commentators is instructive, revealing extensive similarities in their perceptions but also subtle differences between them (Table 4.1). The nearest thing we have to Berg's own opinion is embodied in his tempo markings, which distinguish the thematic areas with great clarity. Interestingly in view of our knowledge of his later music, the succession of tempos traces a wedge-shape, in which gradually increasing speeds alternate with gradually decreasing ones.[19] As a number of commentators have observed, wedge-configurations of pitch are a characteristic feature of Berg's music from at least as early as the *Altenberg Lieder* Op. 4;[20] a tempo wedge similar to that of the Piano Sonata's exposition but on a far larger scale is seen across the six movements of the *Lyric Suite*.

As Bruce Archibald has pointed out, the development and recapitulation of the Piano Sonata fall, like the exposition, into three sections of which the third is in each case the shortest.[21] An important difference, however, is that the development reworks the material of bars 12ff. quite extensively (bars 71–100), whereas the subsidiary themes from bars 30ff.

Table 4.1 Op. 1: Berg's tempo markings for exposition, cf. formal analyses

bar	Berg	Adorno	Redlich	Jarman	Schmalfeldt
1	Mäßig bewegt	MT (antecedent)	A I	S I/i	MT (A)
4	a tempo	MT (consequent)		variant	
12	Rascher als Tempo I	transition? (*or* MT, third part)	A II	S I/ii	false transition, *becomes* MT (B)
17	Tempo I	[transition]			MT (A'), *becomes* transition
30	Langsamer als Tempo I	ST	B I	S II/i	ST 1 (= A)
39	Rasch	CT	B II	S II/ii	ST 2 (= B)
50	Viel langsamer (Quasi Adagio)	*Abgesang*	C	codetta	CT (= A')

Note: MT = main theme; ST = secondary *or* subordinate theme; CT = closing theme.

Sources: Adorno, *Alban Berg*, pp. 42–5; Redlich, *Alban Berg: Versuch einer Würdigung*, pp. 60–61; Jarman, *The Music of Alban Berg*, pp. 31–2; Schmalfeldt, 'Berg's Path to Atonality', pp. 86–9.

and 39ff. are treated briefly in tandem leading back to the recapitulation of the main theme (bars 101–11). The *Abgesang* material – if we accept Adorno's designation – is thus held over until the recapitulation, where it brings the Sonata to a close with the movement's most distant recollection, underlining the nostalgic sense of the whole work. This lingering impression is actually enhanced by the absence of any following movements: the expression of nostalgia's sense of loss thus plays in part upon our understanding of music's formal and generic conventions, in a way that was to become characteristically Bergian.

Looking more closely at the subsidiary and *Abgesang* themes, one of the most striking features on the page is the close relationship between the material of bars 39ff. and bars 50ff. (Example 4.3a). Their identical pitch sequence is, however, heard with two quite different characters, delineated largely through contrasts of rhythm and tempo. This coincidence of material is indicative of Berg's confidence in his ability to articulate similarity into difference. A smaller, more subtle and yet also more outrageous example is to be found at the recapitulation of the subsidiary theme (bar 138), where simply by taking a different note from the B^9 harmony at the start (C$\sharp$, before reverting to F$\sharp$) Berg exposes a connection, at the interval of a tritone, between the head-motives of the principal and subsidiary themes (Example 4.3b). Exchanging the earlier dotted rhythm for even quavers at this point makes the connection less triumphantly obvious, whilst at the same time matching precisely the way the principal theme has been presented at its own recapitulation (bar 111) – at which juncture the change of rhythm is bound to have seemed motivated only by a desire for variety, now transformed into a tight and unexpected coherence.

Example 4.3   (a) Op. 1: bar 39 (*Rasch*); bars 50–51 (*Viel langsamer*)

(b) recapitulation of themes: bars 138–9 (*Langsames Tempo*); bar 111 (*Tempo I*)

Aspects of the musical language

The bar-by-bar musical language of the Piano Sonata has been discussed at length – in different ways and half a century apart, but with remarkable points of contact – by Adorno and Schmalfeldt. Adorno identifies the re-ordering of notes within a motive, and their vertical accumulation into harmonic sonorities, as two characteristic ways in which Berg treats small fragments of material, suggesting that:

> [it] is extremely typical of the Sonata [that motives are] restated in a manner midway between literal and 'retrograde' repetition, which one might call 'axis rotation'; the terse intervals are retained but their succession is altered; [at bar 6] the three-note motive [*a*] begins with the second note, after which comes the first and then the third. Axis rotation is employed so consistently within the Sonata that it does not take much interpretive skill to see it as a prototype for the later serial technique; the motive is treated in the sense of a 'basic idea' [*Grundgestalt*]

> [at the end of the work] the *Abgesang* … clearly exhibits an inclination to present the melodic intervals of the head motive simultaneously as a sonority.[22]

Schmalfeldt takes these ideas further with the supporting conceptual apparatus of pitch-class set theory: she shows in considerable detail that small configurations of pitches, at first presented motivically in the way we have seen, may also be regarded as unordered sets – which is to say, they can be found to reappear (often transposed and perhaps also inverted) with the notes in a different linear order, or indeed vertically as a chord rather than linearly at all. Like Adorno, though without his somewhat premature invocation of serial technique, Schmalfeldt uses this line of argument to link the Sonata with Berg's later compositions, specifically with the String Quartet Op. 3, the clarinet pieces Op. 5 and *Wozzeck*.

Indeed, looking more broadly than just at the Sonata, Berg's music is potentially fertile ground on which to develop a sophisticated counter to the perhaps hastily perceived demarcation between tonal and atonal music which generated such a flurry of both learned polemic and popular misunderstanding through much of the twentieth century. One of the most powerful ideas put forward with this in mind is Mark DeVoto's principle of 'creeping chromaticism' – something which he sees operating in Berg's music from the early songs at least as far as *Wozzeck*.[23] 'Creeping' is an informally descriptive term which is applicable in many musical situations – DeVoto offers examples from Chopin, Schumann, Brahms and a turn of the-century popular song as precedents for Schoenberg and Berg – where chords from a rich harmonic vocabulary seem to be linked in sequence more by the chromatic motion of prominent voices, such as the melody and the bass, than by concepts of root progression. The previous norms of root progression through tonic, dominant and subdominant functions are in any case frequently undermined in late nineteenth-century music, both by the possibility of enharmonic notation obscuring the generative origins of chromaticised chords, and by the versatility of composers in expanding the range of root progressions they could handle convincingly. In Schoenberg's *Harmonielehre* – the 'harmony course' which Berg in effect worked through, prior to its publication, as one of Schoenberg's harmony students – many exercises are devoted to developing a wide-ranging facility in connecting one chord with another: some of the most advanced of these are concerned with 'connections of altered and vagrant chords' (i.e. chromaticised and functionally ambivalent chords) and 'triads connected with all other triads and seventh chords; also, all seventh chords with one another'.[24] Introducing the first of these sections of the book, Schoenberg gives some advice to the student reader:

> [Since] close attention to ... the root progressions often does not assure control over the quality of a progression, control through the voice leading may be substituted ... Thus, in general, the best connections of simple chords with vagrants or of vagrant chords with one another will be those in which the second chord contains, as far as possible, only notes that appeared in the first or are recognisable as chromatically raised or lowered notes of the first. In his first attempts the pupil should make this origin explicit in the voice leading. An E♭ in the second chord should actually appear in the same voice that in the first chord had the E, from which the E♭ came. ... Later, when he is familiar with the functioning of

these phenomena, the pupil may abandon this deliberate expression of the derivation in the voice leading.[25]

This comes close to recommending DeVoto's 'chromatic creeping' as a rule of thumb for the pupil's 'first attempts' – perhaps serving to remind us that Berg's Sonata is still a student work.

Schoenberg also makes it clear that such chords may be handled simply with reference to their own internal construction and characteristic sonorities:

> the pupil will best take all these vagrant chords for what they are, without tracing them back to a key or degree ... [Once] we abandon the desire to explain the derivation of these chords, their effect becomes much clearer.[26]

This concentration on the thing-in-itself is a crucial conceptual step towards recognising even such entities as the whole-tone scale and quartal harmonies (chords built in fourths) as objects to be manipulated in their own right, rather than as interesting end-points of a process of chromatic alteration from conventional chords or scales. But in fact Schoenberg has it both ways: by charting connecting progressions between vagrant chords on the basis of conceiving them as chromatically altered functional chords – which is what he does in the *Harmonielehre* – he allowed both himself (notably in the first Chamber Symphony) and the more gifted of his pupils (notably Berg) to contextualise these new musical artefacts in a richly expanded dialect of tonality. Berg was right at the centre of this: he prepared the index to the first edition of the *Harmonielehre* and seems to have received instruction of an intensity that Schoenberg did not match after its publication.[27]

Adorno chooses to pitch his discussion of how Berg connects quartal harmonies with their triadic surroundings at a different level, stressing that the manner of their contextualisation is historically and expressively charged. He compares Berg's handling of quartal harmonies with Schoenberg's in the Chamber Symphony:

> Fourths opened the Chamber Symphony: chordal in the introduction, melodic in the principal theme. They are expounded abruptly, with all the confidence of conquest. In Berg's Sonata, on the other hand, they first appear in bar 26 in an harmonically formative role [see Example 4.4]. The quartal sonority F♯–B–E is introduced in such a way that the critical note E appears as a suspension to D, that is, 'harmonically foreign' to the tonic chord of the principal key of B minor ... Imperceptibly, ... this quartal trichord gradually emancipates itself until finally revealed (bar 28) as a pure five-note quartal chord. However, with the help of a motivic remnant [a development of the 'axis-rotated' version of *b*]

Example 4.4   Op. 1: quartal harmonies in bars 26–9 (notation simplified)

this chord is slowly altered, note by note, until (bar 29) it is transformed … into an altered dominant of A major. That is how the quartal formation, at its appearance and disappearance, dissolves seamlessly into the tonal flow. … Schoenberg's discovery of quartal sonorities was utopian; Berg discovered them with memory's long, veiled gaze sunk deep into the past, that past which his music, even at its most daring, never forgets to consider.[78]

DeVoto also fastens on this passage of the Sonata, which, as Adorno's description makes clear, is a fine example of 'chromatic creeping'.[29]

But we can be more specific even than this. In the Chamber Symphony, Schoenberg uses quartal harmony not only to set the work on its exhilarating journey but also at formal junctures where, in a more conventionally tonal work, one might expect to find a lengthy prolongation of dominant-quality harmony, analogous (albeit in what is a considerably more elaborate formal design) to the retransition section of a sonata movement. In phenomenological terms, the effect is one of complementarity: a thematically empty prolongation of unresolved dominant-quality harmony is 'made good' by the appearance of a familiar theme played in the movement's most stable tonal area. Filling this kind of slot in a reinterpreted formal schema is a convenient way for quartal harmony to be deployed in the extended tonal style of early Schoenberg and Berg, for whereas tonally functional harmonies can be chromatically altered and contrapuntally obscured by thematic material and yet still be recognised, quartal harmonies once inflected by chromaticism simply lose their identity. In Berg's Sonata, the passage described by Adorno and DeVoto introduces the subsidiary theme in the exposition; there is a touch of quartal harmony in bar 11, just before the 'false transition' theme – which perhaps clarifies the status of this material, after all – and the *Abgesang* is preceded by a passage which features many quartal configurations. The section of the development which reworks the 'false transition' theme is heralded by a passage of pure whole-tone writing – the connection being that, like the quartal chords, the whole-tone scale risks annihilation if chromatically inflected – and the development's reworking of the subsidiary material is preceded by the Sonata's largest climax, built on quartal harmonic foundations akin to those of bars 26–9 but much expanded.[30]

A noteworthy absentee from this list is the retransition itself, which is accomplished harmonically by stealth and thematically by anticipation. One may also point to the angular chromaticism of the sextuplet motive that cues the second subsidiary theme (bar 39) as another means of avoiding naive whole-tone or quartal writing in this work – even if the same pitch sequence, in its slower treatment as the *Abgesang*, is ultimately tamed by a chorale-like chromatic progression of whole-tone chords. This is very different to 'Nacht', with its prominent whole-tone thematic material and radiant bursts of A major, but then the *Lied* as a genre accommodates – demands, even – a more heterogeneous range of musical gesture and a lesser emphasis on balance or complementarity among its materials. Much of the younger Berg's accomplishment as a song composer can be put down to his ability to produce authentically *Lied*-like gestures, and much of the benefit of Schoenberg's teaching can be seen in Berg's new-found ability to mediate among different types of such material and to develop them by constant variation and recombination, whilst still retaining an ear for the expressive turn of phrase.

Four Songs Op. 2

As the surviving manuscripts make clear, Berg continued to write songs while working on his sonata project. Just as serious work on the project seems to have begun only a little after the last of the *Jugendlieder* were composed (the two Hohenberg settings 'Sommertage' and 'Läuterung'), so a later phase of work on the fifth preliminary sonata was coeval with a draft of 'Schlafend trägt man mich', which became the second of the Four Songs Op. 2. Overall, the chronology of Op. 2 is a little clearer than that of the Piano Sonata. It seems that songs two and three were written before the others, to poems 56 and 57 from the collection *Der Glühende* by Alfred Mombert (1872–1942), followed by Op. 2/i, to a poem by the dramatist Friedrich Hebbel (1813–63), and finally by Op. 2/iv, also taken from Mombert's *Der Glühende*. Whereas the origins of songs two and three are roughly contemporary with Berg's work towards the sonata project, song one would seem to postdate the completion of Op. 1, whilst the fourth song was written later still, after the first movement of the String Quartet

Op. 3 had been drafted, early in 1910.[31] Both in their order of composition, then, and in their order of presentation in performance, the Four Songs traverse an apparent boundary between tonal and atonal music. This raises the question of their coherence as a group, which is something one might expect to locate in factors such as a narrative thread running through the substance and imagery of the poetry, large-scale tonal motion across several songs, or the use of shared motives between the songs. To this rather generalised checklist should be added the specific model of Schoenberg's String Quartet No. 2 (1907–8), in which a stylistic journey across the four movements, from tonality into overt atonality, is articulated through the expression of soul-searching and then transcendence, in the two poems by Stefan George which a soprano soloist sings in the third and fourth movements.

In their published order, the poetry of Berg's Op. 2 songs begins with a yearning for total sleep;[32] it continues with an involuntary journey, still in sleep, 'to my homeland', which is explained further as a hero's fairytale return after overcoming 'the strongest of giants' in 'the darkest land'; and ends by presenting a dreamlike state which may or may not be death ('the one dies whilst the other lives: that makes the world so profoundly beautiful'). If already only a little imagination is required to interpret this as the allegorical expression of one who feels propelled by events, from a situation in which good work has been achieved but the task is now done, into a state through which he hopes to have achieved transcendence, then some incidental connections with Schoenberg's works on similar themes supply further correlation. The opening words of Berg's fourth song, 'Warm die Lufte' ('warm [are] the breezes'), recall directly the soprano's opening words in the last movement of Schoenberg's second quartet: 'Ich fühle Luft von anderen Planeten' ('I feel [a] breath from other planets'); and the declamatory style of Berg's song has been likened by several commentators to that of Schoenberg's one-woman music-drama *Erwartung* ('Expectation', 1909), probably cued by the words 'Er kommt noch nicht. Er lässt mich warten' ('He still hasn't come. He's making me wait').[33]

In terms of tonal organisation, the two central songs are clearly linked. Song two ends with a dominant-quality sonority rooted on E♭, at the culmination of a progression around the circle of fifths: the third song opens in a fragmentary A♭ minor, continuing the fifths and resolving the dominant harmony. When the third song ends, now firmly in E♭ major, one may perceive a connection with both the beginning and the end of the preceding song. Had the fourth song been published a minor third higher than it was, it would have begun with the perfect fifth E♭–B♭ in the bass, continuing forward from the second and third songs, and would have ended with a link back to the first song, which begins and ends firmly in D minor (see

Example 4.5   (a) conjectural tonal framework of Op. 2 (song four transposed to E♭/D basis)

(b) actual tonal framework of Op. 2 (as published)

Example 4.5a). Though one ought not to press speculation along such lines too far, not least because the vocal tessitura in bars iv/15–16 is already high and could hardly be transposed upwards, it is fair to suggest that this tonal scheme would have led to Op. 2/iv being perceived ever since as less thoroughgoingly atonal than has been the case. And, setting aside speculation in favour of the true picture (Example 4.5b), what this sequence of observations achieves is to throw into relief the central section of song four, which is in fact a 'song-within-a-song'. After the opening, rooted on the perfect fifth C–G, the voice announces 'I will sing' (bars iv/7–8), and proceeds to relate a crypto-erotic mountain pastoral image, using a musical style reminiscent of Schoenberg's *Das Buch der hängenden Gärten* (1908–9).[34] With the climactic 'Stirb!' ('Die!'), the song-within-a-song comes to an abrupt end, and the music's expanded tonal sense is regained through a quasi-functional succession of dominant thirteenth and augmented ninth chords similar to the harmony of much of the first song.

Consideration of the motivic connections within and between the songs demands closer analysis of each, which may be pursued according to the likely sequence of their composition. The music of Op. 2/iii may be described, on a bar-by-bar basis, in broadly the same terms as apply to the Piano Sonata, but with the proviso that in the more gestural genre of the *Lied* the motivic integration is less continuous: the whole effect is more volatile, in response to the text. Its two principal motives, shown as *a* and *b* in Example 4.6, thus serve not to generate an intricate web of musical material but to provide musical points of reference, to add variety to the

Example 4.6   Op. 2/iii: motives, harmonic framework and 'creeping' voices

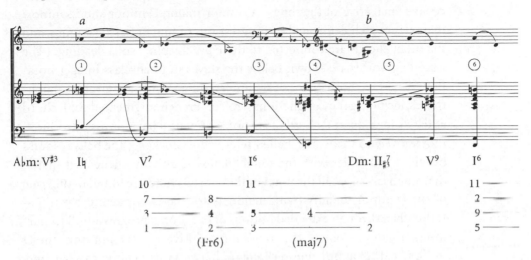

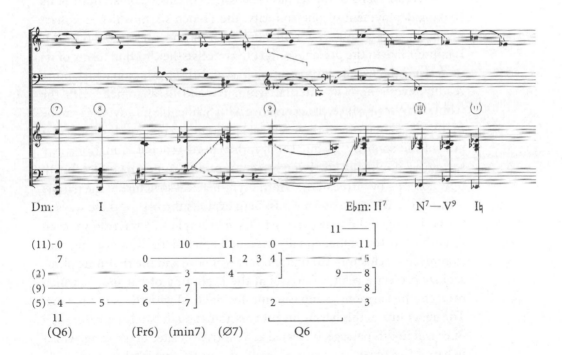

voice-leading and sometimes to assist in covering technically awkward moments. The latter part of motive *a* is in fact a literal inversion of the opening motive *a* of the Piano Sonata, whilst the four unaccompanied vocal notes which begin the song are a variant of the Sonata's motive *b* (we have already seen how this song is related in a more generalised way to the third and fourth preliminary sonatas). As shown in the harmonic reduction on the lower two staves of each system in Example 4.6, the three successive tonal areas of the song – A♭ minor/major, D minor and E♭ minor/major – are each delineated by progressions of functional harmonies, and the other chords are connected to these by 'creeping' voice-leading. (The 'creeping' voices are shown below the staves in pitch-class integer notation[35] and the chord-types of the intervening chords are given in parentheses, including the designations 'Fr6' for 'French' augmented sixth chord and 'Q6' for a quartal chord of six notes.) Quartal harmony is introduced illustratively to the words 'hallen schwer die Glocken' ('the bells resound heavily') and tallies with the tonal context simply by virtue of a shared diatonic basis – i. e., all the notes of the quartal chord are found in the scale of the D minor tonality (with major sixth) that is invoked in bar iii/6 – rather than through extended notions of functional progression. The harmonic rhythm is one of the song's most elusive aspects: not until the D minor triad at bar iii/6 does a change of harmony coincide with a bar-line.

The second song of the set has been widely discussed on account of its striking deployment of one sonority: the French sixth, which is enharmonically equivalent to a dominant seventh chord with lowered fifth.[36] It is appropriate in the present context to conceive the chord in terms of its underlying pitch-class configuration $[0, 4, 6, 10]$,[37] a notation which more readily reveals both its internal symmetry and its alignment with the whole-tone scale, since, in accordance with Schoenberg's advice, it can be manipulated in terms of these features without reference to the tonal origins of the sonority. In tonal usage, the chord generally functions as a secondary dominant, resolving by root motion through a perfect fourth upwards, or – by virtue of the chord's symmetrical structure at the tritone – through a semitone downwards. Berg exploits the first of these ways at the beginning of the song (bars ii/1–3, see Example 4.7), but resolves each 'French sixth' to another equally vagrant 'French sixth', thus evading cues towards tonal closure – though the vocal cadence and the rhythmic phraseology project a point of arrival at the beginning of bar ii/4, at which moment the harmony is enharmonically identical with the very opening. The upper line of this harmonic progression, though barely perceived as a line at all in this passage, is treated as a motive (*c*) later in the song, whilst in bars ii/2–3 the voice adopts a second motive (*d*) that is taken up directly in the piano's transitional passage (bars ii/4–8). Here the harmony continues to be based on $[0, 4, 6, 10]$ chords but in the reverse sequence to the opening; the chords are prolonged and thickened within their respective whole-tone scales, the counterpoint being driven by a near-canon between the hands from bar ii/6 onwards. The texture in this passage is built on a core of parallel major thirds, a model which is found quite frequently in the Piano Sonata, e.g. at bars 5–6 (also in Schoenberg's Chamber Sym-

Example 4.7   Op. 2/ii: opening, showing motives *c* and *d*

phony No. 1 and *Friede auf Erden*, and in some early works by Webern), and which, like 'creeping' but perhaps with even greater longevity, remained part of Berg's compositional palette into a much later period. A new point of arrival is reached at the vocal entry in bar ii/9, supported by a [0, 4, 6, 10] sonority on D, after which the sequence of these chords is interrupted. Successive statements of motive *c* are heard in the voice and piano in bars ii/9–12, and then the material of bars ii/4–8 is taken up again (bars ii/13–14), continuing the sequence of French sixths from the point at which it was interrupted. The palindromic re-use of material is concluded in bars ii/15–18 with a reprise of the opening bars, but varied so as to introduce cross-references both within this song and forward to the next one: first, in bar ii/15, where the faster rate at which the opening chords reappear picks up the rhythm of motive *c* from bars ii/9–12; second, in bars ii/16–17, where bass motion within several of the [0, 4, 6, 10] sonorities between the two potential roots (Gb–C, E–Bb, A–Eb) anticipates the next song's cadential motion between Neapolitan and dominant seventh chords (at bars iii/10–11); thirdly, in bars ii/17–18, through a rhythmic motive in the bass (♩ ♪ ♩ ♩ ♪) which will be heard again in bars iii/2–3 and iii/9–11;[38] and finally, in the metrically incomplete final bar of song two, which is made good by the opening upbeat of song three.

The composition of some of the notable features of these two songs into Op. 2/i served to carry onward Berg's generation of a larger song-cycle. The 6/8 metre of song one, articulated by the exposed rocking bass motion at the beginning (i/1–5), provides an audible precedent for the rhythmic motive, whilst the rocking motion itself anticipates the tritone bass motions found at ii/16–17 and iii/10–11. This is particularly evident at i/7, where the bass also moves through a tritone between two potential harmonic roots of dominant-quality harmony. Example 4.8 shows six examples of this developing harmonic complex from song one, whilst Table

Table 4.2

(a)	i/5–6	0	1	2	3	4		7			10	(t=2)
(b)	i/7	0		2	3	4	6				10	(t=3)
(c)	i/10	0			3	4	6				10	(t=3)
(d)	i/11	0		2	3	4	6		8		10	(t=7)
(e)	i/16–17	0	1	2		4	6	7		9	10	(t=8)
(f)	i/16–17	0	1	2		4	6	7	8		10	(t=7)

Example 4.8   Harmonies in Op. 2/i

4.2 indicates their position in the song and reduces them to pitch-class integer notation (the boxes distinguish notes found in moving melodic parts from those heard as elements of the chord). At i/5–6 (Example 4.8a), the basis in functional harmony is clear, as a chromatically moving line over a stable D^7 chord generates successive sonorities of $D^{9\sharp}$, D^9 and $D^{9\flat}$. At i/7 (Example 4.8b), the perfect fifth is lowered – or, rather, the other notes 'creep' upwards – to transform the underlying basis into the [0, 4, 6, 10] sonority (shown in open noteheads) that will feature prominently in song two, once again with a chromatically moving line above. Some would interpret the successive sonorities produced in this bar as $E\flat^{9\sharp}$, A^{13}, $E\flat^9$ and $A^{13\flat}$, but this highly differentiated tonal sense, already tenuous at i/7, loses explanatory force three bars later (Example 4.8c) when the two alternative 'roots' are heard simultaneously: it is clear from the context, however, that the compound dominant quality of the sonority remains a factor in its deployment as part of a harmonic progression.[39] At Example 4.8d this functional aspect is reduced almost to symbolic status as the bass line moves in perfect fourths upwards (C♯, F♯, B, E) – akin to the opening of song two – but without taking the corresponding [0, 4, 6, 10] harmonies with it; and at i/13–14 the sequence of fourths in the bass continues, not with the A that might have been expected but after a tritone shift to E♭, behind which the tritone link embodied in the [0, 4, 6, 10] sonority hovers unheard. Examples 4.8e and 4.8f are extracted from the harmonically densest passage of the song, and show a continuation of the process seen at Example 4.8c whereby the harmonic basis is expanded by co-opting melodic pitch-classes into it, something which is also found in song two, at bars ii/6–8.

This accumulated density of texture is one strand in a further aspect of the song's construction, as Stephen Kett has shown:[40] both in these terms and more clearly through the progression of its dynamic markings (*ppp–pp–p–mf–*[*p*]*–f–mf–mp–p–pp–ppp–*[*p–mp*]*–pppp*) this song develops the ternary form of song three and the palindromic disposition of material in song two into a more flexible principle of organisation that can be applied to many dimensions of compositional technique. Most strikingly of all, Robert Morgan has illustrated how the focal pitches of the vocal line also follow such a pattern,[41] interacting with motivic configurations such as the A–D which is presented in the unaccompanied bass of i/1 and immediately transformed in the vocal entry. This motive will recur (as *b*) in song three; at its clearest emergence as a motive in song one (i/22–5) it is trans ferred to the top of the texture from the bass in a varied reprise of i/7–10, whilst the voice joins with the inner melodic line of the piano in parallel major thirds, anticipating the textural model of song two, bars ii/6ff. A final revealing detail in this song is to be found in Berg's far more accom plished handling, through Schoenbergian voice-leading, of the same 'Q6' quartal harmony deployed in song three (bars i/18–19, cf. iii/7–9).

Although the sophistication of song one clearly prepares the ground for a coherent cycle, only its less audible features prepare the listener, if at all, for the overt atonality of Op. 2/iv. If we interpret the manuscript evidence to indicate that what prepared Berg himself for the composition of this song was in fact his work on the first movement of the String Quartet Op. 3, then it is clear that on returning to his unfinished song cycle he was sufficiently fluent in deploying what Schoenberg called the 'new re-sources', or 'new means' ('neue Mittel'), to be capable of incorporating features which link Op. 2/iv back to the first three songs. One way in which he assisted himself was by reserving the newest of the 'new resources' for the central song-within a song (iv/9–16); at the song's opening, by comparison, the relationship to the earlier 'means' is clear enough.

First, there are incidental details that allude directly to earlier moments in the cycle: the first four notes of the vocal line, which outline an [0, 4, 6, 10] configuration; the next three notes, which reorder the motivic figure that song three shares with the Piano Sonata; the melody of 'sonnigen Wie-(sen)', which is taken from the previous song (iii/3); and the upper-most piano line in iv/5–6 – perhaps representing the nightingale referred to in the text – which uses the rhythmic motive from songs two and three. Second, there is the construction of the broad piano phrase in the first six bars: this builds significantly on the benefits of Schoenberg's teaching, for having earlier learned a multiplicity of means to bind musical textures and

Example 4.9   Op. 2/iv: opening sonority with whole-tone prolonging motions (bars 1–2) and 'creeping'/canonic transformation into second sonority (bars 3–4)

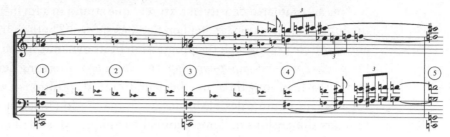

movements together in an extended tonal style, Berg now found himself capable of deploying these techniques in varying combinations separately from the tonal basis, so as to provide, say, motivic coherence in the absence of functional tonal harmony, or to follow recognisable voice-leading in an athematic context. Thus, when the song opens on Neapolitan harmony sustained over the perfect fifth C–G, the prolonging whole-tone motions in bars iv/1–2 lie within the two disjunct whole-tone scales but are nonetheless recognisable as such;[42] the opening sonority is then transformed into the chord that supports the 'nightingale' figure, without obvious reference to familiar harmonic types but through 'creeping' motions in the four upper voices – for the most part strictly chromatic – which incorporate a canonic treatment of the rhythmic motive (Example 4.9). After a descending flourish in iv/6 of a type familiar from Schoenberg's music of the same period, the piano settles on a bare tritone oscillation reminiscent of similar figures in all three of the preceding songs – its rhythm here being essentially a written-out rallentando – against which the vocal setting of 'Ich will singen' ('I will sing') seems entirely *extempore*.

The song-within-a-song falls into three micro-sections: in iv/9–11 the core of the piano texture is a pair of parallel major thirds – once again, a familiar 'resource' – supported, though not tonally contextualised, by major and minor triads. The vocal line at this point features major thirds also, before arpeggiating the A minor triad from the bottom of the piano texture in alternation with notes at chromatically expanding distances from the notes of the arpeggio (Example 4.10a). Over this is heard a piano figure, clearly illustrative of the words 'es schmilzt und glitzert kalter Schnee' ('cold snow melts and glitters'), which oscillates – once more at the tritone – between two open fifths, one of which is the C–G of the song's opening. The next micro-section (iv/12–15) is dominated by an intricate construction in the piano's music which applies the 'creeping' principle in differing ways to selected components of a motivic figure, thus transforming it gradually and perceptibly but without reference to an underlying harmonic basis (Example 4.10b); the transition into this from the preceding

Example 4.10   (a) Op. 2/iv, bar 11: intervallic expansion from A minor triad

schmilzt und glit - zeit kal - ter Schnee,

(b) Op. 2/iv: transformation by multiple 'creeping' in bars 12–15 (piano part)

micro-section is effected by expanding the oscillating major thirds into a miniature wedge motion, whilst transferring the 'melting snow' figure into the bass. The vocal part proceeds without obvious reference to the piano's music, though its gradually rising and widening tessitura follows a path similar in this respect to the motivic transformation. This widening is brought to a dramatic extreme at iv/15 with an outward combination of piano glissandi on black and white key. The final micro-section ensues, restoring the previous registers through downward octave transposition of the treble sonority and upward chromatic creeping in the bass.

As the song-within-a-song concludes, the piano arpeggiates a [0, 4, 6, 10] configuration down to a low Bb, from which point emerges a succession of augmented ninth and dominant thirteenth chords over a bass line of rising fourths (Example 4.11). A progression of this kind has the strong potential to be tonally directed, but in this overtly atonal composition it functions more comprehensively within a network of contextual links, referring back to song one through the harmony, to the opening of song two through the rising fourths, and to motive *a* of song three through the intervallic configuration of the notes above the ascending bass. The vocal part, projecting the poem's clinching line, conforms with these harmonies in the manner of song one, but detaches itself again over the threefold final cadence, part of which (from iv/22) was cited approvingly by Schoenberg in the *Harmonielehre*.[43]

Example 4.11   Op. 2/iv, bars 20–22, piano part

String Quartet Op. 3

The first movement of the String Quartet Op. 3 pursues still further, and in an atonal idiom, the interaction between motivic development and a sonata-form outline that we have seen in the Piano Sonata. Characteristically, Adorno saw profound implications in the progress of this idea:

> What marks the Quartet as a work of genuinely dialectical character is the fact that its architecture emerges from a loyal critique of the architecture that had until then been requisite for chamber music. … Berg met not only the authentic requirements of the form, but also those of his own explosive impulses, and to the end maintained the conflict between them. Not a single element remains that does not receive its rationale entirely from its relationship to the formal whole – and … there is likewise no [aspect of the] form not legitimized by the requirements and impulse of the individual elements. What results from this conflict, however, is nothing less than the *liquidation of the sonata*.[44]

Adorno's interpretation, first published in 1937, and concerned with a work completed in 1910, was conditioned by historical factors – the most obvious of which is that when Adorno was writing, and still more so in 1910, the question of a dichotomy between form and content in an artistic work was far more central to criticism than it is today.[45] A more intractable point – in that it is even less likely to be outmanœuvred through a historically constructed mode of listening – is that an awareness of form, particularly sonata form, was deeply embedded in the minds of educated listeners in the early twentieth century. Adorno's description assumes that the formal model is brought to the music by the listener and through direct experience of the musical argument undergoes a 'loyal critique'. The point is not that this specific work somehow makes sonata form obsolete, but that, on each hearing, it enacts a drama played right on the cusp between an architectural conception of 'form enclosing content' and an organic conception of 'form generated by content'. If awareness of form is not a pro-active part of the listener's mental apparatus, then the dialectic will be unbalanced in favour of the web of motivic correspondences that is woven before one's very ears, and in the general absence of tonal ordering such music may seem single-minded to the point of narrowness. This was not a failing of the work when Berg composed it, but the Cinderella status of the Quartet in Berg's output suggests that subsequent generations have found its assimilation difficult, perhaps for this reason.

On the other hand, it now seems possible that Adorno and others in his day were themselves kept unaware of a potential factor in the Quartet's interpretation. In 1986, the Greek-German musicologist Constantin Floros made the acquaintance of Fritzi Schlesinger-Czapka, a Viennese neighbour of Helene Berg, who passed on to him the following account which she claimed Helene had dictated to her:

> 'The inspiration for Alban Berg's Op. 3 was based on the following events: It was at my parents' house in 1908. Many young people came and went, for my sister and I were sociable girls. We had many suitors, and one of these was Alban Berg. None of the young men got near me except Alban! When my father noticed this, he forbade Alban Berg to visit us, because Alban was prone to illness (he had been an asthmatic since his fifteenth year) and had a profession (musician and composer) which didn't suit my down-to-earth and practical-minded father. Besides, he [my father] was concerned that I too would have a life of worry in store, on account of the chronic illness an asthmatic suffers. The separation hit Alban and me profoundly. Thus Op. 3 came into being. Love speaks in it, and jealousy and indignation over the injustice that was done to us and to our love.'　　　　　　　　　　　　　　Helene Berg[46]

What are we to make of this? Although there seems to be no documentary support for her account, this oral history cannot simply be dismissed; and whether or not there is a connection with Op. 3, there is plenty of evidence to confirm the difficulties placed in the way of the young couple by Helene's father, Franz Nahowski, including a long letter sent to him by Berg in July 1910 refuting his objections to their marriage.[47] This emotional scenario certainly tallies with the sense of anger and frustration that some commentators, even in the absence of specific explanation, have heard in the music of the Quartet. 'With the opening theme [of the second movement]', writes Mosco Carner, 'Berg seems to throw down the gauntlet to imaginary enemies.'[48] According to Adorno, 'Berg liked to say that he wrote the String Quartet … in defiance, after a publishing firm turned down the Piano Sonata.'[49] Given what we know today of the 'secret programmes' of some of Berg's later works,[50] we might readily take this to be the composer's attempt to acknowledge the expressive tone of his Quartet without giving away the motivation for it. Yet we should also observe that Helene Berg's description – if indeed it is hers – is a long way from being a detailed programme. What it purports to outline is no more than an extra-musical inspiration for an abstract composition, in a manner familiar from Schumann and Brahms – less thoroughly developed even than, say, Berlioz's approach to his *Symphonie Fantastique* – and indeed unremarkable for an era in which composers frequently hedged their bets on the competing merits of 'absolute' music and programme music by allowing it to be thought that their works satisfied criteria for both independently.[51]

Whilst the sonata-form outline of the Quartet's first movement is reasonably clear, the form of the second movement has caused confusion among the most respected observers. Carner describes the movement as a rondo with sonata elements; Floros reads it as a sonata form, but with an 'episode' (bars ii/119–42) placed between the development and a 'free' recapitulation. Adorno's idea of a sonata-rondo is accepted by Redlich, who then goes beyond this to suggest that 'the second movement represents a kind of development of the first movement's exposition'.[52] This interpretation has merit on at least three counts: first, because the development section of the first movement is short in length and does not deal with the movement's principal thematic material; second, because themes from the two movements are interrelated; and third, because it points up the direct reappearance of the first movement's opening theme in the second movement, at bars ii/168ff.

Example 4.12 traces some motivic relationships within the thematic materials of the Quartet. The opening theme of the first movement (Example 4.12a) is notable for its rhythms and for its interplay between specific sizes of intervals. The contour and sextuplet rhythm of the second violin's initial flourish are identical with those of a theme in Schoenberg's String Sextet *Verklärte Nacht* which is marked 'angry, vehement' ('wild, leidenschaftlich', Example 4.13); the descending semitone intervals in Schoenberg's theme are transformed here into descending whole tones, and all notes of the gesture but one (C♮) are confined to a single whole-tone scale. This intervallic consistency is taken up by the viola and cello under the violin's sustained B♮ – the viola moving downwards through successive semitone intervals and the cello through perfect fourths. Both of these represent an immediate transformation of the violin's opening three notes, similar to the transformation effected, outside the piece, from Schoenberg's theme: the motion is in each case through a segment of a single *interval cycle*. Berg's awareness of the interval cycles is well documented;[53] an example of their harmonic, as opposed to melodic, use is to be found in the first movement of the Quartet at bars i/98–101, where in a climactic passage the second violin, viola and cello play identical material homophonically, four times over: the first time forming parallel diminished triads, the second time parallel quartal harmonies, the third time parallel augmented triads. In each of these cases, the harmony is formed

Example 4.12   Some thematic and motivic connections in Op. 3

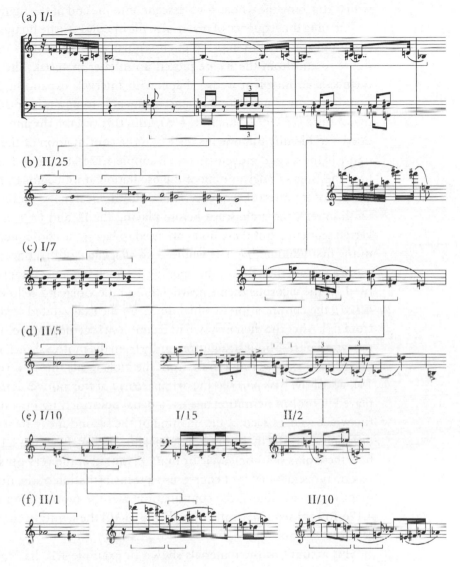

(a) I/i

(b) II/25

(c) I/7

(d) II/5

(e) I/10   I/15   II/2

(f) II/1   II/10

Example 4.13   Schoenberg, *Verklärte Nacht* Op. 4, violin I, bars 137–8 (*wild, leidenschaftlich*)

from a single type of interval; on the fourth statement, the three instruments form parallel harmonies of the type found in the right hand of the
piano at bars iv/20–22 of Op. 2 (see pp. 75–6). Example 4.12b shows how
the Quartet's opening flourish is in turn transformed in the second move-

ment, simply by replacing the whole-tone cycle with perfect fourths, whilst attaching the whole-tone descent onto the end of the figure.

Pursuing the sequence of material at the opening a little further, we find that both the rhythm and the pitch sequence of the violin's oscillating figure to and from the B♮ are picked up in later material. The pitch sequence is an incipient wedge shape, with intervals expanding from the sustained note to a semitone, thence to a whole tone, a minor third and a major third (cf. Op. 2, bars iv/12–15); both this and the rhythm are developed – to identify but one instance – in the continuation of the opening figure in the second movement (see Example 4.12e). Example 4.12c shows how the viola's underpinning of the oscillation at i/4 begins to follow an inverse of its interval sequence (the cello duplicates the violin a major tenth lower); the viola stops before playing the E♭ and G♮ from the inverted sequence, but these notes are used to begin the consequent phrase in the first violin at i/7. The whole-tone allegiance of this phrase is even more apparent than that of the opening: its pitch sequence, in inversion, is used for the vigorous theme heard at ii/5 in the viola and cello (Example 4.12d), the continuation of which picks up the exaggerated wedge shape from ii/2. After the theme shown in Example 4.12c, the first violin continues with a phrase built straightforwardly from the motive shown in Example 4.12e; the answering phrase from the viola treats this in inversion (i/14), whilst the bass part has the original form of the motive; at i/15 this is played in broken figuration against a pedal point, setting up a model for the wider wedges seen at the opening of the second movement (and indeed subsequently in the first). As a final illustration, Example 4.12f shows how the viola's semitone cycle from i/2–3 is used at the very outset of the second movement (it is of course also a transformation of the first movement's opening notes); the continuation uses the motive from Example 4.12e. In a subsequent contrasting theme (ii/10) the semitone intervals are replaced by whole tones.

This account of the materials shown in Example 4.12 has considered merely the relationships between musical ideas that are themselves the basis of further ongoing transformations. There are other thematically differentiated materials which have not been discussed here: indeed, the whole Quartet proceeds on this basis with a remarkable intensity that cannot be reflected in detailed verbal description. Leaving this aside, then, there is an interesting point to be followed up from the identification of a theme from *Verklärte Nacht* as a model. Redlich's discussion convincingly compares various themes from the Quartet with themes from Strauss's *Tod und Verklärung* and *Ein Heldenleben*, and also Wagner's *Tristan und Isolde*;[54] Floros compares some melodic lines from Berg's second movement with passages in Schoenberg's *Das Buch der hängenden Gärten* – a work which Berg knew intimately and had heard at its first performance in Vienna on 14 January 1910[55] – and he, too, raises the spectre of *Tristan*. Much if not all of this could be dismissed as idle speculation (and Adorno was unusually adamant that 'no model can be found')[56] were it not for Floros's identification of an apparently innocuous string quartet sketch by Berg as a model for the theme at i/7 of Op. 3.[57] Not only this, but nearby sketches resemble the theme from *Verklärte Nacht* shown in Example 4.13, according to Floros – though he does not pursue the point. Perhaps even more remarkable is a passage in the first movement of Op. 3 (bars i/126–31) that is adapted from the subsidiary theme of Berg's fifth preliminary piano sonata, a tonal work written immediately prior to his Op. 1.[58] There are strong indications, then, that Berg's earliest atonal venture – for this it was – was achieved, in part at least, by adapting tonal models. Certainly, the methods of interval substitution and expansion we have seen operating in Op. 3 and in bars iv/12–15 of Op. 2 indicate that Berg had the means at his disposal to adapt thematic material away from its harmonic context, an aspect of technique which distinguishes these works from the Piano Sonata.

Of all the passages in Op. 3 that can be related to tonal models, the one which most defies formal integration with the rest of the work is the episode in the second movement, bars ii/119ff. As Floros shows, the thematic material here is akin to a theme from the love duet in *Tristan und Isolde*, heard at Isolde's words 'Barg im Busen uns sich die Sonne'. In Berg's Quartet, the continuation uses this theme in inversion (ii/133ff.), perhaps suggesting that the model was not the love duet, but rather Act III scene 1 of Wagner's opera, in which Tristan, separated from Isolde by the jealous King Marke, is convinced she will return to him but torn asunder by the feelings this situation engenders inside him. Here Wagner, too, uses the theme both in its original form and in inversion, in order to signify Tristan's vacillating emotions. The correlation not only with Berg's handling of the theme but also with his separation from Helene is striking, if one wishes to think of the music in these terms.

At the same time, we should observe that Berg takes up the inversion of the theme for specifically musical purposes: other themes also return in inversion until, following a broad statement of the movement's opening theme (ii/151), the music recapitulates the opening material of the first movement (ii/168). From this point, the movement's latent focus on D as a pitch centre gains momentum – the first violin's repeated melodic cadence in bars ii/217–20 is particularly important in this process – until an extraordinary flourish in the final bar exposes a momentary chord of D minor, a tonality which is known to have had a private significance for Berg and Helene.[59] The tonal focus here distils and balances a less specific extended tonality found in the final pages of the first movement, brought about from bar i/166 by a core of parallel major thirds in a whole-tone dominated texture and in bars i/172–6 and i/180 to the end of the movement through the continual appearance of harmonies akin to those found at bars iv/20–22 of Op. 2. But despite the possible clues, its detailed extra-musical significance remains, like the transcendental interaction of form and motive, imperfectly available to later generations.

5 Berg's aphoristic pieces

Kathryn Bailey

Introduction

In the early part of June 1913 Alban and Helene Berg visited the Schoen-
bergs in Berlin.[1] On the last day of this visit, which was from all reports
otherwise a very happy one, Schoenberg and Berg had a conversation that
was to cause Berg considerable grief and soul searching in the months to
come. It has been generally agreed that at this time Schoenberg criticised
Berg's latest, 'aphoristic' works, although there is no direct evidence to this
effect. In his authorised biography Willi Reich says of this conversation:

> It *must have been* [my emphasis] the aphoristic form of the latest pieces
> – the Altenberg songs and the Four Pieces for Clarinet and Piano, Opus
> 5, completed in the spring of 1913 – that occasioned Schönberg's vehe-
> ment censure.[2]

The assumption is that Reich's information came from Berg himself,
though in that case his use of an uncertain tense is somewhat difficult to
explain.[3] Hans Redlich's reference to the conversation is more circum-
spect. He writes that during Berg's visit to Berlin 'there had ensued a grave
exchange of opinions between master and pupil, which led to a temporary
spiritual crisis'.[4] In any event, whether on this occasion or some other,
Schoenberg does seem to have been severely critical of Berg's work around
this time. We can tell this from a letter written in November 1915, in
which, following what must have been a most devastating meeting with
Schoenberg, Berg attempts to explain his position and to answer a long list
of Schoenberg's grievances, primarily to do with the way in which he conducted his personal life. In this letter he writes, referring to some unspeci-
fied time in the past, 'I naturally took to heart your criticism of the insig-
nificance and worthlessness of my new compositions and your objections
to my piano reductions, and applied that to my subsequent work: the Orchestra Pieces and the Chamber Symphony'.[5]

It only remains to decide which of Berg's 'new compositions' Schoenberg had considered 'insignificant and worthless'. Whether the criticism
came during the Berlin visit in June 1913 or on some other occasion, it is
clear from Berg's reference to 'subsequent work' that it was directed at

works predating Op. 6. And for several reasons the String Quartet Op. 3, finished in 1910 under Schoenberg's tutelage, seems an unlikely candidate. Which leaves only (as Reich has said) the *Altenberg Lieder*, two of which had caused a famous scandal in March of that year,[6] and the Four Pieces for Clarinet and Piano Op. 5.[7] There seems, however, to be no way of knowing for certain that both were under fire.[8]

The *Altenberg Lieder* and the clarinet pieces represent Berg's only experiments in the aphoristic genre. They are often spoken of together because of their chronological proximity as well as the fact that both contain movements of only a few bars' length. This association is to some extent forced, since the two works are essentially rather different. Nevertheless, since they contain the shortest pieces in Berg's œuvre, it is here that we must look if we wish to examine Berg's response to the aphoristic pieces of Schoenberg and Webern.

The aphoristic pieces of Schoenberg and Webern

Perhaps not surprisingly, Webern was the first of the three composers to write pieces of extreme brevity: the earliest were in his Op. 5 for string quartet, written in 1909. Schoenberg's only collection of miniatures, the *Klavierstücke* Op. 19, followed in 1911. By the time the *Altenberg Lieder* were composed, in 1912, Webern had written his Opp. 6, 7 and 8 (for orchestra, violin and piano, and voice and eight instruments, respectively), as well as four of the Bagatelles Op. 9 for string quartet (which he dedicated to Berg) and two of the orchestral pieces Op. 10 (see Table 5.1). The aphorism was a passing phase for all three composers – even for Webern, who continued to compose in this way until after the war – and it was but a brief encounter for both Schoenberg and Berg. Brevity seems to have been almost instinctive for Webern: years later, when the freely unfolding atonality of these early pieces had disappeared in favour of highly structured, often symmetrical twelve-note works in traditional forms, extreme conciseness would still be one of the hallmarks of his style. Berg, on the other hand, was not given to terseness. The aphorism was not a natural mode of expression for him. Anyone who has read his letters will understand this: in his prose, as in his music, his imagination found its true expression in long sentences and sweeping gestures, in repetition and development, in illustration and explanation.[9]

So what do we mean by 'musical aphorism'? The *OED* defines 'aphorism' as 'any principle or precept expressed in few words; a short pithy sentence containing a truth of general import; a maxim'. Chambers adds

Table 5.1 Chronology of aphoristic pieces

	Schoenberg	Webern	Berg
1909			
spring		Op. 5	
end of August		Op. 6	
1910			
June		Op. 7	
August		Op. 8	
1911			
June	Op. 19	Op. 10/i	
July		Op. 10/iv	
summer		Op. 9/ii–v	
1912			
August			Op. 4
1913			
June–July		Op. 9/i, vi	
summer			Op. 5
September		Op. 10/ii	
October		Op. 10/v	
1914			
June		Op. 11	

'an adage'. It is clear that, in appropriating the term for music, we have skewed the meaning to remove its centre of gravity. While no one would question the truth or import of the sort of piece that we have generally agreed to call an aphorism, it seems to me that the absence of a 'principle' or 'maxim' – which might translate in musical terms as 'formula' or 'rule' – is almost an essential. Webern's pieces for cello and piano Op. 11 (lasting for nine, thirteen and ten bars), his Bagatelles Op. 9 (ten, eight, nine, eight, thirteen and nine bars) and the fourth of his pieces for orchestra Op. 10 (only six bars, marked 'Fließend') are surely the epitome of the musical aphorism as it is generally understood – those wisps of music in which one ephemeral gesture follows another for no very apparent reason.

Schoenberg's oft-quoted celebration of Webern's brevity, in his introductory remarks to the Bagatelles Op. 9, 'to express a novel [*Roman*] in a single gesture, a joy in a breath', has sometimes seemed to me somewhat overstated. To be sure, these pieces are complete and self-contained in very small spaces, but a novel (for *novel*, read *sonata* or *symphony*) comprises a complex set of developments and relationships that require time to unfold. Surely the charm of these tiny pieces is not that they are novels, but precisely that they are *not*, that they have denied the necessity to be novels and present the possibility of a work of significance without a superstructure of themes and developments and interrelationships. They seem to me more *haiku* than *Roman* – each the fleeting expression of a single idea. Musically their primary concern appears to be the continual circulation of the twelve notes rather than adherence to any sort of preconceived structure or the unfolding and developing of relationships inherent in the material presented. They have a characteristic look:

- linear construction, though in the main the lines are extremely disjunct, with relatively few chords and nothing approaching the texture of melody and accompaniment

- isolated figures of two to six notes in length in all parts, surrounded by rests, with the interest moving constantly from one part to another

- exaggeratedly wide intervals (the major sevenths and minor ninths that remained Webern's signature, of course, but also much larger intervals) between successive notes of melodic or ostinato figures

- short repeated-note figures, either a single note or two notes alternating

- continually changing timbres as the result of a plethora of playing instructions – *am Steg, pizz.* and *arco, mit* or *ohne Dämpfer, spicc., am Griffbrett* – and numerous harmonics of various sorts

- meticulously controlled dynamics, in many cases – Nos. 1, 2, 3 and 6 – covering a very wide range and alternating suddenly (the fourth and fifth Bagatelles move between *ppp* and *pp* only)

- internal metre changes (in Nos. 1, 4 and 5) and subdivided bars (in No. 2)

- frequent ritardandos and accelerandos and other tempo markings

Conspicuously, there is no canonic imitation, and no use of symmetrical figures. Voices appear to interact with great freedom, without method or constraint, beyond that of the continual even distribution of the twelve pitch-classes.

Schoenberg's own Op. 19 is in a very different style. Perhaps it can be said that, besides their brevity, these two sets of pieces have in common only their lack of an obvious discipline. Events are much more easily followed and understood in the Schoenberg pieces, because voices are for the most part continuous: when interest shifts from one part to another it is in the manner of a fugue, in which first one voice then another has the subject, or a polyphonic texture where an accompanying voice occasionally

comes to the fore with something of melodic interest, rather than occur-
ring, as is the case in Webern, because several voices share, successively, in
the statement of a single idea. Most of the time these pieces can be described as accompanied melody, or as two melodies in counterpoint.
Schoenberg's phrases are much longer than Webern's figures (I question
whether the word 'phrase' has any relevance in Webern's music of this
period); his textures are heavier (note the octaves in the bass in No. 3,
beneath four-note chords at times) and his tessitura generally lower; and
his lines are not disjunct. This describes four of the pieces: two – Nos. 2
and 6 – do not follow the same principles as the others, and only these
come close to Webern's concept of the aphorism. No. 6, a moment briefly
caught, is motionless and ephemeral.[10] And No. 2, thinly textured and
disjunct, presents a single idea: the contrast between the expressiveness of
a few brief, wide-ranging but legato melodic gestures and a dry and static
accompaniment which remains unchanged throughout. It is significant
that, of the six pieces in this opus, this is the one Berg chose to use as a
model. We will return to it later.

The short pieces of Berg's Opp. 4 and 5 (the outer songs of Op. 4 must
be excluded, as they are much larger pieces) look more like the short pieces
of Schoenberg than like those of Webern. Here too, with some obvious
exceptions, lines and voices are continuous and textures sometimes dense.
There are many melodies, sometimes quite generous in length. (See, for
example, the second clarinet piece, in which the clarinet plays a single,
spacious arch which spans the entire piece.) And one of the most characteristic features is the Mahlerian profusion of expressive marks: a myriad
of playing instructions gives meticulous directions about manner and attitude, as well as colour, timbre, dynamics and tempo. The marking
espress. is ubiquitous and apt.

Five Altenberg Lieder Op. 4

Most writers discussing the pieces of Berg's Opp. 4 and 5 see the clarinet
pieces as more truly aphoristic than the *Altenberg Lieder*. Certainly they
are more consistent in their brevity. Although the second of the picture-
postcard songs is probably as close in style to the miniatures being written
by Webern during these years as any of the clarinet pieces, the other songs
are much longer, and all are related thematically,[11] a fact that would seem
to argue against the aphoristic nature of any one of them. For all the brevity of their texts, they are complex works conceived on a grand scale and
concentrated into the space of many fewer bars than they might have

occupied, given the wealth of ideas and techniques they contain.[12] In part, this apparent condensation is achieved simply by packing a large number of notes into each bar – vertically, through writing up to thirty instrumental parts to be played at once, and horizontally, through the subdivision of the beat into very small parts (see the big orchestral sections of the first and last songs: No. 1, bars 1–19 and 25–30; No. 5, bars 20–25 and 30–35). One gets the feeling that Berg was determined to follow his friends into the realm of the miniature but simply could not do it: although he conscientiously trimmed the length of his remarks, his words were too long, and he had too much to say.

Both the outer songs of Op. 4 are in fact quite substantial pieces. The first, the shorter of the two (thirty-eight bars as opposed to fifty-five), opens with nineteen bars of orchestral music of a complexity sufficient for several times this number. In them Berg has made use of his entire very large orchestra, employed numerous variational and developmental devices and introduced, or at least alluded to, most of the materials to be used in the cycle. Subsequently the voice sings three lines related as ABA – the entire song – and the orchestra produces a second climax, louder than the first but texturally simpler, between the second and third of these. There is a seven-bar orchestral liquidation at the end. The fifth song, written before the first,[13] is a passacaglia based on three themes, each of which is the embodiment of a particular technique or process. Both the themes and the techniques they represent are to be found throughout Op. 4, and the techniques are those that are essential to Op. 5 as well: they are among the battery of compositional devices that identify Berg throughout his career.

The opening theme of the passacaglia (see Example 5.1a) is an unadorned short expanding interval series (1–2–3–3: even the interval repetition, which keeps the series from being 'perfect' or predictable, is characteristic of Berg). The theme is stated in its pure form in the first two sections of the passacaglia (v/1–5 and 11–15). When it returns in this form in v/21–5 (played by tuba, fourth horn and contrabassoon as well as piano and harp in a pattern of imitation in which the harp takes each note over from the piano – more *Klangfarbenmelodie* than canon), accompanied by a profusion of triplet and semiquaver versions of itself in the wind and strings, it is following a variation (harp, v/18–19) in which the initial G returns after each successive note is stated, thereby creating a second expanding interval series (1–3–6–9) concurrent with the one that is built into the theme (see Example 5.1b). This idea is later expanded by the voice, in a long melody in which each pair of notes of the harp version from v/18–19 is reversed (A♭–G, B♭–G, C♯–G, E–G) and all the intervening notes filled in each time, thus building up the retrograde form one note at

Example 5.1   (a) Op. 4: first passacaglia theme (v/1–5)

(b) v/18–19, harp

(c) v/25–9

(d) i/20–25 (T4)

(e) i/29–32

(f) iv/9–15

(g) iv/26–9, celesta

a time until the entire theme appears in retrograde in v/29 (see Example 5.1c). (A shorter form of this variation, in a different rhythm and missing the last, complete segment, appears in v/46–50.) The next variation (v/30–35), played by nearly half the orchestra, is again based on the harp version from v/18–19, but here progresses in long note values which are subdivided simultaneously in various ways by different parts of the orchestra. Immediately after this section, in v/36, the theme is verticalised; a more complex verticalisation occurs at the end of the movement, where the chord is assembled note by note.

This theme is also the basis of melodies in the first and fourth songs. It is transposed up a major third and elaborated to form the opening statement of the voice part of the first song (see Example 5.1d), and it also provides the third (and last) vocal line in the same song, where it is treated in the manner of Example 5.1b (see Example 5.1e). In the fourth song (xylophone, iv/10–15) it is built up one or two notes at a time – a straightforward version of the variation shown in Example 5.1c.[14] At the same time the voice, followed by the solo viola, has a slightly decorated version of this in heterophony with the xylophone (see Example 5.1f).

This theme is put to yet another use in the opening orchestral section of the first song, where it governs the ascent of the motive played by the piccolo, first clarinet, glockenspiel, xylophone and half of the *divisi* first violins (i/1–14). The ascent of the flutes and second violin in the same bars follows an expanding interval series (1–2–3–4–5–6–7), which, while not the passacaglia theme, is another example of the technique that gave rise to it. Yet another expanding interval series is seen at the end of the fourth song, where the celesta plays the pattern given as Example 5.1g.

The most obvious aspect of the second passacaglia theme is that it is a twelve-note theme, but perhaps more interesting even than this is its contour, which is typically Bergian and also relates it to the theme just examined. It is composed of two figures: a chromatic wedge followed by a chromatic descent (see Example 5.2a). It is, of course, an expanding interval series. This theme is used less frequently and subjected to less variation than the first. It appears five times in the fifth song (in v/5–10, 10–15, 15–20, 29–35 and 39–45), transposed on one of these occasions (v/15–20), and in several cases with the rhythm slightly changed. The wedge segment is used alone in v/19–24 and v/26–9. The ostinato figure played by the second and third trumpets in the opening section of the first song consists of the first three notes of this theme (transposed). The complete theme, with the opening segments repeated, is the first melody heard in Op. 4, entering over the rising and intensifying ostinatos in i/9–16 (see Example 5.2b).

Although this theme is used less frequently than the first outside the fifth song, the two ideas from which it grew – a twelve-note theme and the chromatic wedge – occur throughout the set in varied forms. The first line of text sung in the first song is introduced and accompanied by several chromatic wedges – in the second clarinet and bass clarinet in i/19–20 and again in i/22, the third and fourth horns in i/21–2, the harp in i/20–24 and

Example 5.2   (a) Op 4: second passacaglia theme (v/5–10)

chromatic wedge _____   chromatic descent _____

(b) i/9–16, violas (and others)

(in a less schematic way) between the inner parts and the bass in i/22–5 – all of which combine to produce a sense of chromatic voice-leading reminiscent of the Wagner or Strauss the song superficially resembles. The first half of the voice's second phrase in the second song (ii/3–4) is a wedge, and the low strings and harp play another in the third song, at iii/12–16. A twelve-note chord is heard at the beginning and end of the third song as background to an eleven-note sung melody (a technique that looks forward to the rising of the moon in Act III scene 2 of *Wozzeck*).

The third passacaglia theme is different again, but, like the others, embodies one of the hallmarks of Berg's music – a series of perfect fourths (see Example 5.3a). Treated more in the manner of the second theme than of the first, this theme appears in slight rhythmic variations throughout the passacaglia (at v/25–8, the most varied appearance, where two voices play versions in short note values in imitation, v/31–6 and 42–6) but is not embellished or given fanciful treatment of the sort seen in Example 5.1.

Like the other passacaglia themes, this theme exerts its influence beyond the passacaglia. It is first encountered in the orchestral introduction to the first song, where it appears in its entirety, as a repeated chromatically ascending ostinato figure in semiquavers and demisemiquavers in the celesta at i/9–13, and continues in a truncated and progressively varied form to i/15 (see Example 5.3b). It is encountered later, moving up through the strings in i/25–7, first in its original form, then its retrograde (displaying the same contour as the original), then in a third form in which the dyads of the original are reversed one at a time, and finally in an imperfect retrograde form in which the fourth and fifth notes are reversed and the penultimate note is missing (see Example 5.3c). In the second song it is played prominently by the solo cello, again in very short note values, leading up to the chord held by the strings in ii/7. It does not make an appearance in either the third or the fourth song.

Like the expanding interval series and the chromatic wedge, which found expression in the first and second themes, however, the *idea* of contiguous perfect fourths, which is the basis of this theme, finds expression

Example 5.3   (a) Op. 4: third passacaglia theme (v/7–12)

(b) i/9–14, celesta

(c) i/25–8

(d) ii/2

(e) ii/8–9, celesta

in other ways as well. Considerable use is made of quartal chords, here juxtaposed rather curiously with augmented triads, in the latter part of the first song (see the horns in i/25–7 and trumpets and trombones (not horns) in i/29, and the second violins, then the harp and finally the trombones in i/31–4). The most important motive in the second song is a pair of descending fourths separated by a semitone (see Example 5.3d).[15] This motive forms the centre of the vocal line that opens the song, at the word 'Gewitterregen'; it returns in the voice part, transposed up a tritone, as the beginning and, at its original pitch, as the end of the final section of the song (the latter coinciding with the return of the word 'Gewitterregen'). Thus the highpoint of the opening section of the song returns as both the climax and the cadence. The voice in the final section, from the climax on, is echoed in canon two octaves lower by the cellos. An additional fourth-figure, also incorporating wedge characteristics, accompanies the canon (see Example 5.3e).

Space does not permit us to examine all the motivic connections in Op.

Example 5.4   (a) Op. 4: ostinato motive (i/1–5)

(b) i/1–6, celesta

(c) i/25–7

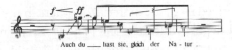

(d) iii/7

4, but I should like to look at one more important motive before passing on to a discussion of other aspects of the work: the ostinato motive in Example 5.4a. All but two of the ostinato figures in the opening of the first song are generated by this motive, through either variation or development. It is imitated (glockenspiel and xylophone), diminished (clarinet and viola), played tremolando (viola) and decorated (first violins); and its retrograde is embellished (celesta, see Example 5.4b). It is also elaborated to produce the second line of the voice part in the first song (see Example 5.4c). It appears again in the outer sections of the third song (voice, at i/7 and 24), where it is transposed down a tone and the notes appear in the order 1–2–5–3–4 (see Example 5.4d).

The second song of this opus, only eleven bars in length, comes the closest of them all to being an aphorism. Yet even here there is a lot going on. The resemblance of the final phrase to the opening one has already been mentioned, as well as the canon in ii/8–11. The similarity of the outer phrases goes beyond the return of the fourth-motive: both combine this motive with another, a turning figure of a semitone and a major third. The second, central phrase is also not unique: the word 'schöner' is set to a long melisma which seems to contain a reference to the setting of the same word in the first song at i/23.[16] A much more definite cross-reference occurs later, when 'Siehe' (the first two notes of the canon) is set exactly as it is in the fifth song (v/35). The ternary form of the movement is articulated by orchestral octave Fs at the beginning and end and a sustained minor ninth chord on F (like an overtone series) just before the return.

Ternary structure is even clearer in the third song, which is more than twice as long as the second: in iii/18–25 the voice repeats exactly its melody from iii/1–8, and this is accompanied on both occasions by the twelve-note chord mentioned earlier. At the opening of the song the chord is in the wind and is played four times (in notes of four beats' length against the voice's 3/4 melody) with the disposition of the twelve notes changing on each repetition – in other words, as a *Klangfarbenharmonie* – then it disappears, one note at a time, in iii/6–8. This scenario is reversed in the last eight bars, where the chord is assembled one note at a time by the strings.[17] The middle section of this song is, like that of the previous one but to a much greater extent, derived from the material of others in the set, as well as its own A section. It begins with the oboe playing a sequential figure that will reappear twice in the fifth song a tone lower (iii/9–11; cf. v/10–12 and v/36–8).[18] During this melody the horns play the first of several descending sixths which foreshadow a further theme used in the fifth song (v/14–16 and later: this theme is often reduced to the descending sixths only, in the fifth song as well as here in the third). The second half of the middle section (iii/12–17) is composed entirely of minor thirds, reminiscent of the first flute and second violin ostinato figure at the opening of the first song, and chromatic descents of a few notes which are clearly derived from the opening melody of this song.[19]

The fourth song is even longer. It is circular only to the extent that it begins and ends with the same two notes played by the first flute in a very high register (the first, played alone, perhaps announcing the fact that the orchestration of this song is more daring than that of any of the others); apart from this it seems to be more or less through-composed, which, if it did not go on for thirty-two bars at a slow tempo, might make it resemble the aphoristic pieces of Schoenberg and Webern more than its companion pieces do. It, too, however, contains cross-references and motivic relationships. Its use of the first passacaglia theme has already been noted; in addition the voice opens with the inversion of the motive that opened the second song. There is a truly amazing *Klangfarben* effect in iv/8–15: a stationary four-note chord (F♯, E♭, C♯, F♮) is played by five dovetailed groups – (i) bass clarinet, violin, horn and oboe; (ii) trombone, bassoon, flute and cello; (iii) bass tuba, bass, viola and trumpet; (iv) bassoon, horn, trumpet and cor anglais; (v) bass clarinet and three clarinets. The last of these groups, the clarinet quartet, continues in a five-bar polyrhythmic descent which brings to mind Stravinsky's *Berceuses du chat* (written shortly afterwards, in 1915–16).[20]

Thus we see a web of motivic relationships and textual responses work-ing hand in hand with a repertoire of compositional devices – techniques that were already an established part of Berg's style by this time – in the five songs of Op. 4. Although the picture-postcard texts are brief and cryp-tic – perhaps aphoristic – the music is none of these. The texture is at times exceedingly dense, not unlike Schoenberg's in his early and middle works; the structures are traditional ones, albeit not handled in a conventional way; the pieces are cyclically related.

Four Pieces for Clarinet and Piano Op. 5

In contrast, the Op. 5 pieces are not motivic.[21] They do not state and vary and develop, as the songs of Op. 4 do; they do, however, use the same compositional devices. In fact each of them is a collection of these pro-cesses and techniques, a composing 'machine' which, once set in motion, automatically produces passages of music without the necessity of themes or motives, though the latter are not ruled out. (The opening of the *Alten-berg Lieder* had operated in much the same way: once all the ostinatos were set in motion and the manner of their ascent determined, the music of the first nineteen bars was virtually fixed.) And this at a time when both Schoenberg and Webern had just abandoned compositional systems of all kinds. Although it has been assumed that it was Berg's purpose in these pieces to emulate the aphorisms of his teacher and his friend, in fact nei-ther set did so. All nine pieces are too dense and highly structured – those of Op. 4 motivically, those of Op. 5 systematically – to be good company for Schoenberg's Op. 19 and Webern's Opp. 9 or 11.

What are the elements of this regimen, the tools that helped Berg to keep atonality in line? They are in fact the devices and techniques he had used from the beginning of his compositional life and that he would con-tinue to use until his death, characteristic shapes and processes that en-sured a personal style of remarkable consistency. The events and shapes of Op. 5 have their forebears in the Piano Sonata; through them, in turn, we get more than a glimpse of what is to come in the operas, the Chamber Concerto, the *Lyric Suite* and the Violin Concerto. What sets the Op. 5 pieces apart is their extreme dependence on these techniques, nearly to the exclusion of any other determining factor.

The most-used device in Op. 5 – as in Op. 4, and perhaps in Berg's music generally – is the expanding or contracting interval series. This was a device also used, but to a much lesser extent, by Webern (see, for in-stance, the canon subject from the fourth piece in *his* Op. 5, composed in

Example 5.5   Webern, Op. 5 No. 4, bar 3

Example 5.6   Berg, Op. 5: i/4, piano right hand

Example 5.7   iii/1–2, clarinet

Example 5.8   i/5, piano left hand

* is the F♯ a printer's error for F♮?

Example 5.9   iii/10–12, piano right hand

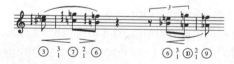

1909 and shown in Example 5.5) and is already familiar to us from Berg's own Op. 4. It rarely takes a simple, direct form in the clarinet pieces (see Example 5.6, where the interval 4 is missing, and Example 5.7, in which the interval 3 is repeated – the latter will be recognised as the series that produced the first passacaglia theme of Op. 4). The end of the clarinet part in the third piece might be described in this way as well: here a long descent uses the whole-tone scale for one bar, subsequently changing to the chromatic scale.[22] Usually this device is applied to the repetition of a whole figure, as in Example 5.8. In Example 5.9 the interval sequence of the figure remains the same for each voice upon repetition, while the distance between the voices increases. In Example 5.10a, repetition of inter-

Example 5.10   (a) Op. 5: ii/5–6, clarinet

(b) iii/12–13, clarinet

Example 5.11   Webern, Op. 5 No. 4, bar 6

Example 5.12   Berg, Op. 5: i/7, clarinet

vals occurs at the end of a series that begins (imperfectly) with alternating larger and smaller intervals; the result is not regular, but it is by no means haphazard – overall interval contraction is clearly the intention. In Example 5.10b only alternate intervals contract, while the major seconds remain. A similar alternating series, in which the intervals of *both* interlocking series change (in this case they expand, though not perfectly), can be seen in the repeating bridge passage of the Webern piece cited in Example 5.11. A more abstract sort of contracting series is seen in Example 5.12, where, although successive intervals do not contract, the entire arpeggio spells out a series of three triads – augmented, major and minor in that order.

When an expanding or contracting interval series is stationary around an axis, the result is the wedge figure, also familiar to us from Op. 4. This takes various forms in Op. 5, as it did there. The simplest is one that expands chromatically in both directions from an axis point, as in Example 5.13, or contracts *towards* a fixed point, as in Example 5.14 (in which, as in

Example 5.13   Op. 5: iv/9–10, clarinet

Example 5.14   i/9, clarinet

Example 5.15   iii/1–3, piano

Example 5.16   iv/9–10, piano

* three positions of 'French sixth' sonority (G♮ and F♮ implied in the third)

Examples 5.10 and 5.11, only alternate intervals change). A particularly complex series of wedges occurs at the beginning of the third piece (iii/1–3, see Example 5.15). Here, four small wedges are written in such a way as to produce two large interval expansion series simultaneously. The distance between the two upper voices, which is constant for each wedge, increases at each repetition (0, 3, 4, 5); the intervals between the outer voices also expand upon each repetition (2–4–6, 4–6–8, 5–7–9, 6–8–10), while the wedge produced by the middle and lower voices is the same (1–3–5) in all cases where there is a third voice. In the middle section of the fourth piece (bars iv/8–11) a contracting wedge is embellished to the point of seeming to meander inwards to the centre (in this case the true axis is a note that is never heard, the C♮ lying between the left hand's B♮ and the right hand's C♯ – see Example 5.16). This accompanies the clarinet's

Example 5.17   Op. 5: i/2–4, piano right hand

Example 5.18   i/4–5, clarinet

Example 5.19   Webern, Op. 5 No. 4, bars 7–9

Example 5.20   Berg, Op. 5: i/6–9, piano right hand

Example 5.13, which has a different axis. The piano's opening figure in the first piece is a similarly aimless-sounding figure which circles briefly around the initial note, A, before moving to E, around which it then circles for two more bars (see Example 5.17). When this has finished the clarinet plays a symmetrical figure around a two-note axis (i/4–5) which, while not in the shape of a wedge, exhibits the same sort of centricity (Example 5.18). Example 5.19 shows a similar figure from the middle section of the already cited fourth movement of Webern's Op. 5. (Indeed, this piece seems to have served as a model – technically, though not structurally – for the pieces in Berg's set.)

If one voice of the wedge is fixed, a sort of half-wedge is the result, like the treatment of Op. 4's first passacaglia theme shown in Example 5.1b, i.e. with a base rather than an axis (see Example 5.20, which begins as a wedge around A complicated by a dramatic interpolation, then becomes a half-wedge based on A). In the third piece of Op. 5 a particular wealth of wedge shapes occupies both foreground and background positions. These are shown in Example 5.21. In the first section of the piece, the bass line (piano, left hand) and the melody (clarinet) produce a highly decorated

Example 5.21   (a) Op. 5/iii, section I

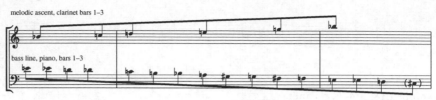

(b) section II

(c) section IV

expanding wedge: see the reduction given in Example 5.21a. (The piano right-hand part during these bars consists of the smaller wedges shown in Example 5.15.) Example 5.21b respells the piano left-hand and clarinet parts at the end of the second section of the same piece (iii/6–8) in order to illustrate more clearly the contracting wedge that occurs there. The final (fourth) section of this piece is the most complex. A graph in which the parts are separated out to make the various wedge shapes more apparent is given as Example 5.21c.

The temporal equivalents of expanding and contracting wedges are repetitions that increase or decrease in length. This lengthening or shortening can come about in two ways: either through a notated ritardando or accelerando, or by adding material to each reappearance or progressively paring it down. Example 5.22 shows three examples of the first of these –

Example 5.22   (a) Op. 5: ii/4, clarinet

(b) iv/11–12, clarinet

(c) iv/11–12, piano

Example 5.23   (a) iii/2, clarinet

(b) iii/16, piano

(c) i/8–9, piano left hand

exact pitch repetitions written in progressively longer note values. A longer passage of this sort can be seen in the piano left-hand part at iii/9–13 (see Example 5.26c, p. 103). The opposite of this, a notated accelerando, is shown in the three extracts of Example 5.23; for yet another see the piano right-hand part in iii/10–12, where the acceleration is mitigated by a *rit.* written above it (Example 5.26b, p. 103). The final section of the fourth piece is a complex combination of notated acceleration and extended repetition. Both the length and the range of the piano figure are increased upon each repetition, while the opening flourish (the complete material of the first statement) is written in progressively shorter note values (except for the second and third occurrences, which are played at the same speed, reminding us of Berg's 'imperfect' expanding interval series): as the

Example 5.24   Op. 5: iv/12–20, piano

(a) bars 12–13

(b) bars 13–14

(c) bars 14–15

(d) bars 15–16

(e) bars 16–20

* Depress silently (harmonics)

extensions far outweigh the acceleration, the net result is lengthening (see Example 5.24). At the same time the clarinet is repeating, in a constant tempo, a series of nine notes (of which, more presently) which is, like the piano music that accompanies it, progressively extended by the addition of material at the end (see Example 5.25).

When the kind of temporal discrepancies just seen between successive repetitions exists between the written metre and that implied by the length of repeating figures, the result is isorhythm of the sort seen in the clarinet part of Example 5.26a, where the beginning of each repetition of a five-note figure advances one-third of a beat. And when these isorhythmic

Example 5.25 Op. 5: iv/13–16, clarinet

(a) bar 13

(b) bar 14

(c) bar 15

(d) bar 16

Example 5.26 iii, section III (bars 9–13)

(a) bars 10–12, clarinet

(b) bars 10–12, piano right hand

(c) bars 9–13, piano left hand

repetitions are combined with a voice that really fits the written metre, as the piano right-hand part does here, the result is two (or more) voices moving at different tempos and/or in different metres. This has been ob-served already, in the opening section of the third of the *Altenberg Lieder* (see p. 94). In the case of the very complex third section of the third clari-

Example 5.27   Op. 5: iv/1–4

Example 5.28   iv/13–16, clarinet

net piece (Example 5.26), this multi-speed situation is exacerbated by the fact that a notated ritardando and a notated accelerando occur simultaneously in the left and right hands of the piano respectively for the entire length of the section. A simpler example, resulting from syncopation rather than isorhythm (because it involves a repeated chord rather than a repeated figure), is shown in Example 5.27.

And, finally, in the last section of the fourth piece Berg uses for the first time a technique that will re-emerge impressively many years later in bars 46–67 of the third movement of the *Lyric Suite*. This technique is rotation, which is a close relative of, but subtly different from, isorhythm: here, in the abstract, the repeating figure advances on the beat, but since each repetition begins on the same part of the beat the repeating figure is treated as a circular construction, rotating one degree on each repetition. The figure in question is the nine notes played by the clarinet in Example 5.25; its successive appearances are displayed in Example 5.28 so as to make clear their rotational relationship.

Such was Berg's repertoire of disciplines in 1913. There were pitch-class restrictions in the Op. 5 pieces as well, though not yet of the sort that would bring his teacher into the spotlight a decade later. Douglas Jarman has pointed out that the pitch collection with which the clarinet opens the first piece is the source for nearly all the subsequent material in the set.[23] The opening two bars of the second piece exemplify the 'synthesis of the horizontal and the vertical' that Webern would refer to so often in later years: the clarinet melody in ii/1–2 is composed of the same five pitch-classes as the two chords played in the right hand of the piano in ii/2 (C, Db, Eb, G, Ab – see Example 5.29). The registral and dynamic climaxes in the same piece (which we will examine in a moment) are supported by a carefully orchestrated chromatic thickening. Only in ii/5–7 are all twelve pitch-classes used; Berg builds to this point carefully, using seven pcs in ii/1–2 (including the initial highpoint), adding an eighth pc in ii/3 and another two just after the second highpoint in ii/4. The remaining two pcs are added in ii/5 (just following the primary registral climax). At the end of the descent from this climax the number of pcs is reduced to seven in ii/7 (from the release of the chord on the second beat and including the first half-beat of ii/8), and finally to only three from ii/8 (second beat) to the end. There is no Bb in ii/1–5, no A♮ between ii/6 (third beat) and ii/9.

The striking resemblance of this movement to the second piece of Schoenberg's Op. 19 has often been remarked upon; a comparison of the two – each the second movement of the opus that represents its composer's only experiment in aphorism – is very instructive. Berg preserves Schoenberg's outline faithfully, but this is fleshed out with a collection of his own techniques, the result being much more complex than the original. It is as if Berg, determined to write a miniature, had copied out his former teacher's piece in order to assure success and then changed the details to make it his own, thereby (unwittingly?) ensuring that it is no longer perceived as aphoristic.

The two pieces are compared in Example 5.29. Both consist of nine bars in common time (though Berg's has an upbeat), both are in a slow tempo and both are very quiet (Berg is more extreme in both cases: 'Sehr langsam' for Schoenberg's 'Langsam', *ppp* for Schoenberg's *pp*). Probably the most striking similarity – and the one most often remarked upon – is the presence of the major third in the piano left hand throughout both movements. The exactness of the correspondence begins to emerge when the progress of these thirds is examined more closely. In both pieces the initial third is a left-hand ostinato which remains stationary until the second beat of bar 4, where a higher one is sounded for the first time, at precisely the same moment in both pieces. There is then a limited alternation of the two thirds over the next three beats (the correspondence of these alternations is shown in Example 5.29). The original third is abandoned by both Berg (in bar 5) and Schoenberg (in bar 6) and subsequently taken up again

Example 5.29   Berg, Op. 5/ii and Schoenberg, Op. 19/ii compared

Berg

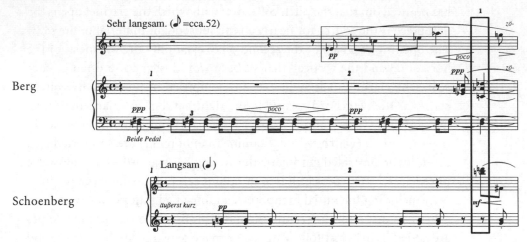

Schoenberg

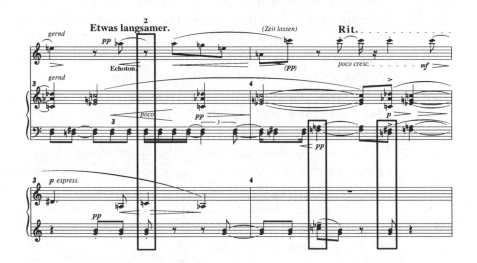

(Schoenberg, bar 7; Berg, bar 8). Both pieces end with the third that opened the piece acting again as an ostinato, and, finally, as part of an augmented triad (Bb, D, F♯) – used alone by Berg, combined with another (G,
B, Eb) by Schoenberg.

Even more remarkable than the resemblance of the ostinatos in thirds is
the exact correspondence of structural events (enclosed in boxes in Example 5.29). Both reach a preliminary highpoint, registrally and dynamically,
on the fourth beat of bar 2 and a second on the third beat of bar 3, on the
way to the primary registral climax, which occurs on the downbeat of bar
5. This is followed, in bars 5–6 (second beat) of both pieces, by a wide-
ranging and rapid descent, leading to the dynamic climax, which occurs
on the third beat of bar 6 in the Schoenberg and a beat later in the Berg.
Both then continue the descent, with falling bass lines in bars 7–8.

Example 5.29
(*cont.*)

Within these almost identical moulds, however, we see two very different pieces, one spare to the point of asceticism, the other a dense mass of notes and ideas, all serving a single large, sweeping gesture in the clarinet. Schoenberg uses a minimum of notes, intervals and rhythms to present a single idea. The melodies of both pieces are wide-ranging, but whereas Schoenberg covers a lot of territory in the space of a few notes, Berg describes an arch of spacious proportions, ascending two octaves over the course of just over three bars, then descending dramatically to a ninth below the starting point over the course of the next three. This is a complex melody consisting of a series of small, definable events or techniques strung together like beads of different colours and shapes to produce a result that is neither homogeneous nor symmetrical but seems right nonetheless. Berg's ostinato of repeated thirds, at first glance similar to Schoenberg's, is on closer inspection also quite different, replacing staccato quavers and rests with a continuous thread which is played legato, using both pedals, with the dynamics and the rhythmic subdivisions constantly changing. (The *espress.* marking in bar 8 is just one sign of the extent to which Berg's accompaniment diverges from its model.) The result of all this activity and variety, added to the generally shorter note values used by Berg, is that a great deal more happens in Berg's piece than happens in Schoenberg's: in spite of the equal length of the two works, Berg's is to all purposes a considerably longer piece.

Aware of the way in which the second piece was composed, one is tempted to search for models for the other movements of Op. 5. In particular, the third, which acts as a scherzo, looks a bit like the first piece of Schoenberg's set, which is in the same spirit.[24] Berg's piece is eighteen bars long, in 6/8 and 3/4 metres (the 3/4 in a middle section), Schoenberg's seventeen bars, mainly in 6/8 with 2/4 occupying a position roughly parallel to Berg's 3/4. In fact both Berg's 3/4 and Schoenberg's 2/4 last for exactly fourteen crotchets. Schoenberg precedes his 2/4 section with one bar of 3/8; in the parallel place Berg writes a note of three quavers' length, played alone as an *Echoton* by the clarinet. The pieces begin with similar quaver upbeats, and both are in four sections, with the third section offering considerable contrast to the other three. But though the two third sections are the same length exactly, this parallel does not extend to the surrounding sections – the structure of the Berg piece (expressed in quavers) is 25+24+28+31, of the Schoenberg 22+12+28+24 – and the similarities seem to end here. While Schoenberg's piece is clearly an ABA form (the division of the first six bars just suggested is largely arbitrary, since these bars are heard as a single section), Berg's, also essentially an ABA but with the first A clearly divided, is, typically, more complex. It seems to me to be best described as a binary scherzo with trio. It is also the only movement of the set in which a motive seems to operate thematically. Example 5.30 shows the complex melodic relationships that bind the sections of this piece together: a variation of the clarinet theme that opens the movement (*a*) is played by the clarinet in the trio (*b*); this variation arises as a slightly varied canonic response to the piano figure that opens the trio (*c*), which in turn is a variation of the opening clarinet melody of the binary form's B section (*d*), thus illustrating the inherent though not obvious relationship between the melodies of sections A and B of the scherzo (*a* and *d*).

There are no other parallels between the movements of Op. 5 and Schoenberg's Op. 19. The most aphoristic piece ever written by Schoenberg, Op. 19 No. 6, especially, finds no resonances in Berg.

Example 5.30   (a) Berg, Op.5/iii: clarinet melody, opening

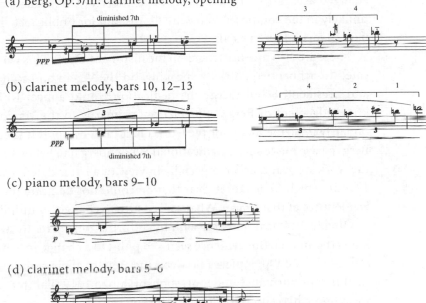

(b) clarinet melody, bars 10, 12–13

(c) piano melody, bars 9–10

(d) clarinet melody, bars 5–6

Conclusion

As we have seen, Berg's two cycles of short pieces share many techniques, though not a style. And they apparently shared in Schoenberg's censure. This is in some ways difficult to understand. After the *Altenberg Lieder's* disastrous and incomplete first performance – indeed because of it – Berg laid the work aside and did not even attempt to have it performed again. It received its first complete performance only in 1953,[25] eighteen years after his death. Although the clarinet pieces did not have to wait nearly so long, they too were not performed immediately, having to wait until 1919, six years after their completion. One is led to suppose that Schoenberg's condemnation of these two works was largely responsible for the length of time between completion and public airing. Yet he had seen – and commented on – the *Altenberg Lieder* in January of 1913, six months before Berg's visit to Berlin. His first judgement of the pieces was contained in a letter dated 14 January: 'they seem (at first glance) remarkably well and beautifully orchestrated. I find some things disturbing at first; namely the rather too obvious desire to use new means ... On the other hand I already have a clear impression of a number of passages, which I definitely like'[26] – not unequivocal praise, but not devastating condemnation either. Although it is clear from the same letter that he has reservations about the work, it is curious that Schoenberg should have condemned in June something to which he had reacted positively in January. Had his opinion changed as a result of the débâcle of 31 March? This seems particularly unlikely in the composer who wore his disdain for public taste like a brilliant many-coloured cloak.

There are also inconsistencies in the history of Op. 5. This work is dedicated to Schoenberg. Strictly speaking, 'to the Verein and to its founder and president, Schoenberg': the dedication would appear to be an acknowledgement of Berg's appreciation, primarily to the Verein and secondarily to Schoenberg, for the work's first performance. It is curious for Berg to have made such a dedication if Schoenberg had heaped censure on the work six years earlier, especially in view of a letter dated 8 September 1914 in which he makes it clear that he could not dedicate the pieces to Schoenberg at that time.[27] What caused him to change his mind?

Obviously, it is impossible with the information currently available to know the answer. But evidence seems to point to a change in Schoenberg's attitude to the Op. 5 pieces between the time of their composition and their first performance under his sponsorship in 1919. This makes sense if we suppose his criticism in the first instance not to have been of the brevity of the pieces, or of Berg's attempt to express himself in a way that Schoenberg thought was foreign to him, as Reich and those who follow him suggest, but of Berg's systematic thinking at a time when both Schoenberg and Webern had kicked over the traces and were embarked on a period of freedom. Could it be that Berg's systematisation of musical materials, which was anathema to Schoenberg in 1913, found more favour with him in 1919 as he approached his own Op. 23, in which he would for the first time compose with note-rows? It would certainly appear that Berg took the step to a more regimented way of composing, where many things were predetermined, ahead of his colleagues. In his case this was a move directly from the strictures of tonality to those of a highly structured atonality, bypassing altogether the period of atonal freedom that formed a step in the progress of both Webern and Schoenberg. Thus the man who has often been considered the least adventurous of the three seems, in one respect at least, to have led the way.

6 Berg, Mahler and the Three Orchestral Pieces Op. 6

Derrick Puffett
St John's College, Cambridge

This chapter is designed as an introduction to Berg's Three Orchestral Pieces Op. 6 – but an introduction from a slightly unusual angle: it considers them in the light of his well-known admiration for Mahler. Whenever this topic has been dealt with before (and it certainly is not new),[1] it has generally been from the perspective of 'influence'. Within the last decade, however, the topic of influence in music has come to assume considerable complexity in itself[2] – to the point where it is hardly possible to undertake a comparative study such as this without involving the reader in a weighty theoretical superstructure. The reader, who may not be interested in theory, quickly turns the page and moves on. It is consistent with this non-theoretical approach that the chapter does not attempt to analyse the pieces in detail. This has already been done elsewhere, though never, in my view, wholly satisfactorily;[3] in any case, the only analysis of these pieces that would seem worthwhile would require far more space – far more words and, in particular, far more graphic illustration – than the present chapter allows. No, what I want to do is to take an indirect and circuitous approach to the subject, like one of those walks in a Vienna park that Berg must have enjoyed, offering outline discussions of the pieces but also suggesting other avenues of approach, other points of orientation, for the reader coming to this marvellous work for the first time.

Berg and Mahler

First a gathering of quotations, all from Berg's letters to Helene:

> ... in the finale of the Mahler symphony [No. 3] ... I gradually felt a sensation of complete solitude, as if in all the world there were nothing left but this music – and me listening to it. But when it came to the uplifting and overwhelming climax, and then was over, I felt a sudden pang ... [1907]

... the link we find between geniuses in all ages, just because they are so 'universal' ... Any number of these links occur to me, like those between Kant and Schiller, Spinoza and Goethe, Nietzsche and both Richard Strauss (Zarathustra) and Mahler (Third Symphony). [1908]

... our gods, Maeterlinck, Strindberg, Mahler, Strauss, and so many others ... [1909]

... the summit where only the noblest ones dwell, where *Parsifal*, Mahler's Ninth, *Faust, Pippa* and a few other masterpieces can alone be created ... [1909]

I have just been passing through the glorious country which sent Gustav Mahler into similar raptures so shortly before his death. The mountains completely under snow right down to the foothills, then green meadows, brown fields, and that sky: almost unbearably beautiful, I wish you could have seen it, you'd have forgotten all the trials of the journey. But now I must watch all this magnificence sad and alone, and ... the sadness won't leave me till tomorrow. The right mood, really, for The Song of the Earth and Second Symphony. [1911]

I have once more played through Mahler's Ninth. The first movement is the most glorious he ever wrote. It expresses an extraordinary love of this earth, for Nature; the longing to live on it in peace, to enjoy it completely, to the very heart of one's being, before death comes, as irresistibly it does. The whole movement is based on a premonition of death, which is constantly recurring. All earthly dreams up to this peak; that is why the tenderest passages are followed by tremendous climaxes like new eruptions of a volcano. This, of course, is most obvious of all in the place where the premonition of death becomes certain knowledge, where in the most profound and anguished love of life death appears 'mit höchste Gewalt'; then the ghostly solo of violin and viola, and those sounds of chivalry: death in armour. Against that there is no resistance left, and I see what follows as a sort of resignation. Always, though, with the thought of 'the other side', which we can see in the *misterioso* on pages 44–45 [bars 376–90], as if in the pure air above the mountains, in the ether itself. Again, for the last time, Mahler turns to the earth – not to battles and great deeds, which he strips away, just as he did in *The Song of the Earth* in the chromatic *morendo* runs-downwards – but solely and totally to Nature. What treasures has Earth still to offer for his delight, and for how long? Far from all strife, in the free, clear air of the Semmering he would make a home for himself, where he could breathe in more and more deeply this purest air on earth [music example: horns, bars 443–4] where his heart, most glorious of human hearts that ever beat, may expand, wider and wider, before it must stop beating for good. [1912?]

On 26th January 1916 [Erwin] Stein will probably be performing Mahler's Third. When I went to see him, he and Steuermann had just

played the third movement: 'Cuckoo has fallen to his death.' Imagine it –
after an age without hearing any music! [1915]

Yesterday's final rehearsal [of Mahler's Third, under Webern] went most
promisingly. ... Do you know the most glorious part? It's in the movement with the female choir, that short bit like a funeral march, where the
whole orchestra is slowly and continuously soaring, then dropping
again, and with it all the time that tragic Bim-Bam. Remember? [1922][4]

These quotations have become so familiar, through reproduction in
essays such as this, that they might in themselves be considered an essential part of Berg reception: anyone who has 'grown up' with them will have
found them shaping his or her experience of both composers. What they
indicate, of course, is not only Berg's high opinion of Mahler (an opinion
shared by most other members of the Schoenberg circle), which placed
him among the 'gods', along with Goethe, Spinoza, etc., or, in other words,
saw in him an artist of 'universal' significance. They also show the extent of
Berg's personal identification with the composer: Mahler's art indeed
cries out for such a response on the listener's part, a phenomenon which
has no doubt helped to ensure his almost 'universal' popularity in the last
thirty years. Such 'identification' could manifest itself in sensitive herme-
neutic criticism, as in Berg's commentary on the Ninth Symphony, and,
presumably, in acute analyses of individual passages, though these have
not come down to us. None of this should offer surprise. Berg was a composer schooled in the rigorous methods of Schoenberg, had been privi-
leged to sit in on the analyses of Mahler movements to which Schoenberg,
doubtless glad to get away from the regular diet of Viennese classics,
treated his students from time to time,[5] and would have been able to carry
out his own analyses on similar lines.

   More surprising are the references to 'Nature'. While such references are
perfectly in keeping with Mahler – indeed, they often echo remarks made
by Mahler himself – they sound less in tune coming from Berg. It is not
that Berg is being insincere: on the contrary, his letters are full of remarks
about nature (or 'Nature'), nature's healing balm etc. The problem is,
rather, that Berg belonged to a generation which could no longer enjoy
quite the same straightforward relationship with nature that Mahler had.
Nature, in its role of repository of innocence (as portrayed at the opening
of Wagner's *Rheingold* or, more relevantly, at the start of Mahler's First
Symphony and in the first part of his cantata *Das klagende Lied*), has no
place in the music of Berg. Berg's music is typically that of the embittered
and world-weary city-dweller, the world of Wozzeck's barracks and *Lulu*
Act III. References to 'the summit where only the noblest ones dwell', the
lofty heights in which one 'gradually feels a sensation of complete solitude', however true they might be to the *spirit* of Mahler (the specific refer-

ence is to the Sixth Symphony, with its 'mountain pastures', cowbells and so on), are bound to seem, in Berg's mouth, a bit of a pose, the sort of idealised views of the countryside one might expect to hear from someone who would be horrified to have to live there. Deeper understanding comes in his remarks on the 'Bim-Bam' movement of Mahler's Third, the movement in which the song of the angels suddenly turns into a funeral march. Here, natural innocence is shown with its inevitable corollary (inevitable for those who live on earth – and most of us, unfortunately, know of no alternative): death and disillusion. This was a lesson Berg learned well.

The 'facts' concerning Berg's relationship with Mahler are also familiar, inasmuch as they have been around in the literature for a long time. Berg's 'first Mahler experience' occurred on 17 February 1901, when he was at the Vienna premiere of *Das klagende Lied* ('a magnificent work!!!!', as he later wrote to Schoenberg).[6] This is interesting in itself, as *Das klagende Lied* was by no means 'contemporary' Mahler: written as long ago as 1880, a precocious piece of juvenilia, it had lain neglected until the composer revived it with some popular success. Berg's reception of Mahler's works thus follows the same broad trajectory as their composition.

The following year he was at the Vienna premiere of the Fourth Symphony: it was after this concert that the famous incident occurred in which Berg stole the conductor's baton, a trophy treasured for life.[7] Reich, the source of this anecdote, reports that Berg hung his portraits of Mahler and Ibsen together, 'my living ideals'.[8] By 1904 Berg had studied Mahler's Second Symphony as well as the works he had heard.[9] In 1907 Mahler left Vienna, and Berg, showing the same dog-like fidelity he had recently begun to show to Schoenberg, was at the station to see him off.[10] It was on this occasion that the two men met for the first time (the conversation between them in which Mahler advised Berg not to become a conductor occurred much later, in 1910).[11] With Mahler in New York for the next three years, Berg's relations with him inevitably took on a less personal, more objective slant.

A professional one, even. In 1910 Berg worked on a four-hand arrangement of Mahler's Eighth Symphony for Universal Edition, a task which, like so many others he undertook, was never completed.[12] And the main musical experiences to come would all occur after Mahler's death. When Mahler was buried in Vienna on 21 May 1911, having burnt himself out in America, Berg was at the funeral. In November the same year he travelled to Munich, with Webern, to hear the posthumous premiere of *Das Lied von der Erde*, along with the Second Symphony, under Bruno Walter (the lyrical letter to Helene); a week later, back in Vienna, he heard the Sixth ('the only Sixth despite the Pastoral', as he wrote to Schoenberg) under Löwe; and, in December, the Second again, the Third and the *Kindertoten-*

lieder.[13] 1912 brought the first performance of the Ninth, again under Walter; Berg attended rehearsals as well as the concert.[14] After all these wonders,[15] life must soon have begun to seem dull. Already in 1912 Berg was complaining to Schoenberg that Mahler's music had started to be forgotten in Vienna.[16]

The first and most significant phase of Berg's Mahler reception was over. Obviously, in the years to come he would hear the works again, refine his understanding, and let his initial enthusiasm settle down into something more 'normal'. But the main process of assimilation had taken place. As it happened, 1912 was an important year in his relationship with Schoenberg and, perhaps, the beginning of a general change of direction. What mattered now was hard work on a variety of projects – no time for hero-worship – one of which, a symphony, would lead straight to the Three Orchestral Pieces.

Why a symphony, of all things? Answering this question takes us back to Mahler.

Mahler's 'world'

Mahler's most famous statement of his aims as a symphonist is surely the view he expressed to Sibelius:

> When we came to speak of the nature of the symphony [Sibelius reported], I used to emphasize my admiration for strictness and style in a symphony and the deep logic which unites all the themes by an inner bond. This was in accordance with my own creative experience. Mahler took a completely opposite view: 'No, the symphony must be like the world. It must embrace everything.'[17]

Mahler's conversation with Sibelius took place in 1907. But he had already expressed a similar view twelve years earlier, to his confidante Natalie Bauer-Lechner: '... to me "symphony" means constructing a world with all the techniques at one's disposal'. This remark came in the context of a discussion of his Third Symphony (1895–6), of which he said: 'My calling it a symphony is really inaccurate, for it doesn't keep to the traditional form in any way ... The eternally new and changing content determines its own form.'[18] Less succinct and memorable than his remark to Sibelius, these statements nevertheless help to bring into focus an important aspect of his creativity, one which clearly left a strong impression on Berg.

Of all Mahler's symphonies, the Third is the one that most coherently realises his vision of the symphony as a 'world'. For many years it was criticised as his *least* coherent, and there are certainly things about it that can appear crude and ill-judged. But even so simple a comment as this betrays a category mistake, a tendency (all too common in his lifetime) to criticise him from the standpoint of so-called absolute music. *All* Mahler's symphonies embody a programme – though this is a word he came to detest. The First and Second, as is well known, depict the life and death of a hero, who is eventually laid to rest (in the finale of the Second) with obsequies involving lines from Klopstock, choirs of angels and an offstage brass band. In the Third, Mahler brings the world itself to life: the passage from winter to summer – a scheme that can be seen to have either Shakespeare or Nietzsche (strange bedfellows!) behind it, depending on which version of the programme one goes by[19] – is accomplished in terms of a creation myth, involving a progress from inanimate matter through flora, fauna and animals to Man and his relationship with God. (The homocentric language is inescapable and very much a part of the work's time.) What is interesting here, among many other things, is that Mahler is dramatising, or giving programmatic expression to, processes that were already an inherent part of abstract, or supposedly absolute, composition: Bruckner, following in the footsteps of Beethoven's Ninth, had made each of his symphonies drag itself out of the primordial slime, starting with simple materials – and always the same 'chaos' metaphor – from which the most monumental structures would be built.

The Third is obviously a *ne plus ultra*. After it, the Fourth, as everyone knows, is a return to classicism – except that it, too, has a programme (albeit an implicit rather than an explicit one), with another 'progress', this time from the world we know to the world beyond. In the first movement an early *Wunderhorn* song, 'Das irdische Leben', whose ostinato treadmill provides a vivid image of daily life, is ground up and destroyed as a necessary preparation for the 'heavenly life' to come. All this was grist to Berg's mill. The four-movement pattern of the Fourth, one of its few truly classical features, returns in the Sixth (another 'heroic' work, the hero being felled by the last of the three famous hammer blows in the finale), but neither this nor either of its five-movement companions, the Fifth or the Seventh, is 'classical' in any conventional sense. By the time of the Eighth, with its unique fusion of medieval Latin and Goethe, we are back to the monumentalism of the Second. As Mahler wrote to Mengelberg: 'Try to imagine the whole universe beginning to ring and resound. These are no longer human voices, but planets and suns revolving.'[20]

It is all gloriously wrong-headed and gloriously of its time. How can a symphony, a musical composition lasting perhaps an hour, possibly be like the world, embracing everything? Yet other artists – Strindberg, with his mystical plays which made such an appeal to the young Berg, the megalomaniac Whitman, fellow composers Ives and Scriabin – shared the same vision. And there were direct musical precedents – to look no further than *Das Rheingold* – for a composer wishing to 'construct a world with all the techniques at one's disposal'. To Berg the challenge must have been irresistible.

Symphonies, syncretism and the concept of the 'piece'

Mahler's influence, though strong, was not the only pressure operating on Berg around 1912. Schoenberg himself was to grapple with a symphony between 1912 and 1914, before giving it up in order to write an oratorio – yet another project that came to nothing, though out of it grew the giant 'fragment' *Die Jakobsleiter* (1917–22). Schoenberg's symphony was itself powerfully influenced by the Mahlerian model, with vocal movements, a 'Dionysiac' scherzo celebrating the beauties of the world (shades of Mahler 5),[21] a *Totentanz* whose very title evokes Mahlerian precedents[22] and material, possibly operatic in origin, related to Balzac's novel *Sera phita*.[23] Little came of this grandiose scheme. Yet Schoenberg had already furnished a model for Berg in his one-movement Chamber Symphony of 1906, a work which the younger man knew intimately. It was this work, it seems, that provided the immediate impetus for Berg's new composition.

At this point some facts are in order. Berg worked on his symphony during 1912 and 1913. On 29 July 1912 he wrote to Webern: 'Just fancy: this winter I intended to compose a big symphonic movement and I had planned to let it end with a boy's voice singing (from the gallery) words from – "Seraphita"! Of course it remained a mere project – as so often happens in my case …'[24] The letter from Webern that elicited this confession was apparently the first Berg knew that Schoenberg had been working on the same subject. It was not until almost a year later, on 9 July 1913 – *after* the composition of the *Altenberg Lieder* and the clarinet pieces, the *Skandalkonzert* of 31 March 1913 and many other events in which he had more than proved his loyalty to the older man – that he was able to nerve himself to tell Schoenberg about his own symphonic ambitions. The context for this was the famous letter in which Berg replied to criticisms his teacher had made at their recent meeting in Berlin:

> The consequences of a careless, nerve-racking lifestyle torment me most now that I'm living very sensibly, abstaining almost entirely from alcohol, nicotine, coffee, and tea. … Unfortunately I have to confess, dear Herr Schoenberg, that I haven't made use of your various suggestions as to what I should compose next. Much as I was intrigued from the start by your suggestion to write an orchestral suite (with character pieces), and

though I immediately began to think of it often and seriously, and did intend to work it out, nonetheless it didn't come about. Again and again I found myself giving into an older desire – namely to write a <u>symphony</u>. And when I intended to make a concession to this desire by beginning the suite with a prelude, I found (upon beginning the work) that it again merely turned into the opening of this symphony. So I simply decided to go ahead with it:– it is to be a large one-movement symphony, naturally including the requisite 4 movements, i.e., sections, with developments, etc. Similar in construction to the Chamber Symphony. Concurrently though, the plan for the suite is sure to mature to the point where I can actually begin writing it, and then your kind suggestion will be realized – though belatedly.[25]

So now we have a suite ('with character pieces') as well as a symphony. On the face of it, the thought of Berg turning out a suite 'in olden style' *à la* D'Albert or Reger is an odd one, though one has only to think of the first scene of *Wozzeck*, not to mention the gavotte in *Lulu*. But let us push the story to a conclusion.

A year further on Berg is still struggling with his composition. But now he is talking, not of a symphony or suite, but of 'pieces':

I've already finished *something* here, the first of the three orchestra pieces, which I'm calling *Präludium*. At present I'm copying the *March* I finished in Vienna into full score and then I have to finish the third piece, called *Reigen* and write that out in full score. There will be only three pieces in all, they are about as long as your Orchestra Pieces and longer.[26]

(The change of tone is striking; Berg is more confident, almost truculent.) And finally, responding wearily to a barrage of new criticisms from Schoenberg, towards the end of 1915, Berg writes:

The 3 Orchestra Pieces really did grow out of the most strenuous and sacred endeavor to compose character pieces in the manner you desired, of normal length, rich in thematic complexity, without striving for something 'new' at all cost, and in this work to give of my best. Perhaps I could have achieved <u>more</u> if I weren't basically such a slow worker and if the war hadn't broken out, bringing with it an initial aversion to composing, as well as a practically doubled workload in connection with my mother's houses and Berghof. But I can't claim that. At any rate, I did what I could.[27]

There is a sort of nobility in such an admission. Fair copies of the *Präludium* and *Marsch* had been sent to Schoenberg in September 1914; *Reigen* followed in August 1915. For a complete performance of the work Berg had to wait until 1930, when Johannes Schüler conducted it in Oldenburg (Webern had performed two movements in 1923).

Time to sort out the threads. At the end of the nineteenth century the symphony – already idealised as *the* supreme musical genre – was, it seems, pulled in two opposing directions. On the one hand there was a tendency towards increased unification and concentration, the direction of the Schoenberg Chamber Symphony. On the other there were the symphonies of Mahler and others in which the musical form became a focus for ideas of a much more diffuse character: here, as we have seen, the ability of the symphony, familiar since Berlioz and Liszt, to absorb ideas from literature and philosophy was stretched to such an extent that it could be asked to embody the *world*. From the Nietzschean panorama – rocks, earth, flowers, beasts, Man – of Mahler's Third to the cliffs and anchorites of the Eighth is but a small step: 'Such syncretism', Clytus Gottwald has written, '… is grounded in the belief that no religion or religious outlook can lay claim to a monopoly of the truth but that, mindful of its crass particularity, can only add its own humble voice to the cry of supplication: "Redeem us from our individuality!"' (Gottwald is writing about *Die Jakobsleiter*).[28] Poor Berg, tossed between the Scylla and Charybdis of his Mahlerian and Schoenbergian affiliations, must sometimes have felt a special sympathy for such 'syncretism'. His troubles were never resolved. The Chamber Concerto of the 1920s is an ultra-concentrated example of the 'unifying' tendency, while his plans for an eight-movement *Lulu Symphony*, towards the end of his life,[29] show the continuing attraction of the 'world'-like, Mahlerian symphonic model.

And now the 'world'-like model collides with the late-Romantic concept of the 'piece'. There is an exquisite irony in the fact that musical ideas conceived in relation to a symphony, most comprehensive of genres, should end up in pieces so neutrally entitled and, on the face of it, so expressively self-contained. The 'piece' has a long history which cannot be rehearsed here. Suffice it to say that after a century of distinguished composition taking in Schubert, Brahms and Grieg, among others, the genre had found a special haven in the work of the Second Viennese School: Schoenberg's Opp. 11, 16 and 19, Webern's Opp. 5, 6, 7, 9, 10 and 11, and Berg's own Op. 5 come immediately to mind. So when Berg decides to style his compositions – enormous as they are – 'pieces', he is contributing to a miniaturist æsthetic whose aims might be thought to run directly counter to his symphonic, 'maximalist' ones. Boulez writes of the beginning of the *Präludium*: 'The instruments *give birth* to a theme' (my emphasis).[30] Quite so: the 'creation' myth of Mahler's Third compressed into a few seconds.

Op. 6 viewed as a whole

Berg's Three Orchestral Pieces form an end-weighted structure whose final part lasts roughly as long as the first two parts put together. This may seem an uncontroversial statement, but it is implicitly at odds with Berg's own analytical comments on the work, as transcribed by Fritz Uhlenbruch for the Oldenburg performance of 1930.[31] According to these, the composer saw the *Präludium* as a symphonic first movement, *Reigen* as a combination of scherzo and slow movement ('in that order!'), and the *Marsch* as a finale. Little scope for disagreement in any of this, one might think. But conventionally – which is to say, habitually throughout the Austro-German symphonic tradition of which Berg felt himself to be an heir – the first movement is far more than a mere introduction, assuming the principal place, and often the centre of gravity, within the multi-movement cycle; scherzo and slow movement, when combined, are expected to add up to something more than a movement with fast and slow elements in it; and a finale is not just something that happens to come last. Berg's comments are the busy composer's typical, offhand response to the programme-note writer, lacking any analytical worth.

As in most late-Romantic symphonic works, there are ample connections among the movements. These have received detailed attention from George Perle and others.[32] One, however, deserves special mention here, the emphatic recollection of the *Präludium* (bars 11–13) towards the end of the *Marsch* (bars 160–61). Mark DeVoto refers to this as a 'flashback'.[33] While the term is vivid and, with its cinematic associations, likely to appeal to anybody seized by the modernist aspects of the work, I don't think it captures the particular flavour of this passage, which, to my ears at least, is much more that of an old-fashioned motto theme (shades of Dvořák and César Franck); this is one of the few moments at which Berg's structure creaks. Each of the movements, in fact, contains a passage which is an extended quotation from one of the others. *Reigen* begins by reworking music from near the end of the *Präludium*.[34] And though it is true to say that each movement takes up and develops material from the movements before, it would be just as true to invert the statement and say that each movement *prefigures* music found in the next one: obviously there is a reciprocal process going on here, such as one finds in the *Lyric Suite* (in other words, it is the *Präludium* 'quoting' the *Marsch* as well as the other way round). This chimes in with the organisation of the *Altenberg Lieder* and one's strong sense – in any Berg work – of all the movements being drawn from a common source.

Going back to the presence of Mahler in Berg's music, one is tempted to try to 'account for' it at every level, to show the effect that Mahlerian thinking had, for example, on the form. But Berg's handling of form is so extraordinary and, in many ways, so *un*-Mahlerian that I want to consider each piece separately. At the stylistic level Mahler's influence is probably best dealt with in terms of rhetoric: broad expressive gesture, the interplay of related and contrasted material, the general trajectory of a movement from its beginning through its climax to its end.[35] Otherwise the enquiry risks getting bogged down in detail. Another way in which it might profitably be limited is to consider each piece in relation to one specific model. In this case the 'model' is interpreted as a *source*, providing thematic ideas, shapes, gestures and (possibly but not necessarily) a form.

The main model for the *Präludium* is obviously the Andante of Mahler's Ninth Symphony.[36] This is evident at once in the movement from silence, through tentative attempts to set out the basic musical ideas, to a fully elaborated texture capable of extreme complexity. Such a pattern is, at one end of the spectrum, a version of the 'creation myth' already exposed, so that one has the sensation of seeing the musical language being assembled as the piece progresses (just as, in a later version of the same myth, Birtwistle begins *The Mask of Orpheus* with a scene invoking the creation of language itself). This is a universal metaphor. But, at the other end of the spectrum, Berg's emergence from silence to noise recalls those pieces by early Romantics whose tentative beginnings suggest a reluctance to leave silence itself behind.[37] The main part of the *Präludium* seems to be a monody, a *Hauptstimme* accompanied by motivic variants and derivatives of itself, almost like a chorale prelude. (Or maybe it's a 'song without words', a Bergian version of Mahler's method in his *Adagietto*.)[38] The general trajectory thus created is a wave form, an overall *crescendo* and *decrescendo* like the Prelude to *Tristan*. In this respect it is similar to one of the 'episodic' *crescendo* sections – not always followed by a *decrescendo*! – in the first movement of Mahler's Ninth. (There are three such episodes in Mahler's scheme.) But the Mahler movement is much more complex, partly because his motives are given much stronger rhythmic and orchestral articulation. (Also, there are more of them; Mahler's is a half-hour piece.) Mahler's method of continually 'reshuffling' his motives is, *pace* Jarman,[39] unknown to Berg. Berg works to a simpler, more single-minded plan: the development of a motive and its transformations. All his motivic offshoots tend to assimilate themselves to the main melody. What gives Berg's music its power is the unifying force of the *harmony*, which is very strongly characterised. From this point of view it deserves comparison with something like the last song of Zemlinsky's Op. 13 (the *Maeterlinck-Gesänge*), which also is heavily influenced by Mahler's Ninth; Zemlinsky's 'reminiscences' stick out much more because there isn't this underlying, strongly characterised harmony.

The title of *Reigen* evokes rounds, spring rounds, *Rondes de printemps*, *Rondes printanières* – all the tradition of maytime dancing, fertility rites and so on. But this is not a Mahlerian tradition. What we have, instead, is a sequence of world-weary *Ländler*, or bits of *Ländler*, with an element of Mahlerian grotesquerie thrown in. The principal model here is the scherzo of Mahler's Seventh. Redlich has an interesting musical example[40] in which he juxtaposes a couple of bars of this scherzo with a couple of bars from *Reigen*. The juxtaposition is persuasive on several counts, not least because the passage from *Reigen* has already isolated itself within the score: in a work notorious for its density, it stands out for its economy, revealing itself as if naked. And of course the example makes graphically clear Berg's absolute dependence on Mahler for the nature of his musical gestures. There is, needless to say, more to *Reigen* than this.

The *Marsch*, finally, leans heavily on a particular Mahlerian precedent, in this case the last movement of the Sixth Symphony. It is not just the hammer blows (Mahler has three, Berg five) but the whole tragic rhetoric of the piece. As Klemperer declared, 'The last movement is really a cosmos in itself; it's [a] tragic synthesis of life and death.'[41] The cosmic imagery is catching! Something will be said below about the style of criticism that Berg's last movement tends to invoke from its commentators. In the meantime let me return to its formal function. One of the most original features of Op. 6 is that thematic material is presented, as it were, incrementally: a great many new themes are added in the second movement, and even more in the third. This puts a huge pressure on the third movement, which is traditionally supposed to recapitulate as much as it presents. In fact the structure implodes, from the sheer weight of its material, before any recapitulation can be implemented. But while the music is racing towards a conclusion, with Berg, as always, trying to reconcile opposites – in this case, the music of the first two movements – the atmosphere is a little like that of the last movement of the Chamber Concerto; less manic, perhaps, and with a doom-laden quality that the later work certainly lacks, but dominated, nevertheless, by the feeling of 'walking on a knife-edge'.

Präludium

The title, an archaic form of 'prelude', poses its own questions. Why should Berg choose to style as a prelude a movement which is obviously integral to the whole, something much more than an introduction? To be sure, other composers have done the same: Franck in his *Prelude, Chorale and*

Fugue, Vaughan Williams in his Fifth Symphony, most recently perhaps Robin Holloway in his Third Concerto for Orchestra. And why the archaic spelling anyway? This must surely be a hangover from the 'suite' idea originally mooted by Schoenberg. In a baroque suite the prelude *is* an integral part of the composition as a whole, the improvisatory beginning of a sequence of movements. Berg's suite is about as un-baroque as one can get, but the idea does still have some residual meaning.

The *form* of the movement is determined by that of the melody: a two-part period structure with introduction and conclusion. I add the qualification 'two-part', which is strictly redundant, because of the melody's length (around twenty-five bars): one can easily lose sight of the overall shape – and many conductors do – when the scale is so large. And the melody itself (bars 15–?41)[42] is at times difficult to follow because it is distributed among so many instruments. This is Schoenberg's *Klangfarben* technique at work, the principle recently developed in the older man's Op. 16 pieces (1909) and adopted by Berg complete with H and N signs; the H signs in fact hold the key to the continuity of the melody.

Example 6.1 lays out the melody as if conceived for one instrument. The first three bars of music with definite pitch (i.e., after the unpitched sounds of the beginning) see the emergence of a three-note motive; call it *a*. This motive consists of a semitone and a minor third, heard first in that order (Fg. 1, bars 6–8) and then, definitively (first half of bar 8), the other way around. As *a* is first stated in this 'prime' form, it is repeated almost immediately in retrograde inversion (muted trumpet). The rest of the introduction consists of three bars of chords with (alto) trombone[43] on top, the first, crashing statement of the 'motto' theme (horns and clarinets, bars 11–13: the motto theme itself consists of two further statements of *a*, in inverted and retrograde forms respectively) and two bars of transition involving the emphatic repetition of a chord (not shown on Example 6.1) in what is usually referred to as a 'fate rhythm' – another gestural idea drawn from Mahler's Ninth. The whole melody lends itself well to motivic analysis of this kind – though it is perhaps more interesting, having made this point, to come at it from another angle.

> A well-balanced melody progresses in waves, i.e. each elevation is countered by a depression. It approaches a high point or climax through a series of intermediate lesser high points, interrupted by recessions. Upward movements are balanced by downward movements; large intervals are compensated for by conjunct movement in the opposite direction. A good melody generally remains within a reasonable compass, not straying too far from a central range.[44]

With the exception of the last point, this quotation – from Schoenberg's *Fundamentals of Musical Composition* – is a remarkably good description

Example 6.1   Op. 6, *Präludium*: Hauptstimme

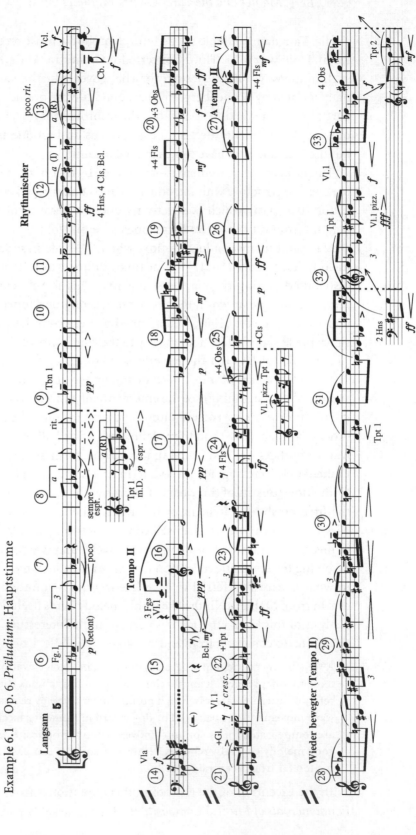

Example 6.1 (cont.)

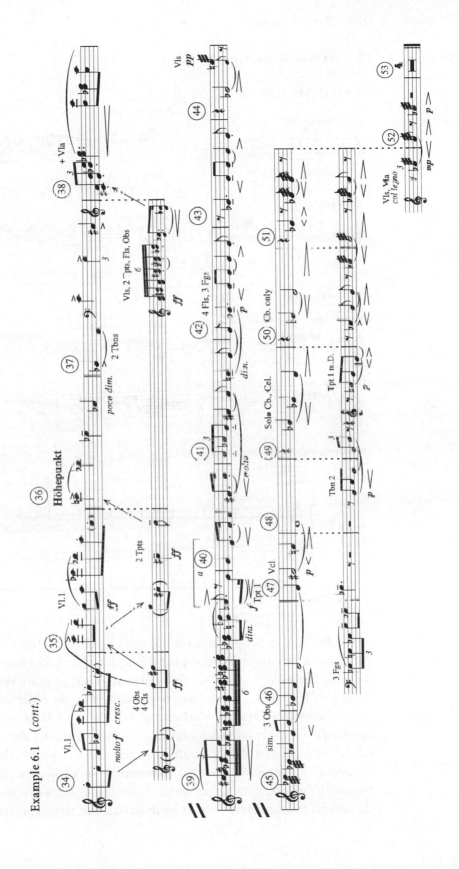

Höhepunkt

Example 6.2　Op. 6, *Präludium*: melody, bars 15ff.

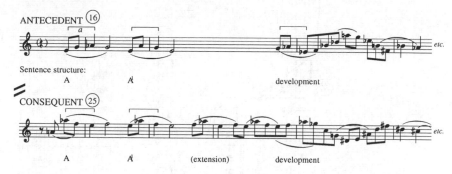

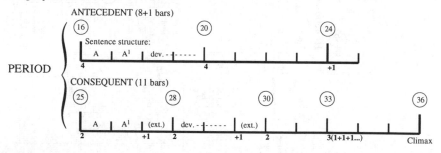

of the *Präludium*. Schoenberg's book wasn't published until long after Berg's death, of course, but there is no reason to think that Schoenberg's teaching, in this respect at least, changed much over the years: the form of the *Präludium* might literally have been dictated by the older man. ('Coherent harmony reinforces relationship', Schoenberg was to write on the same page – another point Berg must have taken to heart.) The construction of the main part of the prelude is severely classical. Within the general framework of the period structure – a modification of the '8+8'-bar archetype, with the first eight-bar phrase extended by one extra bar (bar 24) and the second extended even further by imitation and stretto before coming to a high point or climax (Berg marks it as such in the score) in bar 36 – each half is constructed as a 'sentence',[45] with the initial idea (always a version of *a*) immediately being repeated and developed. Example 6.2 charts the outlines of the sentence structure, together with a comparable example from Beethoven.[46]

The concluding section, after the climax – boundaries are not absolutely clear, for reasons already stated – introduces two 'quotations' (bars 38–9 and 44–6) from the next movement. There is also an 'intertextual' reference, in the miniature funeral march of bars 40–41, to the *Schwerer Kondukt* of Mahler's Ninth ('death in armour', as Berg refers to it in his letter to Helene). Otherwise, the end of the movement is a perfect example of Schoenbergian liquidation, balancing the emergence from silence and tentative motivic formulations of the beginning. Supporting the first, introductory, phrases is a sequence of ten chords (see Example 6.3b). These are presented in three groups of 3+3+4, and the first six (let us refer to them as *a–f*, following Berg's practice in his sketches)[47] return at the end of the piece, rearranged but with the 3+3 ordering maintained. It is these chords that provide the harmony that is such a strongly cohesive force in the Three Pieces.

'Coherent harmony reinforces relationship': the chords not only unify the introductory and concluding sections but supply material for the main section as well. In one of his articles on Op. 6, Mark DeVoto shows how each of the eight bars from 16 to 23 is underpinned by one of the six chords *a–f*, sometimes transposed (curiously, though he labels the chords *a–f* in his music examples, DeVoto doesn't say that this labelling comes from the sketches).[48] (See Example 6.4, p. 129, from DeVoto.) It is an odd way to compose: it is as if one were to take a series of chords from a Bach chorale, stick each one at the beginning of a bar, devise connections from one chord to the next and expect the whole thing to cohere as a continuous harmonic progression. Yet no-one has ever complained that Berg's harmony here is incoherent. And the reason is surely – though DeVoto doesn't make this point – that all the notes *un*accounted for by Berg's (or DeVoto's) lettering are neighbour notes, chromatic passing notes and the like; in other words, the harmonic *progression* is the same as that expressed by the *sequence a–f*, give or take a few embellishments.

Looking at the sequence, then, one wants to know: what makes it work? Example 6.3a lists all ten chords (*a–j*) as they appear in the introductory and concluding sections. The concluding section can probably be discounted – though continuity is significantly enhanced by the fact that the high trombone notes are now transposed down an octave.[49] Example 6.3b repeats the chords from the introduction; and the two remaining systems

Example 6.3 (a) Op. 6, *Präludium*: chords used in Introduction and Coda

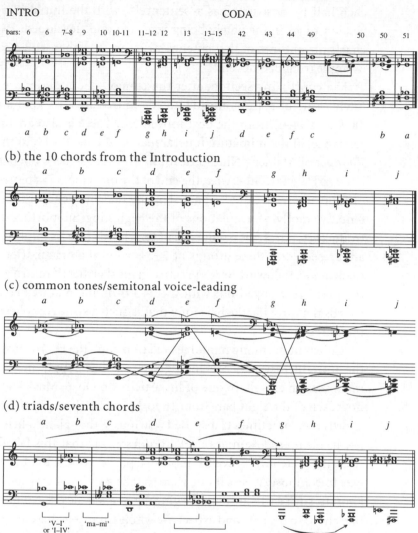

(labelled c and d) show connections between chords, first in terms of common tones and semitonal voice-leading (filled-in notes are the ones that change) and then as suggested by triads and seventh-chords.

Of course the tonal impulse in Berg was strong, as everyone knows. And it is natural to search for explanations of complex harmonic structures in chords whose notes are a third apart. But Example 6.3d is untidy from any point of view. More profitable, surely, to look for explanations in chords based on fourths? These, too, were a favourite sonority of Berg's. Example 6.5a shows three fourth-chords a semitone apart; let them be called I, II and III. 'For the sake of argument' each chord is displayed as consisting of four notes, presumably on the lazy assumption that 3×4 = 12. Yet these

Example 6.4   Op. 6, *Präludium*: elaborated chord progression (from Mark DeVoto, 'Alban Bergs *Drei Orchesterstücke* op. 6')

Example 6.5   Op. 6, *Präludium*: fourth-chords related to interval cycles

(a)

(b)

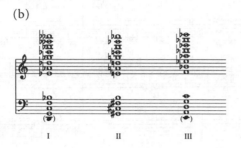

(c)

chords cannot in themselves exhaust the total chromatic, since twelve is not divisible by five (the number of semitones in a perfect fourth). Example 6.5b proposes an alternative model, based on interval cycles of a perfect fourth. Any fourth can be reproduced eleven times before the original pitch-class returns; which is to say, one can relate any fourth-chord to an all-embracing cycle of twelve – which is given here, for convenience, three times (I–III). Think of it like the tuning system of a harp. The harp has a small pool of notes – the diatonic scale – which may be transposed twice: once, at the push of a pedal, a semitone higher, and then (at another push) a semitone higher again. Berg, similarly, can alter the registration of any of the notes in his chords at will, the chords taking their numbering from whichever of the three interval cycles has the notes in the chord closest to the bass (Example 6.5c). Because it is not always a clear-cut matter which of the cycles a particular chordal formation should be related to, 'subjacent' roots (the filled-in notes in the bass) have been added in the case of two of the cycles (see Example 6.5b).

There is, as far as I know, no evidence whatever that Berg composed in this way. Yet the idea has a certain theoretical allure. Six years later he was to send Schoenberg his so-called 'master array of the interval cycles', on which much of George Perle's recent analysis is based;[50] and perfect-fourth cycles are a feature of *Wozzeck*. There is also an extraordinary twelve-note pile-up of fourths in the very next movement of Op. 6, *Reigen* (at bar 66). Berg's imagination was running faster than his theory.[51]

Reigen

Again, the title poses questions. 'Reigen' is conventionally translated as 'round dance': thus *Harvard* and *The New Grove, inter alia*. But what does this mean? Certainly the idea of a springtime frolic doesn't seem to have much to do with Berg. *Duden* offers two meanings, the aforesaid 'round dance' and a haphazard succession of melodies.[52] This is more like it. Furthermore, the title 'Reigen' was often used in respect of nineteenth-century salon music, waltz sequences and the like. There are already hints here of a connection between dance music and banality which would have set Mahler's – not to say Adorno's – mouth watering. It turns out, in fact, that the association of 'Reigen' and 'round dance' is a twentieth-century thing. Friedrich Kluge's *Etymologisches Wörterbuch der deutschen Sprache* (1899) equates 'Reigen' and 'Reihen' – they are the same word in different dialects – describing the dance as one in which people went across the fields in a long row. Its origins obscure (and who would wish for anything else?), it is related to the English ray dance.[53]

There is a much more plausible connection with Schnitzler's *Reigen*. This work (later filmed as *La Ronde*, with music by Oscar Straus), written in 1896–7, was not performed in its entirety until 1920 but in the meantime enjoyed a sensational success through incomplete performances and being circulated in a private edition.[54] Berg had a copy in his library.[55] The subject, as everyone knows, is sexual intercourse (the *theme*, as opposed to the subject, is social and cultural degradation, but that need not concern us). In ten short scenes – a 'haphazard succession of melodies' – a prostitute flirts with a soldier; the soldier flirts with a chambermaid; the chambermaid flirts with the young man of the house; and so on. At the end the prostitute reappears, as if the whole sequence is to start all over again. There is a schematic form here which can be represented thus:

$$(A+B) + (B+C) + (C+D) \dots (Z+A)$$

Mathematicians call this a cyclic form, but cyclic form means something different in music. It might be better to speak of cyclic *permutation* – which also has a different meaning, though one that is not inappropriate in this context. We shall return to these considerations shortly.

The form of *Reigen* – the orchestral piece – is usually characterised as sonata form. Bruce Archibald, who has probably spent more time working on this piece than anyone else in the world, subscribes to this view, most recently, as far as I know, in Jarman's *Berg Companion*. However, he seems unhappy with it: 'Sonata form is not governed here by tonal structure as it was in its roots and at birth, but by melodies, developmental processes, and the balanced structuring of complex sonorities – as might be expected after a century and a half of adventures.'[56] I am not sure why scholars go to so much trouble squeezing their favourite pieces into prefabricated forms when the results are so patently unconvincing, even to themselves.

In this case a simpler approach is more rewarding. It arises out of a perception of some of the most striking moments of the piece – which for me are those moments when fragments of waltz rhythm drift in and out of a dreamlike background, as at the beginning of Ravel's *La Valse* or – a better comparison – the end of the *Valses nobles et sentimentales*.[57] If this implies an episodic, semi-programmatic view of the piece, then such a view is encouraged by the many tempo fluctuations and brusque, unexpected changes of direction which together create a mood close to opera. The opera frequently suggested is of course *Wozzeck*. I am not concerned to write a detailed 'scenario', but one can get a better feeling of the work's character by postulating an imaginary narrative for it than by invoking some abstract form.

Figure 6.1 gives an overview. The movement is framed by an introduction and coda – it would not be quite accurate to call these 'slow', since the introduction already contains tempo modifications and the coda begins more quickly than the music that has immediately preceded it – but the general ternary character is clear. Within the frame, or framework, there is more scope for disagreement. The chart with which Archibald accompanies his analysis is misleading in that it treats all the bars as equal in length: that is to say, it allots an equal space for each of them on the page. This is problematic when we come to the 4/2 section (bars 101–11), where one bar of 4/2 equals four bars of 3/4. By giving each 3/4 bar its proper 'due',

Figure 6.1 Op. 6, *Reigen*

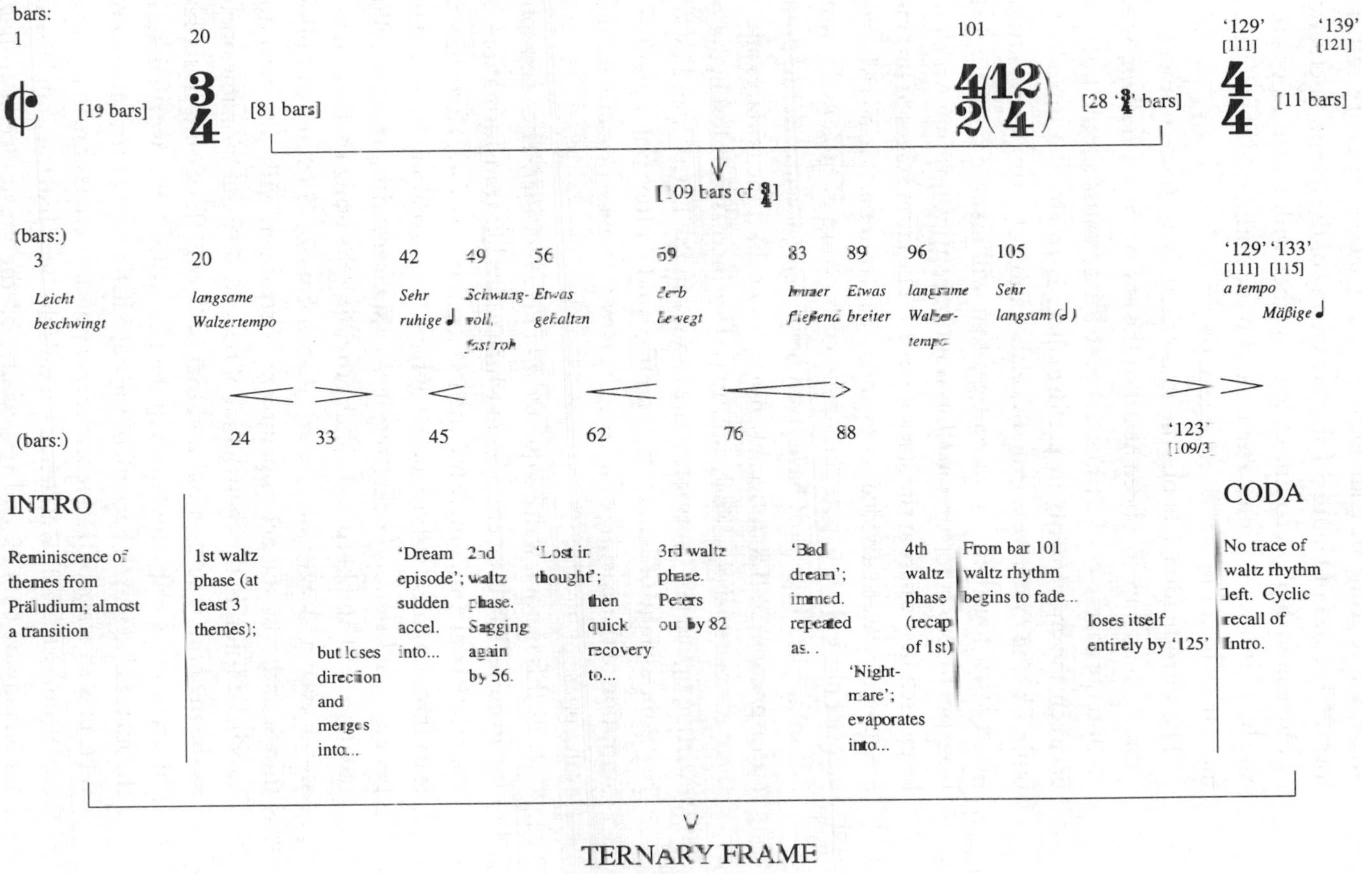

bars:
1   20   '129'   '139'
                                                            [111]   [121]

C   3/4   4/4(12/4)   4/4
[19 bars]   [81 bars]   (2/4)   [11 bars]
                                                    [28 8/4 bars]

                            '129' '133'
                            [111] [115]
                            a tempo
                            Mäßige ♩

(bars:)
3   20   24   33   42   49   56   69   83   89   96   105

Leicht   *langsame*   *Sehr*   *Schwag-* *Etwas*   *Er-b*   *Etwas*   *langsame* *Sehr*
beschwingt   *Walzertempo*   *ruhige* ♩ *voll.* *gefalten*   *Le vegt* *fließend breiter* *Walzer-* *langsam* (♩)
                                                 fest rob   *tempo*

(bars:)
24   33   45   62   76   88   '123'
                            [109/3]

INTRO   CODA

Reminiscence of   1st waltz   'Dream   'Lost in   3rd waltz   'Bad   4th   From bar 101   No trace of
themes from   phase (at   2nd   thought'.   phase.   dream';   waltz   waltz rhythm   waltz rhythm
Präludium; almost   least 3   episode';   Sagging   Peters   immed.   phase   begins to fade… left. Cyclic
a transition   themes);   waltz   again   ou by 82   repeated   (recap   loses itself   recall of
                                        phase.   by 56.   as…   of 1st)   entirely by '125' Intro.
                           but loses   sudden   then   'Night-
                           direction   accel.   quick   mare';
                           and   into…   recovery   evaporates
                           merges   to…   into…
                           into…

TERNARY FRAME

one gets a much better sense of the overall proportions. Specifically, this means acknowledging the full extent of waltz-like material or waltz-like episodes throughout the movement (109 bars of 3/4 as opposed to 81) and perhaps favouring an analytical approach based on genre rather than form.[58] The rest of Figure 6.1 shows as many of the tempo fluctuations as can be comfortably accommodated, together with hairpin signs to indicate brief, local deviations. There are also the outlines of a narrative commentary, which I shall now enlarge upon.

The introduction sets out the main themes of the movement.[59] That some of them have just been heard, at the end of the *Präludium*, gives this section the character of a transition; too long a pause should not be made between the movements in performance. Formally the introduction is built, like the *Präludium*, from the elaboration of a single melody, which pieces itself together, out of motives that will assume great importance later on, before launching itself as a more continuous line which finally loses itself in the bass at the start of bar 14. The latter stages of this melody are shared between divided cellos and violas (four parts in all) whose overlapping phrases anticipate the staggered bowings of Stokowski: working out these phrasings must have given Berg great pleasure. At this point the atmosphere becomes noticeably more dream-like; the fanfares and other thematic material previously announced are increasingly lost in the vague, swirling figuration (but notice the canons in the horns!); and by simple rhythmic sleight-of-hand – not 'metric modulation', but a gradual subsumption of the existing ¢ metre in the new 3/4 – Berg prepares for the first waltz phase of his piece.[60]

Now this is not a waltz sequence *à la Rosenkavalier*. The waltz 'phases' are no more than brief episodes in which waltz-like transformations of the material – sometimes mere fragments – come to the fore. Here there are at least three fragments: the material of bars 20–23 (melody on muted trumpet and first bassoon; orchestration very stylised, with pizzicato cellos on the downbeat and harp and violas providing the waltz rhythm on beats 2 and 3; even a 'sleazy' solo violin), that of bars 24–5 (flutes and oboes in thirds; and now the accompaniment is stronger, with pizzicato double bass in addition to the cellos), that of bars 26–7 (a questionable one, this, as the material is so fleeting) and that of bars 27ff. (violins in sixths and thirds; now the waltz rhythm is in the percussion). It is worth describing the material at length because of the parodistic tone of the music, even at such an early stage of the piece: the entry of the percussion, in particular – bass drum with cymbal attached – recalls the beer-hall music in *Wozzeck*.[61] Yet already by bars 32 and (especially) 33 the music begins to flag; the waltz rhythms are no longer clearly defined; and the accompaniment is starting to resemble the introduction.

Bars 42–9 constitute the first 'dream episode': tempo *sehr ruhig*, wistful solo strings, harp glissandi topped by a triad in the celesta. The whole atmosphere is very close to those episodes in *Wozzeck* that focus on Marie – Marie alone, Marie waiting, Marie brooding like a character in a Muriel Spark novel who knows she is going to die. Then at bars 48–9 there is a sudden acceleration into the next waltz episode. This introduces new stylised patterns, in particular the *Ländler*-like accompaniment in bars 49–51 At this point something very important happens in the thematic structure of Op. 6 as a whole: a theme that has been present since the beginning of the movement (and indeed since the end of the *Präludium* – see Example 6.1, bars 45–6) appears for the first time in inversion (horns, bars 49–51). This inverted form is to play a leading role in the *March*. Berg's manipulation of the structure here brings his work momentarily close to Debussy (cf. the first movement of *La Mer*); the only mystery is why Berg chooses to hide this important event in a *Nebenstimme*.

The *Schwungvoll, fast roh* marking of this episode suggests Strauss, as does the disconcerting G minor cadence of bars 54–5. By 56 (*Etwas gehalten*) things are starting to sag again. The *Ländler* rhythm is kept up, rather oddly, in horns and celesta in bar 56 itself; but from then on Marie seems lost in thought as the solo violin begins an extraordinary virtuoso passage, reminiscent not so much of the later Violin Concerto as of the Marquis's music in Act III of *Lulu*. Against this virtuoso passage is a 'chorale' in the upper woodwind and – important for upcoming ostinatos – a zany trombone line. But now comes the even more extraordinary passage in which the texture fans out in fourths to create the symmetrical twelve-note chord mentioned above. After this the harmony quickly evaporates – what could follow? – and another acceleration leads to the next waltz phase.

This is the nastiest bit of waltz-parody so far, with peremptory trumpet fanfares, 'grotesque' bass drum strokes and the whole bathed in the weird half-light of Mahler's Seventh. One has the sense that parody is being screwed up an extra notch, that the treadmill is being made to run a bit faster. After the inevitable, rapid dispersal of such antics, we have the first of two complementary passages which I think of as 'bad dreams' – further deteriorations of the dream-like episodes mentioned earlier. The first, in bars 83 to 88, may perhaps be thought of as a rumbling anticipation of the second – for everything in this movement, as in much of Berg's music in general, goes from bad to worse. The second ('nightmare') yields the most extraordinary sounds in the cycle – now *this* is calculated noise! – and was one of the passages that earned the praise of Stravinsky. I shall return to these bars later.

From bar 94 the texture lightens and clarifies. The material of the nightmare is gradually overlaid with the waltz from bar 20 – the fourth waltz phase – and this material is in turn overlaid from bar 97 with a '4/2' solo violin. The whole of the 4/2 section is in fact a beautifully calculated wind-down[62] by means of which the waltz material reverts to the character of the opening; and this is effected, technically, by a metric modulation which anticipates the 'monoritmica' in *Lulu* and, indeed, the controlled deceleration of Act III of *Lulu* as a whole. By the time the coda arrives there is no trace of waltz rhythm left. Berg's 'narrative', such as it is, is over; and the rest of the piece is a more or less technical matter of tying up loose ends, recapitulating the opening material in stretto and establishing a sense of closure by means of a slowly accelerating trill and a complex, eleven-note chord.

Two further matters merit discussion. One is Berg's treatment of the ostinato episodes at bars 83 and 89. Here the piling-up of material is worthy of Stravinsky (elsewhere I have coined the term 'ostinato machine' for such constructions):[63] a superimposition of five elements, labelled A–E, the first time round (see Example 6.6a), and, in the even more complex restatement (Example 6.6b), no fewer than six. As if such density were not enough, each element consists of two or more polyphonic voices, not to mention the octave doublings, so that at any given point there may be eight or nine notes sounding. No less complex is the rhythmic structure. As so often in such constructions, the repetition of ostinato units within each element – indicated by beams on Example 6.6 – is primarily regulated not by the metre but by numbers which work against it.

My final point brings us back circuitously to the work's title. In bar 36 the flute has a three-note motive which serves, within the immediate context, to complete a two-bar phrase. The same motive returns in bar 56 – but to begin a phrase (and, indeed, a section). The self-reflecting nature of such a recurrence would generally point to a deeper symmetry. But having puzzled over the passage for some considerable time – though not as long as Archibald – I still have no idea what such a symmetry could be. There is no palindrome of any obvious kind. There is no large-scale repetition. The only thought that occurs to me – in the light of the ostinatos – is that there might be some constant *permutation* of material going on. Unravelling the texture at bar 56, one 'ought' to be able to reassemble it as at bars 83 and 89 – except that the three passages are patently *not* permutations of each other. And at this point further parallels with the Schnitzler play suggest themselves. Maybe a theme, or 'character', that is of only secondary importance in one section assumes greater importance in the next,[64] so that there is a constant turning-over of material (as happens in the ostinato passages)? But this appears not to be the case. And yet: rounds; rows; permutation canons … Could it be that *Reigen* is really a set of variations?

Example 6.6   'Ostinato machines' in *Reigen*

(a) bars 83–8

(b) bars 89–93

Marsch

Discussion of the *Marsch*, like the piece itself, tends to veer off in many different directions. To maintain order, I intend to deal with it under three subheadings: the form of the piece as a whole; thematic approaches to its analysis; and its very individual character or tone, a matter which naturally affects the way people write about it.

The most difficult problem with the *Marsch*, at least for the present writer, is getting a clear sense of the movement as a whole. As with *Reigen*, none of the classical forms seems to apply – a fact which has not prevented many writers from trying to analyse it in terms of sonata form (always the favourite). Carner divides it up as follows:

Introduction	bars 1–32
Main section [Exposition]	bars 33–90
Development	bars 91–126
Reprise	bars 127–54
Coda	bars 155–74

Carner is so apologetic about presenting this 'analysis' that one wonders why he bothers. To call the music at bar 91 a Development (except in the sense that everything in this piece is in a constant state of development, but that is not what Carner means) is an absurd mischaracterisation of what many would hear as the most assertive thematic idea of the piece, while to put the Reprise ('a return that is psychological rather than actual')[65] at bar 127 ignores Berg's own characterisation of bar 126 as the 'climax'.

A more sensitive sonata-form interpretation comes from Jarman, who writes: 'In the "Marsch" ... the three-sectioned sonata design, distinguishable in the background plan of the piece, is exploded by the constant motivic development and the unrelenting presentation of apparently new material; sonata form is here destroyed from within by its own developmental tendencies.'[66] This is certainly an apt description of the 'developmental' aspect of the piece. And the idea of sonata form being 'exploded from within' is an attractive one: one might almost speak of a *deconstruction* of the genre, were it not for the fact that the term has become hopelessly corrupted by those who have sought to apply it to music. However, for a genre to be deconstructed it has to be (at least vaguely) present in the first place, and I see no compelling reason why Jarman's 'background plan' should be sonata form rather than anything else (he doesn't, for example, specify where the 'three sections' begin and end).

Nor do I find DeVoto's 'Chronology of Events in the *Marsch*' very helpful. Though accurate as far as it goes, it resembles the bar-by-bar (or blow-by-blow) descriptions students are usually told to avoid when they begin to do analysis. It gives virtually no idea of the overall shape or of the relations between the sections.[67] In that, there is at least a blessing inasmuch as he does not say that the piece is in sonata form.

So how should one view the piece? I make no bones about saying that I find it the most difficult and perplexing of Berg's instrumental compositions; any comments I have on it must therefore be taken as provisional. But there are hints towards an understanding of it in Berg's own markings. Among the plethora of indications – expressive, instrumental and articulatory – with which Berg litters his score, one finds the markings 'Tempo I', 'II' and 'III'. These are already highly suggestive in that they indicate a segmentation of the piece according to tempo. Now of course the piece is not Stravinsky's *Symphonies of Wind Instruments*: this idea is not applied schematically in formal terms, nor (perhaps surprisingly, given Berg's penchant, even at this relatively early date, for metric modulation) are exact numerical relationships established through the use of metronome marks. Later in life Berg would do all of these things. But at the moment he was content to build a piece around the interaction of three tempos without exploring any further ramifications.

These tempo interactions can be represented on a graph (Figure 6.2). Let it be said at once that this is a crude representation of what goes on, ignoring, for instance, the many local fluctuations in tempo (some of which are actually not much more than a form of written-out rubato). And there is nothing to say that the *difference* in tempo between Tempos I, II and III should be exactly the same, as the graph indicates, or, for that matter, that passages in tempos *outside* of the basic three should be directly relatable to them (of course, they cannot be). But it at least shows – and at a glance – the *extent* of the passages in each of the three main tempos, something which can then be used as a basis for further work.

The next step is to recognise the supreme thematic importance of the material stated at bar 91. This moment asserts itself, to my ears at least, as a point of arrival to which all the previous music seems to act as preparation; its importance is backed up by the fact that it marks the beginning of the first extended passage in Tempo III and (retrospectively) by the long period – thirty bars – for which it remains in this tempo. (There must be further, extra-musical significance in the fact that *Allegro energico*, Berg's tempo direction at this point and also one of his very few Italian markings, is the direction given by Mahler at the start of his Sixth Symphony.) Such a 'point of arrival', if accepted, divides the movement almost exactly into two. It may strain credibility to think of everything that precedes it as an introduction; but there are plenty of historical precedents (or parallels) for a piece whose main thematic material emerges halfway, or more than halfway, through: remember *Tod und Verklärung*, many works by Sibelius and – to get back on the Mahlerian track – the opening movement of Mahler's First Symphony. In addition, it makes better musical sense to

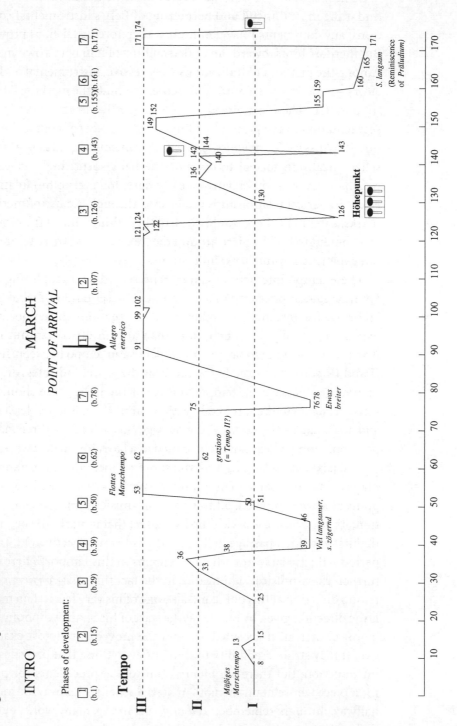

Figure 6.2   Op. 6, *Marsch*

think of the sections as being *cumulative* in effect – part of an inexorable progress towards a goal (Berg's hammer blows!) – rather than as being constrained by the demands of a classical form dependent upon balance.

The segmentation into subsections within the two halves is more subjective; and I have no wish to go through the piece section by section, defending my segmentations in detail, other than to say that each new section is usually marked by the emergence of a solo instrument (solo viola, bar 29; solo cello, bar 39) as well as by a change in tempo. Other segmentations might work equally well or better. What is vital to bear in mind, however, is the overall trajectory of the movement – to use that much overused, Boulezian word – with its inexorable progress towards climax, hammer blows and whatever resolution is indicated by the final fanfares.[68]

The form of analysis most frequently brought to bear on the *Marsch* deals with themes and the relationship between themes. There are obvious historical reasons for this. Schoenberg analysed pieces – to indulge in a vast overstatement – in terms of the relationships between themes; Berg, his pupil, probably composed that way; and to import into the analysis of Berg's music a method devised in association with some other repertoire would be about as sensible as using methods culled from analysing the music of Beethoven to analyse the music of Bali. Nevertheless there are problems. One lies in deciding what exactly is to be called a theme. DeVoto's 'Chronology of Events in the *Marsch*' actually accompanies what he calls a 'Table of Themes', a list of thirty-one thematic ideas with indications as to relationships between them. Again, this is fine *as far as it goes* (it is always possible to find more relationships). The problem arises in deciding the relative status of the thematic ideas. Are all the themes supposed to be of equal importance? Obviously not. So why make the precise distinctions DeVoto does? Some consideration of the difference between themes and motives, and of the difference between thematic relationships and motivic ones (clearly a motive held in common between two themes cannot exist on the same structural level as the two themes), might have been in order. To be fair to DeVoto, he does touch on these problems when he writes:

> It is well to keep in mind that the themes as given here have been assembled and designated with a certain arbitrary exercise of choice, for it is often hard to decide, on the basis of any criteria other than first appearance, whether or not a given melody is more validly characterised by a collateral part, by a collateral harmony, by association with or dissociation from other melodies that occur in succession with it, or by the degree to which subsequent transformations (including fragmentations) are or are not independently used.[69]

A different, though related, problem besets Jarman in his analysis of the *Marsch*. The motivic relations he establishes between themes are for the most part rigorous and convincing.[70] But they lose some of their impact when brought into confrontation with one of the main æsthetic ideas underlying the piece. Let me clarify. Jarman's analysis is underpinned by a commitment to unity (an unfashionable idea nowadays, but none the worse for that): he wants to show how things belong together. Although he never once uses the word unity, the whole drift of his argument is organicist, showing how certain motives pervade the texture, how the apparent chaos conceals a multiplicity of hidden relationships, etc. This comes up sharply against the doctrine of non-repetition that we know to have been one of Berg's principal concerns (as it was of Schoenberg's and Webern's) at the time when he wrote the work. The *Altenberg Lieder* combine 'free atonal' writing with the almost pedantically systematic. The Clarinet Pieces are largely non-repetitive, in spite of certain covert connections between (and within) the pieces; this is the furthest Berg went towards adopting non-repetition as a principle. Somewhere between these two extremes comes Op. 6. The seeming absurdity of analysts trying to find unity through tracing repetitions in pieces that were written out of a desire to avoid repetition – actually a problem endemic in the analysis of atonal music – brings into focus a contradiction within the pieces themselves: the fact that here Berg was attempting to combine two opposing ideas, the avoidance of repetition and the systematic use of techniques (like inversion, canon and so on) that *rely* on repetition. It is this apparent contradiction of aims that makes the pieces – and especially the *Marsch* – so hard to analyse. It also accounts for a certain incoherence in the pieces themselves.

Which has not prevented writers from coming back to them again and again. In his book on *Wozzeck* George Perle has written (the passage has been quoted so often that one could almost recite it from memory):

> The *Marsch* was completed in the weeks immediately following the assassination at Sarajevo and is, in its feeling of doom and catastrophe, an ideal, if unintentional, musical expression of the ominous implications of that event. Fragmentary rhythmic and melodic figures typical of an orthodox military march repeatedly coalesce into polyphonic episodes of incredible density that surge to frenzied climaxes, then fall apart. It is not a march, but music *about* a march, or rather about *the* march, just as Ravel's *La Valse* is music in which *the* waltz is similarly reduced to its minimum characteristic elements. In spite of the fundamental differences in their respective musical idioms, the emotional climate of Berg's pre-war 'marche macabre' is very similar to that of Ravel's post-war 'valse macabre'.[71]

As a characterisation of Berg's music – an evocation of what it is like – this seems to me unexceptionable. The *Marsch* has everywhere been recognised (and this is part of its appeal to both conductors and audiences) as a piece of Mahlerian *Marschmusik* carried to even further extremes. Although Perle does not make the point, the use of 'orthodox' – read 'trivial' – material, whether military or otherwise, is another Mahlerian touch, the further degradation of already degraded gestures providing grist to a view of life that sees in the treadmill (read ostinato) an ultimate symbol of human futility.[72] There would be more of this treatment of military material in *Wozzeck*. But even while accepting Perle's characterisations, one can make distinctions. Even the most barnstorming and apocalyptic Mahler marches, like the finale of the Sixth, are meant 'straightforwardly', i.e. they don't dismantle the genre in the way Berg's does. There is always in Mahler a sense of positive (or positivistic) aspiration that is no longer found in Berg – which means that the quieter, more restful passages are not there either (the peace of the mountain-tops, the episodes with cowbells, which he admired so much in Mahler, were simply out of his reach). However, it is important to distinguish Berg's march-treatment from parody. The march of Op. 6 is definitely not parody;[73] and yet after it there can only be parodies (the marches of David Del Tredici, for example).

Where I differ sharply from Perle is in the implicit value-judgements that his comments carry with them. Because of its association with the Great War, Sarajevo, etc., Berg's march is in danger of becoming a sacred cow. In addition it has, along with the other Op. 6 pieces, the approval of Stravinsky, always a signal for critics to stop thinking for themselves. I find the Three Pieces far from perfect (Stravinsky's word for the *Präludium*),[74] and the *Marsch* the least perfect of the three. It has too many notes (as the Emperor of Austria said of Mozart); and if there is a universe in which such a remark can mean anything, it has to be the universe of the Three Orchestral Pieces. Composers are less squeamish than musicologists in making judgements of this kind. John Adams, for example:

> One of the reasons that Mahler's music is so profoundly successful is that he was a conductor and knew exactly what would work and what wouldn't. By contrast many of the problems with Berg's music result from the fact that he wasn't a performer. Some of his music is wildly overwritten, a problem you don't get with Strauss or Mahler.[75]

If Adams was thinking of any piece in particular, it was surely the *Marsch*: not even the Chamber Concerto can boast such forests of 'unheard' notes.[76] Yet within less than a year, and still without having heard any of his orchestral works performed, Berg was writing more lucidly; for *Reigen* shows a much greater assurance in accomplishing his wishes. If such a judgement, like that of the Emperor of Austria, can be said to mean anything, can it also be said that it may have been the ghost of Mahler, hovering over so much of Berg's music, who helped him towards this success? Precision was Mahler's watchword, in orchestral matters at least, and it may be that his last gift to Berg, transmitted to the latter through a renewed study of Mahler's scores, was a greater sense of what was practicable. If so, then any further enquiry into Mahler's influence on Berg should probably be concentrated in the field of orchestral mastery rather than in the more general areas that have been the focus of this chapter.

7 The musical language of *Wozzeck*

Anthony Pople
University of Lancaster

The phrase 'musical language', though in everyday use, begs many questions and carries a multitude of assumptions. There is naturally a rich and varied literature which attempts to give the topic its due and to work out its detailed implications from a number of perspectives. In this brief chapter, however, the phrase is used in its everyday sense, as a convenient shorthand for the investigation of technical matters in a musical work inasmuch as they relate to what is broadly familiar, embodying an assumption that such ramification of a specific work in a shared context both supports and to some extent reveals a kind of latent musical 'understanding'. In the present context such discussion must also reckon with the fact that *Wozzeck* is an opera, even if the question of genre is far from one-dimensional in this of all such works. The subtitle of Janet Schmalfeldt's impressive monograph on *Wozzeck* – 'harmonic language and dramatic design' – explicitly conjoins the notion of musical language with the idea that operatic music serves a dramatic purpose.[1] Both her book and an earlier study by George Perle seek to relate specific musical configurations to characters, situations and symbols in the drama.[2] As the format of Perle's article acknowledges, this approach owes much to an exegetic line of writing about opera that developed in the post-Wagnerian period. Indeed, the examples of Berg's own guides to Schoenberg's *Gurrelieder* and *Pelleas und Melisande* serve to remind us that during his lifetime such writing frequently spilled over into discussions of non-operatic works.

Writing about the drama of an opera through the music places the drama in a peculiar situation. By rendering it at arms length, giving it a phantom existence that speaks only by virtue of the music's agency, writing in this way endows the drama with the status of something virtual rather than real, and at the same time gives the music the status of something real rather than virtual. It is as if to say that the music serves the drama by *consuming* it – which is indeed a forthright answer to the age-old operatic dilemma of the relative priorities of words and music. In the case of an opera that is composed to a existing free-standing dramatic text, as with Büchner's *Woyzeck* and Berg's *Wozzeck*, such an assessment of the relationship of music to drama represents the most extreme (*apophrades*) of the literary critic Harold Bloom's 'revisionary ratios' – six pragmatic categorisations through which in a famous study of how poets cope with their influences he charts 'the creative mind's desperate insistence on priority'.[3] Appropriating Bloom in this fashion, albeit without associating *apophrades* with the final stages of an artist's career as he does, we might say that to write about *Wozzeck* in this way is to assert that Berg confidently displays his own mastery by overpowering Büchner's text to the point where – as is nowadays surely the common perception – *Woyzeck* the play is unthinkable without *Wozzeck* the opera.[4]

Nonetheless, history can record the play's independent existence. Büchner was only ever a young man – he died in 1837 in his twenty-fourth year – and as well as literature his brilliant and restless mind encompassed radical political activism and the professional medical expertise that had been a family vocation for many generations. The case of Johann Christian Woyzeck would have been known to him through the latter route: in 1821, Woyzeck had killed his partner because she was unfaithful, but pleaded insanity. Medical reports eventually contradicted this and he was executed in 1824. Büchner's play was drafted as a collection of fragmentary scenes shortly before his death and deciphered with enormous difficulty by Karl Emil Franzos for publication in 1879.[5] (Thus there remained two areas of uncertainty in establishing the text of the play: the choice and ordering of scenes, and the detailed reading of the words themselves.) More than thirty years were to elapse before the play's first production in Munich in 1913, by which time – it was Büchner's centenary year – his work had become known in literary circles and was arousing considerable interest. Berg saw the play in Vienna on 5 May 1914 and, moved almost beyond words, resolved immediately to set it to music.[6]

Working from a reprint of Paul Landau's 1909 edition of the play – which without altering the details of Franzos's reading embodied new conjectures about the choice and ordering of the scenes – Berg simply adapted what he saw on the page to form his libretto. Some scenes were omitted, but the order of those that remain is Landau's. Berg made some adjustments of detail in order to retain material from the deleted scenes, but overall, as George Perle succinctly observes, 'the libretto of *Wozzeck* almost literally reproduces the Franzos–Landau text'.[7]

As is well known, Berg's treatment arranges the material into a regular scheme, his three acts each having five scenes. Arguably, this orderly aspect compromises Büchner's creation: viewed through the agency of the opera – or of a scholarly description of the fragments – the play, in its virtual form, is a kind of dramatic mobile, its very formlessness an essential characteristic. But like Berg when fashioning his libretto, stage productions are constrained to render the play as an undeviating chronological entity. This often works poorly in the theatre, but not in Berg. Music gives Berg the capacity for continual cross-references that counterpoint the chronological trajectory of the narrative, indeed throwing it into relief and making a dramatic virtue of its 'inevitability'.

At the same time, this counterpoint was not sufficient for him: in his 1929 lecture on the opera, he made the extraordinary claim that

> although [the final scene] ... clearly moves to cadence on to the closing chord, it almost appears as if it carries on. And it does carry on! In fact, the opening bar of the opera could link up with this final bar and in so doing close the whole circle.[8]

This idea has often been restated without objection, yet it is surely questionable. We can locate here the source of two claims about the drama and the music of the opera. In terms of the wider resonances of the stage action, the implication of Berg's statement is that the tragedy of Wozzeck and Marie could repeat itself in the next generation (and the next, and the next, and so on);[9] it thus amounts to a claim of mythic status for a drama which is actually based on historical fact. Arguably, Büchner's play does not need this particular mythic quality to be a fine and resonant piece of theatre: it achieves this by teasing out a web of possible explanations for Johann Woyzeck's mental state, and by locating the agency of many of those explanations with members of society more respectable and upstanding than the poor soldier himself, none of whom can match his capacity for questioning the nature of the human condition.

Berg's opera, because it subsumes Büchner's play, possesses all of these qualities too, but by explicitly assigning the drama's mythic quality outside time – rather than within the mirror of Woyzeck's society – Berg also aligned his opera with the Wagnerian music-drama project. Inasmuch as the Wagnerian project itself grew from literary origins broadly contemporary with Büchner, there is perhaps another kind of circular closure afoot here that in an uncanny way supports Berg's treatment. Secondly, in musical terms, Berg's proposed 'circular' connection, which must be set against the strongly cadential nature of the end of each of the three acts (the immediately previous point Berg makes in his lecture) would seem to constitute a claim of stylistic integrity across the work from beginning to end – or, at least, from the end to the beginning. This claim is not straightforwardly sustainable, although as Schmalfeldt, Perle and Douglas Jarman have shown, and as will be discussed later in this chapter, it can be supported through detailed analysis.

Table 7.1

drama		music
expositions	*Act I*	*five character pieces*
Wozzeck and the Captain	scene 1	Suite
Wozzeck and Andres	scene 2	Rhapsody
Marie and Wozzeck	scene 3	Military march and lullaby
Wozzeck and the Doctor	scene 4	Passacaglia
Marie and the Drum Major	scene 5	Andante affetuoso (quasi Rondo)
dramatic development	*Act II*	*Symphony in five movements*
Marie and her child, later Wozzeck	scene 1	Sonata movement
the Captain and the Doctor, later Wozzeck	scene 2	Fantasia and Fugue
Marie and Wozzeck	scene 3	Largo
garden of a tavern	scene 4	Scherzo
guard room in the barracks	scene 5	Rondo con introduzione
catastrophe and epilogue	*Act III*	*six inventions*
Marie and the child	scene 1	invention on a theme
Marie and Wozzeck	scene 2	invention on a note
tavern	scene 3	invention on a rhythm
death of Wozzeck	scene 4	invention on a hexachord
	interlude	invention on a tonality
children playing	scene 5	invention on a regular quaver movement

Formal models

Berg's organisation of the action into a regularised sequence of scenes also served a musical purpose which has become well known through the overview of its scenes prepared by his pupil Fritz Mahler, from which Table 7.1 derives.[10] The composer's choice of textbook musical forms is in several cases explicitly related to the dramatic situation through similarities of pacing or in some way metaphorically. For example, as Berg himself said of Act II scene 1:

> The second act … has, as its first musical form, a sonata movement. It is not, perhaps, an accident that the three figures appearing in this scene, Marie, her child and Wozzeck, form the basis of the three thematic groups of the musical exposition – the first subject, second subject and coda – of a strict sonata structure. Indeed the whole of the dramatic development of this jewel scene, the twofold repetitions of certain situations and the confrontation of the main characters, lends itself to a strict musical articulation with an exposition, a first reprise, development and finally a recapitulation.[11]

Rather obviously, and not for the first time in musical history, this takes into the realm of operatic music the principles of the Straussian symphonic poem, with its ambivalent appeal to notions of absolute and programme music. But it also involves a neo-classical aspect, not so much through the use of textbook musical forms *per se*, but rather on account of their stylisation. For example, one cannot imagine Gustav Mahler, Berg's symphonic precursor, composing a 'strict' sonata movement which, like this scene, lasts no more than five minutes in a typical performance.

The distancing from the historical locus of the form which this implies is inevitably more explicit in the case of the first scene of Act I, which through the use of the baroque suite as a formal model, Berg suggests, 'acquires … musically its proper, I should like to say, historical colouring'.[12] Douglas Jarman elucidates this by observing that the use of the 'old-fashioned' form is 'a comment on the Captain's out-dated, traditional and bourgeois moral stance'[13] – in other words, the use of the form is not straightforward antiquarianism, but rather gives scope for an additional level of authorial comment on Berg's part. As the continuation of Berg's sentence makes clear, however, this was not his intention elsewhere in the opera: it was something 'which in this truly timeless drama I naturally did not otherwise keep to';[14] at the same time, one may nonetheless observe an overwhelming quality of stylisation in the Suite, not least in the brevity of its 'movements'. The whole sequence – Prelude, Pavane, cadenza, Gigue, cadenza, Gavotte with two Doubles, Air, and a reprise of the Prelude (much of it in retrograde) – lasts about seven or eight minutes.

One might well ask how recognisable the forms are under such circumstances. Certainly, the opera's formal organisation met initially with incomprehension from some quarters – the Viennese critic Emil Petschnig, for example:

> apart from a few bars of chromatic passagework in 3/8 time … which are supposed to represent the Gigue, a section in [¢] about morality representing the Gavotte and its two Doubles … and a section in 3/2 to which, out of much good will, one might apply the term 'Air', I was unable to discover anything that resembled a Suite or even to discover any of those features that immediately differentiate the old dance forms from one another.[15]

It is easy to belittle such judgements with hindsight, but it is also worth looking a little deeper. The brevity of the forms is of course connected with the brevity of Büchner's scenes, and thereafter is a consequence of Berg's decision to apply a separate musical form to each scene – albeit while grouping them into larger families, notably in the second act. In his brief article 'A Word about *Wozzeck*', Berg explained his reasoning:

> The function of a composer is to solve the problems of an ideal stage director. On the other hand this objective should not prejudice the development of the music as an entity, absolute, and purely musical.

> ... It was first necessary to make a selection from Büchner's twenty-
> five loosely constructed, partly fragmentary scenes ... Repetitions not
> lending themselves to musical variation were avoided. ...
>
> It was impossible to shape the fifteen scenes I selected ... so that each
> would retain its musical coherence and individuality and at the same
> time follow the customary method of development appropriate to the
> literary content. No matter ... how aptly it might fit the dramatic events,
> after a number of scenes so composed the music would inevitably create
> monotony. ...
>
> I obeyed the necessity of giving each scene and each accompanying
> piece of entr'acte music ... an unmistakable aspect, a rounded off and
> finished character. It was imperative to use everything essential for the
> creation of individualizing characteristics on the one hand, and coher-
> ence on the other. Hence the much discussed utilization of both old and
> new musical forms ... .[16]

In other words, the set forms were used primarily in order to give each
scene or interlude 'a rounded off and finished character'; Berg employed
other musical devices to individualise them, to give them 'an unmistak-
able aspect'.

The differentiation is indeed remarkable. The vocal characterisations
and the combinations of characters, the memorable orchestral sonorities
and in some scenes the reduction of the full orchestra to produce a characteristic range of tone colours: all of these things not only differentiate the
scenes from each other but also lend them each an internal coherence. In
Acts I and II at least, it is a moot point whether the coherence of this kind is
more potent than the coherence provided by the stylised forms. Perhaps in
the Passacaglia on a twelve-note theme that supports Act I scene 4 and
through its twenty-one variations mocks the Doctor's obsessiveness, it is
the formal basis rather than the diversity it permits Berg to compose into
the variation sequence that is responsible for holding the scene together –
though the intensity of Büchner's satire also plays its part. But in the tavern scene (Act II scene 4), or the preceding scene between Wozzeck and
Marie – in which the reduction of the orchestra to chamber music proportions and the use of *Sprechstimme* in the vocal parts defines the musical
character – it is surely less the underlying Scherzo and Trio form in the one
case, or the underlying ternary form of the Largo in the other, that gives 'a
rounded off and finished character' to these scenes, but rather the onset
and cut-off of the foregrounded musical characteristics.

This is not to deny the tightness of the formal organisation in many of
the scenes, nor to echo Petschnig's failure to recognise the reference to
traditional archetypes. But in the rich balance of elements that Berg's creativity encompassed, the division of function between the musical foreground and the stylised forms is less clear-cut than the diagram Berg sug-

gested to Fritz Mahler and the explanation he gave in 'A Word about *Woz-zeck*' have seemed to imply. Berg himself came to regret that the opera's use of traditional forms had become the topic of so much discussion: at one point in his 1929 lecture he suggests that 'until now [this] has done as much as the performances to make the opera well known'.[17] His immediate published response to Petschnig was perhaps too robust in its defence of the forms – he claims their 'correctness and legitimacy'[18] – and this may have led in part to the misunderstanding.

There is a further aspect to Berg's formal organisation of the opera that sheds light on his attachment to the idea. This concerns the overall categorisation of Act I as a series of five character pieces and of Act II as a Symphony in five movements. A letter Berg wrote to Schoenberg shortly before he began work on *Wozzeck*, quoted at greater length on pp. 117–18, tells us something of the origin of these models:

> Unfortunately I have to confess, dear Herr Schönberg, that I haven't made use of your various suggestions as to what I should compose next. Much as I was intrigued from the start by your suggestion to write an orchestral suite (with character pieces), and though I immediately began to think of it often and seriously ... I found myself giving in to an older desire ... to write a <u>symphony</u>.[19]

The context for this letter was the sharp criticism Schoenberg had made of Berg's Opp. 4 and 5; its musical consequence was not in fact the Symphony, which never became more than a fragment, but the Three Orchestral Pieces Op. 6.[20] These were in full flow at the time of Berg's fateful visit to see *Woyzeck* in the theatre; in particular Berg's work on the *Marsch* was contemporaneous with his initial musical work on *Wozzeck*, which was concerned with Act II scene 2 and sketches for the third and second scenes of Act I (the latter ended up sharing some material with the *Marsch*).[21] But most of *Wozzeck* was written after his return from war duties at the end of 1918. Act I was finished by 22 July 1919, scenes 1, 3 and 5 of Act II (in addition to scene 2, composed earlier) by the end of August 1920; Act II scene 4 and the whole of Act III were written in 1921, the short score being finished by mid-October; and the full score was completed in April 1922.[22]

Thus by the time he came to write his 'five character pieces' and his 'Symphony' into the substructure of *Wozzeck*, Berg was, chronologically at least, at a distance from Schoenberg's attempts to humiliate him. Indeed, in the interim the older man had relented, even offering Berg the intimate 'Du' form of address in 1918.[23] But if Berg could distance himself from the experience, he seems never quite to have forgiven Schoenberg, who had also more than once expressed opposition to an operatic treatment of *Woyzeck*.[24] The central scene of *Wozzeck* ostensibly pays tribute to Schoenberg, both in its reduced orchestration, which follows the layout of the older man's First Chamber Symphony, and in its use of the *Sprechstimme* device. But in view of the likelihood that the correspondingly central movement of Berg's next work, the Chamber Concerto, is secretly critical of Schoenberg's reaction to *his* wife's unfaithfulness,[25] it is tempting to speculate on the backhandedness of Berg's tribute to his teacher at the very juncture in the opera where Wozzeck challenges Marie to admit her relationship with the Drum Major. The music's reference to Schoenberg is further underscored at the beginning of the scene (bars II/372–3), when several characteristic thematic materials from other scenes are transposed from their customary pitch levels, exposing the interval A–E♭ (in German notation, Schoenberg's initials A. S.) in the bass. Berg's quotation from Schoenberg's Five Pieces for Orchestra at one of the Doctor's sillier moments (bars I/520ff.) may be a further example of a private joke at Schoenberg's expense.[26]

Berg could never overcome the influence of Schoenberg in the way that his opera manages to consume Büchner's play. In terms of Bloom's 'revisionary ratios', what we have here is akin to the third of them, *kenosis*, in which '[the] later poet, apparently emptying himself of his own afflatus, his imaginative godhood, seems to humble himself … but this ebbing is so performed … that the precursor is emptied out also, and so the later poem of deflation is not as absolute as it seems'.[27] However one chooses to express it, one of the nicest ironies is that although Schoenberg told Berg as late as 1923 that he would never be successful with *Wozzeck*, the opera was within a few years of its premiere in Berlin on 14 December 1925 a popular success far greater than Schoenberg had ever achieved himself, or indeed ever would.[28] The even nicer irony is that Berg was suspicious of this success when it came to him, and had apparently to be consoled over it by the likes of Adorno.[29]

Musical materials

In saying, at the end of his lecture on the opera, that his audience should 'forget everything that I've tried to explain about musical theory and æsthetics when you come … to see a performance of *Wozzeck*',[30] Berg did not fully resolve the question of whether, for example, the symphonic structure of Act II is no more than a concept, or whether the act really *is* a symphony, but one from which attention is properly distracted by the drama. Nor is this easy to resolve with hindsight. In musical terms, the expansion of the musical range – to take in a lullaby (scene 1), a fugue (scene 2), folk songs and dance music (scene 4) – does not contradict the symphonic basis, since this kind of genre expansion had been fully established by the Mahlerian symphony. But Mahler's genre expansion was part and parcel of his idea that 'the symphony must be like the world. It must embrace everything.'[31] In *Wozzeck*, on the other hand, each scene is so short as to be only a small corner of 'the world' – 'nur ein Eckchen in der Welt', as Marie sings in Act II scene 1 – and there is a limit to how much each can embrace. Arguably, when borrowed genres appear, it is they, rather than the symphonic types, that tend to dominate the character of the scenes – although in the tavern scene these aspects happily coincide.

Symphonic in a different sense is what Adorno calls 'the inner construction of the music, its fabric [*Gewebe*]':[32] the way in which, as it were, the musical texture is, so very much of the time, 'woven' out of recurrent motivic, harmonic and other ideas. As Adorno goes on to point out, this technique allows the music to outline the 'exceedingly rich, multi-faceted curve of the inner plot … It registers every dramatic impulse to the point of self-forgetfulness.' When Wagner brought this principle into the realm of opera in the 1850s, such musical textures had been associated mainly with the development sections of symphonic movements; but Schoenberg had since shown, in his early compositions such as the Chamber Symphony, that this kind of music could be employed almost ubiquitously in expanded classical forms by means of the combination of formal types and the principle of developing variation. It was this precedent which allowed Berg credibly to present a Wagnerian *Gewebe* as the musical substance of many different movement-types in the second act of *Wozzeck* under the banner of a symphony.

This aspect of the writing does not exclude the borrowed genres, nor is it confined to Act II. Indeed, as Perle and Schmalfeldt in particular have shown, there is a remarkably consistent substructure in the music of *Wozzeck* that interrelates many of the recurrent motives, harmonies and other configurations. The scenes of Act III are termed 'inventions' in Fritz Mahler's table – invention on a theme, a note, a chord, etc. – but this word might have been applied quite as appropriately elsewhere. Act I scene 4 could be called an invention on a twelve-note theme, Act I scene 2 an invention on three chords, and so on. Above all, the endless *Gewebe* shows Berg in a constant state of inventiveness, as he combines, adapts and recombines his characteristic motives, chords, rhythms and other musical devices.

What kind of relationships underpin this network of materials? Douglas Jarman, following a lead given by Berg near the beginning of his lecture,[33] shows how the two cadential chords from the end of Act I (Example 7.1, which follows Jarman in labelling the chords 'A' and 'B') constitute a rich repository of musical configurations.[34] Many of the opera's most

Example 7.1   Cadential chords A and B

Example 7.2   Relationship of Marie's 'Komm, mein Bub!' motive to cadential chord A'

Example 7.3   Relationship of Wozzeck's entrance motive to cadential chord B

prominent motivic and harmonic materials may be related to these chords in a fairly straightforward manner: for instance, Example 7.2 indicates how chord A, expanded by one note (B♭) into chord A' (cf. I/317) and transposed upwards by five semitones, can be split into the two harmonies *p* and *q* which habitually underpin a three-note motive that dominates much of Marie's music in Act I scene 3 (the orchestral presentation of the material at I/363–4 is shown in the example).[35] Example 7.3 shows how the notes of chord B, transposed upwards by a semitone and omitting one pitch (C♮), give the substance of a motive associated both with Wozzeck's entrances on stage (cf. I/427, from the same scene) and, in inversion, his exits.[36] The motive which is indelibly associated from the opera's first scene onwards with Wozzeck's cry of 'Wir arme leut' ('we poor people') is easy to find embedded in the notes of chord B, suitably transposed (see Example 7.4); at the same time, it may be detected among the notes of chord A' (enumerated in Example 7.5a) at the three different transpositional levels shown in Example 7.5b, each of which is four semitones (ic4) apart.

This alerts us to what Allen Forte calls 'the structural importance of ic4 in the opera as a whole',[37] an observation which he makes in consideration of the aggregate of the pitch-classes in the two chords A and B. Only one

Example 7.4   Relationship of Wozzeck's 'Wir arme Leut!' motive to cadential chord B

Wir ar - me Leut!

Example 7.5   (a) Pitch-class content of cadential chord A'

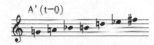

(b) 'Wir arme Leut!' motive embedded in chord A'

other eight-note aggregate, he points out, has the maximum number (seven) intervals of this size among its constituent pitch-classes. Another way of putting this is to describe the aggregate as a combination of two augmented triads plus two other notes a major third apart – a description that applies equally to the other eight-note aggregate to which Forte alludes.[38] Although the two properties are demonstrably corollaries – a situation that repeats itself numerous times with respect to other interrelated pitch materials in this opera – the different descriptions are not exactly interchangeable. Indeed, insofar as it is the mode of description itself which makes available to discussion the thing it describes, a technical nuance such as this can have far-reaching consequences for critical analysis. In particular, the very question of aggregation – of studying the large configurations made up from small ones and seeing the small ones in this light – is one that defines a certain point of view. Broadly speaking, Jarman's analysis works from pre-defined large units (the cadential chords) towards smaller configurations such as the motives seen in Examples 7.2, 7.3 and 7.4. Janet Schmalfeldt's analysis tends to work in the opposite direction, often revealing unsuspected properties of larger aggregates in the *Gewebe* that seem at first sight to arise simply out of a collage of smaller units.

There is no doubt that collages of motivic materials are characteristic of *Wozzeck*, and perhaps of Berg's mature music in general. The classic instance in *Wozzeck* is at the moment of Marie's death, when, as Berg says, 'all the important musical configurations associated with her are played very rapidly ... as at the moment of death the most important images of her life pass through her mind distorted and at lightning speed'.[39] In such in

Example 7.6   (a) Tetrachordal cells *a–d* in Act II scene 1 (after Perle)

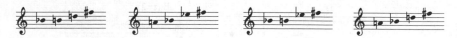

(b) Hexachordal aggregate of cells *a–d*

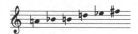

stances the distinct motives themselves must clearly remain in view, but one might also hope for analysis to grant some insight into the particular way in which they are combined. So, if aggregation (and by the same token its opposite, segmentation) are fundamental tools of analysis, a further significant aspect of the discussion that ensues is whether it seeks primarily to define an internal, self-referential consistency in the music, or to point beyond it into external musical norms such as those familiar from tonal music.

In his oft-cited analysis of the music of Act II scene 1, George Perle enumerates a number of tetrachords (shown in Example 7.6a) which he associates with different parts of the formal structure. He further suggests that 'the movement as a whole is based on aggregates of the different cells': one such aggregate is shown in Example 7.6b.[40] The levels of transposition in Example 7.6 are different from Perle's and have been chosen so as to facilitate a comparison between this aggregate and the notes of chord A' (Example 7.5a), from which it can be seen that only one note of the chord is missing from the aggregate of the four-note cells. Janet Schmalfeldt's identification of a number of closely related set-classes associated with Wozzeck (Example 7.7) and Marie (Example 7.8) accomplishes much the same kind of comparison, though on a far larger scale and at a level of detail that cannot be summarised without doing the author a disservice.[41] Schmalfeldt's set-class names have been illustrated here by exemplar sets transcribed into music notation, in both prime and inverse forms (which are sometimes equivalent), highlighting with open noteheads the contrasting symmetrical bases of a (0, 4, 8) augmented triad in the Wozzeck materials and a (0, 3, 6, 9) diminished seventh chord in Marie's, for reasons that will be discussed later in the chapter. Transposition levels of the sets have been chosen to make readily visible some of the inclusion relationships between the set-classes and some of the motivic connections they embody. An analysis seeking primarily to define a network of relationships within the opera itself might fasten almost exclusively on correspondences of this kind: in emphasising the piece-specific nature both of

Example 7.7   Set-classes associated with Wozzeck (after Schmalfeldt)

Example 7.8   Set-classes associated with Marie (after Schmalfeldt)

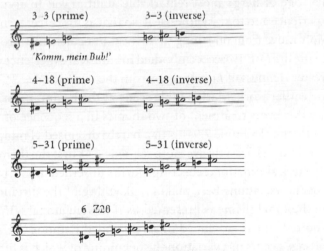

small motivic units and of the larger units they make up in combination, such a view of where the work's coherence lies would fit well with a perception that in *Wozzeck* Berg was essentially working without the shared resources of the common-practice period.

However, both these authors are also well alert to connections beyond *Wozzeck* itself. The sense of tonality in the opera is indeed in many places extremely focused, and Berg's incorporation of passages from two of his own early piano pieces[42] – not to mention parodied folk song and dance

Example 7.9   (a) G minor theme from Act III scene 1 (III/3–6)

(b) Twelve-note theme from Act III scene 1 (III/7–9)

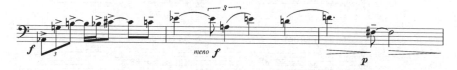

genres – demands that technical analysis of the work should engage with the ramified resources of the vastly expanded tonal language available to Berg at the time. That is to say: not classical tonality, not even Wagnerian tonality, but something yet further developed by, for example, the accretion of new harmonic types such as quartal chords and the whole-tone scale. For one of Berg's most remarkable abilities was to accumulate his own experience and to re-synthesise it, so that as his career went on he did not simply move from one thing to the next but constantly broadened his range to the utmost. *Wozzeck* embodied his musical experience to date; the even greater richness of *Lulu* springs from the same source.

In the earlier work, Marie's Bible scene at the beginning of Act III exemplifies this by its treatment of two themes in a sequence of variations. The first theme (Example 7.9a) is in a barely-disguised G minor; the second (Example 7.9b) is a twelve-note sequence. At first the themes are presented in stark alternation, reflecting Marie's unsettled mood, but over the course of the variations Berg makes a plaything of the distance between the two: the tonal theme is presented as if it were atonal (III/26–8); the twelve-note theme is enveloped in an expanded F minor (III/38–9). The latter passage occurs in a variation the beginning of which is lifted directly from a fragmentary piano piece dating from the period of work that led to Berg's Op. 1: thus, when its theme is revealed, retrospectively as it were, as the model for the G minor theme of this scene, the correspondence with the nostalgia in the text at this point is multi-layered.

One of the most emblematic passages in *Wozzeck* is the opening of Act I scene 2 (see Example 9.3, p. 186). The three chords on which this is based are labelled X, Y and Z (following Perle)[43] in Example 7.10a, which also shows the passing chord (bar I/205) that leads back to a restatement of chord X. Berg's description of the three chords in his lecture is intriguing:

Example 7.10   (a) Chord sequence from Act I scene 2

(b) Pitch-class aggregate of chords in (a)

> The unifying principle of this scene is harmonic: three chords which
> represent the harmonic skeleton of the scene. That such a principle can
> act as a structural element will be admitted by anyone who thinks of
> tonality as a means of building forms and regards these three chords as
> having functions comparable to those of the tonic, dominant and sub
> dominant.[44]

It is clear that Berg felt strongly that these chords could act as a tonal
analogue; less clear why he should relate them to the three basic tonal
functions in the specific order of X as tonic, Y as dominant, Z as subdomi
nant. The climactic placement of Z in the phrase would seem, in the absence of other criteria – that is, if the analogy were a mere contrivance – to
align Z rather than Y with the dominant function. And it must be said that
in tonal music the progression I–IV–V(–I) is far more commonplace that
I–V–IV(–I), and that a standard harmonic sequence might have been expected to establish a tonal analogue more readily than a less standard one.
So if we take Berg at his word there would appear to be more to it than that.
Elsewhere in this book, Patricia Hall shows how an early sketch for the
passage had a continuation that Berg marked 'E♭ major and minor with
unresolved D' (pp. 184–6). She suggests that Berg was in this sense working explicitly with a ten-note aggregate that combined the pitch-classes of
E♭ major and E♭ minor. In the final version, Berg had moved somewhat
away from this: the three chords have a nine-note aggregate, shown in
Example 7.10b. (The notes of the passing chord lie within the same aggregate, perhaps going some way towards confirming its status as a local point
of reference.)

As Example 7.11 indicates, this aggregate could indeed still be formed
by modal mixture: C♯ minor and major combined have these nine notes

Example 7.11   Aggregate of C♯ minor and C♯ major collections

Example 7.12   (a) Cadential chord A' as hexatonic collection plus one note

(b) Aggregate of C♯ minor and C♯ minor/major hexatonic collections

plus one more. But there is a different modal interaction that generates the nine-note aggregate more exactly and relates these chords both to other harmonic materials in *Wozzeck* and to a strand of late nineteenth-century harmonic innovation that embodies the significance of ic4 to which Allen Forte has alerted us in this opera. Example 7.12a reinterprets cadential chord A' as a one-note expansion of the 'hexatonic' collection which is formed from interlocking augmented triads a semitone apart. As Richard Cohn has shown, this collection was known, understood and employed by composers such as Liszt, Wagner, Franck, Brahms and Mahler; it allowed them to shift easily between minor and major tonalities rooted a major third apart, both within and between phrases – though its appearances at the surface of musical textures at this time were apparently rare.[45] Example 7.12b shows how the diatonic scale of C♯ minor and the hexatonic collection that includes C♯ minor and major triads may be combined to produce the nine-note aggregate of chords X, Y and Z. Within this framework, the three chords may be regarded as semitonally altered forms of tonic, dominant and subdominant chords in a hexatonically expanded C♯ minor (Example 7.13), in correspondence with Berg's description. The

Example 7.13   C♯ minor analogue of chords X, Y and Z

Example 7.14   Harmonic outline of opening of D minor interlude (III/320–38)

prototype for chord Z incorporates an appoggiatura motion within the C♯ minor scale (cf. I/243, I/302ff.)

Remarkably enough, the semitonal displacement within chord X links it directly to the highly characteristic opening sonority of the cathartic D minor interlude that plays before the final scene of the opera. (Thus reconstituted as X', it is simply the same chord, a semitone lower.)[46] The first seven bars of this interlude were taken directly from the fourth of Berg's early sonata fragments, in which whole-tone expansions of dominant-quality harmony are prevalent. Example 7.14 shows a harmonic outline of the first nineteen bars of this interlude, over the course of which Berg gradually flexes his stylistic muscles, expanding his musical language before our very ears from the D minor of a 1908 Schoenberg pupil to the three chords X, Y and Z at bars III/337–8. The passage which continues from this point exploits these three chords again, transposed downwards through ic4 (Example 7.15). The putative hexatonic component thus remains constant, while the tonal component shifts to from C♯ to A. It is notable, therefore, that here the chords provide harmonic support for a

Example 7.15   III/339–41, showing chords X, Y and Z

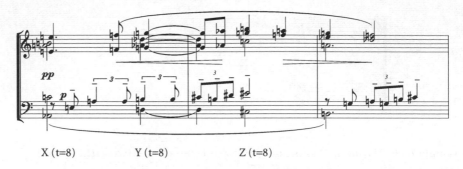

horn melody which duly begins in A major – this is Andres's song from Act I scene 2 – and departs from the key only through whole-tone inflections which outline the augmented triad A–C♯–E♯. Note also how the end of the horn melody is immediately echoed ic4 lower, as is the double appoggiatura to chord Z.

Another small point is revealing in a different way: this is the appearance of chord X at bar III/331 (see Example 7.14 once more), here played without its companions Y and Z, and interpretable in its tonal context as a $C^{13♭}$ chord. It serves as a reminder that a chord of this complexity is likely to be, in Schoenberg's terms, a 'vagrant' harmony which can be interpreted tonally in a number of distinct ways and can thus work effectively within a continually modulating harmonic progression. The appearance of chord X at this moment in the interlude also serves to introduce the sonority itself as the tonal language expands, preparing for the complete statement of the tonal analogue X–Y–Z six bars later.

Hexatonic-diatonic interaction may be sought elsewhere in *Wozzeck*. The harmonies which begin Act I scene 5 (outlined in Example 7.16) combine the C major scale with the hexatonic collection G–B♭–B♮–D–E♭–F♯, and the ostentatious orchestral chords that frame the Drum Major's posturing (bars I/670ff., see Example 7.17) all lie within hexatonic-diatonic aggregates similar to that of chords X, Y and Z – even if some of these inclusion relationships are statistically unremarkable. Yet it is difficult to believe that Berg actually 'used' hexatonic-diatonic interaction, conceived straightforwardly as an interplay of collections, as an explicit part of his compositional technique. This is not to play down the significance of the 'invention on a hexachord' in Act III scene 4[47] – a scene that was composed at a time when, probably influenced by his pupil Fritz Heinrich Klein, Berg seems to have been well aware of ideas about collection-based composition in the current work of Josef Matthias Hauer.[48] It is simply that a more likely explanation is that what might be diagnosed now as collection-oriented hexatonic-diatonic interaction is most likely to have arisen then out

Example 7.16   Harmony at opening of Act I scene 5 (I/656)

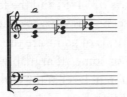

Example 7.17   Harmonies framing Drum Major's boast to Marie (I/670–88)

of a complex of ideas – far less cut-and-dried – involving modal mixture (specifically, adding the minor third and sixth to a major scale or vice versa), together with the long-established norm (it is a cliché in Schubert) of temporary modulation by a major third downwards to the flat submediant, and the association of dominant quality sonorities with a latent whole-tone background in which ic4 is prominent almost by definition.

The legacy of ideological differences in the 1920s and 1930s between the Schoenberg circle and the 'wrong-note' composers such as Stravinsky means even today that to suggest Berg may have created atonal music by adjusting tonal models seems more of an accusation than an analysis. Yet there is evidence of this both in the sketches and in the finished opera, perhaps most clearly embodied by Andres's distorted 'folk song' in the self-same scene that first introduces chords X, Y and Z. The inflection of familiar models is also seen in other ways. Perle, Jarman and Schmalfeldt are among the commentators who have drawn attention to the 'nearly whole-tone' nature of many of the musical themes (such as the oboe melody of the opera's opening bars, and cadential chord B);[49] the 'nearly hexatonic' nature of chord A' (and likewise of A) has been seen earlier in this chapter. In Example 7.7 (adapted from Schmalfeldt's 'Wozzeck' sets), the four-note sets are revealed as an augmented triad plus one note, the five- and six-note sets are 'nearly hexatonic' and the eight note sets are hexatonic plus two notes. The Marie materials in Example 7.8 similarly evade precise alignment with the regular diminished seventh chord (0, 3, 6, 9) and the octatonic collection (0, 1, 3, 4, 6, 7, 9, 10). A significant contrast may be seen here with the ironic connotations Berg finds for 'purity' in passages such as the diatonic C major theme in the Drum Major's march music (albeit over a C♯–G♯ bass, bars I/334–5) and the famous isolated C major chord that is heard in Act I scene 3 as Wozzeck hands over to Marie the pittance he has earned. These kinds of game are the equivalent at the musical surface of Berg's handling of some (if arguably not all) of the formal models he manipulates at a different level of the entire conception. There is a tantalising psychological link here to Berg's well-documented fascination with symmetry, coincidence and numerology.[50] And indeed when all is said and done, the musical balance Berg maintains between the familiar, subtly altered, and the innovative, miraculously cohering, is but one of the wonders of this inspirational score.

PART III

After *Wozzeck*

8 Secret programmes

Douglas Jarman
Royal Northern College of Music, Manchester

In January 1977 the American composer and Berg scholar George Perle made a trip to Mifflinburg, Pennsylvania to visit Dorothea Robetin, the daughter of Herbert and Hanna Fuchs Robettin, who had in her possession a previously unexamined copy of the first published score of the *Lyric Suite* given to her mother by the composer. Annotated in red, blue and green ink by Berg himself and consisting of ninety pages, only eight of which were without some annotation in Berg's hand, this extraordinary document revealed that the work had behind it a detailed extra-musical programme charting the course of a love affair between Alban Berg and Hanna Fuchs-Robettin.

For many years, scholars had known that extra-musical programmes of some kind lay behind much of Berg's music – Willi Reich's description of the programme of the Violin Concerto in the first article ever published about the work[1] and Berg's own 'Open Letter' on the Chamber Concerto[2] had made that much clear. Such things as the sequence of tempo directions that head the movements of the *Lyric Suite* (Allegretto giovale, Andante amoroso, Allegro misterioso and Trio estatico, Adagio appassionato, Presto delirando, Largo desolato), and the various musical quotations from Zemlinsky and Wagner that appear during the course of the work, had already led commentators to indulge in speculation about it.[3] Only with the publication in the summer of 1977 of Perle's articles about his discovery, however, did the precise nature of the programme of what Adorno had called 'a latent opera' and the extent to which the details of the programme were incorporated into and influenced the structure of the final work become clear.[4]

In brief, the *Lyric Suite* documents the love affair of Berg and Hanna from its innocent beginnings (first movement), to their declaration of love (third movement) and finally, in the last movement, to the recognition of the impossibility of its ever developing into anything more permanent. The second movement of the work is dedicated to, and paints a portrait of, Hanna and her two children, Munzo and Dorothea; the fourth movement is a love scene in which the two protagonists exchange their pledge, to a quotation from Zemlinsky's *Lyric Symphony* (where it appears

to the words 'Du bist mein eigen, mein eigen' – 'you are my own, my own'),
and the fifth is a depiction of 'the horrors and pains which now follow, of
the days with their racing pulses, of the painful Tenebroso of the night'.
The last movement was revealed by the annotated score as a setting of 'De
profundis clamavi' from Baudelaire's *Les Fleurs du mal* in a translation by
Stefan George – 'To you, you sole dear one, my cry rises out of the deepest
abyss in which my heart has fallen'[5] – that gradually dies away 'in love,
yearning and grief'.

The revelation of Berg's illicit love affair came as a surprise only insofar
as it overturned the idealistic picture of the relationship between Berg and
his wife Helene that had been painted in all the biographies of the composer published to that point. More extraordinary was the revelation of
the way and the extent to which Berg had used the details of this 'secret
programme' as a means of determining pitch, proportions, tempi and
other technical features of the work. Thus the annotated score revealed
that the four note cell A–Bb–B♮–F, which acts as the main motivic cell of
the work and frequently determines, amongst other things, the choice of
row forms and row transpositions, is derived from the initials of Alban
Berg and Hanna Fuchs converted into German musical notation. A further figuration in the Andante amoroso second movement – the repeated
C♮ in the viola – has its origins in the Robettin family's pet name for
Dorothea, 'Dodo'. Similarly, both the formal proportions and the metronome markings of the whole work are based on two numbers which Berg
particularly associated with himself and Hanna: the number 23, which he
believed to be his own fateful number, and the number 10 which, for some
reason, he associated with Hanna Fuchs.

The Allegro misterioso and Trio estatico of the third movement of the
work can be taken as an illustration of the way in which not only the character of the sections but many of the most important aspects of the structure and the musical material are determined by extra-musical, programmatic considerations.

In the annotated score, only the date '20.5.25' stands at the head of the
movement. That this date refers to the day when Alban and Hanna first
declared, or became aware of, their feelings for one another is confirmed
by the annotation that Berg adds following the word misterioso, 'for everything was still a mystery'. The necessarily clandestine nature of the couple's declaration is reflected in the fact that the four instruments play with
mutes throughout ('like a whisper' says Berg's annotation at the opening
of the movement), even in the Trio in which the dynamic marking is 'sem-
pre *f* possibile'. The movement is an ABA structure with the proportions of
each section determined by Berg's fateful number 23, the first A section
having 69 bars (3×23) and the B section (the Trio) 23 bars. The final A

section is a shortened (46 bars = 2×23) retrograde reprise of the opening section, the significance of the retrograde – which here, as always in Berg's music, acts as a metaphor for negation or denial – being pointed out by the annotation 'Vergessen Sie es … !' ('Forget it … !'). While the number of bars in each section and in the movement as a whole are multiples of Berg's number, 23, the metronome marking of $\downarrow$ = 150 is a multiple of Hanna's 10. Finally, the twelve-note row that forms the basis of the Allegro sections of the third movement derives from that used in the first movement, but now modified by exchanging the fourth and tenth notes of the original so that the notes of the A–B♭–F–H cell appear adjacently. The choice of row forms and transpositions is restricted to those that embody permutations of this cell.

Now that we know of the annotated score, we can see that the relationship between the musical material and the extra-musical programme of the *Lyric Suite* is not unlike that between the musical material and the programme of its immediate predecessor, the Chamber Concerto. In his 'Open Letter' on the Chamber Concerto, which he published in February 1925, some three months before the date inscribed at the head of the Allegro misterioso of the *Lyric Suite*, Berg had drawn attention to the cryptographic and numerological features of the work, describing the way in which the letters of three names 'Arnold Schönberg', 'Anton Webern' and 'Alban Berg' had been used as a source of musical material and the all-embracing role which the resulting number three played in the piece.[6] By giving us detailed, concrete evidence about the way in which the extra-musical programme of the *Lyric Suite* affects the structure and technical aspects of the work, however, Perle demonstrated that the kind of cryptographic and numerological procedures that Berg described in the 'Open Letter' were not confined to the Chamber Concerto, and suggested that there was, at the very least, a strong possibility that Berg might have adopted a similar strategy in works other than the two that we now knew about.

Even with the evidence of the annotated score, however, it would have been difficult to do more than speculate about the programmes of other works had it not, coincidentally, become possible for scholars to gain access to Berg's sketches and manuscripts. In August 1976, five months before Perle's discovery of the *Lyric Suite* score, the composer's widow Helene had died, and gradually over the next year the material from the Berg estate (some of which had already been deposited in the Austrian National Library and some of which remained at the Bergs' flat in Trauttmansdorffgasse) was brought together, catalogued and for the first time made freely available for scholarly study. Now, with the evidence of the sketches, it became clear that, even for the Chamber Concerto, Berg had revealed only a handful of his programmatic secrets. 'If it became known,' Berg had said in his Open Letter dedicating the work to Schoenberg, 'how much friendship, love and a world of human and spiritual references I have smuggled into these three movements, the adherents of programme music – should there be any left – would go mad with joy.'[7]

What Berg had not revealed, but what the sketches for the work make clear, is that 'Friendship', 'Love' and 'the World' are the secret titles of the three movements, and that each of the variations of the first movement depicts a different member of the Schoenberg circle.[8] Nor, understandably, had he told Schoenberg that the Adagio charts the breakdown of the relationship between Schoenberg and his first wife Mathilde following her affair with the painter Richard Gerstl. As Berg's annotations make clear, the large-scale palindromic structure of the second movement represents Mathilde's decline into illness after leaving Gerstl in 1908 and returning to Schoenberg, while the situation between the three of them is alluded to through a reference to the 'Melisande' theme from Schoenberg's own *Pelleas und Melisande* and through a figuration that transforms the letters of the name Mathilde into musical notation.[9] Moreover, as we know from sketches, letters and a variety of internal evidence, the Chamber Concerto also contains a host of other personal allusions, some of which we recognise and understand,[10] some of which we know about without fully understanding their significance,[11] and some of which will perhaps always remain a secret. Starting in the first movement as a kind of Viennese 'Enigma' Variations and ending, perhaps, as a kind of *Heldenleben*, the whole work, in effect, paints a picture of the personal relationships and the professional standing of the Schoenberg school at that time.

After the *Lyric Suite*, the affair with Hanna Fuchs and its musical expression through her cipher B–F and her number 10 were to be among the secrets at the centre of all Berg's remaining compositions. In the following work, *Der Wein*, he returned to the set of Baudelaire poems that had provided the secret text of the sixth movement of the *Lyric Suite* and composed a concert aria that – referring obliquely through its title to Hanna's husband who was a great wine connoisseur and the owner of a famous cellar – takes up again the theme of lost love and the resulting solitude that had been the subject of the Allegro desolato:

> What has it to do with anyone other than you, Hanna, if I say, in 'The Wine of the Lovers', "Let us fly breast to breast, without resting, to my dream land" and these words are accompanied by the lightest of B and F majors? And what can follow then but the song of 'The Wine of the Solitary Man'? That I am and that I remain.[12]

And in the Violin Concerto, Hanna's number stands at the very head of the work, with our attention drawn to it by the wholly superfluous indication

'Introduction 10 bars', while Berg's 23 determines, amongst other things, the point at which the fate rhythm of Part II first appears (bar 23) and the metronome marking ($\bullet = 69$) of the Allegro. The last bar of the Concerto, bar 230, finally unites Alban's and Hanna's numbers.

The Violin Concerto

The Violin Concerto is something of an exception in Berg's output, however, for in this work we have not a 'secret' programme (or even, as in the Chamber Concerto, a 'half-secret' one), but a quite explicit programme that Berg himself made public through his pupil and first biographer Willi Reich. As is well known, the Concerto is dedicated to the memory of – and was designed as a requiem for – Manon Gropius, the daughter of Alma Mahler and Walter Gropius, who died of infantile paralysis in April 1935 at the age of eighteen. According to Reich, the first Part of the Concerto, which consists of an Andante and an Allegretto, paints a portrait of Manon, while the Allegro and the final Adagio of Part II depict her illness and death.[13] This programmatic interpretation of the work springs directly from Berg himself – and indeed many of the words that appear in Reich's description of the Concerto appear in Berg's sketches for Part II, where the annotations 'cries', 'groans' and other programmatic references appear above specific musical figurations; the chord at the climax of the opening Allegro of Part II, for example, is labelled *Lahmungsakkord* – 'Kinderlahmung' being the German name for the illness from which Manon died.

We may well wonder why both Berg's 23 and Hanna's 10 play so prominent a role in the structure of a work about, and dedicated to, Manon Gropius, and, as I have argued elsewhere, there is enough internal evidence in the piece to suggest the existence of another, more autobiographical, programme – a programme in which Berg consciously saw the Concerto as a requiem for himself, as well as Manon, and took the opportunity to write into the work a number of references to both his first love, Marie Scheuchl, and his last love Hanna Fuchs.[14] The sketches for the work make clear, however, that for some considerable length of time Berg had in mind yet another, third, programme and that the idea of the Manon programme occurred to him only when he was some way into the piece.

One of the earliest sketches for the Concerto is a formal plan that Berg made in his diary in March 1935. This shows that, even at that stage, he intended the Concerto to be in two Parts – with Part I consisting of an improvisatory Andante (Berg uses the word 'phantasierend') followed by

a ländler-like Allegretto, and Part II consisting of an Adagio chorale movement separated by a cadenza from a final Allegro rondo. This formal plan,
which predates Manon's death by some five or six weeks, thus shows that
from the outset Berg intended that the Concerto should include a set of
chorale variations, but that he originally thought of these variations as
forming the opening movement of Part II and did not, initially, see them
as having the programmatic significance (or rather the same programmatic significance) that they have in the final work.

The point at which Berg decided to use the Bach funeral chorale 'Es ist
genug' as the basis for the Chorale Variations which form the last movement of the Concerto as we know it, has been a matter of some controversy and discussion. All the evidence suggests, however, that, having decided at the outset that one movement of the piece was to be a set of
chorale variations, the idea of using 'Es ist genug' and of turning the work
into a tone poem in memory of Manon Gropius only occurred to Berg at
quite a late stage in the composition of the piece – well after he had settled
on the note-row of the work, as we can see from a couple of sketches that
show him trying to devise a chorale of his own based on the row of the
Violin Concerto.[15]

The extraordinary thing is that even after Berg had decided to use the
Bach funeral chorale he was for some time reluctant to abandon his original plan of having the chorale movement at the beginning of Part II.
Amongst the sketches is a draft that shows what, at one stage, was Berg's
idea of how the opening of the second Part of the Concerto might work,
the first five bars of the draft corresponding to bars 14–18 of Part II as we
know it, but leading straight into a statement of the Bach chorale, firstly in
C and then, after a change of mind, resketched in D major. Only having
done this – and the draft shows the precise moment at which Berg changed
his mind – did he decide to reverse the order of the last two movements (to
put the Allegro before the Adagio chorale movement) and, taking his pencil and making a heavy line through the sketch, write the reminder 'Über-
gang zu IIb bleibt' – ('the transition to IIb stays') – at which point the
Concerto achieved its final form.[16]

Why was Berg so reluctant to abandon the original formal scheme?
Why – even after he had decided to use the Bach funeral chorale (and thus
presumably having, at least to some extent, settled on the final programme
of the Concerto) – did he for so long cling to the idea that Part II should
open with the Adagio chorale movement and end with an Allegro rondo?
A brisk Allegro is, after all, hardly an appropriate conclusion to a work that
is intended as a requiem. The reason is, as the sketches reveal, that he was
trying to reconcile two extra-musical programmes – that one that we
know and another one that had nothing to do with Manon Gropius but

was there from the beginning, its existence clearly indicated in the earliest sketches for the work.

The original programme of the Violin Concerto first appears on the page in Berg's diary immediately before that on which he outlines the form of the work. Halfway down this page, in the margin, there appear the initials FFFF and, alongside them, the tempo indications Allegro, Largo, Allegretto, Rubato. The meaning of these initials and their relation to the tempo indications is revealed further down the same page where we find the words: 'Die 4 Satzen: Frisch, Fromm, Fröhlich, Frei'– ('The 4 movements: Lively, Devout, Happy, Free') and beneath these words a sequence of roman numerals and tempo indications that show Berg reversing this original order thus:

Frisch	Fromm	Fröhlich	Frei
IV	III	II	I
	(Chorale)	Ländler	Andante

'Frei' (with the indication Andante beneath it) thus became the first movement, 'Fröhlich' the second (with the word 'Ländler' beneath), 'Fromm' ('devout') the third (with the word Chorale beneath) and finally 'Frisch', which became the fourth. The following diary page then outlines the two-part structure of the whole piece with the Chorale ('Fromm') opening Part II.[17]

The difficulties that Berg experienced with the composition of the opening of Part II came about because he wanted to retain the main features of this original plan but, whereas the first half of the plan could be adapted easily enough, the second half was incompatible with the new Manon programme and could only make programmatic sense when the order of the Adagio chorale variations and the Allegro were reversed.

Although the existence of the original FFFF programme is incontrovertible, its significance is unclear and any attempt to understand it raises some uncomfortable questions. The motto 'Frisch, Fromm, Fröhlich, Frei' – which, reversed, forms the original plan of the Concerto – was the motto of the Deutscher Turnverein. This was originally a movement formed in the early nineteenth century by Friedrich Ludwig Jahn, the so-called 'Turnvater Jahn', and concerned with the setting up of clubs devoted to gymnastics. Jahn was a fervent patriot who believed that physical education was a cornerstone, not only of the health, but of the very identity of a nation, and the motto of the Turnverein was a slogan adopted by many German youth and nationalist groups that were active in the early decades of this century. Certainly the distinctive four F symbol, which we find in the first sketch for the Violin Concerto and which had been the symbol of the Deutscher Turnverein since the mid-1840s, and the rhyme 'Frisch,

Fromm, Fröhlich, Frei ist der Deutscher Turnerei' would be well know to any German or Austrian of Berg's generation.

What, then, are we to make of Berg's original plan of basing the Violin Concerto on a slogan associated with German nationalism? We have it on the authority of Adorno[18] that Berg was completely free of the anti-semitism that was such a feature of Viennese life at the period and we know that throughout the 1930s Berg lent his name to and supported the periodical *23* – a periodical that contained a number of outspoken and courageous attacks on the artistic policies, and often on the leading figures, of the Third Reich; yet we also know that, in those passages in Act III scene 1 of *Lulu* that include the Jewish banker, Berg made some additions to Wedekind that both Schoenberg and Erwin Stein regarded as anti-Semitic – additions that were one of the reasons for Schoenberg refusing to complete the orchestration of the opera.

George Perle has argued eloquently, invoking Berg's admiration for Karl Kraus and *Die Fackel*, in defence of Berg's handling of the character of the banker in *Lulu*.[19] Yet, while it is impossible to know for certain why Berg initially chose to base the Violin Concerto on an overtly nationalist slogan, it is difficult to avoid the thought, voiced by Schoenberg in response to the *Lulu* libretto, that in doing so Berg perhaps hoped to find favour with the National Socialist Party.[20] On the other hand, it seems more a sign of political naivety than opportunism to imagine that anything as footling as the addition of a few phrases to the libretto of *Lulu* or the basing of a work on a nationalist motto (and a nationalist motto used backwards at that) would make the chance of performance of these works in the Germany of the Third Reich more likely. The Hindemith affair of 1934, when Goebbels publicly denounced atonality as 'furnishing the most dramatic proof of how strongly the Jewish intellectual infection had taken hold of the national body' had surely shown Berg that it was his musical language that made his work politically unacceptable and placed it firmly in the category of degenerate art – and yet this language remained unaffected by considerations of political expediency.

It is, I think, possible to read a quite different meaning into Berg's intended use of this FFFF motto than that which immediately suggests itself. It is a reading that rests on the fact that Berg, from the outset, chose to use this motto backwards. Backwards or retrograde motion is a particular feature of Berg's music (the Violin Concerto is the only mature work of Berg's that does not include a large scale retrograde or palindrome) and in both the operas and the instrumental music – as Berg's annotation in the third movement of the *Lyric Suite* makes clear – such retrograde motion always has a special symbolic significance in that it is consistently associated with negation or denial.[21]

By the time Berg wrote the Violin Concerto his music was labelled as a manifestation of 'cultural bolshevism' and was no longer played in Germany or even his native Austria. He himself was reviled in the press ('Hindemith', wrote one newspaper at the time of the 1934 affair, wrote music fit only for an atmosphere 'characterised by the names of Alban Berg, Arthur Honegger and Béla Bartók') and was no longer regarded as an indigenous composer.[22] The Violin Concerto, with its ländlers, waltzes and folk tunes, is the most overtly Austrian of all Berg's works and, given the consistent metaphoric significance that Berg attached to retrograde movement, it seems at least possible that in basing the work on the FFFF motto backwards he intended the retrograde to have the same significance as his use of musical retrogrades elsewhere. Berg's reversal of the phrase 'Frisch, Fromm, Fröhlich, Frei' thus symbolises a rejection – albeit a private act of rejection, since no one who heard the piece would ever be aware of the role played by the motto in the structure of the piece – rather than an endorsement, of the nationalism inherent in the motto. It was a rejection that came from a composer whose works were no longer regarded as forming any part of German music, of that narrow nationalism that denied him (and others) a place in the German tradition of which he felt himself so much a part.

The significance of *Wozzeck*

Recent research has accustomed us to the fact that, far from being purely detached essays in technique, much of even the free atonal and twelve-note music of the Second Viennese School has its origins in some kind of subjective programme.[23] For the most part such programmes were 'inspirational forces' which had little effect on the formal organisation of the music[24] and remained private and unrevealed – not least because, by the 1920s, the heyday of programme music was past and a new æsthetic of objectivity was being pursued by the youngest and most radical composers.

Berg's 'programmes', however, are of a different order. Clearly he, like many composers, felt the need for some extra-musical starting point as a way of stimulating his creative imagination; but the detailed autobiographical nature of the programmes, and the way in which these details are embodied in the very structure of the music, make them essentially different from the more generalised programmes that served as a starting point for his colleagues. *Wozzeck* seems to be the crucial work in Berg's adoption of this kind of detailed autobiographical programme. It is significant that there is not a single non-operatic work after *Wozzeck* that does not – and not a single work before it that does – have an extra-musical programme of this kind.[25]

One of the most discussed aspects of *Wozzeck*, and the one to which Berg himself drew most attention and of which he was especially proud, is its use of the forms of 'absolute' instrumental music – and its use of these forms in such a way that they reflect both the psychological and dramatic kernel of the scene and the tiniest detail of the dramatic action while, at the same time, retaining their autonomy as self-sufficient musical structures.[26] Discussing Berg's preoccupation with the technical and formal aspects of his operas, Christopher Hailey has perceptively described the composer's use of such forms in an operatic context as a symptom of his artistic need 'to reconcile the lower impulses of theatre with the requirements of "high art", the sensual self-indulgence of his Viennese heritage with the discipline of the Classical legacy'.[27] It is an observation that is equally applicable to one of the roles which Berg's secret programmes play in the instrumental music, in which the emotional intensity and 'sensual self-indulgence' are not only held in check by, but are themselves transformed into, controlling factors that distance him from the feelings expressed, so that 'subjective elements are transformed into objective restraints which, paradoxically, both embody and curb the subjectivity from which they sprang'.[28]

Wozzeck, like *Lulu*, is full of autobiographical allusions, and it is striking how closely the tactics adopted in the post-*Wozzeck* instrumental music mirror those adopted in the opera. In the opera, Berg chooses to impose 'abstract', self-contained musical forms (albeit forms of which he hoped that the audience would be unaware)[29] onto an existing narrative; in the later non-operatic works, he chooses to impose a narrative (albeit a 'secret' one of which the listener would be unaware) onto the abstract, self-sufficient forms of the instrumental music. Essentially the procedure in both the operatic and instrumental works is identical: the creation of a situation in which the demands of the textual narrative – whether operatic plot or secret programme – and the demands of the autonomous musical structures become identical. Stimulated and inspired by his work on *Wozzeck*, and having succeeded so magnificently in reconciling absolute musical forms with an existing story line, Berg then set about creating secret story lines for the instrumental works; having shaped the libretto of the opera to ensure that it lent itself to be set as sonata forms, passacaglias, variations and so on, he then began to take care to devise secret programmes, shaped in such a way that both the whole and the details were capable of being transformed into satisfactory and 'absolute' musical structures. Many pages of the annotated score of the *Lyric Suite* outline a narrative as detailed as the story line of any opera, and it seems not only possible but likely that in Berg's mind many movements had even more specific programmes than his annotations reveal. Mark DeVoto has drawn attention to

> the final chord of the second movement, Andante amoroso [bar 150], sustained after the pizzicato C's in the cello ('Wie aus der Ferne. Do-Do') have died away. Here the Tristan chord is transposed down a perfect fifth, but otherwise maintains its characteristic spacing. The signification is plain: Hanna's children have run off to play somewhere else, while Alban and Hanna are left to contemplate their love for each other.[30]

Similarly, although according to Dorothea Robetin the love affair between Berg and her mother was never consummated, it is difficult not to wonder whether the passage at bars 51–8 of the Adagio appassionato does not represent such a consummation – whether real or imaginary.

After *Wozzeck*, the invention of some kind of extra-musical story line became so habitual and necessary a part of Berg's working methods that one is inclined to agree with Adorno who, writing to Helene Berg following the composer's death, advised her not to worry about the affair with Hanna since Berg 'didn't write the *Lyric Suite* because he fell in love with Hanna Fuchs but fell in love with Hanna Fuchs in order to write the *Lyric Suite*'.[31] But the adoption of such secret narratives seems to have satisfied a number of needs in Berg's creative and personal psychology and there are, perhaps, additional reasons why he felt it important that the precise details of autobiographical events should be embodied in the music – irrespective of whether or not anyone else ever knew what these events were. They are reasons which, again, first come to the fore in *Wozzeck*.

Reviewing the publication of the diaries of Berg's contemporary and fellow Viennese Arthur Schnitzler, Edward Timms has observed that 'Schnitzler's writings are haunted by evanescence. The painstaking attempt to record how he spent every morning, every afternoon, every evening of his adult life emerges as an attempt to fortify the self against transience and oblivion. It is an exercise in self-confirmation.'[32] Time and the passage of time are central themes of Berg's first opera, and his obsessive recording of the details of his own emotional life in his works can, like Schnitzler's, be seen as an attempt in some way to make permanent the transient, to assert and maintain the reality of individual experience in the face of the fatefully revolving world and endless passage of time that so preoccupy both the Captain and the Doctor in *Wozzeck*.

In a letter to Hanna dated October 1931, Berg distinguishes between the inner person and 'the exterior person, the one I have been forced to present myself as to my fellow human beings ... and who might for a time be fulfilled with the joys of motoring but could never be able to compose *Lulu*.[33] The inner, private Berg was a man who felt – who wanted to feel – that the whole of his life was governed by some strange preordained destiny; a man who would examine tram tickets[34] and postmarks to see whether they contained his fateful number (and would go through extraordinary mathematical convolutions to ensure that they did),[35] who, having worked the number 23 into the structure of the second part of the Violin Concerto, took pains to see that the first part took 23 manuscript pages in the short score; a man eager to accept any theory or to read significance into any coincidence that seemed to confirm his sense that everything was pre-destined. A belief in such things was common in the Vienna of Berg's day, and even without the testament of friends and colleagues like Adorno and Louis Krasner, Berg's letters and compositions themselves provide evidence enough of his interest in numerology, astrology and predestination. Indeed, as I have argued elsewhere, Berg, through purely musical means, identifies not only time but also predestination as central subjects of both *Wozzeck* and *Lulu*.[36]

Berg's first stay with the Fuchs-Robettin family and his first meeting with Hanna came about as a result of his attending a Prague performance of the *Three Fragments from 'Wozzeck'* – pieces, from an opera completed four years earlier, in which the notes of her initials already act as a fate motif. As George Perle has pointed out, 'it is unlikely that a man of Berg's predisposition would have failed to notice what would have struck him as a prophetic coincidence'.[37] Berg's feeling that Hanna Fuchs represented his destiny was further confirmed when, following their meeting, he went back through his earlier works and discovered afresh that the first and last notes of the opening motif of his String Quartet Op. 3 were the notes F♮–B♮ and that the opening bar of the second movement of his newly-composed Chamber Concerto (significantly entitled 'Love' in the sketches) contained both her and his initials.

Berg had already realised that there were similarities between his situation and the situation of the protagonist of Büchner's play *Woyzeck*. 'There is something of me in his [Wozzeck's] character', he wrote to Helene on 7 August 1918,[38] referring ostensibly to the similarities between the world of the down-trodden Wozzeck and his own experiences in the war years – although he cannot have helped, in his own mind at least, thinking of the similarity between himself and Wozzeck as fathers of an illegitimate child by a woman called Marie.[39] The recognition of these similarities might, indeed, have played a role in his deciding to set the play, just as some years later a recognition of the similarities between the names and situations of Alwa and Schön and Alban and Schoenberg, and the similarities between the deaths of Richard Gerstl and Wedekind's painter, must have influenced his decision to set *Lulu*. The meeting with Hanna can only have confirmed the sense that *Wozzeck* not only reflected his own life but in some uncanny way anticipated it.

'Lines, circles, mysterious figures – if only one could read them', sings Wozzeck in Act I scene 4, accompanied by a flurry of inversionally and palindromically symmetrical figurations, of the mysterious patterns that he sees in nature. Wozzeck's obsessions are those of Berg himself, and, as Geoffrey Poole has suggested, 'if the constant recurrence of such patterns in day-to-day life – whether real or imaginary – provided an illusion of order and purpose then that illusion must in its turn have brought a measure of real security'.[40] In 1919, when Berg had already started his work on *Wozzeck*, the Viennese biologist Paul Kammerer published a book entitled *Das Gesetz der Serie* ('The Law of Seriality') in which, believing that 'coincidence rules to such an extent that the concept of coincidence itself is negated' he attempted to set out the unexplored laws of 'seriality'. The final pages of the book express a belief with which Berg would doubtless have agreed. The action of seriality, wrote Kammerer, 'is ubiquitous and continuous in life, nature and cosmos. The law of seriality is the umbilical cord that connects thought, feeling, science and art with the womb of the universe which gave birth to them.'[41]

9 Compositional process in *Wozzeck* and *Lulu*: a glimpse of Berg's atonal method

Patricia Hall
University of California at Santa Barbara

If we compare the inceptions of *Wozzeck* and *Lulu*, the apparent differences outweigh the similarities. They were begun thirteen years apart: *Wozzeck* in 1914 when Berg was relatively unknown, *Lulu* in 1927 after he had become famous from the success of *Wozzeck*. Moreover, this thirteen-year gap is reflected in two dissimilar compositional systems. *Wozzeck* is an atonal opera with latent tonal tendencies, while *Lulu* is a mature twelve-note work employing serial techniques. Berg emphasises these contrasting systems in his writings on the operas: in his lecture on *Wozzeck* (1929), he focuses almost entirely on dramatic, formal and leitmotivic devices,[1] while with *Lulu* he takes pains to justify the unity arising from his cyclically derived twelve-note rows.[2]

It is perhaps surprising, then, to find that the sketches for the two works have identical formats, and that Berg used these formats to accomplish similar goals. This suggests a continuity not only in his working methods, but also between the two compositional systems – atonality and dodecaphony. This chapter will compare the formats of Berg's sketches for *Wozzeck* and *Lulu* – from his earliest work on the libretti to his final compositional sketches – in order to address two analytical questions. First, do the sketches suggest similarities between Berg's atonal and twelve-note technique? And second, might the sketches give us a more precise grasp of Berg's atonal method?[3]

From text to music: Berg's melodic shorthand

In the beginning was the drama. Berg was an avid reader and attender of plays. It was a performance in Vienna of Georg Büchner's *Woyzeck* in 1914 that gave him the subject for his first opera.[4] Similarly, a lecture by Karl Kraus at the private premiere of Frank Wedekind's *Pandora's Box* in 1905 first suggested ideas about character doublings and form that Berg would

Figure 9.1   Sketch for *Wozzeck*, Act II scene 2 (ÖNB, Musiksammlung, F 21 Berg 13/II, p. 61)

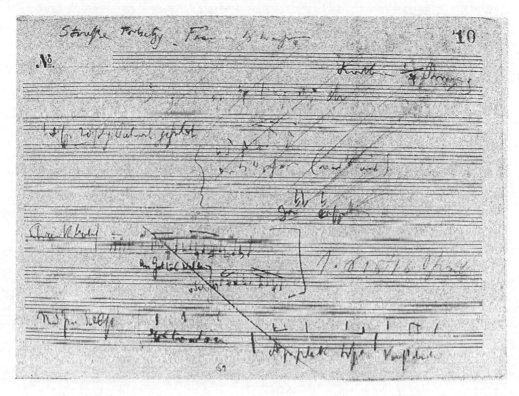

later develop into characteristic features of his operatic treatment of the Lulu tragedies.[5]

Because Berg adapted the libretti for both operas from their respective plays, his own copies of these plays – preserved in the Österreichische Nationalbibliothek – contain the expected underlinings and deletions of text. But they also contain detailed musical annotations that suggest Berg took inspiration for rhythmic, melodic and formal ideas from the printed word. Similarly, his musical sketches are often repeatedly annotated with seminal text fragments. These fragments, through their natural accent or psychological implications, generate important unifying musical motives. For instance, in one of the earliest sketches for *Wozzeck*, shown in Figure 9.1, Berg focuses on the textual fragment 'In vier Wochen' ('In four weeks') to generate an important motivic idea for Act II scene 2. In the centre of the upper margin Berg writes 'Frau in 4 Wochen', and on stave four he experiments with a melodic setting. The abbreviated rhythmic figure on stave seven (♩♪♪♪), which Berg labels 'horror motive' ('Schreckmotif'), reminds us of the psychological bent of many of his sketches. Indeed, he often found it necessary to psychoanalyse primary characters before com-

Figure 9.2   (a) Sketch for *Wozzeck*, Act II scene 2 (F 21 Berg 13/II, p. 76, st. 6–10)

(b) Sketch for *Lulu*, Prologue (F 21 Berg 28/XXV, f. 3ᵛ, st. 1–4)

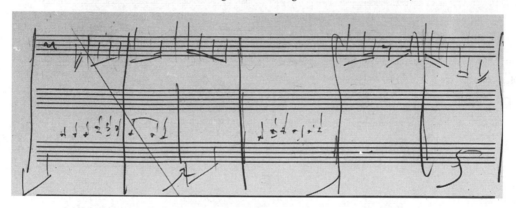

posing their music. One sketch gives a fascinating psychological analysis of the Captain, whom Berg describes as 'a nothing' ('eine Null').[6]

Berg rarely transformed these motivic sketches directly into compositional drafts. Rather, he wrote passages in a rhythmic shorthand, usually focusing on the vocal line. Figure 9.2 shows two rhythmic sketches, one for *Wozzeck* and the other for *Lulu*. Setting aside the obvious differences in handwriting and paper types, the sketching technique is essentially the same. Both sketches feature the rhythmic skeleton and contour of the vocal line in the upper stave. In the *Wozzeck* sketch, with some effort, one can make out the words 'Dr.' in bar 1, 'Sargnagel' ('Coffin nail') in bars 2–3 and 'in 4 Wochen' ('in four weeks') in bar 5. This excerpt, then, is again from Act II scene 2, where the Captain and the Doctor taunt each other until Wozzeck appears on the scene as a more convenient victim for them both (Example 9.1a). The *Lulu* sketch has a distinct rhythm in the vocal line (stave one), and even a few pitches (above stave three, which should be construed with a bass clef). These pitches (C–E–F) express a motive that first appears in the Prologue; indeed, the sketched passage is bars 9–11 (Example 9.1b). Although the pitches are not part of a full twelve-note

Example 9.1   (a) *Wozzeck*, Act II scene 2, bars II/249–54, vocal part (Captain)

(b) *Lulu*, Prologue, bars 9–11, vocal part (Animal Tamer)

row in this sketch, they in fact correspond to the first three notes of the basic series for *Lulu*.

If we compare these sketches with their respective composed passages, it is clear that Berg's shorthand was fairly accurate – that is to say, he would retain essentially the same rhythms and melodic contours in the final version. This suggests that Berg was already familiar in his mind with the melodic line – either from previous thematic sketches, or (in *Lulu*) from charts of twelve-note rows with indications of their thematic potential.[7] By creating this interim stage of composition, Berg was generally able to avoid the ugly battles and constant revision we observe so often in, for instance, Beethoven's sketches.

Pitch collections and centricity

Investigating Berg's compositional sketches can help us to understand his use of pitch collections and centricity in both his atonal and serial writing. This provides insight into the stylistic richness of his music, and into the continuity between his earlier and later compositions.

Berg's sketches for both *Wozzeck* and *Lulu* are frequently hybridised, in the sense that they incorporate features of two or more sketch formats. The sketch for the opening of *Lulu* shown in Figure 9.3 is technically a *compositional sketch* because it features an actual passage of the opera (or at least the passage as Berg envisaged it in 1928 – he later discarded this version altogether).[8] But it is also what Beethoven scholars refer to as a *concept sketch*, because it is more concerned with the 'idea' of the passage

Figure 9.3   Concept sketch for the opening of *Lulu* (F 21 Berg 28/XVI, f. 2)

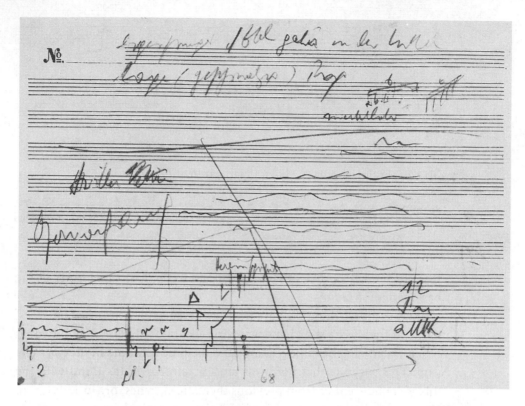

or the depiction of the event than with the actual details of serial or atonal writing. This suggests that Berg often had an æsthetic idea in mind, which he progressively forged by manipulating his atonal or twelve-note materials.

A surprising quantity of the compositional sketches for *Wozzeck* concern Berg's experiments with tonality – not only in the folk idioms that he infuses with a kind of fractured tonality, allowing us to perceive a ländler, a lullaby or a march, but often in passages that analysts have treated as atonal. The sketch transcribed in Example 9.2 shows Berg working on the opening of *Wozzeck*, Act I scene 2, in which Wozzeck and Andres cut reeds together. Like the sketch of the *Lulu* Prologue, this has features of a concept sketch. The 'idea' here is a sonority of five notes, alternating with a high D. The three five-note sonorities that Berg shows in the sketch would eventually evolve into the three chords that appear at the opening of the scene in the definitive version (Example 9.3). Berg spends a substantial amount of time in his famous lecture on *Wozzeck* discussing the unifying properties of these chords, which he likens to a tonal matrix of tonic, dominant and subdominant.[9]

Example 9.2   Transcription of F 21 Berg 13/II, p. 90

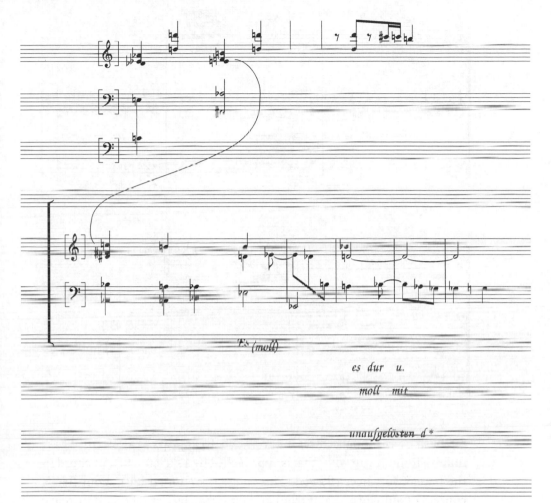

In the centre of the sketch, Berg experiments with a wedge formation which converges on Eb in the bass. He makes the annotation 'Es (moll)' and then 'Es dur und moll mit unaufgelösten d' ('Eb major and minor with unresolved D').[10] The sketch and Berg's annotation reveal two ideas about Berg's concept of atonality in this passage of the opera. First, he is working with a defined collection of notes – Eb minor combined with Eb major. Second, he consciously experiments with unresolved tendency tones within this collection – here, scale degree seven. These tendency tones act as a tonal foil for the collection, giving rise to the unsettling, unresolved quality we associate with atonal music.

Even though modal mixture of major and minor is a common tonal technique, it implies a large collection of notes: ten to be exact. Throw in an accidental or two, and you have all twelve notes. How, then, did Berg

Example 9.3   *Wozzeck*, Act I scene 2, bars I/201–6

establish E♭ as a tonal centre? In the sketch, E♭ appears as a sustained bass note – a tonic, if you will – that is approached by a skeleton of a V⁷ chord in the lower two voices (B♭–A♭). This suggests one final idea about Berg's concept of atonality: that it relies on hierarchy. Berg emphasised primary notes of a key, such as scale degrees one and five, while leaving tendency tones unresolved. With these tensions further articulated by the registral layout and orchestration, there is an eerie quality to the opening of the scene, in which the high D sounds at odds with the rest of the orchestra. Berg presents these chords again at the end of the scene, connected by a scale-like passage in the upper voice. Although it is not clear whether he is really establishing a key centre, our ear nonetheless allows us to hear some of the notes of the upper voice as harmonic, and others as accented passing notes. I have always been moved by this passage – a saving grace for Wozzeck. He may hallucinate and rant like a lunatic, but the music, with its relentless sinking march, reminds us that he is a victim of his environment.

In other tonal sketches for *Wozzeck*, Berg frequently emphasises altered scale degrees not accounted for by mixture. In a sketch for Act III scene 1,

Example 9.4   Transcription of F 21 Berg 13/I, p. 36, st. 3–4

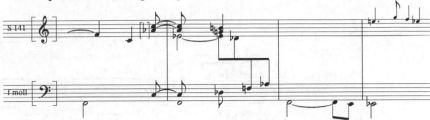

where Marie reads the Bible and ponders her fate, Berg emphasises the pitch B♮, even though he labels the excerpt F minor (see Example 9.4). F minor is strongly established by the sustained F in the bass and scale degree five in the upper voice, but then foiled with the raised scale degree four. The notes B♮ and F♮ then become linked in the motive associated with Marie's death.[11]

Similar extended passages of tonal illusion take place in *Lulu*, very often at emotionally cathartic moments. These 'great tonal moments' often occur when a character finally expresses pent up feelings of love and passion. One such moment occurs when, in Act II scene 1, Alwa finally admits to Lulu that he loves her (Example 9.5). The moment is prepared by a two-bar introduction, and a motion from V^7 to I – to some extent similar to our sketch of the opening of Act 1 scene 2 of *Wozzeck*. Berg has prepared the ground for this passage quite thoroughly. In his sketches he drafts, in flow-chart style, a diagram that shows Alwa's vocal style evolving from the speaking voice without music (his entrance at bar II/239) to the *molto cantabile* of this passage some eighty bars later.[12]

There are certainly inherent tonal elements in the primary row for the Rondo: for that matter, Berg himself refers in his sketches to the minor triad that initiates Alwa's primary row form (the triad can be seen in Example 9.5 at Alwa's first words, 'Eine Seele': C♯–A♮–F♯). But more importantly, Berg voices his rows to maximise this inherent tonality. Note, for instance the F♯ in the bass of bar II/320 which combines with the vocal line to suggest an arrival in F♯ minor. Similarly, at the end of the same phrase, the bass, now transposed, leaps from G♯ to C♯ to enhance the sense of a 'modulation' to C♯ minor. The vocal line, meanwhile, joins the last note of Alwa's series at P$_1$ with the first note of P$_8$ to form a 6–5 suspension (A♯–G♯). This reminds us that Berg's tonal illusion is heavily dependent on metre as well.

Sketches for other passages of *Lulu*, such as the Duet between the Painter and Lulu in Act I scene 1 (bars I/305ff.), show Berg resorting to the elaborate combination of fragments from different series so as to maintain and develop motivic shapes.[13] Here, although he does not abandon serialism, Berg is nonetheless at the outer limits of serial ordering. In

Example 9.5   *Lulu*, Act II scene 1, bars II/318–23

truth, the Duet exhibits the typical motivic variation (elaboration, expansion and contraction of intervals) found in atonal music.

In both his operas, Berg combines elements of tonality, atonality and (in *Lulu*) serial writing, which he fine-tunes depending on the dramatic situation. There is little of this integration in Berg's first serial composition, the song 'Schliesse mir die Augen beide' (1925). In his sketches for the song,[14] Berg compulsively labels almost every note to show its serial order number – it is apparent that he is not enjoying his first foray with the twelve-note method – and the result has always sounded mechanical to me, and un-Bergian. Although Berg's sketches for *Wozzeck* and *Lulu* do not present us with every detail of an easily definable musical language, they allow us to see that as Berg's twelve-note technique evolved forward it also circled backward, enabling him once more to achieve the expressive effects of his earlier atonal and tonal works.

10   Compositional technique 1923–6: the Chamber Concerto and the *Lyric Suite*

Neil Boynton
University of Lancaster

The two major works of the period 1923 to 1926 – the Chamber Concerto (1923–5) and the *Lyric Suite* (1925–6) – embodied major developments in Berg's compositional technique. Between these two scores, Berg composed his second setting of Theodor Storm's poem 'Schliesse mir die Augen beide', which, in a letter to Webern, he described as his 'first attempt at a strict twelve-note composition'.[1] Roughly speaking, the Chamber Concerto is mostly atonal, while the *Lyric Suite* is mostly twelve-note, although the Chamber Concerto does contain 'passages that correspond to the laws [...] for "composition with twelve notes related only to one another"' and, conversely, the second and fourth movements of the *Lyric Suite*, as well as parts of the third and fifth, are 'free' in 'style'.[2] Twelve-note composition thus connects all three of these works and is the central topic addressed in this chapter.

Klein and Hauer

Berg's twelve-note technique has always been recognised as different from that of Schoenberg and Webern, and, as Douglas Jarman writes, 'although characteristics of both Schoenberg's and [Josef Matthias] Hauer's systems can be found in Berg's music, none of his works employs either method exclusively'.[3] The import of this statement has been scrutinised by the American musicologist Arved Ashby, who questions the significance of Hauer's theory of tropes for Berg's twelve-note technique and suggests that 'the concept of additional, systematically derived rows', which in practice sets Berg's technique apart from that of Schoenberg and Webern, originated in the work of Berg's pupil Fritz Heinrich Klein (1892–1977).[4]

 Working from source materials for 'Schliesse mir' II and the *Lyric Suite*, Ashby has documented, among other things, Berg's 'appropriation' of Klein's *Mutterakkord* ('mother chord'), its associated all-interval row, the partitioning of the row into diatonic chords, and Klein's method of deriv-

Example 10.1   (a) Berg to Schoenberg, 13 July 1926: first form of the all-interval row

(b) derivation of 'rows of fourths and fifths'

* ms. has B♮

(c) scale segments and diatonic chords derived from permuted hexachords

ing a second all-interval form of the row from the first – all of which are to be found in the analytical preface to Klein's *Variationen* for piano, Op. 14 (1924).[5] Ashby notes that in a letter to Schoenberg of 13 July 1926, which describes twelve-note techniques employed in the *Lyric Suite*:

> [Berg] repeats many of Klein's points [from the preface to the *Variationen*] and states them in the same order. Tellingly, Klein mentions the capacity of the row for producing scales and a continuous circle of fifths, two characteristics that would prove significant in the first movement of the *Lyric Suite*.[6]

Example 10.1 reproduces the first three of the musical examples from Berg's letter, showing the first form of the all-interval row, the derivation of 'rows of fourths and fifths', and the permuted forms of each hexachord that reveal the derivation of scale segments and diatonic chords.[7]

Ashby also draws an interesting comparison between the twelve-note structure of 'Schliesse mir' II and a twelve-note plan in the sketches for the *Lyric Suite*, both of which centre on the two forms of Klein's row that preserve all eleven intervals. In the analytical preface to the *Variationen*, Klein demonstrates a somewhat idiosyncratic method of deriving the second form from the first;[8] apparently, neither he nor Berg were aware that the two forms are related by inversion.[9] In 'Schliesse mir' II, as Perle notes:

> The sets are unfolded in a manner that provides a structural basis for the binary formal design. The permuted I_8 form [Klein's second form] ... is introduced at the beginning of the second of the two sections in a state-

ment, assigned to the piano, that echoes the statement of P$_5$ [Klein's first form] assigned to the voice in the opening bars.[10]

Ashby points out that Berg's method of deriving the second form of the row, written out in a sketch for the song, is the same as Klein's.[11] In Ashby's view, a sketch for the *Lyric Suite* suggests that

> [Berg] originally conceived the quartet as an unfolding of the relation-ships and differences between Klein's two all-interval rows ... There is every indication here that Berg believed the introduction of Klein's second form of the all-interval row would mark the primary event of the *Lyric Suite* by advancing the segmental variety of the piece to its extreme.[12]

Ashby's ideas on the twelve-note structure of these two pieces are seductive, but he perhaps overstates Klein's contribution to Berg's technique; conversely, the significance of Hauer in general is understated.

In conversation with Hauer in 1924, Schoenberg talked of them both having found the same diamond, which they were looking at from different sides.[13] Indeed, inasmuch as one can speak of twelve-note composition which is neither specifically Schoenberg's nor specifically Hauer's, by a certain point in the early 1920s the principle was considered to some extent common knowledge. Twelve-note composition in this general sense formed part of the conceptual background to Berg's development of 'a personal epistemology of twelve-tone music'.[14] It is perhaps significant that having observed the similarity between Schoenberg's row technique in the third and fourth variations of the third movement of the Serenade Op. 24 and Hauer's canonic techniques,[15] Martina Sichardt is unable to establish whether there had been an exchange of ideas between the two men as early as 1920, when Schoenberg's variation movement was composed.[16] And, since Hauer's *Atonale Musik* for piano, Op. 20, in which he first uses the 'second canonic technique', was composed between 1920 and 1922, it is not possible to show that Schoenberg appropriated Hauer's techniques, nor, *vice versa*, Hauer Schoenberg's. Rather, as their reported conversation acknowledges, it seems likely that both of them arrived independently at more or less the same thing.[17] The independence of their paths must nonetheless be qualified in light of their common theoretical concerns. The same can be said of Berg. It is not surprising, therefore, to find in Hauer's *Etüden* Op. 22 (composed 1922–3)[18] the derivation of fifths and scale segments from the source hexachord which generates Klein's all-interval row (see Example 10.2).

Permutation is perhaps the idea most frequently associated with Hauer's name. Indeed, in discussing the subsidiary sets in the first movement of the *Lyric Suite*, Jarman observes that 'the internal permutations to

Example 10.2   Hauer, *Etüden*, No. 8, bars 73–80

which the two hexachords of the basic set are subjected suggests the trope system of Hauer'.[19] The tonal character of Hauer's atonal and twelve-note music is also striking, particularly in connection with the music of Berg. As early as 1916 Hauer visited Egon Wellesz, a member of the Schoenberg circle, and played him some of his pieces. From this meeting Wellesz reported that each of the short pieces 'represented a *Nomos*, and the *Nomos* consisted of twelve notes […]. This meant that each melody represented the whole compass of the chromatic scale, but the tones were chosen in such a clever way that the layout of a row sounded almost diatonic.'[20] A third feature of Hauer's work is the derivation of rhythm from the particular arrangements of the tropes which he termed *Bausteine* (building blocks).[21] In his 'second canonic technique', the entry of each new note is separated from the entry of the previous note by one unit of duration, a technique which is not dissimilar to Berg's derivation of the two main rhythms of the third movement of the *Lyric Suite*.[22] Example 10.3 reproduces the first *Baustein* of the first example of this technique in *Die Lehre von den Tropen*, which is based on a transposed form of Hauer's Trope 23.[23] It is given first in Hauer's 'twelve-note notation' and then in 'the old notation'. The lines of Hauer's stave system represent the black notes of the piano keyboard, while the spaces represent the white notes.

Whether and how these features of Hauer's work – Schoenberg considered Hauer's pieces more 'examples' than compositions[24] – influenced Berg remains to be decided: the degree to which it is possible to segregate individual contributions from the common theoretical knowledge of the time, as well as the significance thereof, is by no means certain. In considering Berg's appropriation of the new technical possibilities, Regina Busch

Example 10.3   (a) Hauer's second canonic technique: composer's notation

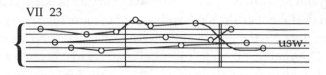

VII 23

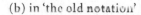

(b) in 'the old notation'

is surely right to place emphasis on what Berg did with the knowledge that was available to him rather than where he got it from, on the stages by which he arrived at his twelve-note technique rather than questions of chronological priority.[25]

Indeed, although the history of F. H. Klein's relationship with Berg has begun to be written, the inchoate nature of this history should strike a note of caution when considering Klein's theoretical writings, and not least in assessing their significance for Berg. Arved Ashby's important research has focused on the time from 1924 onwards; what is known of their association before then is by no means clear. It is not even certain when Klein first came to Berg for lessons: the dates recorded vary between 1917 and 1921, the most probable date being 1918.[26] There is thus a period of at least three years, and more likely six, between the date when Klein came as a pupil to Berg and the composition of Klein's *Variationen* in 1924. Likewise, there are almost as many dates ascribed to Klein's announcement to Berg of his discovery of the *Mutterakkord* as there are accounts of it.[27] As we have seen, Ashby shows that some of the examples in Berg's letter to Schoenberg of 13 July 1926 concerning the twelve-note technique of the *Lyric Suite* are also found in the preface to Klein's *Variationen*, but whether the authorship of the examples common to both can be wholly attributed to Klein cannot be resolved without additional evidence. Writing to Schoenberg and Kolisch, Berg made no secret of his use of Klein's row; but the fact that he did not credit Klein with anything more than this perhaps suggests that Berg did not consider the derivation of a second all-interval row (Klein's 'second form') to be his pupil's intellectual property.[28] Berg was, after all and in spite of his image as a Romantic,[29] fascinated by theoretical experimentation, much more so than Schoenberg or Webern.[30] One suspects further research, in particular an examination of the correspondence between Berg and Klein, would reveal an exchange of ideas between the two.[31]

Continuities in Berg's technique

There is further reason to be cautious about the extent of Klein's contribution to Berg's technique, since, as Douglas Jarman points out, 'in many respects the twelve-note system was simply a codification of some of the techniques which had been a feature of Berg's music from the period of the *Altenberg Lieder* onwards'.[32] The motivic-thematic working in the *Altenberg Lieder* Op. 4 and the Three Orchestral Pieces Op. 6 is suggestive of aspects of Berg's twelve-note technique, including to some degree the concept of row derivation (though not the specific technique of deriving rows according to numerical principles that is used in *Lulu*).[33] Erwin Stein's words – 'he shuffles motifs like a pack of cards, as it were, and makes them yield new melodies. The motifs of the theme reappear, but in a different arrangement'[34] – were written of Mahler, but as Jarman intimates, they might equally be applied to Berg's technique in the Orchestral Pieces.[35]

In the final version of the *Lyric Suite*, Berg did not carry through the idea that introducing the second form of Klein's all-interval row in the third movement would mark the primary compositional event of the work. Indeed, the maximal variety of intervals in Klein's row represents an extreme in Berg's choice of material, contrasting with the mono-intervallic cycles which are a general feature of his music.[36] Instead, the principal rows of the first, third and fifth movements are successively derived by exchanging pairs of notes between the two hexachords, as Berg describes in the 'Nine Pages' (pp. 3 and 6). Yet this process of derivation – 'the actual process of interchange', as Jarman writes – 'is never compositionally unfolded'.[37]

However, there is another technique that *is* involved, among other things, in row derivations that are unfolded compositionally in the *Lyric*

Example 10.4 (a) Berg: *Lyric Suite*, first movement, bars 2–4, violin I

(b) bars 42–4, viola and cello

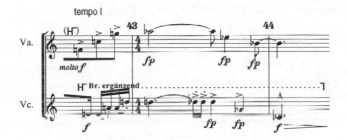

Suite. This is the splitting of a voice into two (or more) parts, three examples of which will be examined here.[38] First, the derivation from Klein's all-interval row of segments of the mono-intervallic cycles of fourths and fifths. As is evident from the stemming and beaming of notes in Berg's letter to Schoenberg of 13 July 1926, this is most directly achieved by splitting the row (see Example 10.1b). Berg shows this compositionally in bars 42–4 of the first movement: the initial statement of this figure, played by the first violin in bars 2–4, is reproduced in Example 10.4a; the split version is reproduced in Example 10.4b.[39]

Splitting occurs again in the third movement, in a manner which reveals more clearly the contrapuntal origins of this technique. The upper notes of the row serve as one voice, the lower notes as a second voice. As with Hauer's second canonic technique, the distance between successive notes is one unit of duration.[40] Berg's example from the 'Nine Pages', in which he draws attention to the rhythms that are produced by the splitting of the row, is reproduced in Example 10.5a; the first occurrence of this splitting in the movement, in which a transposed form of the row is used, is shown in Example 10.5b.[41]

Splitting is used again in the sixth movement, in a way that is contrapuntally and rhythmically similar to the example from the third movement. Here, moreover, it reveals the relationship between the two rows used in this, the final movement of the work. As Jarman explains, at bar 30 an inverted form of the row with which the movement begins (cello, bars 1–2) is split between the two violins, 'in such a way that violin 1 plays the notes of the first hexachord and violin 2 the notes of the second hexachord [of the second row]'; this second row is an inverted form of the row which

Example 10.5   (a) Musical example from Berg's 'Nine Pages on the *Lyric Suite*', p. 4

(b) *Lyric Suite*, third movement, bars 10–12

Example 10.6   (a) Musical example from Berg's 'Nine Pages on the *Lyric Suite*', p. 8

(b) *Lyric Suite*, sixth movement, bar 30

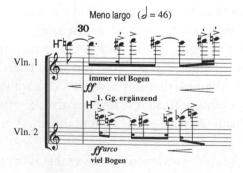

is played by the viola in bars 2–3.[42] Berg also illustrates this relationship in the 'Nine Pages' (p. 8): his example is reproduced in Example 10.6a; the music is reproduced in Example 10.6b.[43]

The technique of splitting shown in these examples from the *Lyric Suite* thus connects the derivation of interval cycles, rhythms and subsidiary rows. A fruitful comparison may be drawn with examples of similar tech-

Example 10.7   (a) Chamber Concerto, first movement, bars 66–8

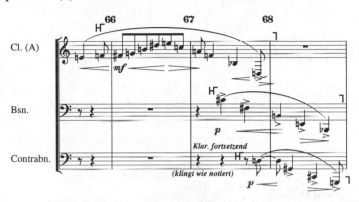

(b) third movement, bars 586–9

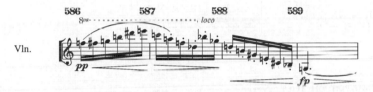

niques from Berg's earlier works. In the second variation of the first movement of the Chamber Concerto, the chain of thirds which is a constructive feature of the *Hauptstimme* in bars 63–6 is split in bars 67–8 in a manner similar to the splitting of the row in the first movement of the *Lyric Suite*.[44] Continuing the clarinet's chain of thirds, the descending arpeggio figure – which from the A♮ at the beginning of bar 67 comprises successively two augmented triads, one major triad and one diminished triad – is broken down in a way that exposes chains of perfect and diminished fifths played by the bassoon and contrabassoon (see Example 10.7a). Splitting thus mediates between chains of thirds and fifths in the Chamber Concerto, just as it mediates between the all-interval row and the segments of the fourth- and fifth-cycles in the first movement of the *Lyric Suite*. The broken line of Example 10.7a is reconstituted as a single line on its reprise in the third movement (violin, bars 586–9, Example 10.7b).[45]

In the Introduction to the third movement, splitting is applied to a descending scalar figure first presented in the *Thema* of the first movement (cor anglais, bar 17). With the introduction of an extra note, C♮, this produces two diminished triads that are registrally differentiated from each other (piano, bar 509). Example 10.8a shows the original cor anglais figure and the *Hauptstimmen* which surround it; Example 10.8b shows the corresponding passage in the third movement. The newly derived diminished triads anticipate the way the minor thirds of the upbeat figure to the first phrase of this passage (bar 507) are expanded into the diminished

Example 10.8   (a) Chamber Concerto, first movement, bars 16–19

(b) third movement, bars 507–13

Example 10.9   *Altenberg Lieder* Op. 4, bars iii/12–16 (partial texture)

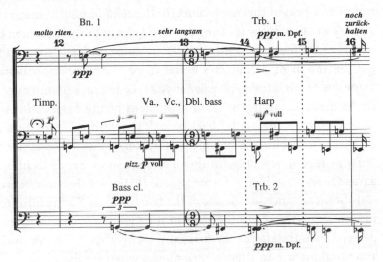

triads of the upbeat figure to the second phrase (bar 510). The splitting
here is also similar to the splitting in the first movement of the *Lyric Suite*:
both examples are concerned with the extraction of segments of interval
cycles. It is more remotely connected with the splitting in the sixth movement of the *Lyric Suite*, insofar as the splitting of the first musical figure
into two parts (*x* alternating with *y*) corresponds to a second musical figure when those two parts are presented successively (*x* followed by *y*). The
transpositional relationship between the simultaneous triads in bar 509 is,
however, different to that between the successive triads in bar 510.

The third of the *Altenberg Lieder* provides an example from significantly earlier in Berg's career. Here, an oscillating figure spanning the interval of a major sixth is introduced in the timpani in bar 12; the figure is
then passed to the strings and finally to the harp. As it is passed through
these instruments the upper note rises chromatically, while the lower note
descends. The chromatic voices implicit in this figure are picked out by the
accompanying instruments: first by the bass clarinet and first bassoon and
then by the two trombones (see Example 10.9).[46] No splitting occurs here:
rather, the contrapuntal implications of the oscillating figure are realised
in the accompaniment. It is the contrapuntal aspect of this example that
suggests an affinity with the splitting of the row in the third and sixth
movements of the *Lyric Suite*.

By comparison with the last three examples, the splitting in the *Lyric
Suite* appears to have a new-found significance – one that is principally,
though not exclusively, attached to the derivation of subsidiary rows. It is
nonetheless difficult to assess the novelty of its significance on the basis of
these few examples; furthermore, one would expect the use of splitting to

be somewhat restricted in the Chamber Concerto, since the principal technical aspect of this work concerns the *combination* of material.

Berg was to employ splitting again in *Lulu*: notably, as Jarman observes, in one of the few 'projected derivations' from the basic row of the opera, the derivation of Schigolch's 'serial trope'.[47] The relation between this trope and Schön's row is revealed in Act I scene 2, in a manner not dissimilar to the splitting in the sixth movement of the *Lyric Suite*, when 'the three chromatic segments of Schigolch's serial trope … are superimposed and arranged to form a statement of Schön's series'.[48] Certainly, the *Lyric Suite* marked a new stage in the development of Berg's technique as regards the way in which rows are related to one another, and represented a significant advance on the use of the two forms of Klein's all-interval row in 'Schliesse mir' II. All the rows in the *Lyric Suite* can demonstrably be derived from the row of the first movement (that is, Klein's row) and the analytical preface to Klein's *Variationen*, whatever the history of its content, describes some of those methods. But, as the examples of splitting show, there are other methods as well.

Aspects of the Chamber Concerto

Consideration of some of the other techniques in the Chamber Concerto may specifically illustrate the advances in twelve-note composition represented by the *Lyric Suite*. It is important to note that the stages by which Berg arrived at the technique demonstrated in the latter work did *not* include composition with twelve notes in a fixed and unalterable order – that is, the use of only *one* row within a work – which, strictly speaking, is the logical premise of what Ashby calls 'the concept of *additional*, systematically derived rows'.[49] Rather, a compositional precedent for the *Lyric Suite*'s use of multiple rows may be seen in the way that the Chamber Concerto abounds with related themes, those of the second movement in particular displaying some of the characteristics of a row in the Schoenbergian sense.[50] If the abundance of themes in the Chamber Concerto corresponds to the multiplicity of rows and subsidiary sets in the *Lyric Suite*, then the new (or, rather, newly applied) techniques in the *Lyric Suite* represent for Berg an advance in the manner by which themes and rows can be related to each other.

In this context, the technique of splitting, by which the relationship between the two rows in the sixth movement of the *Lyric Suite* is demonstrated, is but one resource in a larger technical palette. The principal means by which the relations between themes and motivic-thematic material are fostered in the Chamber Concerto is through the exploitation of

Example 10.10 (a) Chamber Concerto, first movement, bars 6–7, flute

(b) bars 8–10, clarinet

their common segments – a technique famously employed in the *Lyric Suite* through the use of the four-note group A♮–B♭–B♮–F♮.[51] For example, the clarinet melody at bars 8–10 in the *Thema* of the Chamber Concerto's first movement is connected to the beginning of the previous flute melody that contains Berg's cipher by the common notes D♭, D♮ and C♮. As can be seen in Example 10.10, the clarinet melody begins by stating these three notes in retrograde. Raising the analysis to a higher level of abstraction shows that the last four notes of the flute melody (D♭–A♭–D♮–C♮) belong to the same pitch-class set – with prime form (0, 1, 2, 6) – as the first four distinct notes of the clarinet melody (C♮, D♮, C♯, F♯), and that this is the same pitch-class set to which the notorious four-note group of the *Lyric Suite* also belongs.[52] Note also the appearance of diminished triads and whole-tone segments in both flute and clarinet melodies.

A special case of association through common content is presented at the beginning of the third movement. Here, the 'Schoenberg' row with which the *Thema* begins (*Hauptstimme*, bars 1–4, Example 10.11a) is connected with the *Hauptrhythmus* of the second movement.[53] The first four notes of the row are presented as arpeggiated dyads by the piano in bar 481; the fifth note of the row, A♮, is supplied by the violin's statement of the *Hauptrhythmus* (Example 10.11b). After a further two successively diminuted statements of the *Hauptrhythmus*, the first five notes are repeated by the violin and then the sixth note is added (bar 484), a process which recalls the gradual unfolding of the row at the beginning of the first movement.[54]

Example 10.11 represents a special case of association by common content, insofar as the common content is but one pitch. Otherwise, it stands, as could many others in this work, as an example of the association of temporally remote material. As Adorno observes, the formal idea of the third movement of the Chamber Concerto is indebted to that of Schoen-

Example 10.11 (a) Chamber Concerto, first movement, bars 1–4

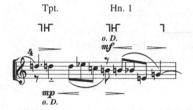

(b) third movement, bars 481–4

Example 10.12 Schoenberg, 'Der Mondfleck' (*Pierrot lunaire*), bar 1, reciter and violin

berg's 'Der Mondfleck', No. 18 from *Pierrot lunaire* Op. 21, in which a continuous form is combined with a palindromic one.[55] The association of material shown in Example 10.11b connects at the outset of the third movement the continuous material of the first movement with the palindromic material of the second. Similarly, in 'Der Mondfleck', the opening phrase of the reciter's continuous music has A♮ as its goal-note and connects *via* this note on the second beat of bar 1 with the ostinato rhythm of the palindromic music of the violin. Reading the rhythm of the first beat of the reciter's music in bar 1 and the first half of the second beat in the violin gives Berg's *Hauptrhythmus*, marked with arrows in Example 10.12. In general, and like the examples of splitting in the *Lyric Suite*, the examples of association in the Chamber Concerto do not solely concern relations between pitch-based phenomena, but also relations between pitch and rhythm: both techniques are used to cut across these often separate domains.

The association of material by pitch content in the Chamber Concerto and the splitting in the *Lyric Suite* are but two examples of the techniques by which the wealth of material, of which Adorno speaks in the earlier works, and which is equally present here, is marshalled.[56] Moreover, the process of combination, which is pursued throughout the third movement of the Chamber Concerto, may be said to represent the technical complement of the splitting in the *Lyric Suite*. The compositional emphasis laid on these techniques in both works throws into relief the secondary status of the twelve-note features *per se*. Although this is equally true of the music of Schoenberg and Webern – insofar as music is, in Webern's words, 'the representation of an idea in notes'[57] – the secondary status is more pointed in Berg's music because of the nature of the ideas themselves. In wishing to dispel the image of Berg as a twelve-note-technical deviant, Ashby is right to promote the idea of Berg's 'personal epistemology of twelve-tone music', but surely we should then hesitate before claiming him as the adherent of yet another theoretical orthodoxy.

11 In the orbit of *Lulu*: the late works

Anthony Pople
University of Lancaster

An opera and its satellites

Work on his second opera dominated the last eight years or more of Berg's life. Yet he accomplished much else besides. To this period also belongs his Violin Concerto – the earliest serial composition to gain the status of a modern classic – together with the concert aria *Der Wein*. Berg also compiled and orchestrated his set of *Seven Early Songs*, prepared a string orchestra version of three movements from the *Lyric Suite*, revised the Three Orchestral Pieces Op. 6 into the form in which they are generally heard, and produced the set of five symphonic pieces known today as the *Lulu Suite*; he also published several articles and carried out some smaller compositional tasks, such as the four-voice canon which he dedicated to the Frankfurt opera house.[1] Most of these projects were touched to a lesser or greater degree by their chronological proximity to the composition of *Lulu*, and in turn the opera bears traces of some of the smaller projects.

Berg began his search for a new operatic subject within a month of the *Wozzeck* premiere, and following a suggestion from his friend Soma Morgenstern he began to consider the 'glassworks fairy-tale' *Und Pippa tanzt!* (1906) by Gerhart Hauptmann (1862–1946).[2] He wrote to Hauptmann's publishers as early as 8 June 1926 about the matter of a royalty agreement,[3] but pending these negotiations he also gave consideration to the two Lulu tragedies of Frank Wedekind (1864–1918) – responding after more than twenty years to the enormous impression that had been made on him as a young man by his literary idol Karl Kraus's private production of the second Lulu play, *Die Büchse der Pandora*, in May 1905. Nor were these the only sources he looked at; but by mid-1927 it seemed that *Pippa* and *Lulu* were the only serious possibilities.[4]

Even before deciding between these alternatives, Berg devised a twelve-note series for his opera, and in a comprehensive chart dated 17 July 1927 he notated various possible ways of deriving useful new configurations from the basic row forms.[5] It may seem a little surprising that he should have felt able to do this at such an early stage without undermining the potential relationships between the as-yet-unwritten music and the as-

yet-undecided drama; but it is also understandable given that the Hauptmann and the Wedekind cover similar ground, albeit in contrasting styles
and settings. *Und Pippa tanzt!* was not unique among Hauptmann's plays
in being set in his native Silesia, nor in its use of a 'fairy-tale' genre to
accommodate erotic fantasy.[6] In contrast, Wedekind's plays adopt a natu-
ralistic tone and a bourgeois setting, which throws into relief the bizarre
and destructive consequences of the characters' feeble attempts to handle
their own sexual instincts, and through ironic farce allows an element of
social satire to play its part in proceedings, as had also been the case with
Wozzeck.

Towards the end of 1927, Berg sought advice in an attempt to resolve his
dilemma between the two texts: whilst Adorno favoured the Wedekind,[7]
others – including Helene Berg – were in favour of *Pippa.* In the end Berg
concurred with the latter view, and he met Hauptmann personally at the
end of January 1928 to discuss the project.[8] Two months later he told
Schoenberg of his plans for the libretto: 'I'll have to make great cuts in
Hauptmann's drama to suit my purpose, indeed, I even intend to combine
the 3rd and 4th (last) acts, thereby somewhat alleviating the weakness of
precisely that portion of the drama.'[9] Berg accomplished more work on
Pippa than is generally recognised. As well as the row-chart, he also made a
number of concept sketches for characteristic musical passages, some of
which were simply taken over into the *Lulu* project.[10] In particular, the
chromaticism that came to be associated with the character of Schigolch
in *Lulu* was originally devised for the not dissimilar Huhn in *Pippa.*[11]
When Berg transferred these sketches to *Lulu,* however, he initially associated the chromaticism with her first husband, the medical specialist Dr
Goll. This sequence of events perhaps explains the otherwise rather
strange moment in the opening section of Act I scene 1 (bars I/112–14)
where the 'Schigolch' row is used as the musical basis for a passage in
which Schön and Lulu discuss her husband.

The halting origins of *Lulu's* serial materials do little, however, to obscure their musical consistency with the *Lyric Suite* and the Chamber Concerto. The all-interval series on which the *Lyric Suite* is based – and also its
forerunner, 'Schliesse mir die Augen beide' – falls into two hexachords, the
second of which is simply the transposed retrograde of the first (Example
11.1a); the first hexachord of the basic series of *Lulu* is none other than a
rotation of this retrograde (see Example 11.1b). While working on the
Lyric Suite, Berg had been excited to realise that triads and other tonalistic
elements could be conceived as embedded configurations within a twelve-
note series,[12] and the early *Pippa/Lulu* sketches show that he tried to ensure the same was possible with the new serial resources he was devising
for the opera.[13] Looking forward as well as back, one can in fact observe

Example 11.1   (a) Diatonic hexachord and its retrograde; hexachord and transposed retrograde combined as twelve-note series for the *Lyric Suite*

(b) Rotated retrograde of hexachord begins basic series of *Lulu*

continuities of technique and substance running all the way through this period. As a number of authors have pointed out, the series of *Der Wein* is highly reminiscent of a scalar series associated with the character of Lulu,[14] and when Berg returned to his opera after composing *Der Wein* he clearly drew on his experiences with the aria. Finally, the Violin Concerto's series, too, has links with that of *Der Wein*, and the overall compositional technique of the work locates it firmly in the orbit of *Lulu*.

Towards a musical language

By the time of the Violin Concerto, Berg had achieved a remarkable fluency of technique. His way of working included a planning stage during which the overall form and character of a work's sections would be determined, and an initial exploration of configurations within the series (or derivable from it) that would fit into his tonally oriented dodecaphonic style – patterns such as scale fragments, arpeggiated triads and other familiar chords. There would be a stage of rough drafting in which details were passed over in favour of fixing the musical flow within broad outlines, and other stages with well-defined objectives, the most crucial of these being the *Particell* (short score), in which virtually all details except the precise instrumentation were determined.[15]

Berg tended to compose with the series by treating it as a source of malleable shapes that could be worked into the continuity of his musical textures. In doing this, he frequently adopted techniques which went beyond the straightforward replication of serial forms that would have arisen had he always played the notes strictly from the first to the twelfth. For example, he might present the elements in a rotated order – that is, starting with an element other than the first and then wrapping round from the last element to the beginning (like traversing a clock face from, say, 9am through to 8pm). Or, he might allocate separate segments from a linear series to the individual voices of a musical texture, thus subordinating the strict order of the notes to the way in which the contrapuntal rhythms interact. Frequently, he would recycle one or more notes just heard (e.g., to present elements from a series in the order 1–2–3–4–2–3–5–6 ...); and in cases where the material was chordally conceived he would sometimes permute the elements within each chord – that is, keeping the chords fixed, but sounding their notes in any order.

All of this serves to maintain a balance between serial correctness and a tangible harmonic and thematic consistency. In particular, the thematic sense of the music often arises through the association of abstract serial shapes with characteristic musical contours and rhythms, and is sustained by the priority given to certain melodic shapes or harmonic elements over the remaining serial pitches. This is especially apparent when pre-existing themes are quoted, such as the opening of *Tristan und Isolde* in the last movement of the *Lyric Suite*,[16] a cabaret song in Act III of *Lulu*,[17] and a Lutheran chorale melody in the Violin Concerto. Very broadly speaking, when a melodic shape is prioritised in this way, the remaining notes of the series tend to be played out in more or less strict order when the texture is highly differentiated in terms of counterpoint or instrumentation, but to be sounded with adjustments to the order – presumably for harmonic reasons – when the texture is more homogeneous.

It is no coincidence that the resulting musical processes very much resemble those of intensive developing variation – the principal difference being that, unlike the initial motivic/thematic statements from which a developing variation texture proceeds, the serial forms and derived configurations remain in theory at least on Berg's sketch-pad, and are thus not necessarily heard as points of departure in the music. But in practice, Berg tended to articulate the formal sections in his late works very clearly, and often to base the thematic openings of such sections closely on the series or on plainly derived configurations, which helps to render the musical processes within each section rather closer to developing variation than they might be otherwise. This also means that the underlying relationships between the thematic materials are well-defined – and it is these relationships, in fact, which remain on the composer's sketch-pad, enshrined in the private derivations of different materials from the series, just as they might in a different way have remained on the sketch-pad of Schoenberg or Berg twenty years previously.

This practice was to some extent evident as early as the Chamber Concerto, as Neil Boynton illustrates in chapter 10.[18] But a systematic investigation of the way in which the concerto's numerous dodecaphonic and near dodecaphonic themes are interrelated, conducted by the American music theorist Philip Lambert, demonstrates among other things that Berg's practice in this regard was not itself systematic.[19] Perhaps more surprising is that at this juncture the small groups of notes that are shared between themes – see, for instance, Example 10.10 (p. 201) – are in general not overtly tonalistic, whole-tone, quartal, octatonic, hexatonic or otherwise familiar. It seems to have been the experience of working with diatonic hexachords in the *Lyric Suite* that sent Berg in this direction, something which was to find its fullest flowering in the second-phase materials of *Lulu*.

The Chamber Concerto was more obviously significant for Berg's development in the way it employs formal combination in conjunction with mirror relationships – inversion and retrograde – similar in ethos to Schoenberg's twelve-note principle but not actually derived from it. Indeed, while the work pays elaborate homage to the Schoenberg circle and makes thematic use of a musical cipher based on the name of **Arnold Schönberg** (as well as those of **Anton Webern**, **Alban Berg**, and, less openly, **Mathilde** **Schoenberg**),[20] several factors indicate that Berg was developing his compositional technique in parallel to Schoenberg rather than on the direct basis of his erstwhile teacher's latest ideas.[21] There is no reason to believe, for example, that in applying mirror relationships to the entire thirty-bar thematic complex of the concerto's opening movement Berg was simply misunderstanding what Schoenberg was doing. This movement, with solo piano (*Thema scherzoso con variazioni*), combines a format of theme and variations with that of a sonata movement. That is to say, the sequence of variations is so characterised as to be capable of being aligned conceptually with the outlines of a textbook sonata form. The sequence of events is as follows:[22]

Theme and variations	*'Sonata movement'*
Theme (30 bars)	'exposition'
Variation 1 (theme reworked for piano solo)	'exposition repeat'
Variation 2 (material recast in retrograde)	
Variation 3 (inversion)	'development'
Variation 4 (retrograde inversion)	
Variation 5 (original, elaborated)	'recapitulation'

The sense in which the theme is subjected to operations of inversion and retrogression is quite free, allowing the music's character to develop in a way that is reasonably independent of the variation format. Example 11.2 illustrates how the opening theme is presented at the end of the retrograde-inversion variation: the spiky piano octaves could hardly form a greater contrast to the rich legato of the cor anglais in its lowest register.

The second movement, with solo violin (*Adagio*), is essentially a palindrome: each half of the movement may be regarded as falling into ternary form, and the whole is equal in length to the first movement at 240 bars. At

Example 11.2   (a) Chamber Concerto, first movement: opening of theme (I/1–3)

(b) end of fourth variation (I/178–80)

the central turning point the solo piano briefly rejoins the ensemble, intoning (on a bottom C♯) what appear to be the twelve strokes of a midnight bell. This portentous moment seems to be in line with the movement's programmatic concern with the fate of Mathilde Schoenberg, who after a long period of decline had died in 1923, fifteen years after her lover Richard Gerstl had committed suicide when she left him to return to her husband.

The final movement, in which both soloists participate (*Rondo ritmico con introduzione*), takes advantage of the precise correspondence in length between the first and second movements. Through a remarkable feat of formal combination, its material is derived from both these movements together, sometimes in alternation and sometimes literally simultaneously. In the abstract, this scheme sounds daunting, and when Pierre Boulez described the work as 'probably the strictest that Berg ever wrote' he was probably alluding to the fact that Berg never attempted the same thing again.[23] By comparison, Berg's use of formal combination in *Lulu* was to be very much looser in both concept and execution.

Within Berg's developing matrix of technical devices and musical processes, a more or less obverse situation applies regarding the derivation of one series from another within the same work. Although the methods he used in the *Lyric Suite* to adapt the series of the first movement so as to create further series for other movements are far from straightforward, they are by no means mechanical.[24] Indeed, the underlying technique of simply exchanging the positions of two or more pitch-classes in one row so as to arrive at a new ordering is essentially arbitrary in nature. In subsequent works, still motivated by a desire for thematic variety underpinned by tangible interrelationships, Berg continued to work with derived series, but the derivational techniques he employed were to become far stricter. This is not yet evident, however, in the initial tranche of materials for *Pippa/Lulu*, as summarised in the row-chart dating from 1927. Although derived configurations are to be found here (some of which are shown in Example 11.3), the means of derivation are largely confined to the extraction of Berg's favoured musical configurations, such as triads and scales.[25] These materials were evidently in Berg's mind as he sketched a setting of the Prologue to the first *Lulu* play, *Erdgeist*, on or around 23 June 1928, since this music deploys several of them, albeit in a fairly rudimentary way.[26] (The *Pippa* project had in the end been made impossible by the exorbitant demands of Hauptmann and his publishers.)

There was further significant preparation to come for Berg's work on *Lulu*, though it may at the time have seemed innocuous. The success of *Wozzeck* gave him an opportunity to raise money by bringing out new arrangements of existing pieces, an enterprise in which the wishes of his publishers also played a part. In the first part of 1928 he prepared a set of *Seven Early Songs* for publication in versions with piano and orchestral accompaniment, and later that year saw the publication of his string orchestra arrangement of three movements from the *Lyric Suite*.[27] Many commentators have construed the *Seven Early Songs* project as a study for *Pippa/Lulu* on account of the characteristic texture of solo soprano and orchestra, and whilst this texture is also found in the *Three Fragments from 'Wozzeck'* (1923–4) it is fair to say that the sound-world of the orchestral songs is far closer to *Lulu* than to the Three Orchestral Pieces, *Wozzeck* or the *Fragments*. At the same time, a more far-reaching consequence of Berg's renewed acquaintance with his earlier manner is to be found in the extensive accommodation with tonality found in the serial works of the *Lulu* period. While working on the *Lyric Suite*, Berg had told Schoenberg of his 'attempt … to write with a strong element of tonality in the strictest twelve-note music',[28] and this attempt is markedly more successful in the works that followed the *Seven Early Songs*.

Correspondingly, the embedding of tonalistic configurations in the serial basis of *Lulu* was the most important technical factor that gave Berg the stylistic freedom to continue a trajectory from the Chamber Concerto and the *Lyric Suite*. But as he worked through Act I scene 1 and the beginning of Act I scene 2, this basis became obscured. Although the music of *Lulu* is through-composed, Berg chose to organise the opera into a sequence of clearly delineated formal sections,[29] most of which are tagged thematically, and this carried implications for the serial technique. He had made prominent use of the row-chart materials in the sections up to and including the Melodrama (I/196–257), deploying each in turn as if simply

Example 11.3   Some configurations found in Berg's 1927 row-chart for *Pippa/Lulu*

(a) Basic series

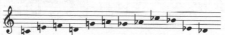

(b) Hexachords superimposed dyadically; adjacent dyads combined as chords

(c) Partitioning into near-chromatic fragments

(d) Identification of embedded triads

(e) Portrait chords (*Bildharmonien*) and associated scalar series

(f) Extraction of dyadic fourths and linear whole-tone hexachords

(g) Extraction of configurations dominated by major and minor thirds

Example 11.4   *Lulu*: opening of Canzonetta (I/258–60), showing deployment of basic series

Example 11.5   *Lulu*: opening of Duet (I/305–6), showing recycling of C major scale fragments

trying them out one by one,[30] but as the composition proceeded he evidently found himself needing to develop additional themes. Significantly, this led him away from the embedded tonal elements as he derived these new themes through ever greater serial convolutions. An early stage is seen in the theme of the Canzonetta (I/258ff., Example 11.4): the opening is based on an inverse form of the basic series in a manner which though difficult to follow aurally is quite clear on paper, whilst conversely its aurally clear development in the subsequent musical texture involves considerable intricacies of serial working.

The Duet (I/305ff.), on the other hand, is serially intricate even at the outset, but here Berg manages to derive a tonal backbone – a C major scale fragment, no less – from conjoined forms of the series. He does this by accumulating notes into the scale figure, which repeats independently of any serial origin to form a core around which new serial notes are deployed (Example 11.5).[31] Similarly, a motivic fragment is conjured from the succession G–Eb–Db, its twofold repetition lending consistency to the end of the phrase.

Der Wein

By the time he returned to Vienna in autumn 1928 Berg had composed 'over 300 bars' of *Lulu*, perhaps up to approximately bar I/414,[32] but at this point in the opera the composition of *Der Wein* interrupted it. Having revised the Three Orchestral Pieces in anticipation of their premiere in Oldenburg,[33] Berg retreated to the Berghof at the end of May 1929 to take up a financially attractive commission from the soprano Ružena Herlinger, with whom he had worked the previous year in Paris.[34] For this purpose it was necessary for him to create another group of row materials, which thus post-date the *Pippa/Lulu* group by about two years: a number of these are summarised in Example 11.6 on the basis of what may be observed in the finished score.

Der Wein has often been construed as a study for *Lulu*. Mosco Carner suggests specifically that it was a study for the 'Lied der Lulu' in Act II scene 1,[35] and Berg would surely have composed the Tango pastiche in *Der Wein* (bars 39–63 and 181–95) with the off-stage jazz band in Act I scene 3 in prospect. Perhaps of greatest importance was that the aria gave him the chance to work in advance with an orchestra that contained some of the special elements he would need for the sound-world of *Lulu*, notably the alto saxophone.[36] He also had the opportunity to try out on a smaller scale, in a text-based composition, something approximating to the over-

Example 11.6   (a) Basic series of *Der Wein* in prime and inverse forms

(b) Trichords superimposed to make harmonic trope

(c) Alternate notes grouped together

(d) Alternate notes treated as half-series; inversion partitioned into chords

(e) Extraction of minor, major and minor/major triads (prime and inverse)

(f) Extraction of voices in parallel fourths

(g) Extraction of whole-tone scale fragments

(h) Extraction of tritone sequence and chromatic motives

all formal shape he had already planned for the opera:[37] the third section of *Der Wein* is an abbreviated recapitulation of the first, and fifty-nine of the second section's eighty-five bars are devoted to a palindrome, the retrograde half of which serves as an orchestral interlude.

Berg had turned to Stefan George's translation of Baudelaire's *Les Fleurs du mal* when composing the secret vocal finale to the *Lyric Suite*.[38] His choice of three more poems from this set for the text of *Der Wein* suggests that this, too, was a composition inspired to some extent by his thoughts of Hanna Fuchs-Robettin. Indeed, in a letter Berg drew her attention to the combination of B major (i.e., 'H') and F major triads at the centre of the work, adding: 'Whom could it have to do with but you, Hanna, when I say ... "Sister, let us flee side by side ... to my land of dreams"'.[39] Whether Hanna would have been flattered by her association with the work as a whole is admittedly questionable. Adorno describes it as 'one great "Ossia"' – because it sets French texts in German translation – and links this observation by means of typical sophistry with what he sees as Berg's synthesis of 'Impressionist' traits into the twelve-note musical fabric of the aria.[40] Yet, as so often with Adorno, this argument need not be taken at face value, but hints at a deeper unease with the work which may be put down to cultural differences over the handling of the seamier images conjured up by Baudelaire, notably in the third of the poems Berg chose to set ('Le vin du solitaire'). Mosco Carner is more honest about his own low opinion of the piece, finding corroboration in a report that 'at the mention of *Der Wein* an apologetic expression would always appear on [Berg's] face', but he also asks: 'did Berg feel a measure of spiritual kinship with this rebellious poet? For [Berg] was also against the moral taboos and moral conventions of his society'.[41] Berg's setting places *Der Wein* midway between the romance of impossible passion and indulgent solitude that is played out in the *Lyric Suite*, and the social analysis of desperate sexuality that is one basis of *Lulu*.

The accessibility of *Der Wein*'s musical language served an important end in unpicking the awkward trend that had been developing in *Lulu*. In the aria, Berg deploys tonalistic configurations almost ostentatiously, both melodically and harmonically, at one and the same time depicting symbolically a world of sleaze and sensation, revelling in it, and perhaps gaining a certain satisfaction from using Schoenberg's serial technique to compose a work that comes closer to the tonality of the *Seven Early Songs* than anything he had written since those sections of *Wozzeck* that were borrowed from his student piano pieces.

Two passages that illustrate this are the very opening of the work (Example 11.7) and the first entry of the voice (Example 11.8). The opening chord makes use of the fact that the basic series of the work, at the pitch

Example 11.7   *Der Wein*: opening (bars 1–3), showing deployment of series

level used here, begins with all seven notes of the ascending scale of D 'harmonic' minor. The first three notes initiate a plodding ostinato in the bass that roots the music on D, while the remaining notes are arranged above so as to mimic the sound of a dominant (minor) ninth chord: the effect is one of dominant harmony over a tonic pedal. The harmonies suggested by the remaining serial notes suggest tonal configurations rooted on A♭ and C♭, which relate to D through the diminished-seventh pattern that is analogously implicated in the V$^{9♭}$ harmony. As would become customary in the Violin Concerto, the continuation of the phrase is built on the inversion of the series, organised so that the initial group of three notes feeds into the ostinato. This sequence is repeated in what follows, and is then developed by taking the ostinato notes from the fourth, fifth and sixth pitches of P$_9$ and I$_{10}$; the music builds in terms of texture and tessitura, leading towards the climax of the phrase.

If anything the passage shown in Example 11.8 is more remarkable: simultaneously ascending and descending forms of the series, both starting on D, envelope the harmonic trope of tritones and chromatic motives shown in Example 11.6h. The rhythmic articulation is such that a classic harmonic sequence round the circle of fifths emerges, finished off with an octatonically outlined link between C^7 and F$^{♯7}$ – something familiar from Rimsky-Korsakov, Scriabin and early Stravinsky among others. Perhaps it was the French–Russian cultural axis that Adorno had in mind when he described the ninth-chords of *Der Wein* as impressionistic.[42] And certainly, the parallel major triads that sweep downwards towards the aria's central 'H/F' moment, and then in retrograde sweep upwards away from it (Example 11.9), bear comparison with the parallel chordal writing that is associated by reputation with Debussy. Yet these triads are serially composed, the harmony and texture being generated with breathtaking simplicity by stating the series simultaneously in three forms that are transpositionally related at the constituent intervals of a major triad.

Example 11.8   *Der Wein*: vocal entry (bars 15–16), showing deployment of series and trope

Example 11.9   *Der Wein*: harmonic summary of bars 131–41, showing parallel major triads

Lulu after Der Wein

After finishing the aria in mid-August[43] Berg was able to devote a month or so to a second bout of work on *Lulu* using the original materials, but he confessed to finding it difficult to make 'one row suffice for a work which lasts several hours'[44] and by the end of September he was back in Vienna, having reached no further than approximately bar I/521.[45]

Example 11.10 *Lulu*: Duettino (I/416–9), showing serial origin

'*Erdgeist* fourths' and remnant (P$_3$)

Ich fin - de, Du siehst heu - te rei - zend aus.   Dein Haar

'*Erdgeist* fourths' and remnant (P$_8$)

It seems likely that the Duettino (I/416ff.) was composed at this time; the serial basis here is extremely convoluted, and it is probably no coincidence that the vocal entry is scarcely if ever pitched accurately in performance. The music is based on the derivation given by Reich for the '*Erdgeist* fourths' motive,[46] making use of an eight-note remnant that is not prominent elsewhere in the opera. Example 11.10 indicates how, even with this basis in place analytically, the construction of the texture seems extraordinarily intricate.[47] It is perhaps hardly surprising that Berg immediately resorts to a rising scale figure in parallel major triads – similar to the central phrases of *Der Wein* – which like that passage is achieved in serial terms by playing a twelve-note series at three different pitch levels simultaneously. (In this case, it is the scalar series associated with the character of Lulu, which may in turn have been the model for the *Der Wein* series.) This way of composing parallel-motion tonal sonorities into serial textures is also found prominently elsewhere in the later sections of *Lulu*: in

Example 11.11 *Lulu*: derivation of selected 'complementary' series from the basic series

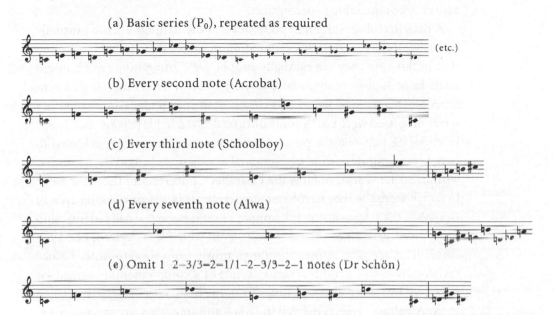

(a) Basic series (P$_0$), repeated as required

(etc.)

(b) Every second note (Acrobat)

(c) Every third note (Schoolboy)

(d) Every seventh note (Alwa)

(e) Omit 1 2–3/3–2–1/1–2–3/3–2–1 notes (Dr Schön)

the Coda to Schön's Sonata, for example (major triads, I/968–72; minor triads, I/972–77), and in the harmonies that underpin the principal theme of Alwa's Rondo (dominant sevenths, I/1027ff. and subsequently).

The third and longest phase of work on the opera began in the summer of 1930, after Berg had found a way of radically expanding the range of serial materials that could be derived from his original row. His pupil Willi Reich had corresponded with him about the 'complementary series' which could be obtained by strict derivation from any given row by taking every second note, or every third note, and so on,[48] and this encouraged Berg to derive a range of additional materials from the basic series of the opera. He gave these materials a function in the musical drama by associating each of the principal characters with a specific serial configuration: for example, four 'complementary' series were associated respectively with the Acrobat, the Schoolboy, Alwa and Dr Schön (see Example 11.11).

In the 1960s and 1970s, controversy arose over the significance of Berg's use of 'complementary series' in this phase of work on *Lulu*. Although there has never been any proper reason to doubt Willi Reich's account of the procedures by which new serial configurations were derived from the basic series,[49] the leading Berg authority George Perle argued strongly that more significant by far are the musical connections between these materials that arise through shared segmental content[50] – a principle familiar from the Chamber Concerto and the *Lyric Suite*. In effect, Perle was challenging the notion that documented but inaudible compositional procedures may be said to 'explain' the music better than aspects one might expect to be amenable to perception.

A detached observer might point out that these things are not mutually exclusive. Indeed, scholarly examination of Berg's sketches has suggested that in this case they are mutually supportive – something which might seem to be highly symptomatic of Berg's ability to synthesise different aspects of his musical world. It is clear that the particular complementary series Berg used were not the only ones he derived in his private sketches.[51] In choosing between the possibilities that arose, he may be reckoned to have kept in mind the kind of segmental associations he had been familiar with in earlier works, notably the Chamber Concerto and the *Lyric Suite*. In fact, it seems he may have begun to develop this way of working even in *Der Wein*: the trope shown in Example 11.6d is hexachordally identical to a permuted version of the basic series from which it is derived, and such ambiguities seem to inform the Tango music from time to time.[52] Since the trope is in fact a rudimentary example of a 'complementary series' – it is derived by taking alternate notes from the basic series of *Der Wein*, just as the Acrobat's series is derived in *Lulu* – and since this particular derivative operation is also found in the *Lyric Suite* (see Examples 10.1 and 10.4, pp. 190 and 195) and in the 'splitting' which may be identified in works composed still earlier,[53] there are grounds for asserting that all these elements of technique that Berg developed in the second phase of work on *Lulu* were latent in his earlier music. Reich's ideas may have broadened Berg's concept of serial derivation, but many of the associated principles were already in his repertoire.

The relation between the audible and the inaudible has also exercised commentators in a different way. In some passages, Berg seems to project before us the actual derivation of one series from another. For example, the Schigolch material (actually dating from the 1927 row-chart) emerges from the basic series at I/458–9 in exactly the way it is presented in Reich's more abstract account. On the other hand, the opening of Schön's Sonata movement seems to some writers to illustrate the generation of Schön's row from the basic series, while to others it seems too loosely structured at the musical surface to project this derivative process into the audible domain.[54] This topic has a broader relevance because of the association of different series with different characters in the drama, and the fact that dependency is one of the crucial topics that motivates the interactions between these characters. And indeed it would appear from the sketches, as described by both Patricia Hall and Thomas Ertelt, that the passage which answers this riddle – with yet another Bergian synthesis – is not the main theme of the Sonata but the Coda (see Example 12.2, p. 235). This music seems to have been composed in a way that clearly displays the abstract link between the two series; at the same time, it expresses the 'possession' or 'belonging' (*Zugehörigkeit*) that fatally entwines Lulu and Schön.[55]

Such calculated precision is entirely in character for Berg, as is the clarity with which many details of the stage action are followed in the orchestral music by means of a technique that became commonplace in soundtracks to animated cartoon films and is known in that context as 'Mickey Mousing'. Berg had previously used this technique to embed secret programmes in the Chamber Concerto and the *Lyric Suite*.[56] In *Lulu*, it is particularly evident when characters are bustling around on stage but are not singing   such as when Countess Geschwitz pretends to leave Schön and Lulu's house early in Act II scene 1, but in fact hides behind a chimney screen, or a little later in the same scene when Lulu's other secret admirers are forced to find hiding places themselves. Motives associated with the characters concerned are heard, in general quite clearly, and the stage action is intended to be synchronised with the music, using these motives as cues. Berg's outline screenplay for the silent film that is shown between the two scenes of Act II pursues this idea at length, choreographing the orchestral interlude and making the cinematic connection explicit.[57]

However, in contrast to such serial and musico-dramatic explicitness of various kinds it must be observed that several of the most notable musical passages in *Lulu* are surprisingly obscure in their serial origins. This is explained in part by Berg's habit, when writing extended works, of reusing serially composed material without necessarily revisiting the finer details of its original derivation. As a result, a process of 'Chinese whispers' is sometimes evident, particularly at the beginnings and ends of such cross-references, and particularly with regard to material which recurs frequently for musico-dramatic effect. One example is the passage known as 'Lulu's entrance music' (George Perle) or 'Freedom music' (Judy Lochhead, in chapter 12). It is music that seems to signify Lulu's freedom to play the seductress, and is first heard in the Prologue when she is brought on stage in the guise of the primeval serpent. But this version of the passage was not actually the first to be composed – indeed it was the last, since Berg composed the opera before the Prologue. The first 'Freedom' passage in the body of the opera occurs in Act II scene 1, at which point its serial basis, though complex, is at least discernable: Berg seems to have targeted the opening diatonic sonority and simply to have worked around it with the remaining notes (Example 11.12). Later appearances – at II/163, 209, 222, 683 (in retrograde), 690, 857, 953, 1001, 1010, 1030, 1033 and 1084, III/1270, and finally three times in the Prologue – sometimes involve minor changes to the harmonies, and often exclude the moving part which in II/145ff. gives the only clear indication of an underlying series.

Example 11.12 *Lulu*: 'Freedom'/'entrance'/'seduction' music (II/145–51, texture simplified)

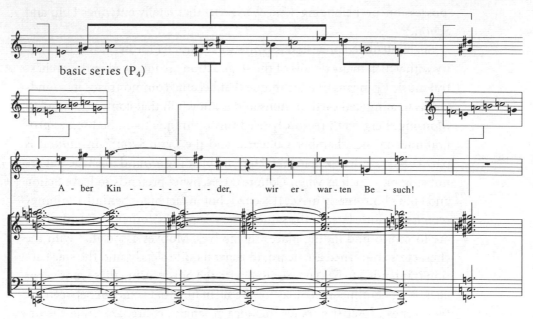

Lulu Suite

Although Berg's progress on *Lulu* was increasingly fluent, it was also unde-
niably slow. Act I was not finished in *Particell* (short score) until July 1931
and Act II until September 1933, more than five years after Berg's first
sketch for the Prologue. In the winter of 1933–4 Berg decided to forego the
pleasures of Vienna for the spartan environment of his 'Waldhaus' in the
country, in order to press ahead with the final act. This sacrifice, together
with the fact that much of the music in Act III is recapitulated from Acts I
and II (and in a far less calculated format than the third movement of the
Chamber Concerto), had the desired effect. *Lulu* was complete, in short
score at least, by April 1934.[58]

After 'overhauling' the *Particell* of the entire opera,[59] Berg began the
task of orchestration by assembling what he called *Five Symphonic Pieces
from the Opera 'Lulu'*. This collection of extracts – known today as the *Lulu
Suite* – gained him performances not only beyond the Nazi sphere of influence but also, in heroic circumstances, under Erich Kleiber in Hitler's
capital city of Berlin. The process of compiling it was undertaken with
great efficiency: Berg simply orchestrated those parts of *Lulu* that were
needed for the suite first of all in order to get them quickly to his publishers, then went back to the beginning of the opera and worked through it.
As Douglas Jarman later discovered, 'the manuscript [of the suite] was
returned to Berg who, to save time and effort, simply dismantled it and

Table 11.1 Movement-plan for the *Lulu Symphony*

I	Allegro (Sonata movement)	I/533–668, I/1209–1361
II	Scherzo (with Trio)	I/351–413
III	Ostinato (film music)	= *Lulu Suite*, second movement (II/652–720)
IV	Rondo	= *Lulu Suite*, first movement (II/243–336, II/1001–1150)
V	Quodlibet	I/463–521
VI	Lied der Lulu	= *Lulu Suite*, third movement (II/491–538)
VII	Variations	= *Lulu Suite*, fourth movement (III/693–740)
VIII	Adagio	= *Lulu Suite*, fifth movement (III/1146–86, I/958–90 and III/1294–1326)

absorbed the different movements of the suite into the full score of the opera at the relevant points'.[60] Happily these included important parts of Act III which he might not otherwise have lived to put into full score. Berg also projected a *Lulu Symphony* with three additional movements which may be located with reasonable certainty from internal evidence in the score of the opera (see Table 11.1).[61] The bar-number locations given here for the movements that Berg never finalised are of course approximate: concert openings would have been required for the Allegro, Scherzo and Quodlibet movements, and also a link between the two parts of the Sonata movement.

Violin Concerto

By this time Berg's income was dwindling as a result of Nazi disapproval of his works (along with those of many other artists), but one ultimately happy consequence was that in 1935 he was forced to accept Louis Krasner's commission for a Violin Concerto in order to keep faith with his publishers, who were giving him regular advances against royalty income that seemed ever more uncertain.[62] The concerto's materials are centred on the series shown in Example 11.13a, the beginning of which may be compared with Example 11.6d, from *Der Wein*. Composing the work occupied him from late April to mid-August, after which he turned again to the scoring of *Lulu*, reaching bar III/268 by the time of his death.[63]

The concerto falls into two parts, each comprising two movements. Part I, after a ten-bar Introduction in which alternate notes are extracted from the series to expose the pristine open strings of the violin (Example 11.13b), takes in an Allegretto movement largely in 2/4 and an Allegretto largely in 6/8. Part II begins with an Allegro movement conceived as an accompanied cadenza and proceeds after an immense climax to a final

Example 11.13 (a) Violin Concerto: basic series (P₇)

(b) Alternate notes generate open-fifths figure, used in solo part, bars I/2–5

Adagio including a series of variations on a Lutheran funeral chorale ('Es ist genug!'), which is quoted in J. S. Bach's harmonisation. This compound binary design marks a departure from the groups of three that had come to dominate Berg's work: the Three Orchestral Pieces Op. 6, the three Acts of both *Wozzeck* and *Lulu*, the three movements of the Chamber Concerto, the three songs of *Der Wein*. What is more, the concerto specifically avoids the cyclic sense of departure and return that is a feature of most of these works. This reflects the strong sense of direction in the 'official' and 'secret' programmes that lie behind the concerto, which Douglas Jarman outlines on pp. 171–5. In its final form, the work may be understood not only as a lament for Alma Mahler's daughter, the eighteen-year-old Manon Gropius – whose death on 22 April 1935 was the catalyst that unleashed the composer's creativity on the work – but also as a covert and intimately autobiographical requiem for Berg himself. This is not to assume that Berg had a premonition of his own death, rather that he might reasonably have anticipated that a work dedicated 'to the memory of an angel' would be played in his own memory at a later date. With this in mind, it would have been consistent with his character for him to have composed into it a number of details that would render such a performance appropriate.

The concerto comes across almost throughout as fluent and accessible. Adorno, always sceptical of such attributes but supportive of Berg, put them down to the speed with which the work was composed, and the fact that it was written on demand.[64] Yet something of the easiness bordering on haste that one finds in certain passages of the concerto – especially, perhaps, in the cadenza movement – may already be found in Act III of *Lulu*, especially in scene 2 (music which Adorno cannot have known well, if at all). This final scene of the opera is dominated by recapitulations of earlier passages, but Berg seems to have spent less time in fashioning the joins between these sections than might be expected of 'the master of the smallest link'.[65] In contrast, the joins in the Violin Concerto are stage-managed with great care.

This is especially apparent in the joins between the Andante and the

Example 11.14 Violin Concerto, Allegretto: opening phrase and continuation (I/104–5, 108)

Allegretto movements in Part I and between the cadenza and the Adagio in Part II. The Andante combines a broad ternary form (ABA') with a palindromic sequence of thematic materials. The figure of open fifths from the Introduction thus returns at the end of the Andante, and a gradual transformation of the musical texture and materials in bars I/94–103, including an anticipation of the Allegretto's 6/8 quaver movement, leads into the scherzando theme at bars I/104ff. (Example 11.14). This theme also extracts a figure of open fifths from the series, but presents it as a repeating bass figure that suggests D minor as a tonal focus (cf. the opening of *Der Wein*, Example 11.7). The following bars illustrate Berg's approach to small-scale structure in this work: the opening phrase is repeated a major seventh higher, with the clarinet melody taken up by the solo violin (bars I/106–7); then, in line with Schoenberg's teaching,[66] the musical 'sentence' pursues an abbreviated development of the first phrase (I/108), introducing harmonic movement, and this is itself immediately repeated at the interval of a tritone before cadencing onto C minor.

One of the concerto's most remarkable features is its use of borrowed thematic materials. As well as the chorale melody, there is a Carinthian folk song, which in the 'official' programme stands for a rustic aspect of 'the vision of the lovely girl in a graceful dance', but which through the words of the song – suppressed in Berg's score – also refers to the composer's youthful affair with a servant girl (of about Manon's age) with whom he fathered a child in his teens.[67] This is presented twice: first as an interlude in the pastoral Allegretto (I/214–28) and then in wistful reminiscence towards the end of the Adagio (II/200–213), where it emerges magically from the chorale variations. The music of the folk song is not incorporated into the serial structure of the concerto; nonetheless, in harmonising it through an alternation of chords functioning in keys a tritone apart, Berg linked it with underlying harmonic features of his style, and with his treatment of the chorale melody.

Example 11.15 Violin Concerto, Adagio: serial counterpoint to opening of chorale (II/136–41)

In fact, presenting the melodic phrases of the chorale in alternate tritone-related keys represents a mid-point in its assimilation, and is how the variations proceed prior to the reminiscence of the folk song. At its initial presentation, the alternation is more stark: the repeating phrases are presented first in serial counterpoint (Example 11.15 shows the opening) and then in Bach's own harmonisation, orchestrated so as to imitate a rustic church organ. Finally, after the folk song has emerged only to vanish once more, there is the suggestion of a synthesis. The Lutheran melody is presented in a chorale-like texture of block chords, but with serial harmony rather than Bach's, while the solo violin's serial lament dissolves into the chorale's final notes. But with the distance between the melody and its setting ever apparent, it may be argued that through stylistic manipulation Berg manages a remarkable thing in these last bars of his last work, presenting the prospect of a final resolution more as a perpetual possibility than as something decisively achievable.[68]

12 Lulu's feminine performance

Judy Lochhead
State University of New York at Stony Brook

Over the past fifty years, much critical attention has been devoted to the character of Lulu, the title figure of Berg's opera *Lulu*. And over that time, critical understanding of the character has changed, the changes motivated by feminist and post-structuralist thought in Europe and the United States. In the first wave of post-war criticism in the 1950s and 1960s, Lulu is characterised as 'the Universal Mistress we all desire to possess or emulate' (Donald Mitchell),[1] and as 'the goddess … "the power of nature, the dæmonic, which never wearies of seducing"' (George Perle).[2] For one critic, Theodor Adorno, Lulu is not the central character of the opera: 'it is not Lulu who is the self out of whose perspective the music comes, but rather Alwa, who loves her'.[3] For Adorno, then, a male voice frames the musical perspective; and for Mitchell and Perle, Lulu herself is incapable of framing a musical perspective because, as a fantasy of male sexual desire, she is an object merely to be possessed (or emulated, if the listener happens to be a woman).[4]

Yet, while depicting her as passive object in one breath, these critics describe her as a powerful and evil force in the next. As either passive object or natural force, Lulu has no agency. Furthermore, in describing Lulu as 'Universal Mistress' and 'goddess', critics draw upon transcendent meanings that effectively invalidate assessment of the type of character she presents. That is to say, since Lulu represents a universal type, the truth or meaning of the type is not an issue.

In the second wave of critical writing in the 1980s and 1990s, the focus turns directly to the meaning of the Lulu character. For some authors, like Karen Pegley, the depiction of Lulu as a '*femme fatale* type' plays a part in the 'operatic tradition which perpetuates women's oppression'.[5] And for others, Lulu's character is a 'projection' of male desire and fear[6] which plays a role in the opera's 'social commentary' by forcing us either to 'reject the piece outright … or face those aspects of ourselves to which we would rather not admit'.[7]

For those who understand the opera as furthering 'women's oppression', the Lulu character is 'authentic' in the sense that she directly embodies social attitudes toward women that have some general currency in the contemporary Western world. From this perspective, critics denounce the Lulu character (and the musical and dramatic forces that give rise to her) as a continuation of negative attitudes toward women. For those who understand the opera as 'social commentary', Lulu depicts characteristics that 'signal' negative attitudes toward women, but those characteristics are not embodied directly: that is, the Lulu character has no authenticity. Rather, the characterisation of her as a *femme fatale*, as a 'dæmonic force of nature', refers negatively to those features. From this vantage point, Lulu's character does not embody any essential feature of 'Woman'. Rather, the Lulu character depicts a social construction of 'Woman', a construction which plays out to tragic and destructive ends in the opera.

The first wave of critics are united in viewing Lulu as an authentic character: she directly embodies the mythic and ambiguous features of 'Woman' that have typically circulated in Western cultures. The second wave of critics differ in their conception of the Lulu character. The conceptual framework of the late twentieth century yields an understanding of Lulu as both a perpetuation and a critique of negative attitudes towards women. The difference between these two understandings turns on whether the meaning of the character is read as authentic or parodic. If Lulu authentically embodies 'Womanly' features that have negative value in the culture, then the character is subject to criticism as a perpetuation of negative attitudes. If the Lulu character depicts those 'Womanly' features in order to criticise them, then Lulu is a parodic figure. The music of *Lulu* plays a central role in this critical scheme of authenticity and parody.

Both the first- and second-wave critics use two recurring musical passages in the opera as evidence for their understanding of the Lulu character. Donald Mitchell argues that one of these imbues 'the operatic Lulu [with] profound and poignant feelings' which are inconsistent with her passive and 'decisively non-developing role' in the drama generally.[8] George Perle, arguing from the same observation of Lulu's musically-projected feelings, understands the emotional content of the music as integral to a character who is essentially inconsistent: she is at once 'the goddess … "which never wearies of seducing"' and the 'human incarnation, the natural, and therefore, innocent woman',[9] the latter susceptible to emotional expression. Leo Treitler, writing in the 1980s, also refers to one of these two passages, calling it the 'radiantly gorgeous music' which 'is a sign of [Lulu's] identity'.[10] Each of these three authors argues from the assumption of a music which authentically expresses human emotion or identity.

But in most of the criticism over the last fifty years there is another kind of observation which implicitly – and only implicitly – contradicts the

idea of an 'authentic' musical expression in the opera. It is a critical discomfort over the relation between musical sound and dramatic action:
'what goes on in the orchestra pit and on the stage fail to match' (Mitchell);[11] 'time after time in *Lulu* we become conscious of the disturbing
difference between the emotional attitude adopted by the music and the
nature of the text to which it is set' (Douglas Jarman);[12] and 'if one is
concentrating on action and character, the music seems completely inappropriate' (Robin Holloway).[13] The discomfort seems to arise from a sense
of disjunction between music that evokes a world of emotional 'beauty',
and dramatic action that – with its murders and suicides, prostitution,
incest and deception – is decidedly not 'beautiful'. While 'irony' and 'pun'
provide some insight into this disjunction of sound and drama, the concepts of authenticity and parody surrounding critical understanding of
the Lulu character provide a more powerful and comprehensive explanation.

The performance of identity

Consideration of whether the Lulu character projects authentic or parodic
attributes hinges on assumptions about personal identity and how it is
constituted. Judith Butler's book, *Gender Trouble: Feminism and the Subversion of Identity* analyses Western concepts of identity and provides a
basis for understanding the assumptions that have driven critical accounts
of Lulu. I shall frame my discussion of Lulu's identity around her work,
linking identity to issues of authenticity and parody. In particular, I shall
use Butler's ideas about the 'performance of identity' as the basis (i) for
arguing that Lulu is a parodic character,[14] and (ii) for demonstrating how
the music of *Lulu* participates in projecting Lulu's dramatic behaviour as a
performance of the 'feminine'.

Two extracts from Butler's book provide a starting point:

1. [What] grounds the presumption that identities are self-identical, per-
   sisting through time as the same, unified and internally coherent?[15]

2. A great deal of feminist theory and literature has nevertheless assumed
   that there is a 'doer' behind the deed. Without an agent, it is argued,
   there can be no agency and hence no potential to initiate a transformation of relations of domination within society.[16]

The first, articulated as a question, suggests that the assumption of unity
and coherence as a basis of identity is ungrounded, and illuminates the

many, often contradictory facets of Lulu's identity. The second raises the issue of agency in a social context; it provides a basis for considering whether the Lulu character is a 'doer' and whether she initiates a transformation in her social situation.

A theme of Lulu's 'non-unified and incoherent' character runs through Wedekind's plays and Berg's opera.[17] The primary difficulty in defining and even describing 'who Lulu *is*' has to do with the impossibility of tracing a single, continuous feature that defines her personality. Critics respond to her contradictory features in diverse ways. Donald Mitchell understands the contradictions as arising from the music and as a failure of Berg's operatic conception. Some other critics respond by theorising different Lulus. George Perle argues that there are two: 'a goddess ... "power of nature"', and a human, 'the natural, and therefore, innocent woman, who represents for all men the ideal fulfilment of sexual desire'.[18] And Leo Treitler argues that there is a 'counterpoint on the stage' between Lulu as a 'prodigy of nature', as she calls herself, and 'a Lulu character that is a complex of roles projected onto it by the men in the drama, out of their own needs, fantasies, and fears about Woman'.[19]

Critics theorising a 'counterpoint' of Lulus must also address the question of agency: is Lulu a 'doer' or is she simply a passive existent, 'a power of nature'? And of the counterpointed Lulus, is there some primary or prior 'identity' which exists as a unified presence behind the other, 'projected' Lulus? In other words, is there an 'authentic' Lulu responsible for her actions?

Both the issue of agency and the question of responsibility in conjunction with agency play a central role in the earliest criticism of the plays and the opera. Donald Mitchell, echoing the sentiments of Wedekind himself, interprets Lulu's behaviour as being without agency: Lulu has 'a decisively non-developing role, "passive" throughout'.[20] But, Mitchell continues, she is deadly in her passivity: 'She is akin to a straight-burning candle flame. The moths clatter their wings, singe themselves and burn themselves to death.' In this formulation, Lulu's destructive and fearful attributes affect the men around her, but these attributes gain their force not through her actions but through her *being*.

While Mitchell considers Lulu 'passive throughout', he also uses language that implies action and personal will. By referring to her as the 'murderer' of Dr Schön, Mitchell ascribes an agency to her character that is at odds with his interpretation of her passivity. George Perle similarly considers Lulu 'responsible' for the deaths not only of Schön but also of the other men who die in the opera, referring to them as Lulu's 'victims'; for Perle, the possibility of 'guilt' is perhaps to be understood in terms of the human Lulu (rather than the goddess Lulu) that he theorises.

The issue of agency arises quite differently for Leo Treitler. Coming to Lulu's defence, he points out that the charge of 'murder' in the matter of Schön's death is inappropriate: 'A good lawyer would plead self-defence.'[21] If Lulu shot Schön in an act of 'self-defence', of 'self-preservation', then we must assume that she had some 'self' – some identity – to 'preserve'. Treitler argues that this identity emerges most prominently in the music – in the sound – of the opera. One passage in particular is crucial: this music 'is a sign of her identity. Through it she says "This is *me*". It fills the air, as her presence fills the stage.'[22] Writing about the same music, George Perle also finds evidence of a wilful subject. He asserts that in imbuing her with human agency the music 'prepares us for [Lulu's] heroic struggle against the Marquis' (who attempts to sell her into prostitution).[23]

The problems critics encounter in attempting to offer understanding of the Lulu character – problems associated with her contradictory attributes, passivity and culpability – derive from underlying notions of identity. In particular, the idea of a unified personality and the idea of personal agency in conjunction with that personality pose significant obstacles to a satisfactory understanding of Lulu. While individual statements by individual critics help to illuminate the dramatic character of Lulu, questions still linger about whether there is some 'authentic' Lulu, some unified identity upon which the other Lulus are projected, about the relationship of these various Lulus to one another, and about the role the music plays in defining her various manifestations of character.

Two additional extracts from Judith Butler's *Gender Trouble* complete the basis of my approach to Lulu's 'feminine performance':

3. [The] 'coherence' and 'continuity' of 'the person' are not logical or analytic features of personhood, but, rather, socially instituted and maintained norms of intelligibility.[24]

4. There is no gender identity behind the expressions of gender; that identity is performatively constituted by the very 'expressions' that are said to be its results.[25]

These extracts, like the two quoted above, form part of Butler's discussion of the difficulties of defining and using the concept of gender in feminist theory. She argues that the difficulties arise from a 'substantive' notion of identity, that is, of the idea that identity is the unified and coherent 'thing' of personhood. Within prior feminist thought, stabilising features such as gender define the substance of identity, a substance which is fixed, unifying and persistent over time. In this conception, the stabilising attributes of identity such as gender are 'essential' traits, immutable properties of the person. The substantive notion of identity and its attendant 'essentialism' make personal agency problematic. If defined by a few stabilising and unifying features that persist through time (e.g., gender), then identity is not a matter of choice: identity is 'being' not 'doing'. The essentialism of the substantive notion of identity is closely linked with the idea of determinism.

Butler argues against the substantive notion of identity precisely because it leads into essentialist notions of gender and makes the idea of agency problematic. Instead, as extracts (3) and (4) suggest, Butler understands identity as a performative result that has no originary, defining source. Performative choices that individuals make and that result in 'identity' arise from 'socially instituted and maintained norms of intelligibility'. In other words, performative choice – 'free-will', agency – is motivated by the needs of an individual within a social context.

Butler's concept of performative choice opens some doors to an understanding of the Lulu character. First, Lulu can be conceived as the bundle of all her contradictory attributes, since the notion of a 'performed' identity can encompass a multiplicity of personality features. Such a conception eliminates the need for a 'contrapuntal' definition of Lulu's identity but at the same time raises two questions about motivation. First, what would motivate a character to perform an identity of contradictory attributes? And second, if performative choices arise from 'socially instituted and maintained norms of intelligibility' why does Lulu choose to perform an identity that stretches the bounds of such intelligibility?[26]

Lulu takes on the role of performer explicitly in her work as a dancer in Act I scene 3, but we may understand her actions throughout the entire opera as implicit performances. Lulu plays the coquette for the Painter in a flirtatious game of chase (Act I scene 1) as a means of responding not only to his but also to her own sexual desires. Her refusal to dance for Schön's fiancée in Act I scene 3 is a performance intended to unmask Schön's duplicitous behaviour toward her. In Act II, she entertains the Acrobat, the Schoolboy and Schigolch as demonstrations of her own 'feminine' prowess. And in Act III scene 1 she attempts to convince the Marquis not to sell her into prostitution with a bourgeois and melodramatic argument about honesty to one's self. In this case, the performance has no effect on the Marquis, and he persists in his own scheme for 'self'.

Throughout, Lulu is motivated by both a 'preservation of self' and the rules of bourgeois society – by the rules of 'social intelligibility'. She performs a 'feminine' role in an effort to gain social status, economic stability, sexual pleasure, family stability and in many instances, she performs for the sheer pleasure of performing. But there is a sense in which her performances are *too* successful, at least in Acts I and II. The performances are exaggerated, the 'femininity' too pronounced: in other words, the performances stretch the boundaries of intelligibility.

Part of Butler's project in *Gender Trouble* is to demonstrate not only that gender and identity are performative choices but also that they are revealed as such by 'the cultural emergence of those "incoherent" or "discontinuous" gendered beings who appear to be persons but who fail to conform to the gendered norms of cultural intelligibility by which persons are defined'.[27] Butler is referring to such cultural practices as 'drag, cross-dressing, and the sexual stylization of butch/femme identities' which parody the socially intelligible gender types – man and woman, masculine and feminine. In other words, these cultural practices reveal gender as performative choice by subverting the comprehensibility of the socially accepted categories of 'gendered norms'.

An extension of Butler's notion of gender parody can illuminate the problematic aspects of the Lulu character. Much of Lulu's dramatic behaviour may be understood as her 'performance of identity'. It is a performance which exaggerates attributes marked as 'feminine': this overabundant *femme fatale* changes her mood too abruptly, her sexually charged seductions are too overt, her allegiance to a moral self too melodramatic. The exaggerations effectively undermine not only the gendered role in which women typically gain their intelligibility but also any sense of Lulu as an 'authentic' character.

The behaviours of the men in the opera similarly parody the masculine response to the *femme fatale* type. They are mesmerised by her bodily appearance too easily, they give in to her seductions too readily. Geschwitz, Lulu's lesbian lover, also falls under the spell of Lulu's 'femininity', 'performing' her own exaggeration of selfless, all-sacrificing love. The parody of the 'feminine' and of the masculine and lesbian behaviours it animates has the effect of revealing the 'feminine' as performance and of subverting it as an 'intelligible' cultural practice.

The playwright Frank Wedekind, as author of the Lulu plays, constructed a parodic character that itself performs the idea of the 'feminine' as *performance*. His character does more than simply parody the 'feminine', however. Through the fate of Lulu, Wedekind comments on the destructive consequences of the 'feminine' and of the social practices that 'institute and maintain' gender identities as 'norms of intelligibility'. I shall return to the issue of Wedekind's social commentary at the end of this chapter, but now turn to how Berg's music plays out this conception of the Lulu character and to how the composer stages his own authorial comment in sound.

Example 12.1   Lulu's 'Freedom' music (Act II scene 2, bars II/1001–3)

Three emblematic musical passages

Critics identify three musical instances as emblematic of the Lulu character. While concurring that these passages play decisive roles in the musico-dramatic characterisation of Lulu, I shall offer an understanding of how the music contributes to this characterisation that differs from earlier critics. In particular, I will show how the music supports the idea of Lulu as a parodic character that performs the idea of the 'feminine' as *performance*. The three passages are (i) Lulu's 'Freedom' music,[28] (ii) the 'Coda' music of the Sonata and (iii) Lulu's Lied.

Since Lulu's Freedom music and the Coda music share certain structural, dramatic and affective features, I consider them together here. Both are recurrent passages that George Perle calls *Leitsektionen*, and he understands the two as 'special *Leitsektionen* that embody concepts governing the work as a whole'.[29] The recurrence of these musical types, their association with significant dramatic moments and their characteristic musical attributes establish their significance for the opera generally. First, a brief description of each.

I name the Freedom music after its occurrence in Act II scene 2 when Lulu, returning home from prison, sings out the passionate cry of 'Freedom'. Example 12.1 cites its opening bars. The Freedom music occurs in several places both before and after the Act II scene 2 statement: in the Prologue when the Animal Tamer brings Lulu onto the stage as a snake; in Act II scene 1 when Lulu, now married to Schön, comes down the grand staircase in his house to greet her 'admirers' (Example 11.12, p. 222); and in Act III scene 2 just preceding Jack's murder of Lulu (there are brief references to it elsewhere in the opera, but I am not counting these as 'occurrences'). As the opening bars of the music suggest, the Freedom mu-

Example 12.2   The Coda music (Act I scene 2, bars I/615–20)

sic is characterised by triadic harmonies – especially in the bass patterns – and by suspension-like melodic figures.

Donald Mitchell, referring to the Freedom music accompanying Lulu's return from prison (Act II scene 2), writes that it is 'perhaps the most moving [music] in the whole opera … Berg's music tells us most beautifully that she has suffered'.[30] And Leo Treitler, writing of the Freedom Music more generally, calls it 'radiantly gorgeous music … which sings her identity'.[31] For these authors, the Freedom music has a 'beautiful' and 'gorgeous' sound which projects Lulu as an authentic and authentically-feeling character.

The Coda music has been similarly characterised as emotionally evocative. Douglas Jarman describes it as the 'rich, Mahlerian Coda theme'[32] and Donald Mitchell points out that '[the] exceptional beauty of this passage leaves us in no doubt as to the depth of Lulu's love', an assessment to which George Perle assents.[33] Example 12.2 cites its first appearance in Act I scene 2. Like Lulu's Freedom music, the Coda music uses triadic sonorities that have tonal associations, and appoggiatura-like melodic figures.[34] And, like the Freedom music, the Coda music is associated with intense and authentic feelings.

The emotional implications of the Coda music arise in part from its initial dramatic associations. It first occurs in Act I scene 2 as the conclusion of the Sonata exposition which literally and metaphorically stages an argument between Schön and Lulu – a confrontation between these two which is metaphorically projected by the opposition of row transpositions associated with each in the first and second theme groups.[35] During the Coda music, Lulu speaks – note how her not singing enhances the melodramatic effect – about her allegiance to Schön, motivating it by the care he showed towards her when she was a young, poor child on the street. The Coda music occurs again as the conclusion of the Sonata's reprise at the end of Act I. After agreeing to cut off his engagement to another woman and marry Lulu, Schön bemoans what he feels to be his impending 'execution', admitting what Jarman calls his 'fatal inability to break free of Lulu'.[36] The Coda music occurs for a last time in the final scene of the opera, just before Jack the Ripper murders Lulu and then Geschwitz. This final statement of the Coda music leads directly and smoothly into a final statement of the Freedom music.

Both the Freedom and Coda musics feature tonally implicative voice-leading in their melodies and make use of triad-based harmonies. Descriptions of the music as 'beautiful', 'gorgeous' and 'memorable' attach to these passages largely because their 'tonal' attributes in a 'non-tonal' context mark them as 'different'. In other words, these passages (as well as some others in the opera) use procedures of tonal music that are sometimes more, sometimes less explicit, but their effect depends on this sounding feature. Berg, having made the compositional decision to use the 'tonal sound' in these passages, did so, we must assume, for musico-dramatic effect. Understanding this effect begins with consideration of the historical context which situates both Berg's compositional choices and the musical significance of those choices.

Compared with the music of the *Lulu* period, Berg's earlier works, such as the *Altenberg Lieder* and *Wozzeck*, demonstrate a more consistent quality of sound: the 'atonal' sound that characterises the Second Viennese School. In the later works, including *Lulu*, he incorporates passages with a tonally-implicative sound, juxtaposing 'tonal' with 'atonal'. In other words, his compositional 'voice' and expressive palette expand. In appropriating a Mahlerian musical style and juxtaposing it with the predominant 'sound' of the opera, Berg employs a particular kind of expressive strategy.

Berg's expanded compositional voice raises a number of questions:

What does the 'tonally-implicative' music express? Does Berg use this Mahlerian style to imbue characters with feeling, to give them heartfelt emotion? Does he imitate this musical style in order to project the kind of expressive content the 'original' Mahler style would have had? Or does he imitate the style in order to parody the expressive content of the original?

A 'Mahlerian' style is not an 'authentic' musical language for Berg in the *Lulu* period; it is one he appropriates. In imitating the style – a style which listeners accept and understand in its 'original' context as having emotional content – Berg does not replicate but rather undercuts the 'authenticity' of this content.[37] Berg's parodic implementation of musical style here reinforces the exaggerated gender roles that Lulu and the other characters inhabit in the drama. The sound of the Freedom and Coda musics parodies a Mahlerian emotional content and undercuts any sense of an emotional authenticity that might attach to the dramatic situation.

The instance of the Freedom music which critics have understood as projecting Lulu's feelings and identity occurs after her escape from prison, an escape organised by Geschwitz, and her subsequent return to Schön's home where Alwa awaits her (Act II scene 2, bars II/1001ff.). The passage that precedes Lulu's 'passionate' display in the Freedom music (II/953ff.) tells us about her illness through its lethargic tempo. The music moves in slow motion as Schigolch escorts Lulu to the room where Alwa waits for her. Immediately upon Schigolch's exit Lulu finds the strength to pour out her emotions on the high B♮ of 'Freedom' and celebrate her liberation (II/1001). But surely Lulu, the consummate performer who has learned her feminine skills well, has other concerns at this moment. She is suddenly left alone with Alwa, the son of the man she has been convicted of murdering, and who gave her up to the police at the end of the previous scene. Lulu cannot be sure of Alwa's feelings towards her in the wake of his father's death, and in order to ensure her own preservation she must utilise her 'feminine' skills to influence Alwa's actions and feelings. Lulu performs her seductive charm through the borrowed expressivity of the Mahlerian style. The sounds pull us, and Alwa, into their seductive orbit. But, while Alwa falls completely under Lulu's Mahlerian allure, the effect on the audience hearing his seduction is quite different. The larger musical context prompts a hearing of the Freedom music as an exaggerated and appropriated 'romantic' sound that, right on cue, pours out Lulu's feelings.

The two prior occurrences of the Freedom music contribute to this hearing. It first occurs in the Prologue and then again in Act II scene 1, in the action preceding Schön's death. These prior occurrences reverberate in the Act II scene 2 version, magnifying the seductive and manipulative implications of Lulu's passionate outburst of 'freedom'.

The Freedom music in the Prologue (bars 44ff.) accompanies Lulu's first on-stage appearance. Having introduced all the other animals which are 'waiting behind the curtain', the Animal Tamer calls for the snake to be brought out: the Freedom music accompanies the Stage Hand, as he carries the soprano who sings Lulu on stage, and then the Animal Tamer as he playfully describes 'this creature created to make trouble … to tempt, to seduce, to poison and to murder without anyone noticing'. The combination of the Mahlerian sound of the Freedom music with the explicit articulation of the 'Woman as Temptress' myth through the Animal Tamer's words and the imagery of the snake has the effect of subverting both the meaning of the myth and the authenticity of the musical style.

The second occurrence of the Freedom music, in Act II scene 1 (bars II/145ff.), restages the myth of 'Woman as Temptress'. Between the end of Act I and the beginning of Act II, Lulu has married Schön, an event which signals the peak of her 'feminine' powers. The potency of her allure is made evident by the male admirers running about Schön's house in this scene. After initial exchanges with Geschwitz and Lulu, Schön leaves the stage, but instead of going to the Stock Exchange as claimed, he stays to spy on Lulu. Thinking her husband has left, Lulu turns her attentions to the admirers running about the house. As the fawning men and boys flutter around her, the Freedom music accompanies her flirtatious banter with the Acrobat (II/209–23). Clearly enjoying the powers of her seductive charms, Lulu engages her admirers in a playful and erotic exchange.

These instances of the Freedom music resound in its occurrence in Act II scene 2. The subversion of musical and mythical meaning from the Prologue's Freedom music and the sense of playfully seductive manipulation from Act II scene 1's version affect its meaning here. Now an escaped convict, Lulu can no longer use her seductive charms merely in play; the efficacy of her allure can mean the difference between freedom and incarceration, between life and death. Lulu chooses to perform the feminine role of 'Woman as Temptress' in order to preserve herself. What is more, hearing the 'Temptress' role as a performance of preservation in the Act II scene 2 version of the Freedom music reinterprets its meaning in prior instances. The later performance recasts earlier presentations of Feminine Myth and Allure as 'deadly serious'.

The Coda music first occurs at the end of the exposition of the Sonata in Act I scene 2 (bars I/615ff.) and is linked to Lulu's love and allegiance to Schön. Throughout the exposition, Schön and Lulu argue. He wants to cut off their relationship; she complains about her life with the Painter, a life of boring comfort arranged and controlled by Schön. Unable to sway Schön through confrontation, she tries emotional seduction. The Mahlerian Coda music creates an emotionally allusive environment in which Lulu can convince Schön of her love for him through reminiscence and declarations of devotion. The Coda music, with its triadic harmonies and 'longing' appoggiaturas, 'changes the subject' from confrontational dialogue to warm sentimentality which will 'melt' Schön's heart. Lulu wields her feminine power in the melodramatic narrative through the 'overpowering' aura of tonal implication.

The effectiveness of Lulu's seductive performance manifests itself in the occurrence of the Coda music at the end of Act I scene 3. Concluding the Sonata's recapitulation, this version of the Coda music (bars I/1356ff.) accompanies Schön's proclamation of what he perceives to be his own impending 'execution'. Unable to free himself from Lulu's feminine powers, Schön gives voice to his powerlessness with the same music that Lulu uses to seduce him, the Coda music. The music which plays out Lulu's feminine power recurs to play out the impotence it effects in Schön. The exaggerated emotional content of Schön's words – 'Now comes the execution' – is magnified by the parodic imitation of a 'romantic' sound.

The musical projection of Lulu as a character that performs a critique of the 'feminine' as a 'socially instituted and maintained norm of identity' derives not only from the parodic imitations of a Mahlerian style in the Freedom and Coda musics but also from another strategy that works something like parody: pastiche. Both parody and pastiche involve the imitation or borrowing of something prior, but pastiche creates its meaning by assembling and juxtaposing prior ideas. While noting the relationship between parody and pastiche, Frederic Jameson suggests that pastiche has none of the 'satirical impulse' of parody.[38] The third of the passages considered by prior critics as emblematic of Lulu's identity, Lulu's Lied, employs a strategy of pastiche.

George Perle in particular focuses on the significance of Lulu's Lied, calling it her 'great aria of self-awareness'.[39] Perle gives a fairly detailed analysis of the Lied's pitch and formal structure, but he does not comment on how these compositional choices relate to the Lied's dramatic significance.

The Lied occurs in the midst of Schön's five-strophe Aria in Act II scene 2 (the Aria occupies bars II/380–490 and 539–51; Lulu's Lied, II/491–538). Schön, presumed out of the house, is in hiding and observes Lulu's flirtatious exchanges with her various admirers. He eventually confronts her soon after Alwa, Schön's son, declares his love for Lulu. After escorting Alwa out of the room, Schön returns and presses Lulu to kill herself. She suggests that divorce is a better solution, but he, quite hysterical by now, will hear nothing of it. Lulu responds with the Lied in which she verbally defends herself. She presents five arguments, each of which corresponds to a formal unit of the Lied:

1. Lulu's worth or value as a person is not diminished because people kill themselves over her

2. Schön went into the marriage with his eyes open

3. Schön has not only fooled his friends over who she is, he has fooled himself

4. Lulu gave up her youth to Schön, which is no less important than his giving up his old age for her

5. Lulu has never tried to be anything other than what she 'is'

The text of Lulu's Lied provides information about her and Schön: Lulu has a strong sense of self and Schön has been deluding himself about her. But beyond that, however, the song provides little detail on how the Lulu character defines herself and what motivates her actions. In other words, the text falls short of the strong statement of 'self-awareness' Perle asserts. Berg's music sheds important light on an understanding of the dramatic role the Lied plays in the opera.

As Perle has noted, the Lied has five phrase units or 'periods'. Each period has an antecedent/consequent phrase structure in which the vocal and instrumental lines of the consequent invert those of the antecedent. In the first period (II/491–7), Lulu sings a melody fashioned from the Basic Series for the antecedent and from the inverted series for the consequent; the orchestra plays chords which are formed from the Basic Series and which are heard in association with Lulu's interactions with the Painter in the opera's first scene.[40] In the second period (II/498–507) the orchestra plays a theme associated with Lulu – the 'Lulu Melody' – based on Lulu's series, which in turn is derived from the trichordal partitioning of the Basic Series into the 'Picture Chords'.[41] This melody forms the thematic basis of the Canon in Act I scene 1 which accompanies a flirtatious game of chase between Lulu and the Painter.[42] The third period (II/508–15) presents an octatonic melody in the vocal part which arises as the top voice of successive statements of the Picture Chords. The fourth and fifth periods re-present in retrograde the melodic strategies of the first and second periods: the fourth period (II/516–21) plays 'Lulu's Melody' as did the second period, and the fifth period (II/522–36) plays a melody based on the Basic Series as did the first period; each of the two parts of this period is extended with statements of the 'Erdgeist Fourths' motive.[43] The Lied's short, concluding music in the orchestra (II/536–8) states a version of a tune, based on Alwa's series, which is featured in music accompanying

Lulu's conversation with him prior to her confrontation with Schön. In the earlier exchange, Lulu sings the tune in inversion as she asks of Alwa: 'Do you love me then?' At the end of the Lied, the tune is supported in the bass by a triad that supports the implied E♭ minor tonality of the tune and states the first three notes of an inverted form of Schön's series.[44]

The various musical references to other characters and earlier events in the opera do not support an understanding of the Lied as a unified statement of Lulu's identity. The Lied refers to musical constructions associated explicitly with Lulu, but even these – unlike the tunes and constructions associated with Schön, Alwa and some of the others in the drama – do not attempt to define an 'authentic' character: the Lulu Melody is based on a linearisation of the Picture Chords, and the Picture Chords, themselves a trichordal partition of the Basic Series, are associated with her depiction as Pierrot. Rather than a musical embodiment of her 'authentic' identity, the Lied is collage-like in its sonorous depiction of recent events in Lulu's life. The character that emerges from this pastiche of past events and associations is self-assured, but her self-awareness is not directed inwards. The music reflects her awareness of the immediate situation: its sounds inform us about her and those people with whom she has had dealings. Lulu knows that she must deflect Schön's hysterical anger: he is raging and has threatened her with death. She presents him with a textual and musical pastiche of prior events that has the immediate goal of defusing his rage, but at the same time this pastiche has the effect of deriding his blustering anger.

Douglas Jarman suggests that the 'disturbing difference between the emotional attitude adopted by the music and the nature of the text to which it is set' is part of *Lulu's* 'subversive' strategy.[45] Robin Holloway also notes the 'subversive' element in Lulu's music when he writes that *Lulu* 'undermines its listeners' obedience to emotive instructions'.[46] Holloway's observation of the subversive element of the opera in general – and, I would add, of the Lulu character in particular – resonates directly with the points I have been making about the Freedom and Coda musics and indirectly with those regarding Lulu's Lied.

As discussion above has demonstrated, the musical and dramatic contexts in which the Freedom and Coda musics occur, and the context of Berg's own compositional history, provide a framework for an understanding of the two musical passages that 'undermines' a 'typical' emotive response to their Mahlerian style. This framework also sets up a larger subversion of the 'feminine' by depicting both the particular emotive response and the feminine identity as performative choices. In the end, the subversive musico-dramatic goals of *Lulu* produce a situation in which 'the disturbing difference between emotional attitude ... and ... text' does not arise. The 'disturbing' effect occurs only if listeners respond 'typically' to the Mahlerian imitation. If listeners hear the Freedom and Coda musics as parodic imitation, then a sense of the Lulu character as critique of the 'feminine' emerges.

While the underlying strategy of subversion operates in Lulu's Lied, the particulars of its deployment are quite distinct from the Freedom and Coda musics. The Lied does not tempt listeners with a 'typical' emotive response, but rather saturates them with a succession of musical associations which simultaneously depict a dramatic history and coolly play out Lulu's response to Schön's hysterical ranting. The music of the Lied does not open a window onto an 'authentic' Lulu whose 'human nature' underlies her 'heroic struggle against the Marquis';[47] rather, it embodies a character whose actions reflect her history, her self-awareness and her strategies for self-preservation.

Berg's own voice

I return now to the issue of Wedekind's social commentary and how Berg's music plays out an authorial comment in sound. Earlier I suggested that Wedekind makes an authorial comment on the destructive aspects of the 'feminine' as performative choice within a patriarchal society through Lulu's murder at the hands of Jack the Ripper. Jack is the one character in the drama over whom Lulu's 'femininity' does not have a mesmerising effect.[48] Her feminine performance does not enchant him but leads instead to her own death. The lesson Wedekind enforces here is not that of a misogynistic patriarchal order but rather that of the devitalising effects of a social order that insists on certain forms of 'feminine' and 'masculine' behaviour. This assessment of Wedekind's commentary is shared by various critics of Berg's opera. Treitler writes that 'The deaths in the opera – and now I mean all of them – are the ravages of socio- and psychosexual struggle.'[49] And Jarman asserts that the opera forces us to pity and identify with 'all the characters helplessly trapped in this grotesque *Totentanz*' and 'to face our moral responsibility for the society depicted on stage'.[50]

Berg, adopting Wedekind's authorial comment, uses the opportunities afforded him by music to make it more palpable and more emotionally direct. The sound of Lulu's death cry and its orchestral aftermath near the opera's end (bars III/1294ff.) compel us to feel intensely the tragedy that is marked by Lulu's death. The shrieking strings stab us, Berg making it painfully clear how we are to feel about this death. Lulu is the symbol of this comprehensive social tragedy since, as archetypal Woman, she bears the

Example 12.3   Fusion of Coda and 'Freedom' musics (Act III scene 3, bars III/1276–81)

greatest social burden: *she* is the scapegoat for society's evil, *she* is Pandora, *she* is Eve. But the tragedy is not hers alone. It belongs to all the men and the women who participate in this '*Totentanz*'.

The effectiveness of Berg's authorial comment arises not simply from his orchestrational skill at the moment of Lulu's death but further from the way he prepares us for this event in the concluding exchange between Jack and Lulu (bars III/1258ff.). Just before they retire to an inner room, Jack tells Lulu that they have no need for the lamp she is carrying – we realise this is so he can wield his knife without her immediate knowledge – and she articulates her desire to be with him. During this exchange the orchestra plays the Coda music which imperceptibly transforms into the Freedom music. The passage climaxes at that point in the Freedom music which juxtaposes two tritone-related triads as Lulu says 'Don't make me beg any longer' (Example 12.3).

Berg's fusing of the Freedom and Coda musics at this crucial moment in *Lulu* attests to the significance of these passages for the opera as a whole. But in this context, their musico-dramatic meanings have been transmuted. The balance of power has changed in this passage. No longer in control, Lulu must now employ the Freedom music – music which was her powerfully seductive medium – to beg. And the Coda music – which she employed to foster Schön's sentimentality – now sets her surrender to Jack's wishes. Rather than exaggerated and melodramatic vehicles for Lulu's feminine performances in order to sway and seduce those who would control her, the Coda and Freedom musics have become sounding commentary on the tragic outcome of the 'socially instituted and maintained norms of intelligibility' that have given rise to Lulu's 'feminine performance'.

Berg's authorial comment on the tragedy of a social order that insists on certain forms of 'feminine' and 'masculine' behaviour operates in two stages: first, by depicting Lulu as an exaggeration of the 'feminine' and thereby demonstrating 'feminine' behaviour as a performative choice through parody of the emotive content implied in the Mahlerian style; and second, by using the parodic music to portray a situation in which the performative strategies are no longer effective. The force of Berg's authorial comment in the orchestral response to Lulu's death arises not simply from the qualitative features of its sounds but from those sounds in conjunction with the transformation of meaning that attaches to the Coda and Freedom musics in the exchange between Jack and Lulu.

Conclusion

Butler's concept of performative choice provides a means for understanding Lulu's various contradictory attributes and her non-unified character. In addition, issues of authenticity surrounding performativity and identity illuminate those musical features of *Lulu* that critics have found 'disturbing' – the disjunction between music and dramatic action. The Lulu character performatively exaggerates her femininity, and her music orchestrates that performance through parody and pastiche. Berg emerges from behind the parodic veil at the opera's end, however. Through the fusing of the Coda and Freedom musics and the shrieking strings that tell us of Lulu's death, Berg makes his position strikingly clear. While Lulu dies literally at the hand of Jack the Ripper, she also dies symbolically from the 'social norms of intelligibility' that dictate certain gendered behaviours. Through parodic exaggeration and pastiche, Berg's music makes us palpably feel the tragic consequences of Lulu's feminine performance.

PART IV

Postscript

13 Berg and the twentieth century

Arnold Whittall
King's College, London

The modern and the plural

As an 'Age of Extremes'[1] with a vigorously diverse mainstream, the twentieth century – in music as in other respects – does not lend itself to straightforward summarising, or the tracing of unambiguously consistent tendencies and trajectories, involving clear-cut lines of influence and dependency. What can be demonstrated, if the musical history of the century is surveyed, are networks of shared concerns which involve many different composers in many different ways, with many degrees of connection and divergence. To tell the story of twentieth-century music with Berg as a central character would require a particularly sensitive interpretation of such networks. The possibility that Berg could be an 'indispensable' figure has nevertheless been acknowledged for some time – for example, in a striking assessment by Pierre Boulez, first published in 1958, and all the more important for the ways in which it modifies Boulez's own earlier (1948) and much more hostile 'reception' of the composer.[2] Observing first that Berg's 'influence' was 'at present less decisive than that of Webern, despite the greater immediate range of his music', Boulez continued:

> It is likely that when the question of modern style becomes more settled
> Berg's influence will be able to make itself felt more profitably. It would
> in any case be superficial to see in Berg no more than a heroic figure rent
> by contradictions or to think of him merely as the culmination of ro-
> manticism on whom it would now be pointless to model oneself. On the
> contrary, by detaching the contradictions that are the key to his work
> from the particular context which gave them birth, it is possible to learn
> from Berg an extremely valuable lesson in æsthetics. His work retains
> intact all its potential for influence; and it is this which makes him
> indispensable to the musical domain of our time.[3]

One of the most revealing aspects of these comments is Boulez's assumption that, at some time in the future, 'the question of modern style' will become 'more settled'. More than thirty years after those comments were written, it might be argued that the main thing to have been 'settled' about 'modern style' is that it remains richly and consistently *unsettled*: what is settled about modern style is that it is, by definition, diverse. More than that, however; of all the earlier twentieth-century masters, Berg is especially prophetic of this plurality, and what Boulez described as Berg's 'diverse æsthetic cargo'[4] now seems an excellent model for a *fin de siècle* in which contrasts between composers who aspire to stylistic and technical synthesis and those who appear to resist such integration are increasingly significant. As will be considered a little more fully later on, Boulez's abiding reservations about Berg tell us much about his own impulses as a composer, centring on a search for synthesis which may appear ultimately more classic than expressionist, or modernist, in æsthetic essence. For Boulez, those 'contradictions' that are the 'key' to Berg's work, and which he appears to see as the source of that work's 'potential for influence', need to be thought of not as modernist fractures which escape ultimate integration, but as classical oppositions or polarities which imply and demand a final synthesis. In revealing comments about the *Lyric Suite*, Boulez has written of 'its certainty and mastery of form, the polished perfection of its instrumental writing' which 'help towards the synthesis Berg was seeking when he wrote the work. He here achieves a rare equilibrium, which was not to be maintained in the works which followed.'[5] It is not mere playing with words to respond that 'synthesis' and 'equilibrium' need not be precisely the same thing. If both possibilities remain viable with respect to the *Lyric Suite*, then this might represent exactly the kind of ambiguity which has helped to make Berg such a powerful presence in later twentieth-century music.

Concerns comparable to those of Boulez can be found in Stravinsky's various remarks on Berg. In his oracular later years, when his own music was achieving a new lease of life through the serial principle, Stravinsky offered this assessment:

> If I were able to penetrate the barrier of style (Berg's radically alien emotional climate) I suspect he would appear to me as the most gifted constructor in form of the composers of this century. He transcends even his own most overt modelling. In fact, he is the only one to have achieved large-scale development-type forms without a suggestion of 'neo-classic' dissimulation. His legacy contains very little on which to build, however. He is at the end of a development (and form and style are not such independent growths that we can pretend to use the one and discard the other) whereas Webern, the Sphinx, has bequeathed a whole foundation, as well as a contemporary sensibility and style.[6]

Stravinsky, at one with Boulez over Berg's 'emotional climate', yet differing over his 'potential for influence', particularly disliked that 'direct expression of the composer's own feelings' evident in *Wozzeck*'s 'D minor' Interlude, and in a characteristically lofty rebuke he declared that 'what disturbs me about this great masterpiece and one that I love, is the level of its appeal to "ignorant" audiences'. For Stravinsky, 'passionate emotion' must be conveyed 'within the most limiting conventions', above all shunning 'the *crescendo molto*'.[7] Stravinsky, of all composers – and he was after all three years Berg's senior – could scarcely have been expected to welcome the prospect that a style so explicitly derived from a late-Romantic, Austro-German *espressivo* would, in the 1960s, continue to attract adherents and even outdo a style reflecting more Webernian sensibilities. But younger composers had more time to spot the trend, and Boulez's partial recantation of his earlier hostility is emblematic of the post-war avant-garde's ability to persuade itself that Berg's was, after all, an authentically modern – that is, complex – voice. Stravinsky himself hinted at this judgement in his 1964 'programme note' for *The Rake's Progress*, describing his choice of an eighteenth-century number opera as model, 'rather than ... musical forms symbolically expressive of the dramatic content (as in the Dædalian examples of Alban Berg)'.[8]

'Dædalian' – intricate, labyrinthine; such terms recur persistently in Berg criticism and analysis. As Boulez reported on his study of the Chamber Concerto:

> I found that there was a lot more to Berg than his immediately accessible romanticism. ... what thrilled me ... was the complexity of his mind: the number of internal correspondences, the intricacy of his musical construction, the esoteric character of many of his references, the density of texture, that whole universe in perpetual motion revolving constantly around itself, all this is absolutely fascinating. It is a universe that is never completed, always in expansion – a world so profound, dense and rich and inexhaustible that one can, after thorough analysis, still come back to it a third or fourth time to find fleeting references that one had not noticed before.[9]

Nevertheless, as noted earlier, Boulez remained resistant to the kind of 'contradiction' he perceived in Berg's attempt to enforce some kind of 'co-existence' between tonal and non-tonal materials: 'To my way of thinking, if one is to preserve certain aspects of the past and to integrate them into our present-day thought, it must be done in the most abstract terms.'[10] Given what might be defined as Boulez's search for a 'new organicism', his reliance on cumulative repetitions and even elements of pitch-centricity in works like *Rituel* (1975) and *Répons* (1983–), it is scarcely surprising to find an implicit lack of sympathy with those æsthetic principles, sometimes termed post-modern, sometimes defined as representing a modernism newly radicalised and reinforced, that have come increasingly into favour in the later decades of the century. In this context, Berg's appeal has been enhanced by the perception that even his most disruptively backward-looking devices – quoting a Bach chorale harmonisation or a Viennese popular song – can set up the kind of irresolvable tensions with their serially-generated, atonal contexts which can now be regarded as the acme of modernist thinking. From this perspective, even an element of what Stravinsky wryly termed 'neo-classic dissimulation' can be invoked, provided it does not extend throughout an entire work, and may well appear a more acceptably modernist mode of expression than anything offered by the Sphinx-like Webern, who, in Boulez's later characterisation, provides 'a truly austere kind of perfection; but [as with Mondrian] when you see it again at a later date, it offers you nothing further'.[11]

Ambiguous laments

The significance of Berg for twentieth-century music since about 1960 is closely bound up with the significance of expressionism, revived and reinvigorated as part of a widespread reaction against the more austere and idealistic initiatives of the immediate post-war years. Indeed, Berg's impact on later composers might be most directly apparent in the way later twentieth-century expressionism tends to find its voice in that rich vein of lament and protest that is the correlative if not the explicit embodiment of sceptical or pessimistic sensibilities. Leo Treitler's formulation – 'One could easily get the impression … that Berg's well-known leaning to symmetrically closed forms and tight motivic networks is not a matter of musical inclination alone but a fatalism about life'[12] – is one manifestation of this idea. Douglas Jarman's judgement of *Wozzeck*, whose 'structure … should be seen as … an assertion of the nothingness which … is the ultimate end of the transient individual human being in the face of the fatefully and endlessly revolving world'[13] is another. Yet to categorise as 'Bergian' all music that evokes dark thoughts, from Birtwistle's melancholic processionals and Lachenmann's most evanescent gestures to Schnittke's more melodramatic outbursts, is dangerously reductive, not least because the expressive context of Berg's music is invariably more complex than the argument that it is essentially or even exclusively 'fatalistic' allows. As will be suggested later, there are usually other, quite different expressive elements present alongside assertions of 'nothingness'. It also needs to be made clear at this stage that Berg's continued appeal, and also his relative closeness to tradition, depend on the fact that he remained a vividly thematic composer: it is not only a matter of those 'tight motivic networks' to which Treitler referred, but also of an expansive melodiousness, and for this reason alone much of the later twentieth century's more abstract, essentially textural expressionism (as in Schnittke and Maxwell Davies) is at a considerable remove from Bergian practice, however close it may approach it in mood and tone. In these cases, indeed, one of Berg's essential concerns is *not* shared.

Simply because Bergian 'fatalism' is something to be offset, challenged, rather than merely established and indulged, Bergian 'ambiguity' seems to have penetrated more pervasively into contemporary musical consciousness. It is worth quoting Jarman at length on the ending of *Lulu*:

> Unlike *Wozzeck*, *Lulu* allows us no easy emotional release. The great D minor interlude in *Wozzeck* ...acts as an emotional catharsis in which the listener responds directly to the power of the music. The end of *Lulu* is more ambiguous. The music of the final pages of the opera has an emotional intensity not unlike that of the *Wozzeck* interlude, but its effect is very different. The music that comes back at this point of the opera is music that brings with it a host of complex and conflicting associations [and the] difference between the luxuriant, elegiac music and the events on stage produces an emotional disorientation that is deeply disturbing; it can also, if we respond to the music and are prepared to give these characters the understanding and compassion that the humanity of Berg's score demands, be humanly restorative.[14]

Jarman is perfectly justified in proclaiming a kind of 'higher' ambiguity in which the unresolved opposition is between the possibility of 'emotional disorientation' and of feeling 'humanly' restored. Yet the possibility that such divergent feelings might be present at the same time suggests a focus on what Robin Holloway has described – again with reference to Act III of *Lulu* – as 'displacement of cause and effect, and sometimes a deliberate rift between them'.[15] That very specifically Bergian tension between the sordid (Lulu's murder) and the sublime (the Countess's brief but exalted declaration of love) at the end of the opera is paralleled at the end of the Violin Concerto by the more abstract but no less palpable combination of sensuality and spirituality, acknowledged by Berg is his simultaneous use of the markings 'religioso' and 'amoroso' (bar ii/222). Displacement, disorientation – these are disturbing experiences, and in Berg the ambivalence is not simply a matter of conflict between disorientation and a 'humanly restorative' experience, but of a tension between apprehensions of order and of chaos which affect structure and expression alike. As Adorno put the point, 'the organizational, rational principle does not eradicate chaos, if anything it heightens it by virtue of its own articulation. With that Berg realized one of Expressionism's most profound ideas; no other musician achieved that to the same degree.'[16] To which one might add, no other musician before a composer like Brian Ferneyhough, in whose work, as Richard Toop has observed, 'much of the forcefulness and richness ...

arises both from the conceptual obstacle courses that the composer sets himself in the realization of individual layers, and from the violent collisions between these layers'.[17] 'Violent collisions' are the acme of a revived expressionism, and composers who seek to shun them – like Boulez – are those who are most remote from Berg in style and æsthetic orientation. Yet it is no less true that the manner in which late twentieth-century 'complex' composers present their own 'violent collisions' is worlds away from the allusive, still essentially romantic idiom of Berg's most personal compositions.

Memory – disintegration?

The paradigm of chaos heightened by rationality may offer a satisfying encapsulation of twentieth-century modernism that is instantly apprehensible in much twentieth-century art, but it leaves responsible criticism with an immensely complex task.

Max Paddison has correctly observed that Adorno's 'analyses of Berg's music are of particular interest because … they take the composer as a paradigm case for the process of "integration through disintegration"'.[18] However, it is no less true that Adorno's analyses do not sustain the kind of deep technical exploration of the Bergian musical fabric through which a clear picture of 'integration through disintegration' might be achieved. Adorno remains most persuasive in his general perceptions, as when he observes that Berg's music 'accomplishes within itself a process of *permanent dissolution*, rather than achieving a "synthesis". … So then, not only does Berg's music start out from the smallest component elements and then immediately further subject these to a kind of "splitting the atom", but the whole character of his music is that of a permanent self-retraction or self-cancelling. Its "Becoming", if I may term it thus – at all events, where it crystallizes-out its idea in its purest form – is *its own negation*.'[19]

As the final stages of this essay will seek to demonstrate, such formulas as these articulated by Adorno can be considered in relation to post-Adornian analytic/critical initiatives and post-Bergian compositional initiatives alike. Some influential writers on Berg appear to use a focus on relations between 'old' and 'new' as a substitute for Adorno's pairing of rationality and chaos, in order to strengthen claims for Berg's role as a continuer of well-established musical traditions. So, for example, Peter Burkholder links Berg's appeal to both connoisseur and lay audience with the kind of 'complete integration of surface rhetoric and inner structure' found in Haydn and Mozart, by way of 'a musical idiom that paralleled the earlier achievement of Haydn and Mozart in its richness of external allusion and internal integration, and wide and lasting appeal.'[20] As Burkholder sees it, 'Berg revitalized the familiar, writing atonal music that preserves and intensifies the emotional expressivity of the common romantic heritage.'[21] Synthesis, it appears, could go no further, and for this very reason Burkholder's reading will seem strained and unpersuasive to those who prefer to stress the tensions, the 'chaos', the particular personal qualities that give Berg's music its unrepentantly expressionistic power.

One problem all critical commentators on Berg confront is the need to balance their perceptions concerning his stylistic and technical consistency (his own 'Bergianism') with acknowledgements of degrees of modernist *dis*integration. The semantic balancing-act that results is illustrated with exemplary clarity in Anthony Pople's monograph on the Violin Concerto, which starts from the premise that 'in the works of Berg's maturity each musical element is simultaneously informed by several different ideologies. The result is not genuinely a synthesis, but gives the illusion of one – just as a mosaic or a pointillist painting may communicate a coherent image from a fine-grained approximation.'[22] Pople then proceeds by way of a narrative seeking to balance the work's integrative and disruptive components, and ends with the characterisation of the concerto as 'a work which simultaneously, and indeed similarly, celebrates both reconciliation and confrontation', and which 'might be said at the same time to have reconciled – and yet not reconciled – those two inseparable and eternal opposites'[23] – an eloquent and persuasive conclusion of which Adorno might well have approved. No less significant in this respect are two important studies by Craig Ayrey which consider the 'peculiar multivalence' of the early Mombert setting, Op. 2 No. 2,[24] and the 'essential ambiguity' of the ways in which serial and tonal elements interact in the second setting of 'Schliesse mir die Augen beide'.[25] As Ayrey demonstrates, this short song provides 'a more ambiguous, more closely integrated tonal-serial structure than the chorale variations of *Lulu*', yet it is nevertheless a '"complicated" structure, since it essentially opposes serial and triadic ... forms'.[26]

Such analytical explorations of the nature and scope of oppositions and interactions in Berg's music can easily be linked with the composer's own aspiration, as set out in his 1929 lecture on *Wozzeck*, 'to have both a great variety and integration'.[27] With its implication of equilibrium between opposites rather than a notable imbalance, this might be regarded as the kind of 'mainstream' manifesto which all later twentieth-century composers who are neither thoroughgoing minimalists nor unremittingly 'complex' could endorse. Nevertheless, as argued earlier, there should be a sense of shared concerns, some element of stylistic association as well as some such purely structural connection, before a composer can sensibly be considered 'Bergian' – some sense of those 'large-scale development-type forms' described by Stravinsky linked with a 'music of lament and protest', perhaps? Yet it cannot be denied that some composers have learned technical lessons from Berg without feeling impelled to echo the expressionistic aspects of his musical style. A particularly striking example of this is George Perle, whose authority as a Berg scholar developed out of a fascination with the kind of 'interval cycle' techniques Perle the composer had been working on in the late 1930s, before he found something similar in Berg's *Lyric Suite*.[28] Even so, Perle's own music has remained more neo-classical than neo-Bergian, setting up the kind of allusive rather than explicit associations with the Master that Robin Holloway has noted in referring to Oliver Knussen's debt to an 'unexpressionistic Berg, one comparable with Ravel (particularly *La Valse*) and (via *Der Wein* and *Lulu*) with American popular music'.[29]

Debts to the expressionistic Berg – however indirect – can be observed with even greater ease. An early example, Dallapiccola's short opera *Il Prigioniero*, completed in 1948, pursues the possibility of co-existence between diverse materials, and between tonal and serial techniques, with what now seems a rather over-heated insistence. The opera nevertheless has something of Berg's expansive melodiousness, and there are elements of ambiguity in the later stages – lament and affirmation, fatalism and faith – even a Bergian blend of sensual and spiritual in the macabre tenderness with which the prisoner is led to his death. What is missing in *Il Prigioniero* is the formal sophistication of *Lulu* and the Violin Concerto, and after 1950 contrasts could increasingly be drawn between Berg's ability to incorporate aspects of the traditionally 'symphonic' into his operas and instrumental works, in ways which enhanced the modernist expressionism of those works, and Schoenberg's more neo-classical approach, as revealed in his concertos for violin and piano. Where Schoenberg was seen as retreating into procedures closer to Brahms than to Mahler – with only the late String Trio and Violin Phantasy offering evidence of a revived expressionism – Berg could be hailed as having effected an imaginative transformation of Mahlerian *Angst* into an authentically twentieth-century language. Indeed, it is scarcely coincidental that the revived expressionism which affected composers as different in age and background as Elliott Carter (1908–) and Peter Maxwell Davies (1934–) coincided with the Mahler revival that began in the 1950s and has sustained an impetus ever since.

A line of development which stemmed from Mahler and Berg, and of-

fered post-war composers a fruitful alternative to more obviously avant-
garde or anti-expressionist tendencies deriving from Webern and Stravinsky, can be traced in many different contexts. It had an undoubted impact
on the music of Hans Werner Henze, while widely-performed operas like
Bernd Alois Zimmermann's *Die Soldaten* (1957–64) and Aribert
Reimann's *Lear* (1975–8) could be regarded as deriving in essence from
the explicitly post-Mahlerian pages of *Wozzeck* or *Lulu*. Yet the validity of
such associations should not obscure the fact that most later composers –
even those who might be placed in the contemporary 'mainstream' – have
tended to avoid Berg's very explicit thematicism. What might be defined
(after Stravinsky) as 'large-scale development-type forms' – Henze's symphonic works or the larger-scale designs of Carter or Maxwell Davies –
unfold with far less evidence of explicit motivic recurrence, however powerful the emotions they create in the process. It is therefore composers
who work most explicitly with aspects of musical memory, not so much
for purposes of pastiche but rather to intensify the confrontation between
something remembered and something contemporary, who have developed a Bergian ethos in the most creative way.

The third movement of Berio's *Sinfonia* (1968–9), which involves the
literal quotation of the Scherzo from Mahler's second symphony, was a
particular landmark in the establishment of a very twentieth-century,
modernist kind of romanticism. It represents a style whose continuation
can be heard with special refinement in one of Berio's very finest works,
Voci (1984) for viola and chamber orchestra, which weaves references to
Sicilian folk-music into a rich yet delicately-shaded harmonic tapestry. If,
as Charles Rosen argues, Beethoven was 'the first composer to represent
the complex process of memory – not merely the sense of loss and regret
that accompanies visions of the past, but the physical experience of calling
up the past within the present',[30] then Berg, and, after him, Berio, are
surely within that Beethovenian tradition which, in essence, succeeds in
intensifying an 'old/new' polarity. Associations on this level can create
some unlikely connections: for example, we might attempt to link Tippett,
by way of his very potent allusions to Beethoven in his Symphony No. 3
(1970–72), with Berg, whose recollections of Bach in the Violin Concerto
no less powerfully 'represent.. the sense of loss and regret that accompanies visions of the past'. Yet it is the quality of 'loss and regret' which is
crucial, and Tippett's context is as different from Berg's as it is from Maxwell Davies's in the final section of his Clarinet Concerto (1990), when a
Scottish folk tune is recalled in a way that cannot quite succeed in elimi-
nating all traces of the composer's own personal musical style. Coupled
with a serial technique that demonstrates a specifically post-Bergian

flexibility about approaches to set-forms as rigidly ordered elements, this atmosphere promotes Maxwell Davies's cause as a composer whose shared concerns with Berg are strong and fruitful. Tippett's, by contrast, are not: in the Symphony No. 3, the impression is created that present-day doubts and ambiguities are challenges to be overcome, rather than feelings to be accepted as inevitable and inescapable.

Rosen also argues that 'the most signal triumphs of the Romantic portrayal of memory are not those which recall past happiness, but remembrances of those moments when future happiness still seemed possible, when hopes were not yet frustrated. … Romantic memories are often those of absence, of that which never was.'[31] Considerations like these can certainly serve to distinguish between the kind of atmosphere created by such modern masters as Carter, Birtwistle or Boulez, and the works of Berio and Maxwell Davies described here. Among the present-day masters of a music of loss and regret which can also create a sense of disturbing disorientation through the sheer force of feeling or of the confrontations engendered, Kurtág, Henze and Schnittke all stand out. In Kurtág's case the laws of the network require acknowledgement of his capacity – in such compositions as *The Sayings of Peter Bornemisza* (1963–8) and *Messages of the Late Miss R. V. Troussova* (1976–80) – for an expressionism several degrees wilder than Berg's, as well as his particular debts to Webern. As for Henze and Schnittke, both are far more prolific than Berg, both far more uneven: yet both show that the power of memory in music extends well beyond the literal quotation of 'old' materials. Schnittke is at his most powerful and intensely post-Bergian in a brief composition like *Stille Nacht* (1978), an 'arrangement' of the carol which turns into a derangement, though a more complex and ambitious work like the Third String Quartet (1983), with its citations of Lassus, Beethoven and Shostakovich, has been described by one commentator in terms that make the Bergian associations irresistible: 'The network of reminiscences, often presenting the quoted material in its original forms, shows how far the music is from a true integration.'[32] Even so, with both Kurtág and Schnittke one may well conclude that the spirit of fatalism is a good deal purer and less ambiguous than is the case with Berg. With Henze, on the other hand, the contrasts between a sense of loss and a serene, even sublime acceptance of loss can seem too mutually accommodating, the tension and conflict diffused rather than positively polarised. In Henze's ten-movement instrumental *Requiem* (1990) the allusions to other composers are far less overt than in an earlier work like *Tristan* (1973), yet simply because there is little of the religious ritual about this music of loss, a degree of association with the spirit, if not the style of Berg's music can still be felt.

The tensions at the centre

Berg is a figure of central importance in twentieth-century music to the extent that the pluralism he pioneered has remained a fundamental factor in its later evolution. Berg was above all a great original in a century as fascinated by, and fearful of, individuality as it has been suspicious of 'slovenly' – yet still potent – tradition. As the century has proceeded, expressionism has shed some of its more surreal overtones and grown ever closer to grim approximations of reality, while resisting the extremes of total decadence and absolute transcendence. The twentieth century may indeed be an 'age of extremes', but in music its preferred strategy of exploring the tensions which arise when advance confronts retreat gives new angles on old genres a special weight. Berg was more resistant of traditional schemes than Bartók, Stravinsky or Schoenberg, less radical in his reorientations than Webern or Varèse. Above all, in the Violin Concerto's use of Bach as a manifest echo of a past that dissonates, creating a tension between old and new, destabilising the sense of progression and leaving closure (goal-arrival) ambiguous, Berg created an image of alienation confronting acceptance whose resonance remains potent and reaches into musical realms far removed from his actual style.

One further composer within Berg's network remains to be mentioned. Like Janáček, Berg helped to legitimise a music which, while technically progressive, could embrace compassionate social 'comment': he helped to legitimise a music in which the 'sordid' and the 'sublime' converge and even fuse. Yet, simply in the sense that they match Adorno's model of 'chaos' heightened by 'rationality' with particular power, the endings of Berg's later works, in their difference from the less ambivalent affirmations of Mahler or Janáček, and in their concern to balance a powerful sense of loss with a spirit of acceptance, speak with a special directness to later, younger composers who also seek to temper their sense of loss with an element of humanistic understanding and engagement. Berg also helped to legitimise a music in which disparate techniques (and even styles) may aspire to integration, within genres (concerto, string quartet, opera) that are renewed by being reshaped. Unlike Janáček, Berg also legitimised a particular concern with the possibilities for symmetrical structuring, and a 'flexible' approach to serialism, in the brave new world of post-tonal composition.

I referred earlier to the remarkable tension between sacred and sensual apparent in the Violin Concerto, and the disconcerting confrontation between sordid and sublime at the end of *Lulu*. But there are other powerfully resonant oppositions, as between personal, private allusions and generic, textural models in the *Lyric Suite* and the no less personal confrontation of raw emotion and constructivism in *Wozzeck* and the Chamber Concerto.[33] This is Berg's world, a world founded on the kind of contradictions to which Boulez, and later musicologists, have referred, and a world in which many other twentieth-century composers – as well as other kinds of musician – have felt, however uneasily, at home. Even if Berg can be held to offer a popularity-generating synthesis, as Burkholder has proposed, this co-exists with an open-ended series of possibilities and tendencies which has all the special fascination of something that is ultimately elusive. Berg may have been particularly progressive in his openness to such modern media as jazz and the cinema and his willingness to bring them within the orbit of his own kind of High Art. Yet it is the tendency of his music – in particular, of his harmony – to gravitate towards sonorities that still suggest the old, romantic world of consonance and dissonance that restrains his progressiveness and enriches his expressive vocabulary. Berg is the very model of the multi-faceted modern master, and the fact that there are a good many other important modern masters seems unlikely to reduce his significance, or even his 'influence', as the twentieth century gives way to the twenty-first.

Notes

Introduction
1 Reich, *Alban Berg*, p. 17.
2 Reich, *Life and Work*, p. 105.
3 See Pople, *Berg: Violin Concerto*, pp. 94–8.
4 Adorno, *Alban Berg*, p. 33.

1 Defining home: Berg's life on the periphery
1 Soma Morgenstern, *Alban Berg und seine Idole; Erinnerungen und Briefe*, ed. Ingolf Schulte (Lüneburg: zu Klampen, 1995), p. 41.
2 In this discussion of Vienna's districts I have drawn upon Felix Czeike (ed.), *Historisches Lexikon Wien*, vols. 1–3 (Vienna: Kremayr und Scheriau, 1992–4) and Christian Brandstätter, Günter Treffer and Anna Lorenz (eds.), *Stadt-chronik Wien: 2000 Jahre in Daten, Dokumenten und Bildern* (Vienna: Verlag Christian Brandstätter, 1986).
3 Alt-Hietzing (Old Hietzing) is the name given to the core of the district that is adjacent to the Schönbrunn grounds. The thirteenth district of Hietzing was created in 1892 by combining the communities of Baumgarten, Breitensee, Hacking, Hietzing, Lainz, Ober St-Veit, Penzing, Unter St-Veit, Schönbrunn, Speising, and parts of Hadersdorf, Hütteldorf, Mauer and Auhof (in 1938 communities north of the Wien river, including Penzing, Breitensee, Baum-garten, Hütteldorf and Hadersdorf-Weidlingau became the fourteenth district of Penzing). In this discussion of the Hietzing Berg knew I have drawn upon Helga Gibs, *Hietzing: Zwischen gestern und morgen* (Korneuburg: Mohl Verlag, 1996) and Erich Alban Berg, *Als der Adler noch zwei Köpfe hatte*, in particular the chapters 'Der Nobelbezirk Hietzing und seine Bewohner', pp. 93–105, and 'Der Kaiser', pp. 141–56.
4 Until 1918 the Lainzer Tiergarten was an Imperial hunting reserve. It was opened to the public in 1919 but did not officially become part of Hietzing until 1956.
5 Soma Morgenstern (1891–1976) gave up his legal career in the mid-1920s to become a columnist and novelist; with the rise of Nazism he left Vienna, set-tling in New York. In his edition of Morgenstern's *Alban Berg und seine Idole*, Ingolf Schulte (p. 41 n. 1) cites registration records to argue that Morgen-stern's move to Hietzing actually took place in January 1921 and that his move to an apartment in Alt-Hietzing (Maxingstraße 30) followed in October of that year. I have chosen to follow Morgenstern's chronology so as not to inter-rupt the flow of his narrative.
6 Morgenstern, *Alban Berg und seine Idole*, pp. 45ff.
7 Adorno, *Alban Berg*, p. 14.

8   Anna Nahowski's diaries relating to her years as the Emperor's mistress have
    been published as *Anna Nahowski und Kaiser Franz Joseph: Aufzeichnungen*, ed.
    F. Saathen (Vienna, 1986). The claim that two of her children were in fact
    fathered by the Emperor has never been subjected to genetic verification.

9   The details of Anna Nahowski's affair with the Emperor are drawn from Erich
    Alban Berg (*Als der Adler noch zwei Köpfe hatte*, pp. 155ff.), who cites Helene
    Berg as his source.

10 Erich Alban Berg, *Als der Adler noch zwei Köpfe hatte*, pp. 95ff.

11 For much of the following discussion of the Berg family I draw on two books
    of reminiscence by Erich Alban Berg: *Der unverbesserliche Romantiker* and
    Alban Berg: Leben und Werk.

12 Smaragda Berg married Adolf Freiherr von Eger on 21 April 1907; they were
    divorced on 23 December of the same year.

13 'Ein junger Künstler wie Sie heiratet nicht die Tochter eines Hofbeamten!';
    'Ein so schönes, vornehmes Mädchen heiratet nicht so einen jungen Bohém-
    ien. Aus dem wird nix.' Morgenstern, *Alban Berg und seine Idole*, p. 65.

14 *Ibid.*, p. 56.

15 For an analysis of Berg's relationship with literary Vienna see chapter 2, and
    also Rode, *Alban Berg und Karl Kraus*.

16 The Vereinigung schaffender Tonkünstler was founded on 23 April 1904 and
    during the course of the 1904–5 season gave two orchestral concerts, the sec-
    ond of which included the premieres of Schoenberg's *Pelleas und Melisande*
    and Zemlinsky's *Seejungfrau*. It also gave four song recitals, the last of which,
    on 11 March 1905, marked the organisation's final concert.

17 During 1904–5 he taught classroom lessons at the Schwarzwald School in the
    first district, where Webern, Horwitz, Jalowetz and Egon Wellesz (all musicol-
    ogy students at the University) were among his pupils. Thereafter he taught
    privately in his ninth district apartment on Liechtensteinstraße 68–70.

18 The suicide was that of the painter Richard Gerstl (1883–1908), who had had
    an affair with Schoenberg's wife. Schoenberg became acquainted with Gerstl in
    1907, at a time when Schoenberg himself was experimenting with painting.

19 Morgenstern, *Alban Berg und seine Idole*, p. 356.

20 Letter to an unidentified woman, quoted in *ibid.*, p. 356.

21 Alban Berg and Helene Nahowski were married on 9 May 1911, although her
    father insisted on a Protestant ceremony to facilitate the divorce he foresaw as
    inevitable.

22 Berg's most significant professional activity was his work for Universal Edi-
    tion, which included preparing the piano-vocal scores for Schoenberg's *Gurre-
    lieder* and Franz Schreker's opera *Der ferne Klang*.

23 In turning down the appointment to the Academy, Schoenberg stated that the
    time was not right for his return to Vienna.

24 Schoenberg's correspondence with Berg offers a detailed account of these years
    (see *The Berg–Schoenberg Correspondence*).

25 Letter of 17 May 1915 (*The Berg–Schoenberg Correspondence*, p. 241).

26 See chapter 5 for a discussion of the musical background to this rift.

27 Morgenstern, *Alban Berg und seine Idole*, pp. 117ff.

28 See chapter 3 for an account of Adorno's personal and intellectual relationship with Berg.

29 Adorno, *Alban Berg*, p. 27.

30 The architect Hermann Watznauer (1875–1939) was a friend of the Berg family and after the death of Conrad Berg assumed the role of Berg's mentor. His biography of Berg was first published by Erich Alban Berg in *Der unverbesserliche Romantiker* (the quoted passage appears on p. 53).

31 Morgenstern, *Alban Berg und seine Idole*, p. 101.

32 *Ibid.*, p. 313.

33 Adorno, *Alban Berg*, p. 31.

34 *Ibid.*, pp. 29ff.

35 Berg was an avid supporter of the football team Rapid which played its matches on the Hütteldorfer Pfannwiese, within walking distance of Berg's home.

36 Adorno, *Alban Berg*, p. 29.

37 Berg helped write the statutes for the *Verein* and served as one of its *Vortragsmeister*, or performance coaches.

38 Adorno, *Alban Berg*, p. 29.

39 See chapters 2 and 5. The *Altenberg Lieder* were not published until 1953.

40 Erich Alban Berg, *Alban Berg: Leben und Werk*, p. 41. In *Der unverbesserliche Romantiker*, p. 155, he dates this incident as having taken place shortly before Berg's death.

41 The journal *23* appeared between 1932 and 1937, a total of thirty-three issues. Berg designed the cover.

42 Johanna Berg died in 1926, Franz Nahowski in 1925, and Anna Nahowska in 1931.

43 Morgenstern, *Alban Berg und seine Idole*, p. 299.

44 *Ibid.*, p. 298.

45 See chapter 8 for a musical perspective on Berg's passion for elaborate secrets.

46 Morgenstern, *Alban Berg und seine Idole*, pp. 376ff.

47 Adorno, *Alban Berg*, p. 16.

48 *Ibid.*, p. 34.

49 Morgenstern (*Alban Berg und seine Idole*, pp. 364, 378) relates the oft-repeated story of how Berg was asked to submit proof of his 'Aryan' ancestry by the German *Reichsmusikkammer*. When challenged by Morgenstern as to why he had complied rather than discard the forms as Krenek had done, Berg is reported to have answered with a sigh, 'Ernst Krenek is not married to Helene', thus compounding his own cowardice through an act of disloyalty to his wife.

50 Adorno, *Alban Berg*, p. 33.

51 See, for instance, Berg's letters to Schoenberg of 13 September 1912 and 10 February 1913 (*The Berg–Schoenberg Correspondence*, pp. 113, 157).

52 See Christopher Hailey, 'Between Instinct and Reflection: Berg and the Viennese Dichotomy', in Jarman (ed.), *The Berg Companion*, pp. 221–34.

2   Battles of the mind: Berg and the cultural politics of 'Vienna 1900'

1 'Die Ohrfeige war so ziemlich das Klangvollste des ganzen Konzertabends.' Werner J. Schweiger, *Peter Altenberg Almanach* (Vienna: Löcker, 1987), p. 34.

For a general assessment of Altenberg see Andrew Barker, *Telegrams from the Soul: Peter Altenberg and the Culture of fin-de-siècle Vienna* (Columbia, SC: Camden House, 1996).

2 See Edward Timms, *Karl Kraus, Apocalyptic Satirist: Culture and Catastrophe in Habsburg Vienna* (New Haven: Yale University Press, 1986), p. 5.

3 See Erich Mühsam, *Namen und Menschen: unpolitische Erinnerungen* (Berlin: Guhl, 1977), p. 126.

4 'Ein besserer Dreibund' was Kraus's term for these three artistic musketeers of *fin de siècle* Vienna.

5 See *Mopp: Max Oppenheimer 1885–1954* (Vienna: Jüdisches Museum der Stadt Wien, 1994), p. 26.

6 Altenberg's evocations of Alban and/or Helene Berg are found in the sketches 'H. N.', 'Bekanntschaft' and 'Besuch im einsamen Park', all found in *Neues Altes* (Berlin: S. Fischer, 1911) from which Berg took the texts for his Op. 4 songs. See David P. Schroeder, 'Alban Berg and Peter Altenberg: Intimate Art and the Æsthetics of Life', *Journal of the American Musicological Society*, 3 (1992), pp. 261–93. See also Rode, *Alban Berg und Karl Kraus*, p. 429. I wish to record here my debt to this important and original study.

7 'Ich verstehe nichts von dieser letzten "modernen Music", meine Gehirn-Seele hört, spürt, versteht nur noch Richard Wagner, Hugo Wolf, Brahms, Dvořak, Grieg, Puccini, Richard Strauss! Aber das moderne Frauenantlitz verstehe ich wie die Bergalm und meinen geliebten Semmering.' Schweiger, *Peter Altenberg Almanach*, p. 35.

8 'Deine Oskar Kokoschka – Else Lasker-Schüler – Arnold Schönberg Vorliebe beweist genau den *Tiefpunkt* deiner *geistig-seelischen Maschinerie.*' Quoted in Willy Haas, 'Aus unbekannten Altenberg-Briefen', *Forum*, 8 (1961), pp. 467ff.

9 'Selbstverständlich und mit innerer Verpflichtung'. ÖNB, Musiksammlung, F 21 Berg 480/7.

10 'Alban, der adeligste Jüngling'. Altenberg to Smaragda Berg, n. d., Wiener Stadt- und Landesbibliothek, 181.213; see also 158.083.

11 'Ich komme als Künstler, zu Ihnen als Künstler —. *Helfen* Sie mir! Ich habe Ihre von mir vergötterete Schwester gekränkt, verletzt —. Legen Sie, *ich flehe Sie an*, ein gutes Wort für mich ein bei der Theuren, damit ich *wieder lebensfähig*, leidensfähig werde —. Möge Gott es Ihnen lohnen. Ich flehe sie an, meine Qualen mir zu *erleichtern!* Smaragda soll mir verzeihen *Ihnen zuliebe.*' ÖNB, Musiksammlung, F 21 Berg 498/1. It has been suggested that Altenberg's extravagant punctuation style may have influenced Berg's own writing practice. See Reich, *Life and Work*, pp. 17–18.

12 In a letter dated 30 August 1909 he writes: 'Gerhart Hauptmann beißt leidenschaftlich seine Fingernägel! Mahler, Lichtenberg, Hauptmann, Altenberg – in eine schöne Gesellschaft bin ich da geraten!!' *Briefe an seine Frau*, p. 132; *Letters to his Wife*, p. 94.

13 Hilmar, *Alban Berg*, p. 42.

14 'Raum 22, die Gustav Klimt-Kirche der modernen Kunst'. Altenberg, 'Kunstschau 1908 in Wien', in *Bilderbögen des kleines Lebens* (Berlin: Erich Reiss, 1909), pp. 115ff.

15   *Briefe an seine Frau*, p. 26; differently translated in *Letters to his Wife*, pp. 34–5.

16   'meine Unkenntnis in Dingen der Malerei u. namentlich Kraus' Verurteilen Klimts [hielt mich] davor zurück, meine Begeisterung für diesen allzu laut werden zu lassen'. Berg to Webern, 14 August 1920, quoted in Rode, *Alban Berg und Karl Kraus*, pp. 61, 395.

17   See *The Berg–Schoenberg Correspondence*, p. 168. Berg offered to send Schoenberg his spare copy.

18   The three songs – 'Traurigkeit', 'Hoffnung' and 'Flötenspielerin' – are among the published *Jugendlieder*. It is not widely appreciated that the third of these early Altenberg songs was also set to a text originally written on a picture-postcard. Berg himself was probably unaware of this. The original postcard with its inscription is still extant at the Galerie St Etienne, New York. See Andrew Barker and Leo A. Lensing, *Peter Altenberg. Rezept die Welt zu sehen* (Vienna: Braumüller, 1994), pp. 204, 409 (n. 25).

19   Altenberg, *Fechsung* (Berlin: S. Fischer, 1915), p. 231.

20   Kurt Blaukopf, *Mahler* (London: Allen Lane, 1973), p. 198.

21   The original manuscript of the sketch is now in the Werner Kraft-Archiv. It was placed in an envelope addressed to 'Herrn *Adolf Loos*, Architekt, für Oskar Kokoschka, Mahler, Semmering an der Südbahn Hotel Panhans'. It is not known whether Loos ever delivered the manuscript to Kokoschka.

22   Altenberg reacted to the withdrawal of his sketch with one entitled 'Hoher Gerichtshof', in which he summarises the contents of the deleted sketch. *Nachfechsung* (Berlin: S. Fischer, 1916), p. 157.

23   See chapters 8 and 11; also Pople, *Berg: Violin Concerto*, p. 28.

24   Timms, *Karl Kraus, Apocalyptic Satirist*, p. 8.

25   See pp. 9–10.

26   Rode, *Alban Berg und Karl Kraus*, p. 160. To describe Werfel and Berg simply as friends – cf. Martin Esslin, 'Berg's Vienna', in Jarman (ed.), *The Berg Companion*, p. 12 – is to oversimplify the issue.

27   'So haben wir denselben Geschmack, was mich sehr freut, denn in einigem geht er ja auseinander: Kraus, *Altenberg*!!' Quoted in Rode, *Alban Berg und Karl Kraus*, p. 392.

28   'Er war edel mit dem Adel einer neuen Zeit, die Peter Altenberg, ihr großer Seher, verkündete: mit dem Adel der Natürlichkeit.' Quoted in Erich Alban Berg, *Der unverbesserliche Romantiker*, p. 186.

29   '[Es] ist klar, daß [Webern] seine Meinung über Karl Kraus, Peter Altenberg, Peter Rosegger, Gustav Mahler und mich nie geändert hat. Das waren seine "Fixsterne".' Quoted in Nuria Nono-Schoenberg (ed.), *Arnold Schoenberg 1874–1951. Lebensgeschichte in Begegnungen* (Klagenfurt: Ritter, 1992), p. 401.

30   Joan Allen Smith, *Schoenberg and his Circle: A Viennese Portrait* (New York: Schirmer, 1986), p. 57. This is a verbatim transcript of a conversation between Deutsch and Smith.

31   'Es wäre so schön, wenn alle Leute, die heute was sind, in einer Stadt beisammen wären, im regsten Verkehr. Schönberg, Klimt, Altenberg, Loos, Kraus, wir, Kokoschka und viele andere.' Quoted in Rode, *Alban Berg und Karl Kraus*, p. 392.

32   'Den Dank für das Beispiel, das Sie mir durch Ihre in allen Kunst- und
       Lebensfragen nachahmenswerte Erscheinung seit meiner Jugend gaben u. auch
       heute noch, wo ich bald 40 Jahre alt bin, immer noch geben. Den Dank für die
       unermeßliche Wonne, die mir Ihr geschriebenes Werk bereitet [...] Den Dank
       für die seelische Stütze, die Sie mir oft u. oft in den unangenehmsten Lebens-
       lagen geboten haben.' Quoted in Rode, *Alban Berg und Karl Kraus*, pp. 10ff.

33   Quoted in Perle, *Lulu*, p. 38.

34   For an English translation of Kraus's lecture see Jarman, *Alban Berg: Lulu*,
       pp. 102–12. These words are sung in the opera at Act II, bars 319–23 (see
       Example 9.5, p. 188).

35   Berg followed Franzos's spelling, *Wozzeck*, which can be attributed to a mis-
       reading of Büchner's script. See Perle, *Wozzeck*, pp. 25–37.

36   Egon Friedell, 'Die Altenberg-Anekdoten', in E. Friedell (ed.), *Das Altenberg-
       buch* (Vienna: Verlag der graphischen Wiener Werkstätte, 1921), pp. 417–25. In
       a letter to Helene in Autumn 1909 Berg mentions going to the 'Fledermaus'
       (*Briefe an seine Frau*, p. 145).

37   *Die Fackel*, 274 (February 1909), pp. 1–5 (Altenberg's 50th birthday article). In
       a letter to Helene of August 1910, Berg compared Altenberg's *Was der Tag mir
       zuträgt* and *Märchen des Lebens* with the prose poems of Baudelaire (*Briefe an
       seine Frau*, p. 184).

38   Weininger was the author of the great succès de scandale *Geschlecht und Char-
       akter* (*Sex and Character*). In 1903 he committed suicide, aged twenty-three, in
       the house in the Schwarzspanierstrasse where Beethoven died. The house was
       demolished for redevelopment in 1904. There is evidence that Altenberg's
       views were articulated before the publication of *Geschlecht und Charakter*. See
       Andrew Barker, 'The Persona of Peter Altenberg: "Frauenkult", Misogyny and
       Jewish Self-Hatred', in J. A. Parente and R. E. Schade (eds.), *Studies in German
       and Scandinavian Literature after 1500: A Festschrift for George Schoolfield*
       (Columbia, SC: Camden House, 1993), pp. 129–39.

39   Timms, *Karl Kraus, Apocalyptic Satirist*, p. 69.

40   Karl Rykl, quoted in *The Berg–Schoenberg Correspondence*, p. 52 n. 2.

41   *Briefe an seine Frau*, p. 150; *Letters to his Wife*, p. 101.

42   'Mein Tintenfäßchen ist aus braunem Glas, fabelhaft leicht zu reinigen, kostet
       2 Kronen, und heißt noch dazu "Bobby", also jetzt "Robert". Es ist daher ein
       Kunstwerk, es erfüllt seinen Zweck, stört Niemanden und ist schön braun.'
       Altenberg, *Vita Ipsa* (Berlin: S. Fischer, 1918), p. 48. This inkwell is now in the
       Historisches Museum der Stadt Wien, Inv. Nr. 94.605/1, 2.

43   Jens Malte Fischer, *Fin de Siècle: Kommentar einer Epoche* (Munich: Winckler,
       1978), p. 22.

44   Carl E. Schorske, *Fin de Siècle Vienna: Culture and Politics* (New York: Alfred
       A. Knopf, 1980), pp. 116–80.

45   An English version of Kraus's text is available in Harold B. Segel, *The Vienna
       Coffee House Wits* (West Lafayette: Purdue University Press, 1994), pp. 65–85.

46   Kraus's dislike of Klimt may have been conditioned by the enthusiastic sup-
       port the painter received from Hermann Bahr, most loathed and most savagely
       treated of all Kraus's literary foes.

47   Christopher Hailey has suggested that Schoenberg's 'aggressive' identification
with tradition is linked to his awareness of being an autodidact trained outside
the official Viennese institutions ('Berg and the Viennese dichotomy', in
Jarman (ed.), *The Berg Companion*, p. 224). See also chapter 1.

48   Rode, *Alban Berg und Karl Kraus*, p. 418.

49   Peter Haiko and Mara Reissberger, 'Ornamentlosigkeit als neuer Zwang', in A.
Pfabigan (ed.), *Ornament und Askese im Zeitgeist des Wien der Jahrhundert-
wende* (Vienna: Brandstätter, 1985), pp. 110–19.

50   Patrick Werkner, *Egon Schiele: Art, Sexuality and Viennese Modernism* (Palo
Alto: Society for the Promotion of Science and Scholarship, 1994), p. 66.

51   *Ibid.*

52   Hermann Broch, *Hofmannsthal und seine Zeit* (Frankfurt: Suhrkamp, 1974),
pp. 7–15.

53   Adolf Loos, 'Potemkin City', in *Spoken into the Void: Collected Essays 1897–
1900* (Cambridge, MA: MIT Press, 1982), pp. 95–103.

54   Altenberg to Samuel Fischer, n. d., Wiener Stadt- und Landesbibliothek,
199.208/1–5.

55   *The Berg–Schoenberg Correspondence*, p. 170.

56   *See* Rode, *Alban Berg und Karl Kraus*, p. 429.

57   *The Berg–Schoenberg Correspondence*, p. 171 n. 3; *Die Fackel*, 374–5 (May
1913), p. 24.

58   *The Berg–Schoenberg Correspondence*, p. 52.

59   In 1912 the painter Egon Schiele, who shared Loos's and Altenberg's fascination with the 'child woman', served 24 days in prison for circulating obscene
drawings. Earlier charges of abducting and raping a minor had been dropped.
See Werkner, *Egon Schiele*, p. 68.

60   *Adolf Loos: Festschrift zum 60. Geburtstag* (Vienna: Lanyi, 1930), p. 9. The page
is reproduced in Erich Alban Berg, *Alban Berg: Leben und Werk*, p. 216.

61   'in den unangenehmsten Lebenslagen […] von meiner mehr als 3jährigen
Militärdienstzeit nicht zu reden', Rode, *Alban Berg und Karl Kraus*, p. 10.

62   See Berg's letter to Schoenberg of 8 October 1914 (*The Berg–Schoenberg Correspondence*, pp. 218–20). In 'Untergang des Franzosentums', Altenberg described the French as 'sham romantics and heartless megalomaniacs in this
earthly madhouse'. For an explanation of Kraus's initial reticence, which had
personal as well as political grounds, see Timms, *Karl Kraus, Apocalyptic
Satirist*, pp. 266ff.

63   'Wann hebt die größere Zeit des Krieges an – der Kathedralen gegen
Menschen!' *Die Fackel*, 404 (December 1914), p. 11.

3   Berg and Adorno

1   Theodor W. Adorno, *GS* 13, i.e. vol. 13 of *Gesammelte Schriften*, ed. G. Adorno
and R. Tiedemann (Frankfurt: Suhrkamp, 1970–), p. 340.

2   See Jan Maegard, 'Zu Th. W. Adornos Rolle im Mann/Schönberg Streit', in R.
Wiecker (ed.), *Gedenkschrift für Thomas Mann 1875–1975* (Copenhagen:
Verlag Text und Kontext, 1975), pp. 216–17. Admittedly this is a retrospective
judgement and Schoenberg was not always the most fair-minded judge. See

also Thomas Mann's letter to Jonas Lesser of 15 October 1951 (*Briefe*, ed. E. Mann, vol. 3 (Frankfurt: Fischer, 1965), pp. 225–8); also Jürgen Habermas's two essays on Adorno in *Philosophisch-Politische Profile* (Frankfurt: Suhrkamp, 1971).

3 *The Berg–Schoenberg Correspondence*, p. 335; Adorno, *GS* 13, p. 361.

4 An early account of Adorno's compositions is René Leibowitz, 'Der Komponist Theodor W. Adorno', in M. Horkheimer (ed.), *Zeugnisse: Theodor W. Adorno zum 60. Geburtstag* (Frankfurt: Europäische Verlagsanstalt, 1963), pp. 355–9; for more recent commentary see *Musik-Konzepte*, vols. 63–4, ed. H.-K. Metzger and R. Riehn (Munich: edition text+kritik, 1989) and the essay by Siegfried Schibli issued with the CD recording WER 6173–2 (Mainz: Wergo, 1990).

5 As late as 1938 he was writing that 'according to our theory there will be no war' (Adorno–Benjamin, *Briefwechsel, 1928–1940*, ed. H. Lonitz (Frankfurt: Suhrkamp, 1994), p. 328) and even in early 1939 he is not convinced that war will come (*ibid.*, pp. 388–90).

6 Leo Löwenthal, 'Erinnerungen an Adorno', in L. von Friedeburg and J. Habermas (eds.), *Adorno-Konferenz 1983* (Frankfurt: Suhrkamp, 1983), p. 390.

7 Reich, *Alban Berg*, pp. 21–7 ('Klaviersonate, op. 1'), pp. 27–31 ('Vier Lieder, op. 2'), pp. 31–5 ('Sieben frühe Lieder'), pp. 35–43 ('Streichquartett, op. 3'), pp. 47–52 ('Vier Stücke für Klarinette und Klavier'), pp. 52–64 ('Drei Orchesterstücke, op. 6'), pp. 91–101 ('Lyrische Suite für Streichquartett'), pp. 101–6 ('Konzertarie "Der Wein"').

8 Wiesengrund began publishing essays under the name 'Theodor Wiesengrund-Adorno' in the 1930s, but people who knew him continued to refer to him and address him as 'Wiesengrund'. Berg refers to him exclusively in this way. By 1943 he is 'Dr. Adorno' (see Thomas Mann, *Die Entstehung des 'Doktor Faustus'* (Frankfurt: Fischer, 1949), pp. 31–5 *et passim*).

9 Adorno, *Philosophie der neuen Musik* (Tübingen: J. C. B. Mohr, 1949). Eng. trans. of 2nd edn (Frankfurt: Europäische Verlagsanstalt, 1958) as *Philosophy of Modern Music*, trans. A. G. Mitchell and W. V. Blomster (London: Sheed and Ward, 1973). Repr. as vol. 12 of *GS*.

10 Mann describes the writing of the novel and his relations with Adorno in great detail in *Die Entstehung des 'Doktor Faustus'*.

11 Adorno, *GS* 18, pp. 488, 491; *GS* 13, p. 402. Both Berg and Leverkühn find it difficult to focus their general æsthetic interests and confine them to music, both are interested in numerology, etc. Mann adds that in both the real music of Berg and the imaginary music of Leverkühn dissonance is the expression of the serious and spiritual, while harmony and tonality ('das Harmonische und Tonale') stand for hell or the world of the commonplace (Mann, *Tagebücher*, ed. P. Mendelssohn and I. Jens, 9 vols. (Frankfurt: Fischer, 1979–93), *1946*, p. 769). None of this really amounts to much.

12 'Die Deitschen fressen immer nur Dreck' (Adorno, *GS* 18, p. 489); cf. *GS* 13, p. 340, *GS* 20, p. 553.

13 Leverkühn rejects the tempting offers of the French impresario Fittelsberg to enter 'le grand monde', maintains his artistic integrity and stays put in his rural retreat. Berg didn't imagine that a concert in Paris would threaten his integrity: he gave one in 1928 (see Jarman, *The Music of Alban Berg*, p. 10 n. 2).

A few more such performances in the 1930s would have allowed Berg to buy an even more powerful car. It is hard to imagine Leverkühn buying a car.

14   Mann, *Tagebücher, 1949–1950*, p. 580.

15   Adorno's end was as grotesque, in its way, as those of Berg, Webern and Schoenberg. Throughout the 1950s and early 1960s he had kept up a steady stream of social and cultural criticism, but he seems to have been surprised by the German student movement of the mid- and late 1960s and quickly distanced himself from it. A number of incidents – such as his public handshake with the burly police chief who organised the removal of students occupying his Institute for Social Research – caused consternation among members of the left. Finally, a group of women students decided to stage an 'Adorno love-in'. Stripping to the waist, they performed a parody of the Flower Maidens scene from *Parsifal*, dancing in an erotically suggestive way around Adorno as he entered the lecture-hall and pelting him with flowers. This was an extremely astute tactic. Adorno prided himself on not being a prude, but the 'love-in' was too much for him. Shielding his eyes from the sight of the women's breasts with his leather briefcase, he left the lecture-hall – without (for once) speaking. He left for a holiday in Switzerland without trying to lecture again and died there of a heart-attack.

16   For a good full-length treatment of Adorno's views on art see Susan Buck-Morss, *The Origin of Negative Dialectics: Theodor W. Adorno, Walter Benjamin, and the Frankfurt Institute* (New York: Macmillan, 1977). The best discussion of Adorno's theory of music is Max Paddison, *Adorno's Æsthetics of Music* (Cambridge: Cambridge University Press, 1993). See also Raymond Geuss, review of Adorno's *Æsthetic Theory*, *Journal of Philosophy* (1986), pp. 732–41.

17   See the last section of the final poem ('Le Voyage') in Baudelaire's *Les Fleurs du mal*.

18   See W. Benjamin, 'Zentralpark', in *Illuminationen* (Frankfurt: Suhrkamp, 1977), p. 247.

19   There might seem to be strong similarities between these views of Adorno and those held by Schoenberg. Schoenberg, too, rejects the idea that the artist is trying to realise beauty, and claims that art must be 'true' ('Die Kunst soll nicht schmücken sondern wahr sein', Willi Reich, *Arnold Schönberg oder Der konservative Revolutionär* (Vienna: Fritz Molden Verlag, 1968), p. 44; cf. Adorno, *GS* 18, p. 62). Schoenberg also gives a central place to the 'necessity' of artistic production (see *Harmonielehre*, 3rd rev. edn (Vienna: Universal Edition, 1922), chapter 22; *Stil und Gedanke: Aufsätze zur Musik*, ed. I. Vojtech (Frankfurt: Fischer, 1976), p. 73). However, when Schoenberg speaks of 'truth' he usually seems to have in mind authenticity of expression, that a musically elaborated form of an original inspiration ('Einfall') is *true to* that 'Einfall' and hence an authentic expression of the composer (*Stil und Gedanke*, p. 6). This notion of truth of expression is completely different from Adorno's Hegelian idea of 'truth'. For Adorno, the expressionist self and its 'Einfalle' are not the absolute to which art must be true (*GS* 12, p. 52). Crudely put, the composer may have a worthless 'Einfall', and an authentic elaboration of it won't make it a work of art. Similarly, when Schoenberg speaks of 'necessity' he seems usually to mean the composer's inner need for self-expression, not the neces-

sity of a particular solution to the puzzle the material presents. On freedom and necessity see Adorno's two essays 'Reaktion und Fortschritt' (*GS* 16) and 'Stilgeschichte in Schönbergs Werk' (*GS* 18), both from the 1930s.

20 Adorno, *GS* 12, pp. 13–19.

21 Stravinsky's published comments on political matters over the course of a long lifetime present a no less contradictory picture than do his remarks on many other matters. In the 1930s and 1940s he seems to have had little time for Hitler but quite a lot of time for Mussolini and some sympathy for Franco, though his words and actions are perhaps easier to reconcile with an instinct for self-preservation than with a strong and consistent political stance. See 'Stravinsky's Politics', in Vera Stravinsky and Robert Craft (eds.), *Stravinsky in Pictures and Documents* (New York: Simon and Schuster, 1978), pp. 547–58. [Ed.]

22 In the 'Preface' to *Philosophie der neuen Musik*, Adorno states that the book can be seen as an 'excursus' to *Dialektik der Aufklärung*, a book he wrote jointly with Max Horkheimer in the early 1940s.

23 The most concise and accessible account of this work is in David Held's *Introduction to Critical Theory: Horkheimer to Habermas* (Berkeley: University of California Press, 1980), chapter 5; see also Paul Connerton, *The Tragedy of Enlightenment: An Essay on the Frankfurt School* (Cambridge: Cambridge University Press, 1980).

24 It is precisely this that Schoenberg seems to want to deny by denying that there is a twelve-note system and insisting that he had invented a method or technique: 'One must follow the series; but nevertheless one composes as freely as before' ('Man muss der Grundreihe folgen; aber trotzdem komponiert man so frei wie zuvor', *Stil und Gedanke*, p. 80). Schoenberg always said that Adorno had missed the point (see his letter of 27 July 1932 to Rudolf Kolisch: *Stil und Gedanke*, p. 150). Adorno tries to defend himself in the 'Vorrede' to his *Moments Musicaux* (in *GS* 16). If the method of composing with twelve notes related only to each other is *just* a method and 'not the only route to the solution of the new problems' (Maegard, 'Zu Th. W. Adornos Rolle', p. 218) then one of the main assumptions of *Philosophie der neuen Musik* is undermined. Note that there is another (and much less plausible) version of Schoenberg's famous dictum, namely: 'One follows the series, but composes just as before' ('Man folgt der Grundreihe, komponiert aber im übrigen wie zuvor'). Twelve-note composition might well be 'just as free' as tonal composition, but it is very hard to believe it can be just like it.

25 Adorno, *Philosophy of Modern Music*, pp. 68–9. *GS* 12: 'Das Subjekt gebietet über die Musik durchs rationale System, um selbst dem rationalen System zu erliegen.' (p. 68); 'Die neue Ordnung der Zwölftontechnik löscht virtuell das Subjekt aus.' (p. 70).

26 Adorno, *GS* 14, p. 9.

27 Adorno, *GS* 12, pp. 122–6.

28 Adorno, *GS* 18, p. 668. Note that Adorno is constantly praising Berg's 'economy' (e.g. *GS* 18, p. 462).

29 Adorno, *Philosophy of Modern Music*, p. 30. 'Die einzigen Werke heute, die zählen, sind die, welche keine Werke mehr sind.' *GS* 12, p. 37.

30   For details see Jarman, *Alban Berg: Lulu*, chapters 1 and 2.

31   Including, apparently, Schoenberg (*The Berg–Schoenberg Correspondence*, p. 365).

32   'I cannot say with certainty whether it is I who first pointed him toward *Lulu*, as it now seems to me upon reflection; in such cases it is easy to err out of narcissism' (*Alban Berg*, p. 26). This is so uncharacteristically modest one might be tempted to think there is something to it. In any case since we know that Berg attended a performance of *Die Büchse der Pandora* in 1905, almost twenty years before he first met Adorno (who, after all was only born in 1903), Adorno can at most imply that he drew Berg's attention to the operatic possibilities of a play which the composer already knew well.

33   Given Berg's evident fascination with ways in which music can emerge gradually from noise (see Adorno, *GS* 13, pp. 416–21; also Perle, *Wozzeck*, p. 10) it is a shame that we will never hear Pippa's musical glass.

34   See Adorno–Benjamin, *Briefwechsel*, p. 398.

35   Repr. in Jarman, *Alban Berg: Wozzeck*, p. 138.

36   Repr. in *ibid.*, p. 156.

37   See Perle, *Wozzeck*, pp. 25–37.

38   Adorno, *GS* 12, p. 37.

39   Adorno, *GS* 16, p. 94: 'jedes Stück Bergs war seiner Unmöglichkeit abgelistet'.

40   Adorno, *GS* 12, p. 37.

41   Friedrich Cerha, 'Some Further Notes on my Realization of Act III of *Lulu*', in Jarman (ed.), *The Berg Companion*, pp. 261–7.

42   Adorno, *GS* 13, p. 452.

43   Adorno, *GS* 18, p. 458, 654; *GS* 13, pp. 325–30.

44   Adorno, *GS* 18, pp. 667–70; cf. *GS* 13, p. 355.

45   Adorno, *GS* 13, p. 440.

46   Adorno, *GS* 18, pp. 467, 475; *GS* 16, pp. 88–90.

47   See Nietzsche's discussion of 'active' and 'passive' pessimism in *Der Wille zur Macht*, ed. P. Gast and E. Förster-Nietzsche (Stuttgart: Kröner, 1964), pp. 10–96.

48   Adorno, *GS* 13, p. 346.

49   Adorno, *GS* 18, p. 461; *GS* 16, pp. 90–96. This, of course, is just what Boulez objects to in his early essay 'Incidences actuelles de Berg' (1948) – Boulez playing Baudelaire, as it were, to Adorno's Hegel (Eng. trans. as 'The Current Impact of Berg (the Fortnight of Austrian Music in Paris)', in *Stocktakings from an Apprenticeship*, trans. S. Walsh (Oxford: Clarendon, 1991), pp. 183–7).

50   Adorno, *GS* 18, p. 500: 'Das Stehen-Lassen der Brüche zwischen Moderne und Spätromantik ist angemessener als begänne die Musik absolut von vorn; eben damit fiele sie dem undurchschauten Gewesenen zur Beute.'

51   See Pople, *Berg: Violin Concerto*, pp. 98–9.

52   Adorno, *GS* 18, p. 500; *GS* 13, p. 350; *GS* 15, p. 340.

53   Adorno, *GS* 18, pp. 499–501; *GS* 13, p. 349. Contrast this again with Boulez's 'The Current Impact of Berg'.

54   Adorno, *GS* 16, p. 86.

55   Adorno, *GS* 18, p. 500; cf. *ibid.*, pp. 667–70.

56   For instance in the open letter to Schoenberg about the Chamber Concerto

(Eng. trans. in Reich, *Life and Work*, pp. 143–8, and in *The Berg–Schoenberg Correspondence*, pp. 334–7).

57   Robert P. Morgan, 'The Eternal Return: Retrograde and Circular Form in Berg', in Gable and Morgan (eds.), *Alban Berg*, pp. 111–49.

58   Adorno, *GS* 12, p. 10.

59   Adorno, *GS* 4, p. 281; *GS* 12, pp. 122–6.

60   See Douglas Jarman, 'Alban Berg, Wilhelm Fliess, and the Secret Programme of the Violin Concerto', in Jarman (ed.), *The Berg Companion*, pp. 181–94.

61   Adorno, 'Aberglaube aus zweiter Hand', in *GS* 8, pp. 147–76.

62   Adorno, *GS* 13, pp. 22–3.

63   *Ibid.*, pp. 342–3.

64   *Ibid.*, p. 347. Oddly enough, Adorno, who throughout his life was known to his friends as 'Teddie', was also very much 'like' his name. If Berg was an alpine chapel, the short, stout Adorno, who spoke continuously in an over-articulated voice, was an animated teddy-bear, who kept trying to cover himself in as many glittering ornaments as possible.

65   Adorno admits this to Benjamin (see Adorno–Benjamin, *Briefwechsel*, pp. 344–5).

4   Early works: tonality and beyond

1   'An Leukon', in Reich, *Alban Berg*, appendix, pp. 14–15.

2   Letter to Emil Hertzka (managing director of Universal Edition, Vienna), dated 5 January 1910. Arnold Schoenberg, *Letters*, ed. Erwin Stein, trans. Eithne Wilkins and Ernst Kaiser (London: Faber, 1964), p. 23.

3   Ten years Alban's senior, Watznauer filled a void left by the recent death of his father Conrad Berg (1846–1900) and the absence of his eldest brother Hermann (1872–1921) in the United States. Berg's letters to Watznauer give ample evidence of a consuming interest in the arts and a readiness to indulge in passionate responses to works of literature and music.

4   Watznauer's biography is published with expansions and commentary in Erich Alban Berg, *Der unverbesserliche Romantiker*, pp. 9–117. The chronology of the songs is reproduced on pp. 152–3.

5   'Liebe', 'Im Morgengrauen', 'Grabschrift' and 'Traum' are published in the *Jugendlieder* (Vol. I nos. 21–3, Vol. II no. 1); an excerpt from 'Wandert, ihr Wolken' may be found in Nicholas Chadwick, 'Berg's Unpublished Songs in the Österreichische Nationalbibliothek', *Music and Letters*, 52 (1971), p. 130.

6   This is the date given by Watznauer (Erich Alban Berg, *Der unverbesserliche Romantiker*, p. 68) and by Willi Reich on Watznauer's authority. Whilst publishing Watznauer's chronology intact, Erich Alban Berg himself suggests independently that the song was performed in public by Smaragda Berg, accompanied by her brother, on 12 April 1905 (*Der unverbesserliche Romantiker*, pp. 58, 150).

7   The concert programme is reproduced in Erich Alban Berg, *Alban Berg: Leben und Werk*, p. 107.

8   'The Teacher's Testimonial', in Reich, *Life and Work*, p. 28.

9   Chadwick, 'Berg's Unpublished Songs', p. 137.

10 Adorno writes, though almost certainly without knowledge of the manuscript evidence: 'One could well imagine that [Op. 1] came about in response to the assignment "sonata movement"' (*Alban Berg*, p. 40).

11 Reich, *Alban Berg*, p. 10.

12 Hilmar, *Katalog*, p. 75.

13 Perle, *Wozzeck*, p. 2. It is indeed difficult if not impossible fully to correlate the contents of the manuscript sources and sketches of Opp. 1–3 (as described in Hilmar, *Katalog* and Floros, *Alban Berg*, p. 156) with the dates given in many apparently authoritative general commentaries.

14 This is the view expressed by Ulrich Krämer in his essay issued with the CD recording JD 643–2 (Zurich: Jecklin–Disco, 1990).

15 See pp. 161–2.

16 Redlich, *Alban Berg: Versuch einer Würdigung*, p. 355 n. 47. The fact that Polnauer did not begin his studies with Schoenberg until 1909 perhaps supports the dating of Op. 1 to that year, although it is of course entirely possible that he heard the anecdote from Berg subsequently.

17 By Adorno, for example (*Alban Berg*, pp. 40–42).

18 *Ibid.*, p. 43. For a lucid commentary on and development of Adorno's analysis, see Max Paddison, *Adorno's Æsthetics of Music* (Cambridge: Cambridge University Press, 1993), pp. 158–68 and 279–84.

19 See Berg's letter to Robert Lienau Verlag, 26 June 1920, transcription and facsimile in Rosemary Hilmar (ed.), *Katalog der Schriftstücke von der Hand Alban Bergs, der fremdschriftlichen und gedruckten Dokumente zur Lebensgeschichte und zu seinem Werk* [*Alban Berg Studien*, 1/ii] (Vienna: Universal Edition, 1985), pp. 122–4.

20 See chapter 5; also Douglas Jarman, 'Alban Berg: The Origins of a Method', *Music Analysis*, 6 (1987), pp. 273–88.

21 Bruce Archibald, 'Berg's Development as an Instrumental Composer', in Jarman (ed.), *The Berg Companion*, p. 94.

22 Adorno, *Alban Berg*, pp. 43, 46.

23 Mark DeVoto, 'Alban Berg and Creeping Chromaticism', in Gable and Morgan (eds.), *Alban Berg*, pp. 57–78.

24 Schoenberg, *Theory of Harmony*, trans. Roy. E. Carter (London: Faber, 1978), pp. 258–67, 360–65.

25 *Ibid.*, pp. 258–9 (translation adapted).

26 *Ibid.*, p. 258.

27 See Clara Steuermann reporting the views of her late husband, the Schoenberg pupil Eduard Steuermann (1892–1964), and Eduard Steuermann's own words quoted from an interview with Gunther Schuller, in Joan Allen Smith, *Schoenberg and his Circle: A Viennese Portrait* (New York: Schirmer, 1986), pp. 138–9.

28 Adorno, *Alban Berg*, p. 41.

29 DeVoto, 'Alban Berg and Creeping Chromaticism', p. 67. See also his discussion in Walter Piston, *Harmony*, 4th edn, revised and expanded by Mark DeVoto (New York: Norton, 1978), p. 491.

30 Max Paddison sees a model for this passage in the Prelude to Wagner's *Tristan und Isolde* (*Adorno's Æsthetics of Music*, pp. 279–84).

31   See Steven Kett, 'A Conservative Revolution: The Music of the Four Songs Op. 2', in Jarman (ed.), *The Berg Companion*, pp. 69–70; Floros, *Alban Berg*, p. 156; Hilmar, *Katalog der Musikhandschriften*, pp. 45, 48, 75; also Watznauer's chronology (in Erich Alban Berg, *Der unverbesserliche Romantiker*, p. 76). We should be wary of the latter source, however, as Watznauer assigns all four of the Op. 2 songs to 1908, and mistakenly attributes the poem of Op. 2/i to Hohenberg rather than Hebbel.

32   This topic may have suggested itself to Berg by way of an exhibition at the Viennese Secession in 1909 which featured the painting *Die Schlafenden* by Josef Engelhart (1864–1941). See Kett, 'A Conservative Revolution', p. 70.

33   Adorno, *Alban Berg*, p. 49; Mosco Carner, *Alban Berg: The Man and the Work*, 2nd edn (London: Duckworth, 1983), p. 100; DeVoto, 'Berg the Composer of Songs', in Jarman (ed.), *The Berg Companion*, p. 44.

34   Stephen Kett also draws this comparison with Schoenberg's cycle ('A Conservative Revolution', p. 82).

35   C♮ = 0, C♯/D♭ = 1, … B♮/C♭ = 11. This standard notation follows the work of the influential American music theorist Allen Forte.

36   The classic analysis of the song in these terms is found in Craig Ayrey, 'Berg's "Scheideweg": Analytical Issues in Op. 2/ii', *Music Analysis*, 1 (1982), pp. 189–202. Ayrey interprets '[an] image of the piece as complete and self-referential', suggesting that 'hierarchical repetition proceeds from the projection of the vertical symmetry of the first chord's set … onto a foreground linear paradigm, and thence through the complete structure' (p. 200).

37   This is to say, in untransposed form, [C, E, F♯/G♭, A♯/B♭] (the chord can of course be formed on any of the twelve chromatic pitches). The notation [0, 4, 6, 10] does not of itself identify a 'root' for the chord; if the chord appears in a context that allows it to be interpreted as tonally functional, then either C or F♯/G♭ (at the untransposed pitch-level) would be regarded as the root, depending on the details of the voice-leading.

38   See Jarman, *The Music of Alban Berg*, p. 148.

39   Schoenberg's discussion of his Ex. 342 in *Theory of Harmony*, pp. 418–19, similarly invokes a linkage of dominant-quality sonorities at the tritone in explaining a chord from *Erwartung*; his Ex. 342a presents exactly the three upper voices of Berg's Op. 2/i, bar 5, indicating that Schoenberg thought of the augmented ninth (F♮) as a dissonance which is resolved through the melodic motion to E.

40   Kett, 'A Conservative Revolution', p. 74.

41   Robert P. Morgan, 'The Eternal Return: Retrograde and Circular Form in Berg', in Gable and Morgan (eds.), *Alban Berg*, pp. 134–6.

42   I am ultimately grateful to Christopher Wintle for insisting on this point, albeit differently nuanced, in a public exchange of views, though the analysis given here synthesises his observations with others I have made previously. See Anthony Pople, 'Secret Programmes: Themes and Techniques in Recent Berg Scholarship', *Music Analysis*, 12 (1993), pp. 392–4, and Christopher Wintle and Douglas Jarman, 'Recent Berg Scholarship: Responses to Anthony Pople', *Music Analysis*, 13 (1994), pp. 310–12. Stephen Kett also identifies the whole-tone planes of motion in 'A Conservative Revolution', pp. 82–3.

43 Schoenberg, *Theory of Harmony*, p. 420.

44 Adorno, *Alban Berg*, p. 54. The emphasis is Adorno's.

45 In music, this was one strand in a wider discussion: see Carl Dahlhaus, *The Idea of Absolute Music*, trans. Roger Lustig (Chicago: University of Chicago Press, 1989), esp. chapter 2.

46 Floros, *Alban Berg*, pp. 154–5.

47 *Letters to his Wife*, pp. 106–11. Not everything in this letter was entirely accurate: Berg occasionally stretched the truth in order to make a point. But, perhaps fortunately, its intended recipient never read it: it was placed unopened in Helene's room. Their enforced separation ended in early September of that year and the couple were married on 3 May 1911. The Quartet had received its first performance, privately, a few weeks earlier on 24 April.

48 Carner, *Alban Berg*, p. 118.

49 Adorno, *Alban Berg*, p. 53.

50 See chapter 8.

51 See, for example, Dahlhaus, *The Idea of Absolute Music*, chapter 9 ('The Idea of the Musically Absolute and the Practice of Program Music').

52 Redlich, *Alban Berg: Versuch einer Würdigung*, p. 63.

53 The terminology is George Perle's ('Berg's Master Array'). This article is based on an interpretation of Berg's letter of 27 July 1920 to Schoenberg (*The Berg–Schoenberg Correspondence*, p. 283).

54 Redlich, *Alban Berg: Versuch einer Würdigung*, pp. 64–5.

55 Floros, *Alban Berg*, pp. 165–6.

56 Adorno, *Alban Berg*, p. 53.

57 Floros, *Alban Berg*, pp. 156–8.

58 See DeVoto, 'Alban Berg and Creeping Chromaticism', pp. 72–3.

59 Berg to Helene, 16 July 1909 (*Briefe an seine Frau*, p. 71; *Letters to his Wife*, p. 62).

5   Berg's aphoristic pieces

1 The date of this visit was 4–11 June (*The Berg–Schoenberg Correspondence*, p. 179 n. 1).

2 Reich, *Life and Work*, p. 41. This statement is difficult to reconcile with Reich's own chronology (p. 113), which gives 'summer 1913' as the date of composition of Op. 5.

3 Regina Busch (in a personal communication) expresses doubts, based on the same uncertainty of language that attracts my attention, that Reich and Berg ever talked about this meeting – had the information come from Berg himself surely Reich would have said so – and remarks further that the relationship between Reich and Schoenberg was not such that they would have been likely to speak of it. During the preparation of this chapter I became fascinated by the dearth of authoritative information concerning either the subject of this meeting or the date on which Berg finished his Op. 5. In the course of trying to pin down the sources of the meagre (but confidently offered) information contained in the first-generation books on Berg I corresponded with several scholars whose generosity in sharing their knowledge was as impressive as their readiness to devote time to answering my questions: my warmest thanks

to Bruce Archibald, Regina Busch, Mark DeVoto, Christopher Hailey and Douglas Jarman.

4 Redlich, *Alban Berg: The Man and His Music*, p. 234. The original German-language edition speaks of '[eine] Krise in Bergs geistiger Existenz' (*Alban Berg: Versuch einer Würdigung*, p. 302). Redlich's use of the word 'spiritual' in the English version (one might expect 'intellectual') is a bit odd, unless he was of the opinion that the criticism was of something more personal than the style of Berg's latest compositions. This interpretation of the meeting seems to me a very likely one, in view of the impatience with Berg's personal habits that is expressed repeatedly in Schoenberg's letters to him.

5 *The Berg–Schoenberg Correspondence*, p. 256. Berg made piano reductions of Franz Schreker's *Der ferne Klang* in 1911 and Schoenberg's *Gurrelieder* and the two vocal movements of Schoenberg's Second String Quartet in 1912.

6 This concert, conducted by Schoenberg in the Musikvereinsaal on 31 March, broke into a riot during the performance of Berg's songs and could not be finished. It was one of the best documented scandals in recent concert history, leading to lawsuits and a good deal of caricature and critical comment (see p. 24). Berg kept Schoenberg posted on the aftermath of the concert in letters of 2, 3, 4, 7–8, 16 and 24 April and 6 May (*The Berg–Schoenberg Correspondence*, pp. 166–76). According to Reich, Berg was so dispirited as a result of the hostile reception given his two songs that he wrote in a letter to Webern, 'The whole thing is so loathsome that one would like to fly far away' (Reich, *Life and Work*, pp. 40–41). He never sought another performance for the work, and it was not done again during his lifetime.

7 During this time Berg had also written bits of a symphony which remained unfinished. It is not certain that Schoenberg had seen this work, and in any case it would not have shared the 'aphoristic' style of the Op. 4 and Op. 5 pieces – as can be seen from the page of the extant *Particell* fragment reproduced in Hilmar, *Katalog*, p. 159.

8 Having acknowledged receiving Schoenberg's 'censure' during the Berlin visit, it is surprising that Berg should have written, in his long and heartfelt letter of late November 1915, that 'The 1st time I noticed your dissatisfaction with me was during the Amsterdam trip' (*The Berg–Schoenberg Correspondence*, p. 256). This presumably refers to Berg's tour with Schoenberg and others to Prague, Leipzig and Amsterdam which took in a performance of the latter's Five Orchestral Pieces Op.16 in Amsterdam on 12 March 1914 (*ibid.*, p. 203 n. 1). Berg wrote to Helene from there on 10 March, but his letter gives no inkling yet of any disagreement with Schoenberg (*Briefe an seine Frau*, pp. 244–7, *Letters to his Wife*, pp. 152–4); it does, however, mention the clarinet pieces, which Berg had promised to send to some Dutch musicians. In a slightly later letter to Helene, Berg explains his proposal to dedicate the Three Orchestral Pieces Op. 6 to Schoenberg, who 'has long been due for a large-scale work dedicated to him … He asked for it outright in Amsterdam … He "ordered" it, in fact' (letter of 11 July 1914, *Briefe an seine Frau*, p. 253; *Letters to his Wife*, p. 159). [Ed.]

9 Schoenberg chides him for his verbal extravagance in a letter dated 28 November 1913: '… *be more concise*. You always write so many excuses, parenthetical asides, "developments," "extensions," and stylizations that it takes a long time

to figure out what you're driving at' (*The Berg–Schoenberg Correspondence*, p. 196).

10   According to Schoenberg this piece was inspired by the sun's appearance from behind a cloud at the funeral of Gustav Mahler. It is a picturesque setting, almost entirely without motion or activity.

11   Mark DeVoto sees the motivic organisation of the *Altenberg Lieder* as their 'pervasive, distinguishing feature' ('Alban Berg's Picture-Postcard Songs', PhD diss., Princeton University, 1967, p. 7).

12   For analyses of Op. 4 see DeVoto, 'Alban Berg's Picture-Postcard Songs'; also his 'Some Notes on the Unknown *Altenberg Lieder*', *Perspectives of New Music*, 5/i (Fall/Winter 1966), pp. 37–74, and 'Berg the Composer of Songs', in Jarman (ed.), *The Berg Companion*, pp. 47–66. See also René Leibowitz, 'Alban Berg's Five Orchestral Songs after Postcard Texts by Peter Altenberg, Op. 4', *The Musical Quarterly*, 34 (1948), pp. 487–511; Adorno, *Alban Berg*, pp. 62–7; and Rolf Urs Ringger, 'Zur formbildenden Kraft des vertonten Wortes', *Schweizerische Musikzeitung*, 99 (1959), pp. 227–9 (an analysis of the second song only). The Altenberg texts are discussed by David C. Schroeder in 'Alban Berg and Peter Altenberg: Intimate Art and the Æsthetics of Life', *Journal of the American Musicological Society*, 46 (1993), pp. 261–94.

13   See DeVoto, 'Alban Berg's Picture-Postcard Songs', p. 91; and Jarman, *The Music of Alban Berg*, pp. 5–6.

14   DeVoto believes this was the first song to be written. See DeVoto, 'Alban Berg's Picture-Postcard Songs', p. 91 and Jarman, *The Music of Alban Berg*, pp. 5–6.

15   This anticipates the figure in *Lulu* that analysts have agreed to call 'Basic Cell I' (see Perle, *Lulu*, p. 87; Jarman, *The Music of Alban Berg*, p. 86). Jarman discusses the importance of *Lulu*'s Basic Cells I and III in this song in 'Alban Berg: The Origins of a Method', *Music Analysis*, 6 (1987), pp. 280–84.

16   DeVoto, 'Alban Berg's Picture-Postcard Songs', p. 70.

17   The two lines of text concerned are subtly different: 'Über die Grenzen des All blicktest du sinnend hinaus' ('You gazed pensively over the edge of the world') and 'Über die Grenzen des All blickst du noch sinnend hinaus' ('You are still gazing …'). The twelve-note chord used to accompany the initial statement, in the past tense, is gradually recalled as the statement of continuation in the present tense unfolds.

18   This musical quotation probably points out a textual similarity: in song three, 'Hattest nie Sorge um Hof und Haus!' ('Not a care for house and home!'); in song five, '… hier sind keine Menschen, keine Ansiedlungen' ('… here are no people, no settlements').

19   See also p. 199.

20   Both these events are in response to the text. The static *Klangfarben* chord accompanies the text 'Ich habe gewartet, gewartet, oh, gewartet!' ('I have waited, waited, oh, waited!'), while the clarinets tumbling down in helter-skelter fashion immediately after usher in the text 'Die Tage werden dahinschleichen' ('The days will slip away').

21   These pieces are discussed by Adorno (*Alban Berg*, pp. 67–71), Bruce Archibald ('Berg's Development as an Instrumental Composer', in Jarman (ed.), *The Berg Companion*, pp. 106–10), William Devotis ('Vier Stücke für Klarinette und

Klavier, Op. 5', *Musik-Konzepte 9: Alban Berg Kammermusik II*, ed. Heinz-Klaus Metzger and Rainer Riehn, July 1979), Diether de la Motte (*Musikalische Analyse mit kritischen Anmerkungen von Carl Dahlhaus* (Kassel: Bärenreiter, 1972), pp. 131–45) and Wallace Berry (*Musical Structure and Performance* (New Haven: Yale University Press, 1989), chapter 4).

22 Similar substitutions of one interval cycle for another in the String Quartet Op. 3 are discussed on pp. 78–80.

23 Jarman, *The Music of Alban Berg*, pp. 23–4.

24 Adorno sees a resemblance between this movement and the *fourth* of Schoenberg's set (*Alban Berg*, p. 71). This discrepancy is as good evidence as any for the degree to which the Berg pieces deviate from their models.

25 Jarman, *The Music of Alban Berg*, p. 3 n. 2.

26 *The Berg–Schoenberg Correspondence*, p. 143.

27 This letter accompanied a copy of the Three Orchestral Pieces Op. 6, which were dedicated to Schoenberg. In this letter he said 'For four years it has been my secret but no less fervent wish to dedicate something to you … Unfortunately my hope of writing something … to dedicate to you without angering you, eluded me for several years' (*The Berg–Schoenberg Correspondence*, p. 214).

6 Berg, Mahler and the Three Orchestral Pieces Op. 6

1 See, for example, Redlich, *Alban Berg: The Man and his Music*, esp. pp. 50–51, 57, 65–6, 71, 140–42; Reich, *Life and Work* (many separate references). It is worth noting the Mahlerian sympathies of both writers, Reich having been a pupil of Berg and Redlich having worked on the fringes of the Schoenberg circle between the wars. Other writers who have emphasised Mahler's influence on the Op. 6 pieces are René Leibowitz, *Schoenberg and his School*, trans. D. Newlin (New York: Da Capo, 1975), p. 153, and Adorno, *Alban Berg*, p. 7. For a recent study of Mahler's influence on *Wozzeck*, see Patrick Lang, 'Mahler, mein lebendes Ideal: zum Einfluss Gustav Mahlers auf Berg und *Wozzeck*', in Beat Hanselmann (ed.), *Berg Wozzeck: der Opernführer* (Munich: PremOp, 1992), pp. 191–208.

2 Landmark publications are Joseph Straus, *Remaking the Past: Musical Modernism and the Influence of the Tonal Tradition* (Cambridge, MA: Harvard University Press, 1990), and Kevin Korsyn, 'Towards a New Poetics of Musical Influence', *Music Analysis*, 10 (1991), pp. 3–72. Both acknowledge the influence of Harold Bloom's work in literary theory, or, rather, take Bloom's work as a starting-point. Bloom's main contributions here are *The Anxiety of Influence: A Theory of Poetry* (London: Oxford University Press, 1973), *A Map of Misreading* (Oxford: Oxford University Press, 1975) and *Poetics of Influence* (New Haven: Schwab, 1988).

3 The principal sources here are Jarman, *The Music of Alban Berg*, pp. 37–46, and two articles by Mark DeVoto: 'Alban Bergs Drei Orchesterstücke op. 6: Struktur, Thematik und ihr Verhältnis zu *Wozzeck*', in Rudolf Klein (ed.), *Alban Berg Studien*, 2 (Vienna: Universal Edition, 1981), pp. 97–106, and 'Alban Berg's "Marche macabre"', *Perspectives of New Music*, 22/ii (1984), pp. 386–447. There is also an article by Michael Taylor, 'Musical Progression in the "Präludium" of

the Three Orchestral Pieces op. 6', in Jarman (ed.), *The Berg Companion*, pp.
123–39; unfortunately Taylor's detailed analysis does not get beyond bar 15.

4   *Letters to his Wife*, pp. 32, 37–8, 63, 90, 134, 147–8, 181, 300. Some editorial
inconsistencies have been preserved.

5   Berg refers to some of these occasions in his letters to Schoenberg: see *The
Berg–Schoenberg Correspondence*. Schoenberg's analytical comments on the
Andante of Mahler's Sixth Symphony, the work to which Berg makes special
reference, are preserved in 'Gustav Mahler', *Style and Idea*, 2nd edn, ed.
Leonard Stein (London: Faber, 1975).

6   *The Berg–Schoenberg Correspondence*, p. 87.

7   Reich, *Life and Work*, p. 19. See also Erich Alban Berg, *Alban Berg: Leben und
Werk* (Frankfurt: Insel, 1976), p. 104

8   Reich, *Life and Work*, p. 17.

9   Hilmar, *Alban Berg*, p. 178.

10   Reich, *Life and Work*, p. 25; Hilmar, *Alban Berg*, p. 42.

11   Reich, *Life and Work*, p. 34; Hilmar, *Alban Berg*, p. 48.

12   Hilmar, *Alban Berg*, p. 57.

13   *Ibid.*, p. 56.

14   *Ibid.*, p. 87. See also *The Berg–Schoenberg Correspondence*, p. 98. Of the four-
hand arrangement of the Ninth, Berg wrote: 'This is music no longer of this
world. Mysteriously beautiful and magnificent.' (*The Berg–Schoenberg Correspondence*, p. 96.)

15   See also Berg's comments on a performance of the Eighth Symphony: *The
Berg–Schoenberg Correspondence*, p. 79.

16   *Ibid.*, p. 118.

17   Quoted in Kurt Blaukopf, *Mahler: A Documentary Study* (London: Thames and
Hudson, 1976), p. 250.

18   Natalie Bauer-Lechner, *Recollections of Gustav Mahler*, trans. D. Newlin, ed.
P. Franklin (London: Faber, 1980), p. 40.

19   See the fascinating chart showing eight of the versions it went through, in
Henri Louis de la Grange, *Mahler* (London: Gollancz, 1976), pp. 798–9.

20   Letter of 18(?) August 1906, in *Selected Letters of Gustav Mahler*, ed. Knud
Martner (London: Faber, 1980), p. 294.

21   A famous list of contents for the *Fourth* Symphony gives movement five as a
scherzo in D major with the subtitle 'Der Welt ohne Schwere'. This is generally
assumed to have 'become' the Scherzo of the Fifth. See Paul Bekker, *Gustav
Mahlers Sinfonien* (Berlin, 1921), p. 145, and Donald Mitchell, *Gustav Mahler:
The Wunderhorn Years* (London: Faber, 1975), p. 139.

22   Schoenberg's full title for this section was *Totentanz der Prinzipien*. Its high
moral and religious concerns are, it must be admitted, about as far from
Mahler as can be imagined.

23   On Schoenberg's symphony, see (for an outline of its likely contents) Josef
Rufer, *The Works of Arnold Schoenberg* (London: Faber, 1962), trans. D. Newlin,
pp. 115–18, and (for a more searching discussion) Alan P. Lessem, *Music and
Text in the Works of Arnold Schoenberg* (Ann Arbor: UMI, 1979), pp. 177–80.

24   Quoted in Redlich, *Alban Berg: The Man and his Music*, pp. 65–6. The sketches

are published in the Berg Collected Edition: see *Sämtliche Werke, Separatum: Symfonie-Fragmente*, ed. Rudolf Stephan (Vienna: Universal Edition, 1984).

25   *The Berg–Schoenberg Correspondence*, p. 182.

26   *Ibid.*, p. 212.

27   *Ibid.*, p. 257.

28   Programme note to Boulez's recording, Sony SMK 48 462, p. 6.

29   See p. 223; also Jarman, *The Music of Alban Berg*, p. 12.

30   Notes to CBS recording, CBS 72614.

31   Paraphrased in Reich, *Life and Work*, p. 115.

32   See, for example, Perle's comments in *The New Grove Dictionary of Music and Musicians*, ed. Stanley Sadie, Vol. 2 (London: Macmillan, 1980), p. 527.

33   DeVoto, 'Marche macabre', p. 105.

34   The note to the Philharmonia score, by 'F. S.' [Friedrich Saathen], claims that the entire second movement is a reworking of No. 1, but this is an exaggeration.

35   This chapter will not go any further in the direction of a *stylistic* investigation of the Berg/Mahler relationship: Reich, Redlich and others have done this, and it is only too easy to add to the list of 'parallel passages'.

36   I say 'obviously' because this has been recognised by most critics of Berg.

37   Cf. Charles Rosen, *The Romantic Generation* (New York: HarperCollins, 1995), *passim*.

38   According to Mengelberg, Mahler composed his *Adagietto* on the basis of a poem which was then deleted from the score. Mengelberg's conducting copy, into which he wrote the words, is reproduced in *Gustav Mahler: Adagietto*, ed. Gilbert E. Kaplan (New York: Kaplan, 1992), p. 20. Berg is known to have composed the finale of his *Lyric Suite* the same way (see p. 168).

39   Jarman, *The Music of Alban Berg*, p. 45. The reference is to Erwin Stein's description of Mahler's motivic technique, which he compares to the shuffling of a pack of cards. Although one might find isolated examples of this in Berg's Op. 6, Mahler's use of the technique is and remains, as far as I have been able to discover, unique.

40   Redlich, *Alban Berg: The Man and his Music*, p. 71.

41   *Conversations with Klemperer*, ed. Peter Heyworth (London: Gollancz, 1973), p. 33.

42   There has to be a query about the end of the melody because it leads so naturally into the closing section.

43   The passage was written for alto trombone in the first, unpublished version; when Berg revised the score in 1929 he rewrote it for the tenor instrument.

44   Arnold Schoenberg, *Fundamentals of Musical Composition*, ed. Gerald Strang and Leonard Stein (London: Faber, 1967), p. 16.

45   See Schoenberg, *Fundamentals*, chapters 5 and 8.

46   The diagram in Example 6.2 shows how Berg avoids symmetry by adding one-bar phrases, thus displacing the two-bar phrases so that they fall across the usual 4+4 divisions.

47   These are known to me only through the music examples in Taylor, 'Musical Progression', pp. 126ff. Incidentally Taylor is the only author to get the period structure of the melody right.

48 DeVoto, '*Drei Orchesterstücke*', pp. 99–101.

49 The chords thus spaced sound very like the chords from Schoenberg's 'Farben', Op. 16 No. 3.

50 See Perle, 'Berg's Master Array', and subsequent writings. Berg's actual array, in the form of a music example, is reproduced both in Perle's article and in *The Berg-Schoenberg Correspondence*, p. 283.

51 Some comments of a critical nature should be made at this point. The *Präludium* is very hard to grasp aurally. For one thing, it is almost impossible to 'hear' the chords, apart from the odd triadic/seventh-chord formation onto which the ear gratefully latches. Vertically, for the most part, I can't hear it at all, and I doubt that Berg could. Playing through it note by note on the piano helps. The proliferation of motives/lines from around bar 34 to the climax is quite overwhelming. The ear can't possibly take it all in. In preparing this chapter I made a reduction of the score, to help; but in some ways following the score is easier because then the breakdown of H and N, etc., is clear at a glance. Æsthetically bars 34–6 might as well be 'noise', the unpitched batterings one associates with Varèse (and with which the opening of Berg's work is often, and wrongly, compared). Then at bar 37 there is an incredible clarification: the music can be reduced onto four (!) staves again; suddenly things make sense. The calculation involved in the progression from the very first sounds to the melody, and in the descent from the climax to the end, is amazing, wonderful. The evaporation of the chord in bars 51–3, pitch by pitch, is equally good. But the ascent to the climax is hard to fathom because of the mass of detail; and it's all essential, *thematic* detail. In the 1960s, incidentally, this climax became a byword for (pointless) thematic complexity among young British composers when a page of it – actually, p. 12 of the Philharmonia score – was reproduced in one of those symposia on twentieth-century music so popular at the time. For months afterwards every aspiring composer's manuscripts were black with notes.

52 Vol. 5 (1980), p. 2130. I am indebted to Alfred Clayton for this reference.

53 For this see the *Oxford English Dictionary*, compact edition (New York: Oxford University Press, 1971), Vol. 2, p. 2424, which refers to Chaucer, *House of Fame* (1374–85), Book III, lines 1233–6:

> Ther saugh I famous, olde and yonge,
> Pipers of the Duche tonge,
> To lerne love-daunces, sprynges,
> Reyes, and these straunge thunges.

The Works of Geoffrey Chaucer, New Cambridge Edition, ed. F. N. Robinson, 2nd edn (London: Oxford University Press, 1957), p. 294.

54 Arthur Schnitzler, *Reigen*, in *Dramatische Werke*, Vol. 1 (Frankfurt: Fischer, 1962).

55 See Rode, *Alban Berg und Karl Kraus*, p. 468.

56 Bruce Archibald, 'Berg's Development as an Instrumental Composer', in Jarman (ed.), *The Berg Companion*, p. 116. Archibald's work on *Reigen* goes back to the early 1960s.

57 Ravel's *La Valse*, like Berg's *Marsch*, is traditionally viewed as a metaphor for the collapse of European civilisation after 1914. For a fascinating account of

how Ravel 'attacks' the basic foundations of the waltz in ways comparable in some respects to Berg's in *Reigen* see George Benjamin, 'Last Dance', *The Musical Times*, 135 (1994), pp. 432–5.

58   Berg's system of bar numbering is idiosyncratic in that he numbers each of the four subdivisions of bar 101 separately but then gives only one number for each subsequent bar (105ff.). Figure 6.1 treats Berg's bar 106 as '109'–'112', Berg's 107 as '113'–'116', and so on through to the double bar line after Berg's bar 110 (i.e. '125'–'128').

59   There are too many of them to be listed, or even labelled, here. The interested reader will find the main relationships clearly set out in Perle's article in *The New Grove*.

60   The move from ¢ to 3/4 is very well done and effected almost entirely through the harmony; there is no percussion, and not even a pizzicato downbeat till the waltz starts at bar 20. The cross-rhythms of the violins in bars 17–19 confuse the ear but do not actually set up a 3/4 pattern, and ¢ persists (small stave) until bar 24.

61   Berg later declared *Reigen* to be a study for the tavern scene in *Wozzeck*. See Mosco Carner, *Alban Berg: The Man and the Work*, 2nd edn (London: Duckworth, 1983), p. 144.

62   This takes place in four stages:

 bars 94–9 The first four-bar phrase of waltz emerges from the 'noise' of the second ostinato passage;

 bars 98–100 the second four-bar phrase, actually shortened to three and overlaid from bar 97 with the new '4/2' (i.e. there is a one-bar overlap);

 bars 101–4 the first bar of actual 4/2, notated as four 3/4 bars separated by broken lines;

 bars 105–10 six 4/2 bars (= twenty-four '3/4' bars).

The pedals, the harmonic rhythm and the dissolution of the 3/4 metre all contribute to the elegiac tone.

63   Derrick Puffett, *Debussy's Ostinato Machine*, Papers in Musicology, No. 4 (Nottingham: Nottingham University, 1996).

64   There is an obvious link with the *Lyric Suite* here. Could this work have a connection with Schnitzler that even George Perle was unaware of?

65   Carner, *Alban Berg*, p. 146.

66   Jarman, *The Music of Alban Berg*, p. 177.

67   For instance, of bar 91 he writes: '*New section*. March character resumed.' DeVoto, 'Marche macabre', p. 399.

68   Stravinsky's word for them, 'protest', is perfect and indicates non-resolution. See *Stravinsky in Conversation with Robert Craft* (Harmondsworth: Penguin, 1962), p. 87.

69   DeVoto, 'Marche macabre', p. 408.

70   Jarman, *The Music of Alban Berg*, pp. 37–46.

71   Perle, *Wozzeck*, p. 18. Perle's reference to Ravel's 'valse macabre' is unfortunate in that it sets off irrelevant echoes of Saint-Saëns.

72   The final expression of this world-view in Berg is the street-organ in Act III of

Lulu which grinds out its trivial melodies as Lulu plies her trade as a prostitute in London.

73 Though there must be an element of deliberate gigantification in it: cf. the Cyclops episode of Joyce's contemporaneous *Ulysses*.

74 *Stravinsky in Conversation*, p. 87.

75 John Adams in interview with Nick Kimberley, *Gramophone*, June 1996, p. 23.

76 Examples are bars 70–72, 76–7, 102–6 and most of 115–26. That some thinning-out occurred before the *Marsch* went into print is evidenced by two copies in the Pierpont Morgan Library, both of which have passages in an even thicker orchestration than that which Berg allowed to survive.

7 The musical language of *Wozzeck*

1 Schmalfeldt, *Berg's Wozzeck*.

2 George Perle, 'Representation and Symbol in the Music of *Wozzeck*', *Music Review*, 33 (1971), pp. 281–308. See also Perle, *Wozzeck*, chapter 4 (pp. 93–129).

3 Harold Bloom, *The Anxiety of Influence: A Theory of Poetry* (New York: Oxford University Press, 1973), pp. 13–16.

4 Bloom, *The Anxiety of Influence*, p. 16: 'the new poem's achievement makes it seem to us ... as though the later poet himself had written the precursor's most characteristic work' (something of Bloom's association of *apophrades* with a poet's final works is perhaps to be observed in the critical surprise and admiration that often ensues when a young-ish composer's *first* opera is judged successful). A number of authors have sought to apply Bloom's ideas directly to music, notably Kevin Korsyn, 'Towards a New Poetics of Musical Influence', *Music Analysis*, 10 (1991), pp. 3–72, and Joseph N. Straus, *Remaking the Past: Musical Modernism and the Influence of the Tonal Tradition* (Cambridge, MA: Harvard University Press, 1990).

5 For an English translation of Franzos's moving account of his struggles to decipher Büchner's work in the face of extraordinary practical difficulties and to present it faithfully despite the interference of Büchner's brother Ludwig, see Jarman, *Alban Berg: Wozzeck*, pp. 111–29.

6 See Jarman, *Alban Berg: Wozzeck*, p. 1.

7 Perle, *Wozzeck*, p. 38. A direct comparison between Berg's libretto and the Landau edition may be made in English translation, in *Wozzeck: Alban Berg* [Opera Guide 42, ed. N. John] (London: Calder, 1990), pp. 61–110.

8 Jarman, *Alban Berg: Wozzeck*, p. 156. A translation of Berg's lecture is given on pp. 154–70.

9 See pp. 44–5.

10 This table forms the basis of discussions in, for example, Reich, *Life and Work*, pp. 120–42 (Reich reports that Fritz Mahler's table 'was suggested by Berg himself'); Perle, *Wozzeck*, pp. 43–89 (bibliographical sources of the table are identified on p. 43); and Jarman, *Alban Berg: Wozzeck*, pp. 41–50.

11 Eng. trans. in Jarman, *Alban Berg: Wozzeck*, pp. 162–3.

12 'Diese erste Szene erhält dadurch ... auch musikalisch das ihr zukommende, ich möchte sagen, historische Kolorit'. Repr. in Redlich, *Alban Berg: Versuch einer Würdigung*, p. 316 (for the entire lecture see pp. 311–27).

13 Jarman, *Alban Berg: Wozzeck*, p. 43.

14 '... an das ich mich in diesem wahrhaft zeitlosen Drama natürlich sonst nicht hielt'. Redlich, *Alban Berg: Versuch einer Würdigung*, p. 316.

15 Emil Petschnig, 'Creating Atonal Opera', Eng. trans. in Jarman, *Alban Berg: Wozzeck*, pp. 143–9 (the quoted passage is on p. 144). Originally published in *Die Musik*, 16 (1924), pp. 340–45.

16 Repr. in Jarman, *Alban Berg: Wozzeck*, pp. 152–3. Originally published in *Modern Music*, November–December 1927.

17 Eng. trans. in Jarman, *Alban Berg: Wozzeck*, p. 158.

18 Berg, 'The Musical Forms in my Opera *Wozzeck*', Eng. trans. in Jarman, *Alban Berg: Wozzeck*, pp. 149–52 (the quoted passage is on p. 152). Originally published in *Die Musik*, 16 (1924), pp. 587–9.

19 Letter of 9 July 1913, Berg to Schoenberg (*The Berg–Schoenberg Correspondence*, p. 182).

20 See chapters 5 and 6.

21 See Mark DeVoto, 'Alban Bergs *Drei Orchesterstücke* op. 6: Struktur, Thematik und ihr Verhältnis zu *Wozzeck*', in Rudolf Klein (ed.), *Alban Berg Studien*, 2 (Vienna: Universal Edition, 1981), pp. 97–106.

22 Jarman, *The Music of Alban Berg*, pp. 7–8.

23 See Berg's letter to Schoenberg, 24 June 1918 (*The Berg–Schoenberg Correspondence*, p. 268).

24 Perle, *Wozzeck*, p. 192 n. 23.

25 See pp. 169–70.

26 See Perle, *Wozzeck*, p. 123.

27 Bloom, *The Anxiety of Influence*, pp. 14–15.

28 For an account of the early stage history and reception of *Wozzeck*, see Jarman, *Alban Berg: Wozzeck*, pp. 69–78.

29 Adorno, *Alban Berg*, p. 10.

30 Eng. trans. in Jarman, *Alban Berg: Wozzeck*, p. 170.

31 See pp. 115–117.

32 Adorno, *Alban Berg*, p. 87.

33 Eng. trans. in Jarman, *Alban Berg: Wozzeck*, p. 155.

34 Jarman, *The Music of Alban Berg*, pp. 47–63.

35 *Ibid.*, p. 62.

36 *Ibid.*, p. 51.

37 Allen Forte, *The Structure of Atonal Music* (New Haven: Yale University Press, 1973), p. 17.

38 The aggregate of the cadential chords is (1, 2, 3, 5, 6, 7, 9, 11) in integer notation – belonging to Forte's set-class 8–24. The comparable set-class (8–19) has the prime form (0, 1, 2, 4, 5, 6, 8, 9).

39 Eng. trans. in Jarman, *Alban Berg: Wozzeck*, p. 167. See Derrick Puffett's analysis of this passage in 'Berg and German Opera', in Jarman (ed.), *The Berg Companion*, pp. 197–200.

40 Perle, *Wozzeck*, pp. 145–55. The quoted passage is from p. 145. Example 7.6 may be compared with Perle's Examples 114 and 115 (p. 146).

41 Schmalfeldt, *Berg's Wozzeck*, pp. 120–21, 206.

42 See p. 58.

43   Perle, *Wozzeck*, p. 139.

44   Eng. trans. in Jarman, *Alban Berg: Wozzeck*, p. 160.

45   Richard Cohn, 'Maximally Smooth Cycles, Hexatonic Systems, and the Analysis of Late-Romantic Triadic Progressions', *Music Analysis*, 15 (1996), pp. 9–40.

46   David Fanning has described how Berg explored in his sketches the similarity between the (unaltered) chord X and the opening chord of the D minor interlude, in 'Berg's Sketches for *Wozzeck*: A Commentary and Inventory', *Journal of the Royal Musical Association*, 112 (1987), pp. 284–5.

47   A detailed analysis of this scene may be found in Jarman, *Alban Berg: Wozzeck*, pp. 52–8.

48   See chapter 10.

49   Perle, *Wozzeck*, pp 155–8; Jarman, *The Music of Alban Berg*, pp. 57–8, *Alban Berg: Wozzeck*, p. 46; Schmalfeldt, *Berg's Wozzeck*, pp. 48–59.

50   See chapter 8.

8   Secret programmes

1   *Neues Wiener Journal*, 31 August 1935; subsequently revised in *Anbruch*, XVIII/9 (September/October 1935), pp. 250–52 and *Schweizerische Musik Zeitschrift*, 75 (1935), pp. 735–7.

2   *Pult und Taktstock*, 2 (February/March 1925), pp. 23–8.

3   See Constantin Floros, 'Das esoterische Programm der Lyrischen Suite: Eine semantische Analyse', *Hamburg Jahrbuch für Musikwissenschaft*, Band I (Hamburg, 1975), pp 101–45.

4   George Perle, 'The Secret Program of the Lyric Suite', *The International Alban Berg Society Newsletter*, 5 (June 1977), pp. 4–12; enlarged as 'The Secret Programme of the Lyric Suite', *The Musical Times*, 118 (1977), pp. 629–32, 709–13, 809–13.

5   Eng. trans. by Douglass M. Green, *The International Alban Berg Society Newsletter*, 5 (June 1977), pp. 13–23.

6   Eng. trans. by Cornelius Cardew, in Reich, *Life and Work*, pp. 143–8.

7   *Ibid.*, p. 148.

8   Berg's sketches show that the first four variations represent, respectively, Eduard Steuermann, Rudolf Kolisch, Josef Polnauer and Erwin Stein; the fifth represents 'the others who follow after, want to overtake etc.' See Brenda Dalen, 'Freundschaft, Liebe, und Welt: The Secret Programme of the Chamber Concerto', in Jarman (ed.), *The Berg Companion*, pp. 142–50.

9   Dalen, 'Freundschaft, Liebe, und Welt', pp. 160–71.

10   Thus the solo violin's pizzicato notes in bars 111–12, its only appearance in the first movement, are a reference to Kolisch's habit, when playing a concerto, of quietly testing his tuning in this way before his first entry; similarly, the piano figuration at bars 775–80 refers to F. H. Klein by quoting his 'Mother chord' (see chapter 10).

11   As, for example, the significance of one sketch which suggests that the three movements represent or are in some way associated with three places – Vienna, Trahütten and Baden.

12   Berg to Hanna Fuchs, 4 December, 1929, quoted in Floros, 'Alban Berg und Hanna Fuchs: die Geschichte einer unglücklichen Liebe und ihre Auswirkung-

en auf Bergs Schaffen', *Österreichische Musik Zeitschrift*, 50 (1995), p. 790. See also pp. 216–17.

13   Reich, *Life and Work*, pp. 178–9.

14   Douglas Jarman, 'Alban Berg, Wilhelm Fliess and the Secret Programme of the Violin Concerto', *The International Alban Berg Society Newsletter*, 12 (Fall/Winter 1982), pp. 5–11.

15   Both Constantin Floros, in 'Die Skizzen zum Violinkonzert Alban Berg', *Alban Berg Studien*, 2 (Vienna: Universal Edition, 1981), pp. 118–35, and Anthony Pople, in *Berg: Violin Concerto*, have argued that the presence of the final phrase of 'Es ist Genug' on a sketch headed 'Akkorden und Cadenzen' (a sketch which includes the 'ritmico' material of Part I, bars 140ff.) indicates that Berg had, at an early stage, decided on using the Bach chorale. The 'Akkorden und Cadenzen' sketch, however, is part of a double page, the opposite page of which, linked to the 'Akkorden und Cadenzen' sketch by a series of arrows, shows Berg working out the harmonization of the chorale at Part II, bars 214ff.

16   The relevant page is reproduced as Faksimile 4 of *Alban Berg: Sämtliche Werke*, 5/2 (Vienna: Universal Edition, 1996).

17   Floros ('Die Skizzen zum Violinkonzert Alban Berg', p. 119) misreads the word 'Fromm' as 'Traum' and consequently ignores the FFFF annotation and its significance. This reading is followed by Pople in *Berg: Violin Concerto*, p. 30. I am grateful to Regina Busch for her help in freshly deciphering Berg's sketch.

18   Adorno, *Alban Berg*, p. 11.

19   Perle, *Lulu*, pp. 284–9.

20   *Ibid.*, p. 286.

21   See Jarman, *The Music of Alban Berg*, pp. 230–41.

22   See Reich, *Life and Work*, p. 286.

23   See, for example, Walter B. Bailey, *Programmatic Elements in the Works of Arnold Schoenberg* (Ann Arbor: UMI Research Press, 1984) and Hans Moldenhauer, *Anton Webern: A Chronicle of his Life and Work* (London: Gollancz, 1978).

24   Bailey, *Programmatic Elements*, p. 98.

25   This, of course, does not preclude the possibility that more general extra-musical 'inspirational forces' lie behind some of the earlier, pre-*Wozzeck* pieces. Constantin Floros, for example, has suggested in *Alban Berg*, pp. 153–64, that the String Quartet Op. 3 has a programme concerning Berg's love for Helene (see chapter 4). As presented by Floros, however, the proposed 'programme' of Op. 3 is so generalised as to be essentially different in both nature and function from the programmes of the post-*Wozzeck* works.

26   See pp. 148–50.

27   Christopher Hailey, 'Between Instinct and Reflection: Berg and the Viennese Dichotomy', in Jarman (ed.), *The Berg Companion*, p. 230.

28   Jarman, *The Music of Alban Berg*, p. 230.

29   See Berg, 'A Word about Wozzeck', in Jarman, *Alban Berg: Wozzeck*, p. 153.

30   Mark DeVoto, quoted in Perle, *Style and Idea in the Lyric Suite of Alban Berg* (Stuyvesant: Pendragon, 1995), p. 50.

31   Adorno to Helene Berg, 16 April 1936, in Hilmar and Brosche (eds.), *Alban Berg 1885–1935*. See also pp. 21–2.

32 *The Times Literary Supplement*, 30 April 1982, p. 475.

33 Perle, 'The Secret Programme of the Lyric Suite', pp. 811–12.

34 Floros, 'Alban Berg und Hanna Fuchs', p. 781.

35 See, for example, Berg to Schoenberg, 10 June 1915: 'I received your first telegram … on 4.6! [4 June] (46 = 2×23) The telegram bore the number Berlin-Südende 46 (= 2×23) 12/11 (12+11 = 23). The 2nd telegram bore the number 24/23 and was sent off at 11:50 (1150 = 50×23).' (*The Berg–Schoenberg Correspondence*, p. 245.)

36 Jarman, *The Music of Alban Berg*, pp. 223–41. For another perspective on this aspect of Berg's thought see pp. 48–9.

37 Perle, 'The Secret Programme of the Lyric Suite', p. 812.

38 *Briefe an seine Frau*, p 376; *Letters to his Wife*, p. 229.

39 Erich Alban Berg, 'Eine natürliche Tochter: zur Biographie Alban Berg', *Frankfurter Allgemeine Zeitung*, 21 May 1975.

40 Geoffrey Poole, 'Berg's Fateful Number', *Tempo*, 179 (December 1991), p. 2.

41 Paul Kammerer, quoted in Arthur Koestler, *The Case of the Midwife Toad* (London: Pan, 1971), p. 141.

9 **Stages of compositional process in Wozzeck and Lulu**

1 For an English translation of Berg's lecture see Jarman, *Alban Berg: Wozzeck*, pp. 154–70.

2 See Willi Reich, 'Alban Berg's *Lulu*', trans. M. D. Herter Norton, *Musical Quarterly*, 22 (1936), pp 383–401, and *Life and Work*, pp. 156–77. These accounts were based on discussions between Reich and Berg that took place in 1934; the music examples stem principally from Berg himself.

3 This chapter is part of an ongoing study of the sketches for *Wozzeck* held in the Österreichische Nationalbibliothek. An earlier version of it was read as a paper at the West Coast Conference of Music Theory and Analysis held at the University of British Columbia, Vancouver. I would like to thank my audience for their thoughtful comments, many of which I have incorporated

4 In the production Berg saw, and in the edition stemming from Paul Landau's critical edition from which he developed his libretto, the play was entitled *Wozzeck*; subsequently, Büchner scholars have preferred to read the spelling *Woyzeck* from the playwright's almost illegible handwriting. See Perle, *Wozzeck*, pp. 25–37.

5 For an English translation of Kraus's lecture see Jarman, *Alban Berg: Lulu*, pp. 102–12. Bryan R. Simms has identified additional likely sources of ideas on role doubling and formal structure in Wedekind's tragedies ('Berg's *Lulu* and the theatre of the 1920s', *Cambridge Opera Journal*, 6 (1994), pp. 147–58); nonetheless, the enormous and sustained influence of Kraus on Berg's cultural outlook in general and his interpretation of these plays in particular is well attested (see chapter 2).

6 ÖNB, Musiksammlung, F 21 Berg 13/vii fol. 6v.

7 See chapter 11; also Volker Scherliess, 'Alban Bergs analytische Tafeln zur *Lulu*-Reihe', *Die Musikforschung*, 30 (1977), pp. 452–64, and Patricia Hall, 'The Progress of a Method: Berg's Tone Rows for *Lulu*', *The Musical Quarterly*, 71 (1985), pp. 500–519.

8   See Thomas F. Ertelt, '"Hereinspaziert …" Ein früher Entwurf des Prologs zu
Alban Bergs *Lulu*', *Österreichische Musik Zeitschrift*, 41 (1986), pp. 15–25, and
Douglass M. Green, 'A False Start for *Lulu*: An Early Version of the Prologue', in
Gable and Morgan (eds.), *Alban Berg*, pp. 203–13.

9   See pp. 158–62. For an English translation of Berg's comments see Jarman,
Alban Berg: Wozzeck, p. 160.

10   In his article 'Berg's Sketches for *Wozzeck*: A Commentary and Inventory',
Journal of the Royal Musical Association, 112 (1987), pp. 280–322, David
Fanning misreads 'unresolved' ('unaufgelöste') as 'superimposed'.

11   See Jarman, *Alban Berg: Wozzeck*, pp. 29–30, 38 and 53; also Perle, *Wozzeck*,
pp. 105–6 and 135–40.

12   See the upper margin of the sketch for Act II scene 1, bar 242 (ÖNB, Musiksammlung, F 21 Berg 29/i).

13   See pp. 212–13; also Hall, 'The Sketches for *Lulu*', in Jarman (ed.), *The Berg
Companion*, pp. 235–59.

14   ÖNB, Musiksammlung, F 21 Berg 15/i.

10   Compositional technique 1923–6: the Chamber Concerto and the *Lyric Suite*

1   Berg, letter to Webern, 12 October 1925, quoted in Jarman, *The Music of Alban
Berg*, p. 9. Berg first set this poem to music in 1907 (see Reich, *Life and Work*, p.
109; also Hilmar, *Katalog*, pp. 45, 47; and Floros, *Alban Berg*, pp. 227–9).

2   Berg, open letter to Schoenberg, Eng. trans. by Cornelius Cardew in Reich, *Life
and Work*, pp. 143–8 (p. 147); first published as 'Alban Bergs Kammerkonzert
für Geige und Klavier mit Begleitung von dreizehn Bläsern', *Pult und Taktstock*,
2/ii–iii (1925), pp. 23–8. 'Nine Pages on the *Lyric Suite*', in Ursula von Rauchhaupt (ed.), *Schoenberg–Berg–Webern: The String Quartets, a Documentary
Study*, translations by Eugene Hartzell (Hamburg: Deutsche Grammophon
Gesellschaft, 1971), pp. 102–13 (p. 102); a revised and more complete German
edition is given in Berg, *Glaube, Hoffnung und Liebe*, ed. Frank Schneider,
Reclams Universal-Bibliothek, 899 (Leipzig: Reclam, 1981), pp. 236–53 ('Neun
Blätter zur "Lyrischen Suite für Streichquartett"').

3   Jarman, *The Music of Alban Berg*, p. 81.

4   Arved Ashby, 'Of *Modell-Typen* and *Reihenformen*: Berg, Schoenberg, F. H.
Klein, and the Concept of Row Derivation', *Journal of the American Musicological Society*, 48 (1995), pp. 67–105 (p. 72).

5   Published by the composer. Ashby surmises that Berg's copy (Vienna, Österreichische Nationalbibliothek) 'is perhaps the last extant'; on the history of the
work's publication, see Ashby, 'Of *Modell-Typen*', pp. 74–5.

6   *Ibid.*, p. 83. See Jarman, *The Music of Alban Berg*, pp. 82–3, 129.

7   Examples 10.1a–c have been transcribed from the facsimiles reproduced in
The Berg-Schoenberg Correspondence, p. 349.

8   Fritz Heinrich Klein, preface to *Variationen* for piano, Op. 14 (1924), Fig. 22;
quoted in Ashby, 'Of *Modell-Typen*', p. 86.

9   Ashby, 'Of *Modell-Typen*', p. 90. Likewise, both Berg and Klein believed Klein's
all-interval row to be the only such row (*ibid.*, pp. 88–9). Several comprehensive accounts of all-interval rows and their properties appeared during the
1960s and 1970s. See Hanns Jelinek, 'Die krebsgleichen Allintervallreihen',

Archiv für Musikwissenschaft, 18 (1961), pp. 115–25; Herbert Eimert, *Grundlagen der musikalischen Reihentechnik* (Vienna: Universal Edition, 1964), pp. 39–86; Stefan Bauer-Mengelberg and Melvin Ferentz, 'On Eleven-Interval Twelve-Tone Rows', *Perspectives of New Music*, 3 (1965), pp. 93–103; and Robert Morris and Daniel Starr, 'The Structure of All-Interval Series', *Journal of Music Theory*, 18 (1974), pp. 364–89.

10 Perle, *Lulu*, p. 7. For a harmonic analysis of this song, see Craig Ayrey, 'Tonality and the Series: Berg', in J. Dunsby (ed.), *Models of Musical Analysis: Early Twentieth-Century Music* (Oxford: Blackwell, 1993), pp. 81–113.

11 Ashby, 'Of *Modell-Typen*', p. 90, p. 86 (Klein, Fig. 22) and p. 93 (transcription of Berg's sketch, Fig. 8). The sketch is held in Vienna, ÖNB, Musiksammlung, F 21 Berg 116, fol. 1. See also Joan Allen Smith, 'Some Sources for Berg's "Schliesse mir die Augen beide" II', *International Alban Berg Society Newsletter*, 6 (1978), pp. 9–13.

12 Ashby, 'Of *Modell-Typen*', pp. 92, 94–5; F 21 Berg 76/V, fol. 11. A second sketch contains a plan for the work showing the introduction of Klein's second form in the third movement (Ashby, 'Of *Modell-Typen*', p. 96; F 21 Berg 76/V, fol. 8).

13 Reported in Walter Szmolyan, *J. M. Hauer* [Österreichische Komponisten des XX. Jahrhunderts, 6] (Vienna: Lafite, 1965), p. 49. Cf. Felix Greissle: 'he said, you know, he and Hauer had found from another side almost the same thing', interview transcribed in Joan Allen Smith, *Schoenberg and His Circle: A Viennese Portrait* (New York: Schirmer, 1986), p. 203.

14 The phrase is Ashby's ('Of *Modell-Typen*', p. 103).

15 See Josef Matthias Hauer, *Zwölftontechnik. Die Lehre von den Tropen* [Theoretische Schriften, 2] (Vienna: Universal Edition, 1926), pp. 10–18. An example of the second canonic technique is given in the present chapter (Example 10.3).

16 Martina Sichardt, *Die Entstehung der Zwölftonmethode Arnold Schönbergs* (Mainz: Schott, 1990), pp. 55–74 (esp. pp. 72–4). See also Rudolf Stephan, 'Zur Entstehung der Zwölftonmusik', in Günter Schnitzler (ed.), *Musik und Zahl. Interdisziplinäre Beiträge zum Grenzbereich zwischen Musik und Mathematik* (Bonn: Verlag für systematische Musikwissenschaft, 1976), pp. 159–70.

17 For more on the dating of the composition of Schoenberg's variation movement see Sichardt, *Die Entstehung der Zwölftonmethode Arnold Schönbergs*, p. 56. An analysis by Berg of the third movement of Schoenberg's Serenade is located amongst the sketch material of the Chamber Concerto (see Hilmar, *Katalog*, pp. 55, 102; two pages from this analysis are reproduced in facsimile on pp. 184–5); cf. Ashby, 'Of *Modell-Typen*', p. 70 n. 12.

18 These are the dates given in Szmolyan's work list (*J. M. Hauer*, p. 71); Stephan gives 1922 in 'Über Josef Matthias Hauer', *Archiv für Musikwissenschaft*, 18 (1961), pp. 265–93 (p. 290). Like Berg's Chamber Concerto, Hauer's *Etüden* are dedicated to Schoenberg on the occasion of his fiftieth birthday.

19 Jarman, *The Music of Alban Berg*, pp. 83–4. Example 10.1c in the present chapter corresponds to the first of these sets; the second is produced by placing the partial rows outlined by Berg (Example 10.1b) successively within each hexachord so as to produce the complete cycle of fifths when read from left to right (the retrograde of this set is played *pizzicato* by the cello in bars 8–9).

Ashby is admittedly cautious in ascribing the authorship of these derivations to Klein: 'Berg's … use of the circle-of-fifths row in the Allegretto giovale of the *Lyric Suite* does not necessarily show that he did any more than adopt Klein's all-interval row and two derivations therefrom … It would not have taken Berg long to notice the circle of fifths in the row, given what George Perle has called his "characteristic preoccupation with interval cycles" discernible as early as the op. 2 songs' ('Of *Modell-Typen*', p. 85; Perle, 'Berg's Master Array').

20   Egon Wellesz, *The Origins of Schönberg's Twelve-Tone System: A Lecture […] January 10, 1957* (Washington: The Louis Charles Elson Memorial Fund, 1958), pp. 7–8.

21   Regina Busch notes that Berg knew the term *Baustein* as one that stemmed from Hauer ('Einige Bemerkungen zur Zwölftonkomposition bei Schönberg, Berg und Webern', in Rudolf Stephan, Sigrid Wiesmann and Matthias Schmidt (eds.), *Arnold Schönberg: Neuerer der Musik. 3. Internationale Schönberg Kongreß. Duisburg 1993* (Vienna: Lafite, 1997), pp. 114ff.). See also Sichardt, *Die Entstehung der Zwölftonmethode Arnold Schönbergs*, pp. 72–3. I am grateful to Regina Busch for supplying me with a typescript of her paper.

22   Hauer, *Die Lehre von den Tropen*, pp. 13–14; Berg, p. 4 of the 'Nine Pages'.

23   The entire example is reproduced in Szmolyan, *J. M. Hauer*, p. 61.

24   Schoenberg, *Theory of Harmony*, trans. Roy E. Carter (London: Faber, 1978), p. 433. Schoenberg's remark appears in a footnote to the revised edition of 1922, for which Berg prepared the index. Berg comments on the new additional material in a letter to Schoenberg of 12 June 1922 (*The Berg-Schoenberg Correspondence*, pp. 314–16).

25   Busch, 'Einige Bemerkungen zur Zwölftonkomposition'.

26   Compare Christian Baier, 'Fritz Heinrich Klein: Der "Mutterakkord" im Werk Alban Bergs', *Österreichische Musikzeitschrift*, 44 (1989), pp. 585–600 (p. 585); Hilmar, *Alban Berg*, p. 147; Erich Alban Berg, *Der unverbesserliche Romantiker*, pp. 96, 165; Ashby, 'Of *Modell-Typen*', p. 72; *The Berg–Schoenberg Correspondence*, p. 317 n. 1; Smith, *Schoenberg and His Circle*, p. 277; Dave Headlam, 'Fritz Heinrich Klein's "Die Grenze der Halbtonwelt" and *Die Maschine*', *Theoria*, 6 (1992), pp. 55–96 (p. 57). The dates vary from some time after 1917 to 1921 (the date of 1921 is given in *The Berg–Schoenberg Correspondence*); Klein's own account reproduced in Erich Alban Berg's book (though this is not the only account by Klein) states that after having attended Schoenberg's composition seminar at the Schwarzwald School (in 1917–18, according to Baier) he went to study with Berg, but leaves open the time that had elapsed between the two events.

27   Compare Erich Alban Berg, *Der unverbesserliche Romantiker*, pp. 96–7; Hilmar and Brosche (eds.), *Alban Berg 1885–1935*, pp. 163–4 (No. 391: letter from Klein to Berg, March 1922); Ashby, 'Of *Modell-Typen*', p. 87; Baier, 'Fritz Heinrich Klein', p. 589. The dates given are 1920, 1922, 1922 and 1923, respectively. Note that the twelve-note, all-interval chord given by Klein in the letter to Berg of March 1922 is not the same as either of the two forms of the *Mutterakkord* in the Preface to the *Variationen* (Fig. 23; Ashby, 'Of *Modell-Typen*',

p. 86), the first of which appears earlier in the piano version of *Die Maschine* (facsimile reproduced in Headlam, 'Fritz Heinrich Klein's "Die Grenze der Halbtonwelt" and *Die Maschine*', p. 68). *Die Maschine* is also discussed at some length by Hans Oesch, 'Pioniere der Zwölftontechnik', in *Basler Studien zur Musikgeschichte* [Forum Musicologicum, 1] (Bern: Francke, 1975), pp. 273–304). Note also that in a letter written to Berg in March 1922, Klein says he arrived at this, 'the first' twelve-note, all-interval chord, through permuting the *Mutterakkord* (Hilmar and Brosche (eds.), *Alban Berg 1885–1935*, p. 163; ÖNB, Musiksammlung, F 21 Berg 935/I [1 Doppelbl.]). This is obscured in Ashby's translation: 'I admit this chord originated as a sudden idea; but it is scientifically incontestable that in the course of the permutation of the interval figures of the chord ['des Mutterakkordes'], it *must* eventually appear at some time!' (Ashby, 'Of *Modell-Typen*', p. 87 (for orig. text see p. 87 n 41); letter from Klein to Berg, 28 March 1922, F 21 Berg 935/I, fol. 2).

28   The process of placing intervals in reversed order, one by one, by which Klein demonstrates the derivation of the second form of his all-interval row (Fig. 22, quoted in Ashby, 'Of *Modell-Typen*', p. 86) is essentially the same as that used by Berg in the first of the Four Songs Op. 2. For a diagrammatic representation of the retrograde structure of this song, see Robert P. Morgan, 'The Eternal Return: Retrograde and Circular Form in Berg', in Gable and Morgan (eds.), *Alban Berg*, pp. 111–49 (Example 3, p. 134). Baier details the arrangements between Berg and Klein concerning the acknowledgement of the use of Klein's row in the scores of the Chamber Concerto (the row appears in the piano, bars 775–80), 'Schliesse mir' II and the *Lyric Suite*; only the acknowledgement for 'Schliesse mir' II was published with the score ('Fritz Heinrich Klein', pp. 593, 595, 597).

29   An 'incorrigible Romantic' in his own words, as handed down by his nephew, Erich Alban Berg (*Der unverbesserliche Romantiker*, pp. 7–8).

30   See Jarman, *The Music of Alban Berg*, pp. 224–5; Busch, 'Einige Bemerkungen zur Zwölftonkomposition'.

31   ÖNB, Musiksammlung, F 21 Berg. Most of the letters from Berg to Klein have been destroyed (Ashby, 'Of *Modell-Typen*', p. 74 n. 24).

32   Jarman, *The Music of Alban Berg*, p. 79. In considering whether characteristics of Berg's twelve-note music might be seen in a latent form in his earlier music, Busch suggests a revision of Jarman's notion of 'codification' inasmuch as it implies a general subordination of harmonic phenomena to motivic-thematic ones, and cites cases in both the atonal and twelve-note music where it is perhaps not possible to decide what is the primary determinant of the music – at least it is not obvious that the motivic considerations or the ordered row are primary ('Einige Bemerkungen zur Zwolftonkomposition'). Compare also Adorno's comments on Berg's thematic *Leitharmonien* in his essay 'Bergs kompositionstechnische Funde', *Quasi una Fantasia* (Frankfurt: Suhrkamp, 1963), pp. 257–9; Eng. trans. by Rodney Livingstone (London: Verso, 1992). Ann Shreffler brings an alternative historical model, proposed by the art historian James Ackerman, to bear on the evolution of Webern's twelve-note composition: 'evolution in the arts should not be described as a succession of steps

toward a solution to a given problem, but as a succession of steps away from
one or more original statements of a problem' ('"Mein Weg geht jetzt vor-
über": The Vocal Origins of Webern's Twelve-Tone Composition', *Journal of
the American Musicological Society*, 47 (1994), pp. 275–339 (pp. 279–80)).

33   See chapters 5 and 6; also Ernst Křenek, 'Fünf Orchesterlieder nach
Ansichtskartentexten von Peter Altenberg op. 4', in Reich, *Alban Berg*, pp. 43–
7; Jarman, *The Music of Alban Berg*, pp. 34–46; and Mark DeVoto, 'Some Notes
on the Unknown *Altenberg Lieder*', *Perspectives of New Music*, 5 (1966), pp. 37–
74. One aspect of Klein's methods that is striking in relation to the derivation
of rows in *Lulu*, but receives no comment from Ashby, is the phrase he uses to
describe the derivation of the fourths- and fifths-form: 'connecting every
second note produces perfect fourths or fifths' (Ashby, 'Of *Modell-Typen*', pp.
82–3; 'jeder zweite Ton miteinander verbunden, ergibt reine Quarten oder
Quinten'). Although Klein's emphasis seems to be more on the interval cycles
than on the numerical principle, this description may be compared, in particular, with Berg's derivation of the Acrobat's series in *Lulu* (see chapter 11).

34   Erwin Stein, *Orpheus in New Guises* (London: Rockliff, 1953), p. 7; Jarman,
The Music of Alban Berg, p. 45.

35   See, however, Derrick Puffett's comments on p. 121. [Ed.]

36   See Perle, 'Berg's Master Array'.

37   Jarman, *The Music of Alban Berg*, p. 126.

38   The material on splitting in the *Lyric Suite* presented here draws on Jarman's
work on the derivation of subsidiary sets (*ibid.*, pp. 126–30).

39   *Ibid.*, p. 129 (Ex. 162).

40   The use of these rhythms in the third movement is analysed by Jarman,
The Music of Alban Berg, pp. 156–8; and Douglass M. Green, 'The Allegro
misterioso of Berg's *Lyric Suite*: Iso- and Retrorhythms', *Journal of the
American Musicological Society*, 30 (1977), pp. 507–16.

41   Example 10.5a and the other examples from the 'Nine Pages' in this chapter
have been transcribed from the facsimiles reproduced in Willi Reich, *Alban
Berg: Bildnis im Wort* (Zürich: Die Arche, 1959), pp. 45–54.

42   Jarman, *The Music of Alban Berg*, pp. 127–8 (Ex. 160); and Perle, *Serial Composition and Atonality*, 5th edn (Berkeley: University of California Press, 1981),
pp. 72–4 (Ex. 104).

43   Reich's transcription of the 'Nine Pages' in *Alban Berg: Bildnis im Wort* omits
the parenthetical note beneath the example (see facsimile, p. 53); Schneider
transcribes this only partially and erroneously in his edition of Berg, *Glaube,
Hoffnung und Liebe*, p. 244. The best version is to be found in the marginalia of
Redlich's copy of Reich's book (Lancaster, University Library, Redlich Collection): '(NB Similarities between the tail-ends of the half-series and the beginnings of the rows exploited. Particularly at the conclusion at the entries of the
first four forms!)'; '(NB Ähnlichkeiten der Ausläufer der Halbreihen und An-
fänge der Reihen ausgenützt. Besonders am Schluß bei den [Einsätzen] der 4
ersten Formen!)'. The detail to which this comment refers is omitted in Example 10.6a, but is visible, albeit indistinctly, in the facsimile in Reich, *Alban
Berg: Bildnis im Wort*, and is included in Schneider's transcription. In an autograph score of the *Lyric Suite* in which the last movement is inscribed with the

text of Baudelaire's 'De profundis clamavi', pencilled arrows indicate the course of the first row through the parts of the two violins at bar 30 (ÖNB, Musiksammlung, F 21 Berg 23/I; facsimile reproduced in Hilmar and Brosche (eds.), *Alban Berg 1885–1935*, p. 87).

44 Similar examples are to be found in bars 138–40, 145–7, 281 and 663–5. The material at bars 663–5 (third movement) represents the reprise of the material at bars 145–7 (first movement).

45 This correspondence and others like it reflect the overall design of the Chamber Concerto, whereby the third movement inventively re-uses the materials of the first and second movements in orderly combination, effecting this not only by means of free composition but also through techniques such as splitting (see pp. 208–9). [Ed.]

46 See chapter 5 for an extended discussion of 'wedging' in Berg's Opp. 4 and 5.

47 Jarman, *The Music of Alban Berg*, pp. 118–24, 130. See also Rudolf Stephan, 'Drei Autographe von Alban Berg', in Hans Jörg Jans, Felix Meyer and Ingrid Westen (eds.), *Komponisten des 20. Jahrhunderts in der Paul Sacher Stiftung* (Basle: Paul Sacher Stiftung, 1986), pp. 148–56 (facsimiles of the three pages of analytical notes Berg prepared for Reich after completing the opera are reproduced (pp. 152–4); the derivation of the '*Schigolch-Chromatik*' (Schigolch's 'serial trope') from the basic row is shown at the top of the first page (p. 152)); and Thomas F. Ertelt, *Alban Bergs 'Lulu': Quellenstudien und Beiträge zur Analyse* [*Alban Berg Studien*, 3] (Vienna: Universal Edition, 1993), pp. 69–74.

48 Jarman, *The Music of Alban Berg*, p. 92 (Ex. 115), p. 128 (Ex. 160).

49 Ashby, 'Of *Modell-Typen*', p. 72 (emphasis added).

50 See Jarman, *The Music of Alban Berg*, pp. 73–4.

51 *Ibid.*, pp. 73–9; and Philip Lambert, 'Berg's Path to Twelve-Note Composition: Aggregate Construction and Association in the Chamber Concerto', *Music Analysis*, 12 (1993), pp. 321–42. See also pp. 168–9.

52 A different analysis of these two melodies is offered by Lambert; it is, nevertheless, one that aims to show their common segmental content ('Berg's Path to Twelve-Note Composition', pp. 324–6).

53 The *Hauptrhythmus* is first stated at bar 297 by the contrabassoon and trombone.

54 Adorno termed this gradual unfolding 'Kapuzinern', referring to a children's game of cloaking and revealing 'in which the word "Kapuziner" is disassembled and put back together again: Kapuziner – Apuziner – Puziner – Uziner – [...] – Er – R – Er – [...] – Puziner – Apuziner – Kapuziner' (*Alban Berg*, pp. 3–4, 95). See also Busch, 'Einige Bemerkungen zur Zwölftonkomposition'.

55 Adorno, 'Bergs kompositionstechnische Funde', p. 271.

56 *Ibid.*, pp. 263–7.

57 Anton Webern, *Der Weg zur Neuen Musik*, ed. Willi Reich (Vienna: Universal Edition, 1960), p. 18 (7 March 1933); Eng. trans. by Cornelius Cardew as *The Path to the New Music* (Bryn Mawr, PA: Presser, 1963). The emphasis on the techniques of association and splitting call to mind Rudolf Stephan's summing up of the twelve-note features in *Lulu*: 'the twelve-note aspect is hardly of interest to the opera's listeners, especially as musically speaking it is scarcely anywhere of less significance than in this work' ('der Zwölftonaspekt ist für die

Hörer der Oper kaum von Interesse, zumal er musikalisch kaum irgendwo weniger bedeutet als in diesem Werk'), quoted in Volker Scherliess, 'Alban Bergs analytische Tafeln zur Lulu-Reihe', *Die Musikforschung*, 30 (1977), pp. 452–64 (p. 452).

11   In the orbit of *Lulu*

1   The canon is based on a theme from Schoenberg's comic opera *Von heute auf morgen*. See Craig Ayrey, 'Introduction: Different Trains', in C. Ayrey and M. Everist (eds.), *Analytical Strategies and Musical Interpretation* (Cambridge: Cambridge University Press, 1996), pp. 26–31.

2   See Thomas F. Ertelt, *Alban Bergs 'Lulu': Quellenstudien und Beiträge zur Analyse* [*Alban Berg Studien*, 3] (Vienna: Universal Edition, 1993), p. 26.

3   Rosemary Hilmar, *Katalog der Schriftstücke von der Hand Alban Bergs, der Fremdschriftlichen und gedruckten Dokumente zur Lebensgeschichte und zu seinem Werk* [*Alban Berg Studien*, I/2] (Vienna: Universal Edition, 1985), p. 22.

4   Ertelt, *Alban Bergs 'Lulu'*, pp. 27–9.

5   Friedrich Cerha, *Arbeitsbericht zur Herstellung des 3. Akts der Oper 'Lulu' von Alban Berg* (Vienna: Universal Edition, 1979), p. 7.

6   See p. 44.

7   Adorno, *Alban Berg*, pp. 26–7.

8   Alma Mahler Werfel, *And the Bridge is Love*, trans. E. B. Ashton (London: Hutchinson, 1959), p. 174.

9   Letter to Schoenberg, 30 March 1928 (*The Berg–Schoenberg Correspondence*, p. 366).

10   Ertelt, *Alban Bergs 'Lulu'*, pp. 11–24.

11   *Ibid.*, pp. 21–3.

12   See chapter 10.

13   Ertelt, *Alban Bergs 'Lulu'*, pp. 39–40.

14   This has been pointed out, for example, by Dave Headlam in 'The Derivation of Rows in Lulu', *Perspectives of New Music*, 24/i (1985), p. 212.

15   This is one reason – another, very clearly, being Friedrich Cerha's musicianship and scholarly integrity – why we can be confident that there is an overwhelming degree of authority in the published Act III of *Lulu*.

16   See Perle, *Lulu*, p. 14.

17   See Jarman, *The Music of Alban Berg*, pp. 144–5.

18   See pp. 200–201.

19   Philip Lambert, 'Berg's Path to Twelve-Note Composition: Aggregate Construction and Association in the Chamber Concerto', *Music Analysis*, 12 (1993), pp. 321–42.

20   See pp. 169–70.

21   See chapter 10.

22   For an English translation of Berg's tabular presentation of the form of the Chamber Concerto see Redlich, *Alban Berg: The Man and His Music*, pp. 124–5.

23   Boulez, prefatory note to the study score (UE 12419). It is interesting to note that Berg's 'strictness' in the Chamber Concerto is not dissimilar to Boulez's

own technique in *Le marteau sans maître*, another work in which an elaborately layered pre-compositional plan was executed in a way that allowed for freedom at the musical surface. See Lev Koblyakov, *Pierre Boulez: A World of Harmony* (Chur: Harwood, 1990).

24   See pp. 169, 195–6.

25   See Volker Scherliess, 'Alban Bergs analytische Tafeln zur *Lulu*-Reihe', *Die Musikforschung*, 30 (1977), pp. 452–64.

26   Ertelt, '"Hereinspaziert ...": Ein früher Entwurf des Prologs zu Alban Bergs *Lulu*', *Österreichische Musik Zeitschrift*, 41 (1986), pp. 15–25; Douglass M. Green, 'A False Start for *Lulu*: An Early Version of the Prologue', in Gable and Morgan (eds.), *Alban Berg*, pp. 203–13; see also pp. 183–4. Almost all of the musical ideas in this sketch were eventually discarded when a new Prologue was written after the rest of the opera had been completed.

27   Six of the seven songs that Berg chose had also found their way into an earlier, unpublished collection of 'Ten Songs from the Year 1907' [sic] which he made for Helene in 1917. The exception is 'Traumgekrönt', the text of which he quoted to Helene in a letter during their courtship (17 August 1907: *Letters to his Wife*, p. 26). The manuscripts of the seven songs are missing from the (second) volume of early songs, entitled 'Alte Lieder', which according to Rosemary Hilmar (*Katalog der Musikhandschriften*, pp. 44–5) Berg had bound in the 1920s. Since Berg wrote to Schoenberg on 30 May 1926 that with the money from the *Wozzeck* royalties he and Helene 'have had all our unbound scores and books bound' (*The Berg–Schoenberg Correspondence*, p. 347) it could be that he had made his selection for the *Seven Early Songs* project by this time.

28   Letter to Schoenberg (27 June 1926), cited in Ursula von Rauchhaupt, *Schoenberg, Berg, Webern, die Streichquartette: eine Dokumentation* (Hamburg: Deutsche Grammophon, 1971), p. 92.

29   See Perle, *Lulu*, pp. 68–77.

30   See Ertelt, *Alban Bergs 'Lulu'*, pp. 49–80.

31   See Hall, 'The Sketches for *Lulu*', in Jarman (ed.), *The Berg Companion*, pp. 248–53; Pople, 'Secret Programmes: Themes and Techniques in Recent Berg Scholarship', *Music Analysis*, 12 (1993), pp. 384–7.

32   Berg had abandoned the early Prologue sketch without completing it, though he had planned how it would end and the first scene of the opera itself begin (see Greene, 'A False Start', pp. 212–13). It is not clear whether or not the figure of 'over 300 bars' which he reported to Schoenberg in a letter of 1 September 1928 (*The Berg–Schoenberg Correspondence*, p. 373) makes an allowance for the Prologue; assuming it does not, then the first scene and orchestral interlude of the opera together comprise 329 bars (I/86–414) after which there is a musical hiatus, making it seem reasonably likely that this was the extent of Berg's work on the opera during 1928.

33   Letters to Schoenberg, 17 January and 7 May 1929 (*The Berg–Schoenberg Correspondence*, pp. 382, 387).

34   *The Berg–Schoenberg Correspondence*, p. 365 n. 3. Berg's fee for *Der Wein* was 5,000 schillings.

35 Mosco Carner, *Alban Berg*, 2nd edn (London: Duckworth, 1983), p. 110.

36 It should perhaps be underlined that although the musical substance of the early part of *Lulu* precedes *Der Wein*, its orchestral realisation does not.

37 Patricia Hall's studies of this aspect through the Lulu sketches confirm that he had given early consideration to this ('Role and Form in Berg's Sketches for *Lulu*', in Gable and Morgan (eds.), *Alban Berg*, pp. 235–59).

38 See p. 168.

39 Letter of 4 December 1929 to Hanna Fuchs-Robettin, quoted in Perle, *Lulu*, p. 139. See also p. 170. The low D♭ that Berg places under the H–F triads at the centre of *Der Wein* constitutes an intriguing link to the tolling bass C♯s at the centre of the Adagio of the Chamber Concerto, and to *Lulu*, bars III/1006–7 (the pause for breath before Lulu defies Alwa and Geschwitz to return to the streets alone).

40 Adorno, *Alban Berg*, pp. 117–18, 119–20.

41 Carner, *Alban Berg*, pp. 108, 110. The anecdote about Berg's 'apologetic expression' stems from the publisher Hans W. Heinsheimer (see Erich Alban Berg, *Alban Berg: Leben und Werk*, p. 34).

42 Adorno, *Alban Berg*, p. 118.

43 Letter to Schoenberg, 26 August 1929 (*The Berg–Schoenberg Correspondence*, p. 388).

44 Letter to Webern, 20 September 1929, quoted in Patricia Hall, 'The Progress of a Method: Berg's Tone Rows for *Lulu*', *Musical Quarterly*, 71 (1985), p. 500.

45 See Hall, 'The Progress of a Method', p. 512 and p. 518 n. 19. There is a double bar line at I/521, two bars before one of the second-phase series appears.

46 Reich, *Life and Work*, p. 164.

47 I am grateful to Patricia Hall for information that sheds light on this passage.

48 Reich, *Life and Work*, pp. 79–80; Hall, 'The Progress of a Method', pp. 501–2.

49 Reich, *Alban Berg*, p. 113.

50 Summarised in Perle, *Lulu*, pp. 93–127; see also Jarman, *Alban Berg: Lulu*, pp. 68–73.

51 Hall, 'The Progress of a Method', pp. 501–10.

52 Specifically, the notes 1–6 of the trope are a transposition (t=4) of notes 2–7 of the basic series.

53 See pp. 196–9.

54 See, for example, Hall, 'The Sketches for *Lulu*', pp. 244–5; Manfred Reiter, *Die Zwölftontechnik in Alban Bergs Oper Lulu* (Regensburg: Gustav Bosse Verlag, 1973), pp. 44–5; Jarman, *The Music of Alban Berg*, pp. 119–20.

55 Hall, 'The Sketches for *Lulu*', pp. 253–6; Ertelt, *Alban Bergs 'Lulu'*, pp. 91–8 and 108–16. See chapter 12 for a discussion of the wider dramatic significance of this passage.

56 See chapter 8.

57 See Perle, *Lulu*, pp. 150–56.

58 For further details of the *Lulu* chronology during 1934 see Cerha, *Arbeitsbericht*, pp. 4–6.

59 Some changes were certainly made during this process. Among the more significant were amendments to bars I/98–9 and I/119–23, which had been

composed before Alwa's and Schön's series had been derived from the basic series. Berg now incorporated these serial forms, enhancing the characterisation achieved in both passages. See Hall, 'The Progress of a Method', pp. 515–18; Ertelt, *Alban Bergs 'Lulu'*, pp. 62–5, 74–7.

60   Jarman, *Alban Berg: Lulu*, pp. 7–8.
61   *Ibid.*, p. 131; see also Anthony Pople, review of Friedrich Cerha (ed.), *Alban Berg, Lulu, Act 3*, [etc.], *Journal of the Royal Musical Association*, 114 (1989), p. 258.
62   Berg also prepared an arrangement of the second movement of the Chamber Concerto for violin, clarinet and piano, early in 1935. See David Congdon, '*Kammerkonzert*: Evolution of the Adagio and the Trio Transcription', *Alban Berg Studien*, 2 (Vienna: Universal Edition, 1981), p. 154.
63   Further details of the chronology of the Violin Concerto and Berg's final illness may be found in Pople, *Berg: Violin Concerto*, pp. 26–41.
64   Adorno, *Alban Berg*, p. 21.
65   This is the subtitle of Adorno's *Alban Berg*.
66   Arnold Schoenberg, *Fundamentals of Musical Composition*, ed. Gerald Strang and Leonard Stein (London: Faber, 1967), pp. 58–9. See also pp. 123–7.
67   Reich, *Life and Work*, p. 178; Pople, *Berg: Violin Concerto*, pp. 33–4.
68   See p. 48; also Pople, *Berg: Violin Concerto*, pp. 98–102.

12   Lulu's feminine performance

1   Donald Mitchell, 'The Character of Lulu', *The Music Review*, 15/iv (1954), pp. 268–74 (p. 270).
2   George Perle, 'The Character of Lulu: A Sequel', *The Music Review*, 25/iv (1964), pp. 311–19 (p. 317).
3   Adorno, *Alban Berg*, p. 130.
4   I do not mean to exclude the possibility of Lulu as a fantasy of female (homosexual) desire, a possibility which is in fact realised in Wedekind's drama itself. But rather, I mean to reflect the perspective of the three male critics quoted.
5   Karen Pegley, 'Musical Characterization of Women in *Lulu*: A Feminist Deconstruction' (given at the annual meeting of the American Musicological Society, Oakland, 1990), p. i.
6   Leo Treitler, 'The Lulu Character and the Character of *Lulu*', in Gable and Morgan (eds.), *Alban Berg*, pp. 261–86 (pp. 274–5).
7   Jarman, *Alban Berg: Lulu*, pp. 91 and 101.
8   Mitchell, 'The Character of Lulu', p. 272.
9   Perle, 'The Character of Lulu: A Sequel', p. 318.
10   Treitler, 'The Lulu Character', p. 263.
11   Mitchell, 'The Character of Lulu', p. 274.
12   Jarman, *Alban Berg: Lulu*, p. 95.
13   Quoted in *ibid.*, p. 37.
14   Others have observed that Berg employs allusion and parody in his later music. For instance, in *Berg: Violin Concerto*, Anthony Pople writes: '*Lulu* is littered with subtle examples of momentary allusion, and shot through with music which from moment to moment suggests something else' (p. 13).

15   Judith Butler, *Gender Trouble: Feminism and the Subversion of Identity* (New York: Routledge, 1990), p. 16.

16   *Ibid.*, p. 25.

17   The topic of Lulu's inconsistencies is discussed in all the sources cited here. I have chosen not to recapitulate those inconsistencies.

18   Perle, 'The Character of Lulu: A Sequel', pp. 317–18, quoting Kierkegaard's description of Don Giovanni with the phrase 'power of nature'. Critics of Wedekind's plays also theorise multiple Lulu characters. For instance, in *The Sexual Circus: Wedekind's Theatre of Subversion* (New York: Blackwell, 1987) Elizabeth Boa identifies 'The Three Faces of Lulu': she (i) 'is an allegorical spirit of nature', (ii) 'embodies and externalizes dreams and fantasies in a non-realist manner comparable to Expressionist theater', and (iii) 'is a mimetic character … from a low-life milieu … destroyed by bourgeois society' (p. 54).

19   Treitler, 'The Lulu Character', p. 274.

20   Mitchell, 'The Character of Lulu', p. 272.

21   Treitler, 'The Lulu Character', p. 269.

22   *Ibid.*, p. 263.

23   Perle, 'The Character of Lulu: A Sequel', p. 319.

24   Butler, *Gender Trouble*, p. 17.

25   *Ibid.*, p. 25.

26   I frame the discussion here as if Lulu were not a dramatic character. Later, I shall raise the issue of Wedekind as author of the Lulu character and Berg as composer of her musical projection.

27   Butler, *Gender Trouble*, p. 17.

28   My understanding of the Lulu character has prompted the designation 'Lulu's Freedom Music'. Other scholars have adopted different names in keeping with their understanding of Lulu: Treitler refers to the musical type as 'Lulu's Music' and Perle calls it 'Lulu's Entrance Music'. See also pp. 221–2.

29   Perle, *Lulu*, p. 79.

30   Mitchell, 'The Character of Lulu', pp. 272–3.

31   Treitler, 'The Lulu Character', p. 263.

32   Jarman, *Alban Berg: Lulu*, p. 87. The 'Mahlerian' features of Berg's music have been discussed by many commentators (see chapter 6). In this chapter I will refer to the quality of sound projected by both the Freedom and Coda Musics with the adjective 'Mahlerian'.

33   Mitchell, 'The Character of Lulu', p. 273 and Perle, *Lulu*, p. 79.

34   Both Jarman and Perle describe the tonal implications of Lulu's Freedom Music and the Coda Music in detail: Jarman, *The Music of Alban Berg*, pp. 94ff. and Perle, *Lulu*, pp. 131–9.

35   I have described the details of this metaphorical opposition in an unpublished paper, 'Lulu: Ways of Being Twelve-Tone'.

36   Jarman, *Alban Berg: Lulu*, p. 87.

37   My colleague Joseph Auner has pointed out that Mahler's music itself often projects a parodic or, perhaps better, ironic surface. Adorno affirms this aspect of Mahler's music in *Mahler: A Musical Physiognomy*, trans. Edmund Jephcott (Chicago: Chicago University Press, 1992): '[Mahler's] experiential core, bro-

kenness, the musical subject's feeling of alienation, seeks to realize itself æs-thetically by articulating the outward form not as immediate but as also bro-ken, a cipher of the content, which is reciprocally influenced by the fractured form. In his work the musical phenomena are no more to be taken literally than the experiential core can directly become musical structure' (p. 33). And: 'Mahler's music does not express subjectivity, but in it the latter takes up its stance toward objectivity' (p. 25).

38 Frederic Jameson, 'Postmodernism and Consumer Society', in Hal Foster (ed.), *The Anti-Æsthetic: Essays on Postmodern Culture* (Port Townsend, WA: Bay Press, 1983), p. 114, quoted in Butler, *Gender Trouble*, p. 138.

39 Perle, *Lulu*, p. 81. The Lied is repeated in a shortened version in the duet be-tween the Marquis and Lulu in Act III scene 1.

40 Perle (*ibid.*, pp. 106–9) calls these the 'Painter's Chords'. See Example 11.3b, p. 211.

41 See Reich, *Life and Work*, p. 162; also Perle, *Lulu*, pp. 110–12. It is Perle's termi-nology that is used here. See Example 11.3e, p. 211.

42 For a discussion of this canon see Craig Ayrey, 'Introduction: Different Trains', in Craig Ayrey and Mark Everist (eds.), *Analytical Strategies and Musical Inter-pretation: Essays on Nineteenth- and Twentieth-Century Music* (Cambridge: Cambridge University Press, 1996), pp. 1–32 (pp. 21–5). [Ed.]

43 See Reich, *Life and Work*, p. 164; also Perle, *Lulu*, pp. 87–9. Perle refers to this motive as 'Basic Cell I'.

44 Perhaps more obviously at this point, the Eb minor triad also states the first three notes of Alwa's series in its prime form. The close trichordal connection between the two rows is noted by both Jarman (*The Music of Alban Berg*, pp. 92–3) and Perle (*Lulu*, p. 97).

45 Jarman, *Alban Berg: Lulu*, p. 95

46 Quoted in *ibid.*, p. 96.

47 Perle, 'The Character of Lulu: A Sequel', p. 319.

48 The same could perhaps be said of the Marquis who attempts to sell Lulu into prostitution for his own personal gain. She manages to escape from him, how-ever.

49 Treitler, 'The Lulu Character', p. 273.

50 Jarman, *Alban Berg: Lulu*, p. 98.

13   Berg and the twentieth century

1 Eric Hobsbawm, *Age of Extremes: The Short Twentieth Century, 1914–1991* (London: Abacus, 1995).

2 Pierre Boulez, 'The Current Impact of Berg' (1948), and 'Alban Berg' (1958), in *Stocktakings from an Apprenticeship*, trans. Stephen Walsh (Oxford: Clarendon Press, 1991), pp. 183–7, 243–58.

3 *Ibid.*, pp. 257–8.

4 *Ibid.*, p. 249.

5 *Ibid.*, p. 255.

6 Igor Stravinsky and Robert Craft, *Conversations with Igor Stravinsky* (London: Faber, 1979), pp. 71–2.

7   Stravinsky and Craft, *Dialogues* (London: Faber, 1982), pp. 124–5.

8   Stravinsky, 'The Composer's View', in Paul Griffiths, *Igor Stravinsky: The Rake's Progress* (Cambridge: Cambridge University Press, 1982), p. 2.

9   Boulez, *Conversations with Célestin Deliège* (London: Eulenberg, 1975), p. 24.

10 *Ibid.*, p. 25.

11 *Ibid.*, p. 24.

12 Leo Treitler, *Music and the Historical Imagination* (Cambridge, MA: Harvard University Press, 1989), p. 282. See also pp. 48–9.

13 Jarman, *Alban Berg: Wozzeck*, p. 68.

14 Jarman, *Alban Berg: Lulu*, pp. 100–101.

15 Robin Holloway, 'The Complete *Lulu*', *Tempo*, 129 (1979), p. 37.

16 Adorno, *Alban Berg*, p. 23.

17 Richard Toop, 'Ferneyhough's Dungeons of Invention', *The Musical Times*, 128 (1987), p. 626.

18 Max Paddison, *Adorno's Æsthetics of Music* (Cambridge: Cambridge University Press, 1993), p. 158.

19 *Ibid.*, p. 171.

20 J. Peter Burkholder, 'Berg and the Possibility of Popularity', in Gable and Morgan (eds.), *Alban Berg*, pp. 32–3.

21 *Ibid.*, p. 53.

22 Pople, *Berg: Violin Concerto*, p. 7.

23 *Ibid.*, p. 102.

24 Craig Ayrey, 'Berg's "Scheideweg": Analytical Issues in Op. 2/ii', *Music Analysis*, 1 (1982), p. 190.

25 Ayrey, 'Tonality and the Series: Berg', in J. Dunsby (ed.), *Early Twentieth-Century Music* [Models of Musical Analysis] (Oxford: Blackwell, 1993), p. 109.

26 *Ibid.*, p. 111.

27 See Jarman, *Alban Berg: Wozzeck*, p. 157.

28 See George Perle, 'Reflections (1990)', in *The Right Notes: Twenty-Three Selected Essays* (Stuyvesant, NY: Pendragon Press, 1995), pp. 183–7.

29 Holloway, 'Where the Wild Things Are', *Tempo*, 137 (1981), p. 37.

30 Charles Rosen, *The Romantic Generation* (Cambridge, MA: Harvard University Press, 1995), p. 166.

31 *Ibid.*, pp. 174–5.

32 Hugh Collins Rice, 'Further thoughts on Schnittke', *Tempo*, 168 (1989), p. 13.

33 For further discussion of these issues see Peter Cahn, 'Klassizismen bei Berg', in W. Osthoff and R. Wiesend (eds.), *Colloquium Klassizität, Klassizismus, Klassik in der Musik 1920–1950, Würzburg 1985* (Tutzing: Schneider, 1988), pp. 95–138.

Select bibliography

Adorno, Theodor W., *Alban Berg: Master of the Smallest Link*, trans. J. Brand and C. Hailey
(Cambridge: Cambridge University Press, 1991)
Alban Berg: Briefe an seine Frau, ed. Helene Berg (Munich: Langen- Müller, 1965)
Alban Berg: Letters to his Wife, ed., trans. and annot. Bernard Grun (London: Faber, 1971)
The Berg–Schoenberg Correspondence, ed. Juliane Brand, Christopher Hailey and Donald
Harris (London: Macmillan, 1987)
Berg, Erich Alban, *Alban Berg: Leben und Werk in Daten und Bildern*, 2nd edn (Frankfurt
am Main: Insel, 1976)
Als der Adler noch zwei Köpfe hatte: Ein Florilegium 1858–1918 (Graz: Edition
Kaleidoskop, 1980)
Der unverbesserliche Romantiker: Alban Berg 1885–1935 (Vienna: Österreichischer
Bundesverlag, 1985)
Floros, Constantin, *Alban Berg: Musik als Autobiographie* (Wiesbaden: Breitkopf und
Härtel, 1992)
Gable, David and Robert P. Morgan (eds.), *Alban Berg: Historical and Analytical Perspec-*
tives (Oxford: Clarendon, 1991)
Hilmar, Rosemary, *Alban Berg, Leben und Wirken in Wien bis zu seinen ersten Erfolgen als*
Komponist (Vienna: Böhlau, 1978)
(ed.), *Katalog der Musikhandschriften, Schriften und Studien Alban Bergs im Fond Alban*
Berg und der weiteren Handschriftlichen Quellen im Besitz der Österreichischen
Nationalbibliothek [*Alban Berg Studien, 1/i*] (Vienna: Universal Edition, 1980)
Hilmar, Rosemary, and Günter Brosche (eds.), *Alban Berg 1885–1935: Ausstellung der*
Österreichischen Nationalbibliothek, Prunksaal, 23. Mai bis 20. Oktober 1985 (Vienna:
Österreichische Nationalbibliothek in Zusammenarbeit mit der Universal Edition,
1985)
Jarman, Douglas, *The Music of Alban Berg* (London: Faber, 1979)
Alban Berg: Lulu (Cambridge: Cambridge University Press, 1991)
Alban Berg: Wozzeck (Cambridge: Cambridge University Press, 1989)
(ed.), *The Berg Companion* (Houndmills: Macmillan, 1989)
Perle, George, 'Berg's Master Array of the Interval Cycles', *Musical Quarterly*, 63 (1977),
pp. 1–30
The Operas of Alban Berg, vol. 1: *Wozzeck* (Berkeley: University of California Press,
1980)
The Operas of Alban Berg, vol. 2: *Lulu* (Berkeley: University of California Press, 1985)
Pople, Anthony, *Berg: Violin Concerto* (Cambridge: Cambridge University Press, 1991)
Redlich, Hans F., *Alban Berg: The Man and his Music* (London: John Calder, 1957)
Alban Berg: Versuch einer Würdigung (Vienna: Universal Edition, 1957)
Reich, Willi, *Alban Berg. Mit Bergs eigenen Schriften und Beiträgen von Theodor*
Wiesengrund-Adorno und Ernst Křenek (Vienna: Reichner, 1937)
The Life and Work of Alban Berg, trans. C. Cardew (London: Thames and Hudson, 1965)
Rode, Susanne, *Alban Berg und Karl Kraus: Zur geistigen Biographie des Komponisten der*
'Lulu' (Frankfurt am Main: Peter Lang, 1988)
Schmalfeldt, Janet, *Berg's Wozzeck: Harmonic Language and Dramatic Design* (New Haven:
Yale University Press, 1983)

Index